Motor Learning and Performance

From Priniciples to Application

FIFTH EDITION

Draft. Not for Distribution.

Richard A. Schmidt

Timothy D. Lee

Human Kinetics

Library of Congress Cataloging-in-Publication Data

Schmidt, Richard A., 1941- author.
 Motor learning and performance : from principles to application / Richard A. Schmidt, Timothy D. Lee. -- Fifth edition.
    p. ; cm.
 Includes bibliographical references and index.
 I. Lee, Timothy Donald, 1955- author. II. Title.
 [DNLM: 1. Learning. 2. Motor Activity. 3. Kinesthesis. 4. Psychomotor Performance. BF 295]
 BF295
 152.3'34--dc23
                         2013014793

ISBN-10: 1-4504-4361-3 (print)
ISBN-13: 978-1-4504-4361-6 (print)

Copyright © 2014 by Richard A. Schmidt and Timothy D. Lee
Copyright © 2008, 2004, 2000 by Richard A. Schmidt and Craig A. Wrisberg
Copyright © 1991 by Richard A. Schmidt

All rights reserved. Except for use in a review, the reproduction or utilization of this work in any form or by any electronic, mechanical, or other means, now known or hereafter invented, including xerography, photocopying, and recording, and in any information storage and retrieval system, is forbidden without the written permission of the publisher.

Permission notices for material reprinted in this book from other sources can be found on page \bb\

The web addresses cited in this text were current as of June 19, 2013, unless otherwise noted.

Acquisitions Editor: Myles Schrag; **Managing Editor:** Katherine Maurer; **Assistant Editor:** Susan Huls; **Copyeditor:** Joyce Brumfield; **Indexer:** \bb\; **Permissions Manager:** Dalene Reeder; **Graphic Designer:** Nancy Rasmus; **Graphic Artist:** Dawn Sills; **Cover Designer:** Keith Blomberg; **Photograph (cover):** © mauritius images/age fotostock; **Photo Asset Manager:** Laura Fitch; **Visual Production Assistant:** Joyce Brumfield; **Photo Production Manager:** Jason Allen; **Art Manager:** Kelly Hendren; **Associate Art Manager:** Alan L. Wilborn; **Art Style Development:** Jennifer Gibas; **Illustrations:** © Human Kinetics; **Printer:** Courier Companies, Inc.

Printed in the United States of America   10 9 8 7 6 5 4 3 2 1

The paper in this book was manufactured using responsible forestry methods.

Human Kinetics
Website: www.HumanKinetics.com

United States: Human Kinetics
P.O. Box 5076
Champaign, IL 61825-5076
800-747-4457
e-mail: humank@hkusa.com

Canada: Human Kinetics
475 Devonshire Road Unit 100
Windsor, ON N8Y 2L5
800-465-7301 (in Canada only)
e-mail: info@hkcanada.com

Europe: Human Kinetics
107 Bradford Road
Stanningley
Leeds LS28 6AT, United Kingdom
+44 (0) 113 255 5665
e-mail: hk@hkeurope.com

Australia: Human Kinetics
57A Price Avenue
Lower Mitcham, South Australia 5062
08 8372 0999
e-mail: info@hkaustralia.com

New Zealand: Human Kinetics
P.O. Box 80
Torrens Park, South Australia 5062
0800 222 062
e-mail: info@hknewzealand.com

E5868

Jack A. Adams (1922-2010) was a giant in motor learning research. His passing marks a sad personal loss for us as well as a huge professional loss to motor learning research across the world. This book is dedicated to Jack's memory in appreciation for all he taught us.

Contents

Preface x
Acknowledgments xx

1 Introduction to Motor Learning and Performance x
How skills are studied

Why Study Motor Skills? xx
The Science of Motor Learning and Performance xx
▶ Focus on Research 1.1 Franklin M. Henry, Father of Motor Behavior Research xx
Defining Skills xx
Components of Skills xx
Classifying Skills xx
▶ Focus on Research 1.2 Error Scores in Discrete Tasks xx
▶ Focus on Research 1.3 Error Scores in Continuous Tasks xx
Understanding Performance and Learning xx
Summary xx
Learning Aids xx

PART I Principles of Human Skilled Performance

2 Processing Information and Making Decisions xx
The Mental Side of Human Performance

Information-processing approach xx
Reaction time and decision-making xx
▶ Focus on Research 2.1 Donders' Stages of Processing xx
▶ Focus on Research 2.2 Hick's Law xx
▶ Focus on Application 2.1 Light Switches xx
▶ Focus on Application 2.2 Strategies for Anticipating xx
▶ Focus on Research 2.3 Assessing Anticipation Skills xx
Memory systems xx
Summary xx
Learning Aids xx

3 Attention and Performance   xx
Limitations on Information Processing

▶ Focus on Application 3.1 William James on Attention   xx
What Is Attention?   xx
Limitations in Stimulus Identification   xx
Limitations in Response Selection   xx
▶ Focus on Research 3.1 Distracted-Driving Research   xx
Limitations in Movement Programming   xx
▶ Focus on Research 3.2 The Double-Stimulation Paradigm   xx
Decision-Making Under Stress   xx
▶ Focus on Application 3.2 Automotive Panic   xx
Summary   xx
Learning Aids   xx

4 Sensory Contributions to Skilled Performance   xxx
Feedback Processing in Motor Control

Sources of Sensory Information   xx
Processing Sensory Information   xx
▶ Focus on Application 4.1 Error Correction in Batting   xx
Principles of Visual Control   xx
▶ Focus on Research 4.1 "Blindsight" Reveals Dorsal- and Ventral-Stream Processing   xx
▶ Focus on Research 4.2 Gaze Control   xx
▶ Focus on Application 4.2 Visibility in Night-time Car-Truck Accidents   xx
Audition and Motor Control   xx
▶ Focus on Application 4.3 When Vision Degrades Performance   xx
Summary   xx
Learning Aids   xx

v

5 Motor Programs · xxx

Motor-Program Theory   xx
Evidence for Motor Programs   xx
- ▶ Focus on Research 5.1 The Henry-Rogers Experiment   xx
- ▶ Focus on Application 5.1 Checked Swings in Baseball   xx
- ▶ Focus on Research 5.2 Initiating a Motor Program   xx

Motor Programs and the Conceptual Model   xx
Problems in Motor-Program Theory: Novelty and Storage   xx
Generalized Motor Program Theory   xx
- ▶ Focus on Research 5.3 Invariances and Parameters   xx
- ▶ Focus on Research 5.4 Relative Timing in Locomotion   xx
- ▶ Focus on Application 5.2 Relative Timing Fingerprints   xx

Summary   xx
Learning Aids   xx

6 Principles of Speed, Accuracy and Coordination · xxx
Controlling and timing movements

Speed-Accuracy Trade-offs   xx
- ▶ Focus on Research 6.1 Fitts Tasks   xx
- ▶ Focus on Application 6.1 Fitts' Law in Everyday Actions   xx

Sources of Error in Rapid Movements   xx
Exceptions to the Speed-Accuracy Trade-Off   xx
Analyzing a Rapid Movement: Baseball Batting   xx
Accuracy in Coordinated Actions   xx
- ▶ Focus on Application 6.2 Coordination in Golf Putting   xx
- ▶ Focus on Research 6.2 Coordination as a Self-Organization Process   xx

Summary   xx
Learning Aids   xx

7 Individual Differences · xxx
How people differ in their performance capabilities

The Study of Individual Differences   xx
Abilities versus Skills   xx
Are Motor Abilities Connected?   xx
- ▶ Focus on Application 7.1 The Babe (Mildred "Babe" Zaharias)   xx
- ▶ Focus on Research 7.1 Correlation: The Statistic of Individual Differences   xx

Abilities and the Production of Skills   xx
Prediction and Selection Based on Ability   xx
- ▶ Focus on Research 7.2 The Relative-age Effect   xx

Summary   xx
Learning Aids   xx

Contents

PART II Principles of Skill Learning

8 Introduction to Motor Learning — xxx
Concepts and Methods in research and application

Motor Learning Defined   xx
How is Motor Learning Measured?   xx
▶ Focus on Research 8.1 Learning Curves: Facts or Artifacts?   xx
▶ Focus on Application 8.1 Self-Assessments of Learning   xx
Distinguishing Learning from Performance   xx
Transfer of Learning   xx
Summary   xx
Learning Aids   xx

9 Skill Acquisition, Retention, and Transfer — xxx
How expertise is gained

Skill Acquisition   xx
▶ Focus on Application 9.1 Principles of Golf Practice   xx
▶ Focus on Research 9.1 Learning Never Ends   xx
▶ Focus on Application 9.2 Fitts and Bernstein Learn to Play Ice Hockey   xx
Skill Retention   xx
Transfer of Learning   xx
▶ Focus on Application 9.3 Teaching for Transfer of Learning   xx
▶ Focus on Research 9.2 Game Systems for Virtual Training   xx
Summary   xx
Learning Aids   xx

10 Organizing and Scheduling Practice — xxx
How the structure of practice influences learning

Context and Considerations for Practice   xx
▶ Focus on Application 10.1 Mental Practice in Stroke Rehabilitation   xx
Organizing Practice and Rest   xx
Variable versus Constant Practice   xx
▶ Focus on Research 10.1 Especial Skills: An Exception to Variable Practice?   xx
Blocked versus Random Practice   xx
Summary   xx
Learning Aids   xx

11 Augmented Feedback — xxx
How providing extra information influences learning

Feedback Classifications   xx
Functions of Augmented Feedback   xx
▶ Focus on Research 11.1 Revising Ideas about How Feedback Works   xx
How Much Feedback Should Be Given?   xx
▶ Focus on Research 11.2 Augmented Feedback from Video Replays   xx
When Should Feedback Be Given?   xx
▶ Focus on Application 11.1 Physical Guidance in Stroke Rehabilitation   xx
▶ Focus on Application 11.2 Physical Guidance in Learning to Swim   xx
Summary   xx
Learning Aids   xx

Glossary   xxx
References   xxx
Index   xxx
About the Authors   xxx

Draft. Not for Distribution.

Preface

Most of us feel tremendous excitement, pleasure, and perhaps envy when we watch a close race, match, or performance, focusing on the complex, well-controlled skills evidenced by the players or musicians. In these situations, we marvel at those who must succeed in executing their skill "on the spot"—at how the person with high-level skills is able to excel, sometimes under extreme "pressure" to do so.

This book was written for people who appreciate high-level skilled activity and for those who would like to learn more about how such incredible performances occur. Thus, readers in fields related directly to kinesiology and physical education (such as teaching and coaching) will benefit from the knowledge provided here. But the material extends far beyond these fields and should be relevant for those who study rehabilitation in physical and occupational therapy, as well as for instructors and facilitators of many other areas in which motor skills play an important role, such as music, ergonomics, and the military. The text is intended for beginners in the study of skill and requires little knowledge of physiology, psychology, or statistical methodologies.

The level of analysis of the text focuses on motor *behavior*—the overt, observable production of skilled movements. Of course, there are many scientific areas or fields of study involved in the understanding of this overt skilled behavior. Any skill is the outcome of processes studied in many different fields, such as neurology, anatomy, biomechanics, biochemistry, and social and experimental psychology; and this text could have focused on any number of these fundamental fields. But the focus of the text is broader than the fundamental fields that support it. The focus is *behavioral*, with the major emphasis on humans performing skills of various kinds. To be sure, we will talk about these other levels of analysis from time to time throughout the book in an attempt to explain what processes or events occur to support these high-level skills. Therefore this text should be appropriate for courses in elementary motor learning and motor performance in a relatively wide group of scientific areas.

Throughout the text, we construct a conceptual model of human performance. The term "model" is used in a variety of ways in many branches of science, and models are found frequently. A model typically consists of a system of parts that are familiar to us; when assembled in a certain way, these parts mimic certain aspects of the system we are trying to understand. One example is the pump-and-pipe model of our circulatory system, in which the heart is represented by a pump and the arteries and veins are pipes of various diameters and lengths. One could actually construct the model (although some models are purely conceptual); such a model could be used in classroom demonstrations or "experiments" on the effects of blood pressure on capillaries of the "hand."

Our first goal in writing this text was to build a strong, general, conceptual understanding (an overview) of skills. We believe that instructors, coaches, therapists, and trainers, as well as others dealing with the learning or teaching of skills, will profit greatly from such a high-level conceptual understanding of skilled behavior. In striving toward this goal, we have adopted (assumed) the idea that skills can be understood, for the most part, through the use of concepts concerning information and its processing. We set about to build a conceptual model that would capture (or explain) many of the intricacies of skilled motor performance. We begin this process by considering the human as a very simple input–output system; then gradually, as we introduce new topics in the text, we expand the model by adding these new concepts. Gradually, by building on knowledge and concepts presented in earlier parts of the text, we add increasing complexity to the conceptual model. Simply presenting the finished conceptual model would make it very difficult for students to understand, and we hope that the systematic process of constructing the model, assembled with parts as they are presented in the text, forms a logical basis for increasing the model's complexity. This construction process should make the final version of the model maximally understandable.

Our second goal was to organize the book in the best way to aid student understanding based on our many years of teaching experience. The text is divided into two parts. After the introduction to the study of motor skills in chapter 1, part I, examines how the motor system works by investigating the major principles of human performance and progressively developing a conceptual model of human actions. The focus is mainly on human performance as based on an information-processing perspective; but motor learning cannot be ignored, so it is mentioned briefly in various places. Chapter 2 discusses the nature of information processing, decision making, and movement planning. Chapter 3 considers the concepts of attention and memory. Chapter 4 concerns the information received from various sensory sources that are relevant to movement. Chapter 5 examines the processes underlying the production of movement, with particular attention to the role of motor programs. Chapter 6 considers the basic principles of performance that form the "building blocks" of skilled performance—analogous to the fundamental laws of physics. Finally, in chapter 7, the concern shifts to the differences in movement abilities among people and how these differences allow the prediction of success in new situations; differences among components in the conceptual model help in understanding these differences among people. On completion of part I, the student should have a reasonably coherent view of the conceptual and functional properties of the motor system. These principles seem appropriate for maximizing the performance of already learned skills. Part II of the text uses the conceptual model to impart an understanding of human motor *learning* processes. Much of this discussion uses the terms and concepts introduced in part I. This method works well in our own teaching, probably because motor learning is usually inferred from changes in motor behavior; therefore, it is easy to discuss these changes in terms of the behavioral principles from part I. In this second part, chapter 8 treats some methodological problems unique to the study of learning, such as how and when to measure performance, which also have application to measuring performance in analogous teaching situations. Chapter 9 considers broad issues of learning, retention, and transfer, such as the important role of practice. Chapter 10 concerns the issue of how and when to practice, dealing with the many factors that instructors can control directly to make practice more effective. Finally, chapter 11 deals with the critical topic of feedback, examining what kinds of movement information students need for effective learning, when it should be given, and so on. By the end of the text, readers will have a progressive accumulation of knowledge that, in our experience, provides a consistent view of how skills are performed and learned.

Many real-world examples of motor performance and learning principles are discussed in the main body of the text. In addition, we've included Focus on Application sections set off from the main textual materials. Strategically located directly after pertinent discussions of principles, these sections indicate applications to real-world teaching, coaching, or therapy. We wanted to write a text that could be used by performers, teachers, coaches, physical therapists, and other instructors in various fields to enhance human performance in real-world settings. To meet this goal, we have worked to focus the text on the topics most relevant to practical application.

As a third goal, we wanted a presentation style that would be simple, straightforward, and highly readable for those without extensive backgrounds in the motor performance area. As a result, the main content does not stress the research and data that contribute to our knowledge of motor skill acquisition and performance. Important points are occasionally illustrated by data from a critical experiment, but the emphasis is on an integrated conceptual knowledge of how the motor system works and how it learns. However, for those who desire a tighter link to the basic data, we have included sections called Focus on Research, which are set off from the main text and describe the important experiments and concepts in detail.

Finally, we demanded that the principles discussed should be faithful to the empirical data and thought in the study area. From decades in doing basic research in motor learning and motor performance, we have developed what we believe to be defensible, coherent, personal viewpoints (conceptual models, if you will) about how skills are performed and learned, and our aim was to present this model to the reader to facilitate understanding. Our viewpoints are based on a large literature of theoretical ideas and empirical data, together with much thought about competing ideas and apparently contradictory research findings. We have tried to write from this perspective as we would tell a story. Every part of the story can be defended empirically, or it would not have been included. Our goal has been to write "the truth," at least as we currently understand it and as it can be understood with the current level of knowledge. We have included a brief section at the end of each chapter describing additional readings that provide competing viewpoints and additional scientific justifications.

Students will find a range of learning aids within each chapter, including chapter-opening outlines, objectives, and lists of key terms, as well as an end-chapter summary of the activities in the accompanying web study guide and "Check Your Understanding" and "Apply Your Knowledge" questions. Instructors using this text in their courses will find a wealth of updated ancillary materials at www.humankinetics.com/MotorLearningAndPerformance, including a presentation package and image bank, instructor guide, and test package.

This fifth edition of Motor Learning and Performance extends the approach used in the previous four editions. As with the previous editions, we have tried to integrate the latest new findings together with the research and findings that have remained relevant for longer periods of time. But this edition could also be considered quite different as well. In many ways, this fifth edition returns to the approach adopted in the first edition, of providing a theoretical and conceptual basis for motor performance and learning that could be applied as broadly as possible. Since motor learning and performance are probably the most widespread activities that humans from all walks of life experience on a daily basis, our goal was to touch on as many of these applications as possible. The generality and limitations of these principles represent a core of human existence, and we hope that our treatment of them in this book resonates well with each person who reads it.

Richard A. Schmidt
Human Performance Research
Marina del Rey, California

Timothy D. Lee
Department of Kinesiology
McMaster University, Hamilton, Ontario

Draft. Not for Distribution.

Student and Instructor Resources

Student Resources

Students, visit the free web study guide, available at www.humankinetics.com/MotorLearningAndPerformance. The web study guide has been fully revised for the fifth edition to offer a more focused and interactive set of activities to aid learning. The activities in this study guide will help you to assess and build your understanding of concepts from each chapter of the text as you study.

In each chapter of the web study guide, you will be presented with a series of two to four interactive activities that test your understanding of important concepts. These include matching, multiple-choice, and diagram-based activities. For each chapter, you will be also be presented with a situation-based exercise that prompts you to take your knowledge beyond the classroom by using principles of motor control and learning to analyze an activity. There is no single right answer for the situation-based problems, but it is important to provide evidence and reasoning to support your ideas. Each situation-based exercise includes sample student answers and critiques of those answers to guide you as you develop your analysis. By completing the exercises included in this study guide, you will build your knowledge of important concepts from the textbook and learn to apply that knowledge to real-world situations.

Instructor Resources

The instructor guide, test package, chapter quizzes, presentation package, and image bank are free to course adopters and are accessed at www.humankinetics.com/MotorLearningAndPerformance.

Instructor Guide

The instructor guide includes chapter summary notes for preparing lectures and ideas for presenting topics and engaging students in class discussions, as well as practical laboratory activities. Sample essay questions are also provided for potential testing or student assignments.

Test Package

The test package includes more than 230 true-or-false, multiple-choice, fill-in-the-blank, and short-answer questions that can be used to create exams. The test package is available for download in Respondus and LMS formats as well as in Rich Text Format (.rtf) for use with word processing software.

Chapter Quizzes

New for the fifth edition, these ready-to-use 10-question quizzes help assess students' comprehension of the most important concepts in each chapter. Chapter quizzes can be imported into learning management systems or be used in RTF format by instructors who prefer to offer a written quiz.

Presentation Package

The presentation package includes more than 230 PowerPoint text slides that highlight material from the text for use in lectures and class discussions. The slides can be used directly in PowerPoint or can be printed to make transparencies or handouts for distribution to students. Instructors can easily add, modify, and rearrange the order of the slides as well as search for images based on key words.

Student and Instructor Resources

Image Bank

The image bank, included with the presentation package, includes most of the figures, content photos, and tables from the text, sorted by chapter, which can be used to develop a customized presentation.

Acknowledgments

This edition of *Motor Learning and Performance* owes a debt of gratitude to many people. It was Rainer Martens who first conceptualized the idea, and his encouragement led to the publication of the first edition (Schmidt, 1991). Sincere thanks go to Craig Wrisberg, who coauthored the next three editions (Schmidt & Wrisberg, 2000, 2004, 2008). Over the years the authors have worked with many wonderful editors at Human Kinetics, who made the sometimes tedious process much more enjoyable, for which we are very grateful. For this edition we would especially like to thank Myles Schrag and Kate Maurer for their efforts in seeing this project through to completion. We also thank Liz Sanli for her hard work on the book's ancillaries and Jasmine Caveness and Dianne Hopkins for their contributions to the task of copyediting and several other efforts. And lastly, we thank our wives, Gwen Gordon and Laurie Wishart, for their understanding and support of the work that went into not only producing this book, but all of our various endeavors.

Draft. Not for Distribution.

Credits

Figures

Figure 2.6 Reprinted, by permission, from R.A. Schmidt and T.D. Lee, 2011, *Motor control and learning: A behavioral emphasis,* 5th ed. (Champaign, IL: Human Kinetics). 65; Data from Merkel 1885.

Figure 2.7 Reprinted, by permission, from R.A. Schmidt and T.D. Lee, 2011, *Motor control and learning: A behavioral emphasis,* 5th ed. (Champaign, IL: Human Kinetics). 65; Data from Merkel 1885.

Figure 2.8 Reprinted, by permission, from R.A. Schmidt and T.D. Lee, 2011, *Motor control and learning: A behavioral emphasis,* 5th ed. (Champaign, IL: Human Kinetics). 70.

Figure 2.9 Reprinted, by permission, from J.A. Adams and S. Dijkstra, 1966, "Short-term memory for motor responses," *Journal of Experimental Psychology* 71: 317.

Figure 3.3 Reprinted from D.J. Simons and C.F. Chabis, 1999, "Gorillas in our midst: Sustained inattentional blindness for dynamic events," *Perception* 28: 1059-1074. By permission of D.J. Simons and C.F. Chabis.

Figure 3.5 Part *a* reprinted, by permission, from R.A. Schmidt and T.D. Lee, 2011, *Motor control and learning: A behavioral emphasis,* 5th ed. (Champaign, IL: Human Kinetics), 108; part *b* reprinted, by permission, from R.A. Schmidt and T.D. Lee, 2011, *Motor control and learning: A behavioral emphasis,* 5th ed. (Champaign, IL: Human Kinetics), 110; Data from Davis 1959.

Figure 3.7 Reprinted from M.I. Posner and S.W. Keele, 1969, Attentional demands of movement. In *Proceedings of the 16th Congress of applied physiology* (Amsterdam, Amsterdam: Swets and Zeitlinger). By permission of M.I. Posner.

Figure 3.8 Reprinted, by permission, from R.A. Schmidt and T.D. Lee, 2011, *Motor control and learning: A behavioral emphasis,* 5th edition. (Champaign, IL: Human Kinetics). Data from Weinberg and Ragan 1978.

Figure 4.7 Reprinted, by permission, from D.N. Lee and E. Aronson, 1974, "Visual proprioceptive control of standing in human infants," *Perception & Psychophysics* 15: 529-532.

Figure 4.11 Reprinted, by permission, from T.J. Ayres, R.A. Schmidt et al., 1995, Visibility and judgment in car-truck night accidents. In *Safety engineering and risk analysis--1995*, edited by D.W. Pratt (New York: The American Society of Mechanical Engineers), 43-50.

Figure 5.3 Reprinted with permission from *Research Quarterly for Exercise and Sport*, Vol.24, 22-32, Copyright 1953 by the American Alliance for Health, Physical Education, Recreation and Dance, 1900 Association Drive, Reston, VA 20191.

Figure 5.4 Reprinted, by permission, from R.A. Schmidt and T.D. Lee, 2011, *Motor control and learning: A behavioral emphasis,* 5th edition. (Champaign, IL: Human Kinetics), 183.

Figure 5.5 Part *a* reprinted, by permission, from R.A. Schmidt and T.D. Lee, 2011, *Motor control and learning: A behavioral emphasis,* 5th edition. (Champaign, IL: Human Kinetics), 195; part *b* reprinted, by permission, from R.A. Schmidt and T.D. Lee, 2011, *Motor control and learning: A behavioral emphasis,* 5th edition. (Champaign, IL: Human Kinetics), 195; Data from Slater-Hammel 1960.

Figure 5.6 Reprinted from W.J. Wadman, 1979, "Control of fast goal-directed arm movements," *Journal of Human Movement Studies* 5: 10. By permission of W.J. Wadman.

Figure 5.8 Adapted from T.R. Armstrong, 1970, *Training for the production of memorized movement patterns: Technical report no. 26* (Ann Arbor, MI: University of Michigan, Human Performance Center), 35. By permission of the Department of Psychology, University of Michigan.

Figure 5.9a and b Reprinted, by permission, from R.A. Schmidt and T.D. Lee, 2011, *Motor control and learning: A behavioral emphasis,* 5th edition. (Champaign, IL: Human Kinetics), 212.

Figure 5.10a and b Reprinted, by permission, from D.C. Shapiro et al., 1981, "Evidence for generalized motor programs using gait-pattern analysis," *Journal of Motor Behavior* 13: 38.

Credits

Figure 5.11 Adapted, by permission, from J.M. Hollerbach, 1978, *A study of human motor control through analysis and synthesis of handwriting.* Doctoral dissertation, (Cambridge, MA: Massachusetts Institute of Technology).

Figure 5.12 Reprinted from M.H. Raibert, 1977, *Motor control and learning by the state-space model: Technical report no. A1-TR-439* (Cambridge, MA: Artificial Intelligence Laboratory, Massachusetts Institute of Technology), 50. By permission of M.H. Raibert.

Figure 6.1 Adapted from *Categories of human learning,* A.W. Melton (Ed.), P.M. Fitts, Perceptual-motor skills learning, categories of human learning pg. 258.

Figure 6.2 Reprinted, by permission, from R.A. Schmidt and T.D. Lee, 2011, *Motor control and learning: A behavioral emphasis,* 5th ed. (Champaign, IL: Human Kinetics), 226. Data from Fitts 1954.

Figure 6.3a and b Adapted from P.M. Fitts, 1954, "The information capacity of the human motor system in controlling the amplitude of movement," *Journal of Experimental Psychology* 47: 381-391.

Figure 6.4 Reprinted, by permission, from R.A. Schmidt et al., 1979, "Motor-output variability: A theory for the accuracy of rapid motor acts," *Psychological Review* 86: 425. Copyright © 1979 by the American Psychological Association.

Figure 6.5 Reprinted, by permission, from R.A. Schmidt et al., 1979, "Motor-output variability: A theory for the accuracy of rapid motor acts," *Psychological Review* 86: 425. Copyright © 1979 by the American Psychological Association.

Figure 6.8 Reprinted, by permission, from R.A. Schmidt and D.E. Sherwood, 1982, "An inverted-U relation between spatial error and force requirements in rapid limb movements: Further evidence for the impulse-variability model," *Journal of Experimental Psychology: Human Perception and Performance* 8: 165. Copyright © 1982 by the American Psychological Association.

Figure 6.9 Reprinted, by permission, from R.A. Schmidt and T.D. Lee, 2011, *Motor control and learning: A behavioral emphasis,* 5th ed. (Champaign, IL: Human Kinetics), 238.

Figure 6.12 Reprinted, by permission, from P.A. Bender, 1987, *Extended practice and patterns of bimanual interference.* Unpublished doctoral dissertation (Los Angeles, CA: University of Southern California).

Figure 6.13a and b Reprinted, by permission, from T.D. Lee et al., 2008, "Do expert golfers really keep their heads still while putting?" *Annual Review of Golf Coaching* 2: 135-143.

Figure 6.14 Reprinted from *Physics Letters A, Vol.118,* J.A.S. Kelso, J.P. Scholz, and G. Schöner, "Nonequilibrium phase transitions in coordinated biological motion: Critical fluctuations," pg. 281, copyright 1986, with kind permission of Elsevier.

Table 7.2 by permission, from J.N. Drowatzky and F.C. Zuccato, 1967, "Interrelationships between selected measures of static and dynamic balance," *Research Quarterly* 38: 509-510.

Figure 7.4 Reprinted, by permission, from E.A. Fleishman and W.E. Hempel, 1955, "The relation between abilities and improvement with practice in a visual discrimination task," *Journal of Experimental Psychology* 49: 301-312. Copyright © 1955 by the American Psychological Association.

Figure 8.2 Reprinted, by permission, from J.A. Adams, 1952, "Warm up decrement in performance on the pursuit-rotor," *American Journal of Psychology* 65(3): 404-414.

Figure 8.3 Reprinted, by permission, from C.J. Winstein and R.A. Schmidt, 1990, "Reduced frequency of knowledge of results enhances motor skill learning," *Journal of Experimental Psychology: Learning, Memory and Cognition* 16: 677-691. Copyright © 1990 by the American Psychological Association.

Figure 8.4 Adapted, by permission, from H.P. Bahrick, P.M. Fitts, and G.E. Briggs, 1957, "Learning curves—facts or artifacts?" *Psychological Bulletin* 54: 256-268. Copyright © 1957 by the American Psychological Association.

Figure 9.3 Adapted, by permission, from R.A. Schmidt and T.D. Lee, 2011, *Motor control and learning: A behavioral emphasis,* 5th ed. (Champaign, IL: Human Kinetics), 451; Adapted from MacKay, 1976, personal communication.

Figure 9.4 Reprinted, by permission, from E. Neumann and R.B. Ammons, 1957, "Acquisition and long term retention of a simple serial perception motor skill," *Journal of Experimental Psychology* 53: 160. Copyright © 2011 by the American Psychological Association.

Figure 9.5 Reprinted from E.A. Fleishman and J.F. Parker, 1962, "Factors in the retention and relearning of perceptual motor skill," *Journal of Experimental Psychology* 64: 218. Copyright © 1962 by the American Psychological Association.

Figure 10.1 Adapted, by permission, from B.A. Boyce, 1992, "Effects of assigned versus participant-set goals on skill acquisition and retention of a selected shooting task," *Journal of Teaching in Physical Education* 11(2): 227.

Figure 10.2 Reprinted, by permission, from R. Lewthwaite and G. Wulf, 2010, "Social-comparative feedback affects motor skill learning," *Quarterly Journal of Experimental Psychology* 63: 738-749.

Figure 10.3 Reprinted, by permission, from G. Wulf, 2003, "Attentional focus on supra-postural tasks affects balance learning," *Quarterly Journal of Experimental Psychology* 56A: 1191-1211.

Figure 10.4 Reprinted, by permission, from D.M. Ste-Marie et al., 2012, "Observation interventions for motor skill learning and performance: An applied model for the use of observation," *International Review of Sport and Exercise Psychology* 5(2): 145-176.

Figure 10.6 Reprinted, by permission, from R.A. Schmidt and T.D. Lee, 2011, *Motor control and learning: A behavioral emphasis,* 5th ed. (Champaign, IL: Human Kinetics), 365. Data from Baddeley and Longman 1978.

Figure 10.7 Reprinted from L.E. Bourne and E.J. Archer, 1956, "Time continuously on target as a function of distribution of practice," *Journal of Experimental Psychology* 51: 27.

Figure 10.10 Reprinted, by permission, from K.M. Keetch, R.A. Schmidt, T.D. Lee, and D.E. Young, 2005, "Especial skills: Their emergence with massive amounts of practice," *Journal of Experimental Psychology: Human Perception and Performance* 31: 970-978. Copyright © 2005 by the American Psychological Association.

Figure 10.11 Adapted, by permission, from J.B. Shea and R.L. Morgan, 1979, "Contextual interference effects on the acquisition, retention, and transfer of a motor skill," *Journal of Experimental Psychology: Human Learning and Memory* 5: 179-187. Copyright © 1979 by the American Psychological Association.

Figure 10.12 Reprinted with permission from *Research Quarterly for Exercise and Sport,* vol. 68, pg. 103. Copyright 1997 by the American Alliance for Health, Physical Education, Recreation and Dance, 1900 Association Drive, Reston, VA 20191.

Figure 10.14 Adapted with permission from *Research Quarterly for Exercise and Sport,* vol. 68, pg. 357-361. Copyright 1997 by the American Alliance for Health, Physical Education, Recreation and Dance, 1900 Association Drive, Reston, VA 20191.

Figure 11.3 Reprinted with permission from *Research Quarterly for Exercise and Sport,* Vol. 78, pg. 43, Copyright 2007 by the American Alliance for Health, Physical Education, Recreation and Dance, 1900 Association Drive, Reston, VA 20191.

Figure 11.4 ©Bob Scavetta. Reproduction is forbidden without the written permission of the copyright holder.

Figure 11.5 Reprinted, by permission, from R.A. Schmidt and T.D. Lee, 2011, *Motor control and learning: A behavioral emphasis,* 5th ed. (Champaign, IL: Human Kinetics), 401; Data from Kernodle and Carlton 1992.

Figure 11.6 Reprinted, by permission, from C.J. Winstein and R.A. Schmidt, 1990, "Reduced frequency of knowledge of results enhances motor skill learning," *Journal of Experimental Psychology: Learning, Memory, and Cognition* 16: 910. Copyright © 1990 by the American Psychological Association.

Figure 11.9 Reprinted, by permission, from W. Yao, M.G. Fischman, and Y.T. Wang, 1994, "Motor skill acquisition and retention as a function of average feedback, summary feedback, and performance variability," *Journal of Motor Behavior* 26: 273-282.

Figure 11.12 Adapted, by permission, from Schmidt and Lee, 2011, *Motor control and learning: A behavioral emphasis,* 5th ed. (Champaign, IL: Human Kinetics), 387. Adapted from Armstrong 1970.

Figure 11.13 Reprinted, by permission, from S.P. Swinnen et al., 1990, "Information feedback for skill acquisition: instantaneous knowledge of results degrades learning," *Journal of Experimental Psychology: Learning, Memory, and Cognition* 16: 712. Copyright © 2011 by the American Psychological Association.

Figure 11.14 Reprinted from M.A. Guadagnoli and R.M. Kohl, 2001, "Knowledge of results for motor learning: Relationship between error estimation and knowledge of results frequency," *Journal of Motor Behavior,* 33: 217-224.

Photos

Page \bb Courtesy of Jack Adams.

Page \bb © Zumapress/Icon SMI

Page \bb © Jerome Brunet/ZUMA Press

Page \bb MOCK – Reprinted, by permission, from Weinberg, R.S., and Gould, D. 12003, Foundations of Sport and Exercise Psychology, Champaign, IL: Human Kinetics, 10.

Page \bb © Lee Mills/Action Images/Icon SMI

Page \bb © Human Kinetics/J. Wiseman, reefpix.org

Page \bb © Cliff Welch/Icon SMI

Page \bb © Human Kinetics

Page \bb © Human Kinetics

Credits

Page \bb ©Chris Ison/PA Archive/Press Association Images

Page \bb © Human Kinetics

Page \bb © Human Kinetics

Page \bb Reprinted from D.J. Simons and C.F. Chabis, 1999, "Gorillas in our midst: Sustained inattentional blindness for dynamic events," _Perception_ 28: 1059-1074. By permission of D.J. Simons and C.F. Chabis.

Page \bb © Zuma Press/Icon SMI

Page \bb © Human Kinetics

Page \bb © Zuma Press/Icon SMI

Page \bb © Jim West/Age Fotostock

Page \bb © Human Kinetics

Page \bb © Human Kinetics

Page \bb ©Photo courtesy of Philip de Vries.

Page \bb Reprinted from D.N. Lee and E. Aronson, 1974, "Visual proprioceptive control of standing in human infants," _Perception & Psychophysics_ 15: 529-532. By permission of D.N. Lee.

Page \bb All four photos © Human Kinetics

Page \bb © Ed Bock/Lithium/age fotostock

Page \bb © Tonyi Mateos/Age Fotostock

Page \bb © Human Kinetics

Page \bb © Zumapress/Icon SMI

Page \bb © Human Kinetics

Page \bb © STOCK4B/Age Fotostock

Page \bb © Human Kinetics

Page \bb © Human Kinetics

Page \bb © Human Kinetics

Page \bb © Human Kinetics

Page \bb © Human Kinetics

Page \bb © Zumapress/Icon SMI

Page \bb Everett Collection Inc./age footstock (BABE)

Page \bb © Javier Larrea/Age Fotostock

Page \bb © Human Kinetics

Page \bb © A. Farnsworth/Age Fotostock

Page \bb © Human Kinetics

Page \bb © Human Kinetics

Page \bb © Martin Rickett/PA Archive/Press Association Images

Page \bb Courtesy Timothy D. Lee.

Page \bb © Human Kinetics

Page \bb © Human Kinetics

Page \bb © George Shelley/Age Fotostock

Page \bb Courtesy Richard A. Schmidt

Page \bb © Norbert Michalke/ imagebroker/age footstock

Page \bb © Zuma Press/Icon SMI

Page \bb © GEPA/Imago/Icon SMI

Page \bb © Human Kinetics

Page \bb © Tony Ding/Icon SMI

Page \bb © Denis Meyer/Age Fotostock

Page \bb © Human Kinetics

Page \bb © Human Kinetics

Page \bb © Laura Leonard Fitch

Page \bb © Tim Ockenden/PA Archive/Press Association Images

Introduction to Motor Learning and Performance

How Skills Are Studied

KEY TERMS

absolute constant error (|CE|)
absolute error (AE)
closed skill
constant error (CE)
continuous skill
discrete skill
open skill
root-mean-square error (RMSE)
serial skill
skill
tracking
variable error (VE)

CHAPTER OUTLINE

Why Study Motor Skills?
The Science of Motor Learning and Performance
Defining Skills
Components of Skills
Classifying Skills
Understanding Performance and Learning
Summary

CHAPTER OBJECTIVES

Chapter 1 provides an overview of research in human motor skills with particular reference to their study in motor learning and performance. This chapter will help you to understand

- ▶ the scientific method in skills research,
- ▶ different taxonomies used to classify skills,
- ▶ common variables used to measure motor performance, and
- ▶ the rationale for developing a conceptual model of motor performance.

In 2012, a petite American girl named Gabrielle ("Gabby") Douglas captivated the sport world with her feats in women's gymnastics at the London Olympic Games, and, almost instantly, she became a role model for many young girls who suddenly wanted to learn gymnastics. The "flying squirrel," as she is fondly called by her teammates, won the gold medal in the women's all-around competition—arguably the pinnacle in women's gymnastics. In the 1980s Jim Knaub, who had lost the use of his legs in an accident, won several important marathons in the wheelchair division, earning our heartfelt respect. From the 1970s into the '90s, David Kiley earned the title "King of Wheelchair Sports" by (a) winning five gold medals in the 1976 Paralympic Games in Canada; (b) climbing the highest mountain in Texas; (c) playing on the United States men's wheelchair basketball team five times; and (d) competing at the highest level in tennis, racquetball, and skiing. And, since the Woodstock music festival in 1969, Johnny Winter, who is arguably (at least according to the second author) the world's best guitarist, continues to amaze audiences with his skills and versatility. These and countless other examples indicate that skills are a critical part of human existence. How people can perform at such high levels, how such skills are developed, and how you can develop some approximation of these skills in yourself, your children, or your students—all of these questions generate fascination, encouraging further learning about human movement.

A description of the study of motor performance and learning starts here. The overview presented in this chapter introduces the concept of skill and discusses various features of its definition. The chapter then gives examples of skill classification schemes important for later applications. Finally, to help you understand skills effectively using this book, the logic behind the book's organization is described: first, the principles and processes underlying skilled performance, followed by how such capabilities can be developed with practice.

The remarkable human capability to perform skills is a critical feature of our very existence. It is almost uniquely human, although various animals relatively high on the evolutionary scale can be trained to produce what you might call skilled behaviors (e.g., circus dogs doing somersaults, bears riding bicycles). Without the capacity for skilled performance, we could not type the page we are preparing now and you could not read it. And for students involved in physical education and kinesiology, coaching, physical (or speech or occupational) therapy, chiropractic, medicine, or human factors and ergonomics, here is the opportunity to learn about the fundamentals of a wide variety of sports and athletic endeavors, music, and simply ordinary everyday actions that are so strongly fascinating and exciting. Human skills take many forms, of course—from those that emphasize the control and coordination of our largest muscle groups in relatively forceful activities like soccer or tumbling, to those in which the smallest muscle groups must be tuned precisely, as in typing or repairing a watch. This text generally focuses on the full range of skilled behavior because it is useful to understand that many common features underlie the performance of skills associated with industrial and military settings, sport, the reacquisition of movement capabilities lost through injuries or stroke, or simply the everyday activities of most people.

Most humans are born with the capability to produce many skills, and only some maturation and experience is necessary in order to produce them in nearly complete form. Walking and running, chewing, balancing, and avoiding painful stimuli are some examples of these relatively innate behaviors. But imagine what simple and uninteresting creatures we would be if these inherited actions were all that we could ever do. All biological organisms have the remarkable facility to profit from their experiences, to learn to detect important environmental features (and to ignore others), and to produce behaviors that were not a part of their original capabilities. Humans seem to have the most flexibility of all, which allows gains in proficiency for occupations as chemists or computer programmers, for competition in music or athletics, or simply for conducting

Johnny Winter, who is (according to this book's second author) the world's best guitarist, demonstrating just one of his nearly unlimited variety of motor skills.

daily lives more efficiently. Thus, producing skilled behaviors and the learning that leads to their development are tightly intertwined in human experience. This book is about both of these aspects of skills—skilled human performance and human learning.

This book is *not* about skills in which the degree of success is determined by deciding which of many already learned actions the performer is to do. When the laboratory rat learns to press a bar at the presentation of a sound, the rat is not learning how to press the bar; rather, the animal is learning when to make this already learned bar-pressing action. As another example, in the card game of poker, it does not matter *in what fashion* the various cards are played (i.e., moved). What matters is cognitive decision making about which card to play and when to do it. The study of these kinds of decision-making processes falls mainly into fields such as experimental psychology and cognitive neuroscience, and these processes are deliberately not included here.

Why Study Motor Skills?

Because skills make up such a large part of human life, scientists and educators have been trying for centuries to understand the determinants of skills and the factors that affect their performance. The knowledge gained is applicable to numerous aspects of life. Important points apply to the instruction of skills, where methods for efficient teaching and effective carryover to life situations are primary concerns. There is also considerable applicability for improving high-level performances, such as sport, music, and surgical skills. Of course, much of what coaches and music and physical education teachers do during their professional activities involves, in one way or another, skills instruction. The practitioners who understand these skill-related processes most effectively undoubtedly have an advantage when their "subjects" begin their trained-for activities.

Other application areas can be emphasized as well. There are many applications in training skills for industry, where effective job skills can mean success in the workplace and can be major determinants of satisfaction both with the job and with life in general. Teaching job skills most effectively, and determining which of a large number of individuals are best suited to particular occupations, are common situations in which knowledge about skills can be useful in industry. Usually these applications are considered within human factors (ergonomics). The principles also apply to physical therapy and occupational therapy settings as well, where the concern is for the (re)learning and production of movements that have been lost through head or spinal cord injury, stroke, birth defects, and the like. Although all these areas may be different and the physical capabilities of the learners may vary widely, the principles that lead to successful application are generally the same.

The Science of Motor Learning and Performance

It is not uncommon that as an area of interest grows, the systematic study of the principles involved also develops. Motor learning and performance is no different, in that a science has emerged that allows the formalization of terms and concepts for others to use. When we use the word "science," what do we mean?

The concept of a science implies several things: (a) the active use of theory and hypothesis testing to further our knowledge; (b) a certain "infrastructure" that involves books and journals, scientific organizations that deal with both the fundamental aspects of the science and ways to apply the knowledge to real-world situations, and granting agencies to provide funds for research; and, of course, (c) the existence of courses of study of the area in universities and colleges.

Theories and Hypotheses

Certainly at the heart of every science are theories that purport to explain how things work. A theory is a human-made structure whose purpose is to explain how various phenomena occur. The theorist conjures up what are called *hypothetical constructs*—imaginary elements, or pieces, that interact in various ways in the theory. The theorist then describes the ways in which the hypothetical constructs interact with each other so as to explain some empirical phenomenon. Then, using logical deduction, scientists determine certain predictions that the theory makes in its current form. These predictions form the basis of hypotheses that can be tested, typically in the laboratory. These hypotheses take the form of statements such as "If I ask learners to practice under condition x, then learning should be enhanced."

Theories are typically tested by doing experiments, which determine whether or not the hypothesis predicts what happens. In the field of motor learning and performance, these experiments typically take the form of having at least two groups of subjects randomly assigned to experimental treatments, with one group performing a task under condition x (as in the example just mentioned) and the other group performing under some other conditions that are reasonably well understood (sometimes called a "control condition"). If, in this example, the group practicing under condition x outperforms the group in the control condition, then we say that the hypothesis is supported. However, a given theory might predict an outcome that would make sense for several different theories, so an experiment that supports a hypothesis is not always the strongest type of evidence. What is usually far stronger is if the results come out *contrary* to the prediction; this leads to the logical inference that the theory must be incorrect, allowing us to

Focus on RESEARCH 1.1

Franklin M. Henry, Father of Motor Behavior Research

Before World War II and during the 1950s and 1960s when much effort was directed at military skills such as pilotry, most of the research in movement behavior and learning was done by experimental psychologists using relatively fine motor skills. Little effort was devoted to the gross motor skills that would be applicable to many sports. Franklin M. Henry, trained in experimental psychology but working in the Department of Physical Education, at the University of California Berkley, was filling this gap with a new tradition of laboratory experimentation that started an important new direction in research on movement skills. He studied gross motor skills, with performances intentionally representative of those seen on the

Franklin M. Henry (1904-1993).

playing fields and in gymnasiums. But he used laboratory tasks——that enabled the rigorous study of these skills employing methods analogous to those used in experimental psychology. He examined a number of research problems, such as the differences among people, practice scheduling, the mathematical shapes of performance curves, and the roles of fatigue and rest in performance.

Henry's influence on the fields of physical education and kinesiology was widespread by the 1970s and 1980s.

reject one of the possible theories. This is so because a theory cannot "survive" for long if something predicted from it turns out not to be the case. Because of this difference in the power of the ways in which hypotheses are tested, scientists tend to search out predictions from a theory that might not hold if tested in the laboratory.

What Kinds of Skills Have Been Studied?

The science of motor learning and performance has been used to study many varieties of skills. In the very beginning (research and writing done in the early 1900s, or perhaps slightly before), two types of investigations can be identified: (a) investigations of relatively complex, high-level skills such as telegraphy and typing (e.g., Bryan & Harter, 1897, 1899), and (b) studies by biologists and physiologists concerning the fundamental mechanisms of neural control of muscle, muscle force production (Fullerton & Cattell, 1892), and the study of nerves and the nervous system (Fritsch & Hitzig, 1870; Sherrington, 1906).

Defining Skills

As widely represented and diverse as skills are, it is difficult to define them in a way that applies to all cases. Guthrie (1952) provided a definition that captures most of the critical features of skills that we emphasize here. He defined **skill** as "the ability to bring about some end result with maximum certainty and minimum outlay of energy, or of time and energy" (p. 136). Next, we consider some of the important components (or features) of this definition.

First, performing skills implies some desired environmental goal, such as holding a handstand in gymnastics or being able to walk again after a stroke. Skills are usually thought of as different from *movements*, which do not necessarily have any particular environmental goal, such as idly wiggling one's little finger. Of course, skills consist of movements because the performer could not achieve an *environmental* goal without making at least one movement.

Second, to be skilled implies meeting this performance goal, this "end result," with maximum *certainty*. For example, while playing darts a player makes a bull's-eye. But this by itself does not ensure that he is a skilled darts player, because this result was achieved without very much certainty. Such an outcome could have been the result of one lucky throw in the midst of hundreds of others that were not so lucky. To be considered "skilled" requires that a person produce the skill reliably, on demand, without luck playing a very large role. This is one reason why people value so greatly the champion athlete who, with but one chance and only seconds remaining at the end of a game, makes the goal that allows the team to win.

Third, a major feature in many skills is the minimization, and thus conservation, of the energy required for performance. For some skills this is clearly not the goal, as in the shot put, where the only goal is to throw the maximum distance. But for many other skills the minimization of energy expenditure is critical, allowing the marathon runner to hold an efficient pace or allowing the wrestler to save strength for the last few minutes of the match. We evolved to walk as we do, in part, because our walking style minimizes energy expenditure for walking a given distance. This minimum-energy notion applies not only to the physiological energy costs but also to the psychological, or mental, energy required for performance. Many skills have been learned so well that the performers hardly have to pay attention to them, freeing their cognitive processes for other features of the activity, such as strategy in basketball or expressiveness in dance. A major contributor to the efficiency of skilled performance is, of course, practice, with learning and experience leading to the relatively effortless performances so admired in highly skilled people.

Finally, another feature of many skills is for highly proficient performers to achieve their goals in minimum time. Many skills have this as the only goal, such as a swimming race. Minimizing time can interact with

To be skilled implies that a person can produce an end result with a high degree of certainty. For example, an expert darts player can consistently throw the dart close to his target.

the other skill features mentioned, however. Surgeons who conduct invasive surgery need to work quickly to minimize the opportunity for infections to enter the body. Yet surgeons obviously need to work carefully, too. Speeding up performance often results in imprecise movements that have less certainty in terms of achieving their environmental goals. Also, increased speed generates movements for which the energy costs are sometimes higher. Thus, understanding skills involves optimizing and balancing several skill aspects that are important to different extents in different settings. In sum, skills generally involve achieving some well-defined environmental goal by

- maximizing the certainty of goal achievement,
- minimizing the physical- and mental-energy costs of performance, and
- minimizing the time used.

Components of Skills

The elegant performance of the skilled dancer and the artistic talents of an expert sculptor may appear simple, but the performance goals actually were realized through a complex combination of interacting mental and motor processes. For example, many skills involve considerable emphasis on sensory–perceptual factors, such as detecting that a tennis opponent is going to hit a shot to your left or that you are rapidly approaching a car that has suddenly stopped on the road ahead of you. Often, sensory factors require the split-second analysis of patterns of sensory input, such as discerning that the combined movements of an entire football team indicate that the play will be a running play to the left side. These perceptual events lead to decisions about what to do, how to do it, and when to do it. These decisions are often a major determinant of success. Finally, of course, skills typically depend on the quality of movement generated as a result of these decisions. Even if the situation is correctly perceived and the response decisions are appropriate, the performer will not be effective in meeting the environmental goal if she executes the actions poorly.

These three elements are critical to almost any skill:

- Perceiving the relevant environmental features
- Deciding what to do and where and when to do it to achieve the goal
- Producing organized muscular activity to generate movements that achieve the goal

The movements have several recognizable parts. Postural components support the actions; for instance, the arms and hands of a surgeon need to be supported by a stable "platform" in order to perform accurately. Body transport, or locomotion, components move the body toward the point where the skill will take place, as in carrying a package of shingles up a ladder to place on the roof of a house.

It is interesting, but perhaps unfortunate, that each of these skill components seems to be recognized and studied in isolation from the others. For example, sensory factors in perception are studied by cognitive psychologists, scientists interested in (among other things) the complex information-processing activities involved in seeing, hearing, and feeling. Sometimes these factors are in the realm of psychophysics, the branch of psychology that examines the relationship between objective physical stimuli (e.g., vibration intensity) and the subjective sensations these stimuli create when perceived (loudness). Factors in the control of the movement itself are typically studied by scientists in the neurosciences, cognitive psychology, biomechanics, and physiology. Skill learning is studied by yet another group of scientists in kinesiology and physical education, in experimental or educational psychology, or in the field of human factors and ergonomics. A major problem for the study of skills, therefore, is the fact that the several components of skill are studied by widely different groups of scientists, often with little overlap and communication among them.

All of these various processes are present in almost all motor skills. Even so, we should not get the idea that all skills are fundamentally the same. In fact, the principles of human performance and learning depend to some extent on the *kind* of movement skill to be performed. So, the ways in which skills have been classified are discussed next.

Classifying Skills

There are several skill classification systems that help organize the research findings and make application somewhat more straightforward. These are presented in the following sections.

Open and Closed Skills

One way to classify movement skills concerns the extent to which the environment is stable and predictable throughout performance. An **open skill** is one for which the environment is variable and unpredictable during the action. Examples include most team sports and driving a car in traffic where it is difficult to predict the future moves of other people. A **closed skill**, on the other hand, is one for which the environment is stable and predictable. Examples include swimming in an empty lane in a pool and drilling a hole in a block of wood. These "open" and "closed" designations actually mark only the end points of a continuum, with the skills lying in between having varying degrees of environmental predictability or variability (see Gentile, 2000, for a fuller discussion).

This classification points out a critical feature for skills, defining the performer's need to respond to moment-to-moment variations in the environment. It thus brings in the subprocesses associated with perception, pattern recognition, and decision making (usually with the need to perform these processes quickly) so the action can be tailored to the environment. These processes are arguably minimized in closed skills, where the performer can evaluate the environmental demands in advance without time pressure, organize the movement in advance, and carry it out without needing to make rapid modifications as the movement unfolds. These features are summarized in table 1.1.

Discrete, Continuous, and Serial Skills

A second scheme for classifying skills concerns the extent to which the movement is an ongoing stream of behavior, as opposed to a brief, well-defined action. At one end of this dimension is a **discrete skill**, which usually has an easily defined beginning and end, often with a very brief duration of movement, such as throwing a ball, firing a rifle, or turning on a light switch. Discrete skills are particularly important in both sport and daily actions, especially considering the large number of discrete hitting, kicking, and throwing skills that make up many sport activities, as well as everyday skills of fastening buttons, writing your signature, and tying your shoelaces. Discrete skills often result in a measured outcome score, which can be combined with other scores to result in several types of "error" scores, discussed in Focus on Research 1.2 and 1.3.

At the other end of this dimension is a **continuous skill**, which has no particular beginning or end, the behavior flowing on for many minutes, such as swimming and knitting. As discussed later, discrete and continuous skills can be quite different, requiring different processes for performance and demanding that they be taught somewhat differently as a result.

One particularly important continuous skill is **tracking**, in which the performer's limb movements control a lever, a wheel, a handle, or some other device to follow the movements of some target-track. Steering a car involves tracking, with steering wheel movements made so the car follows the track, defined by the roadway. Tracking movements are very common in real-world skills situations, and much research has been directed to their performance and learning. Tracking tasks are sometimes scored using a particular error score, called root-mean-square error (RMSE) presented in detail in Focus on Research 1.3, "Error Scores in Continuous Tasks."

Between the polar ends of the discrete-continuous-skill continuum is the **serial skill**, which is often thought of as a group of discrete skills strung together to make up a new, more complicated skilled action. See table 1.2 for a comparison summary. Here the word

TABLE 1.1 Open and Closed Skills Continuum

Closed skills ←		→ Open skills
Predictable environment	**Semipredictable environment**	**Unpredictable environment**
Gymnastics	Walking a tightrope	Playing soccer
Archery	Steering a car	Wrestling
Typing	Playing chess	Chasing a rabbit

TABLE 1.2 Discrete–Serial–Continuous Skills Continuum

Discrete skills	Serial skills	Continuous skills
Distinct beginning and end	**Discrete actions linked together**	**No discrete beginning or end**
Throwing a dart	Hammering a nail	Steering a cart
Flipping a light switch	Assembly-line work	Swimming
Shooting a rifle	Gymnastics routine	Tracking task

Focus on
RESEARCH 1.2

Error Scores in Discrete Tasks

Quite frequently in research, we are called on to generate a method for computing an accuracy score for a given subject who was attempting a series of trials on a test requiring accuracy, often involving discrete tasks. As we shall see here, there are various ways to do it.

Assume that you are testing subjects on a throwing task, in which subjects have to throw a ball exactly 50 ft away from where they are standing. Two hypothetical subjects perform this task for five trials, and the following are the results:

Subject	Trial 1	Trial 2	Trial 3	Trial 4	Trial 5
Chester	46	52	39	55	60
John-Lee	40	54	48	46	49

Which of these two subjects was more skillful in this task? The problem here is to generate a single number that accurately reflects their skill in the task (a throwing accuracy "score"), based on those five throwing trials. Several candidate measures are possible.

Constant Error (CE)

The most obvious way to determine which subject was more accurate is to compute the error deviation of each throw, relative to the target, and then calculate the average of these error deviations. For example, on trial 1, Chester's error score was -4 (his throw was 46 ft, and thus, 4 ft short of the target). The error score on the second trial was +2 (his 52-ft throw as 2 ft too far). After the error scores for each trial are computed the mean can then be calculated to determine the average error deviation. This is termed the subjects' average **constant error**. The interpretation is that Chester tended to overthrow the 50 ft target by 0.4 ft; John-Lee tended to underthrow the target by 2.6 ft.

The formula for constant error is

$$CE = [(\Sigma X_i - T) / N]$$

where: Σ = the "sum of," i = trial number, X_i = score for the ith trial, T = the target distance, and N = the number of trials.

Absolute Error (AE)

Another relatively obvious way to combine the scores into a single number is to consider the *absolute value* (i.e., with the sign ignored or removed) of the error on each trial, and take the average of those error scores for the various trials. For example, for Chester the first trial has an error of –4 ft; when we take the absolute value, the first trial has an absolute error of 4 ft; the second trial has an error of +2 ft, whose absolute value is 2. If we do this procedure for the remainder of the trials for Chester, and all the trials for John-Lee, the computed average absolute error for Chester is 6.4; for John-Lee it is 4.2. Here, with the direction of the errors being disregarded, the interpretation is that Chester was off-target more than was John-Lee.

The formula for average **absolute error (AE)** is

$$AE = [(\Sigma \ |X_i - T|) / N]$$

where: Σ, i, X, T, and N are defined as before for constant error, and the vertical bars (|) mean "absolute value of."

Variable error (VE)

The third measure of skill is actually a measure of the subject's inconsistency—that is, how different each individual score was in comparison to his average (CE) score. To compute **variable error (VE)**, we square the difference between each trial's error score and the subject's own constant error $[(X_i - CE)^2]$, sum those over all of the trials, and divide by N. Now, since these are squared values, we return them to their original state by computing the square root of this value.

In this example, for Chester's first trial, the difference between X_1 and Chester's average CE (which was +0.4) is $[(-4 - (+0.4)] = -4.4$ ft, which, when squared, is 19.36 ft. For the second trial, the difference between X_2 and Chester's average CE is $[(+2) - (+0.4)] = 1.6$ ft, which, when squared, is 2.56 ft. Now do the same thing for trials 3, 4, and 5; add up all five squared differences; divide this number by $N = 5$; then take the square root of that number; and you finally have VE. The score is interpreted as the inconsistency in responding, that is, how variable the performance is about the subject's own CE. Of course when computing the value for John-Lee, we would use his CE (which was -2.6) in the computations. The computed VE score for Chester was 7.3 ft, and for John-Lee the VE was 4.5 ft. The interpretation is that even though Chester's average throw was closer to the goal than was John-Lee's average throw, Chester was more inconsistent in those throws than was John-Lee.

The formula for variable error is

$$VE = \sqrt{[(\Sigma X_i - CE)^2 / N]}$$

where Σ, X, i, CE, and N are defined as before, and $\sqrt{}$ is the square root.

AE was employed as a measure of error very frequently until investigators Schutz and Roy (1973) pointed out some statistical difficulties with it. Today, investigators tend to use CE (as a measure of average bias, or directional error) and VE (as a measure of inconsistency). Sometimes investigators use a statistic called **absolute constant error** (abbreviated |CE|) instead of CE for a subject's measure of bias. The |CE| is simply the average absolute value of the computed CE score as defined previously. The advantage is that |CE| retains the magnitude of average deviation from the target, but prevents two scores from "canceling out" when subjects are averaged together to present a group score. Much more on these error scores is presented in chapter 2 of Schmidt and Lee (2011).

Swimming in an empty pool lane is an example of a closed, continuous skill.

"serial" implies that the order of the elements is usually critical for successful performance. Shifting car gears is a serial skill, with three discrete shift lever action elements (along with accelerator and clutch elements) connected in sequence to create a larger action. Other examples include performing a gymnastics routine and most types of cooking. Serial skills differ from discrete skills in that the movement durations tend to be somewhat longer, yet each component retains a discrete beginning and end. One view of learning serial skills suggests that the individual skill elements present in early learning are somehow combined to form one larger, single element that the performer controls almost as if it were truly discrete in nature (e.g., the smooth, rapid way a gymnast shifts from one maneuver to another on the rings).

Understanding Performance and Learning

In some ways, skilled performance and motor learning are interrelated concepts that cannot be easily separated for analysis. Even so, a temporary separation of these areas is necessary for presentation and making eventual understanding much easier. Many of the terms, principles, and processes that scientists use to describe the improvements with practice and learning (the subfield of motor learning) actually come from the literature on the underlying processes in the production of skilled motor performance (the subfield of human performance; the field of motor behavior often includes both motor learning and human performance). Therefore, whereas at

Focus on
RESEARCH 1.3

Error Scores in Continuous Tasks

Continuous tasks, like tracking, are capable of producing many error scores on a single trial. Consider figure 1.1 as an example of a portion of a single trial of a tracking task for one subject. The blue track represents the stimulus goal, such as a highway lane along which a driver might navigate a car. The red line represents the exact (unmarked) center of the track from edge to edge. The dotted line represents a subject's tracking behavior, in this case, how close to the center of the road the car is maintained. How can skill be measured in this single trial of a continuous performance?

A common method used by researchers who study tracking tasks is to compute a measure called **root-mean-square error (RMSE)**. One does this by computing the distance of the subject's tracking response from the target line at set distance-points along the track (e.g., every 10 ft of highway traveled) or, more commonly, at a constant interval of time along the track (e.g., every 100 ms). This method effectively "slices" the movement into equal intervals of tracking behavior, from start to finish.

With each "slice" of the track, the researcher then computes how far the subject's tracking position is from the target. Since the red line in figure 1.1 represents the center of the track, it is convenient to define the red line as the "zero" position. Therefore, if the subject is to the right of the target, the measure is given a positive error value; if the tracking position is to the left of the target, the measure gets a negative value. The root-mean-square error score is computed by first calculating the squared deviations for each measured position along the track, then taking the square root of the sum of those scores.

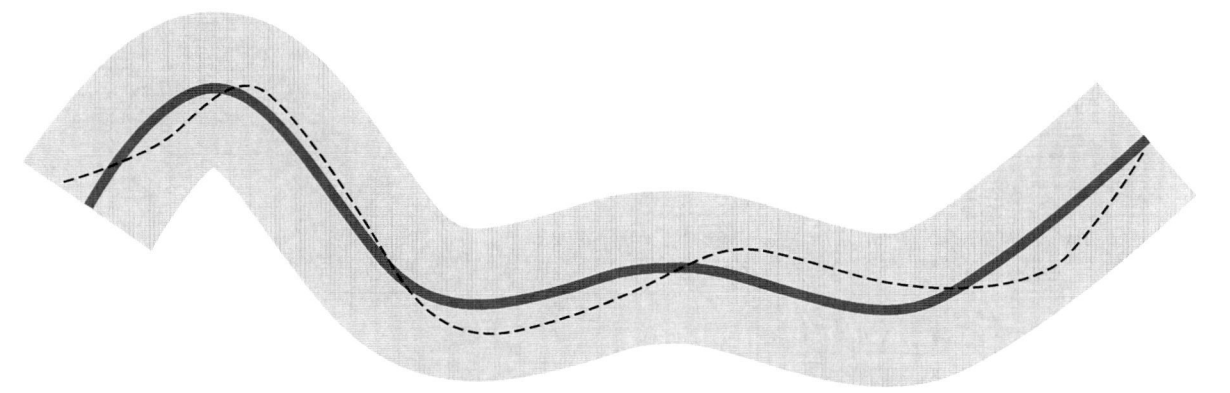

FIGURE 1.1 Measuring RMSE in a tracking task. The blue line represents the "track" (such as a highway lane); the red (solid) line represents the unmarked center of the lane, and can be considered the subject's goal track. The blue (dotted) line represents the subject's performance in attempting to follow the red line.

The RMSE is a more complex measure of performance than any of the error scores for discrete tasks, because it represents two components of behavior. The RMSE reflects both the subject's bias tendency (e.g., on average, to drive closer to the right edge of the lane than the left edge) as well as inconsistency in the tracking behavior (how variable the performance tends to be). It is well recognized as a very good measure of how effectively the person tracked.

first glance it might seem most logical to treat motor learning before motor performance (a person has to learn before performing), it turns out to be awkward to present information on learning without first having provided this background performance information.

For this reason this book is organized into two parts, the first of which introduces the terminology, concepts, and principles related to skilled human performance without very much reference to processes associated with learning. The principles here probably apply most strongly to the performance of already skilled actions. Having examined the principles of how the motor system produces skills, the discussion turns to how these processes can be altered, facilitated, and trained through practice. This involves motor learning, whose principles apply most strongly to the instruction of motor skills.

When studying motor-skill performance and learning, it is helpful to understand where each concept fits into the complex process of performing a skill. For this reason, and to help apply skills information to a variety of settings, this book develops a conceptual model. This model represents the big picture of motor performance; and as new topics are introduced, they are added to the model, tying together most of the major processes and events that occur as performers produce skills. Models of this type are critical in teaching and in science because they embrace many seemingly unrelated facts and concepts, linking real-world knowledge with the concepts being discussed.

Models can be of many types, of course, such as the plumbing-and-pump model of the human circulatory system and the variety of balls that model the structure of atoms, the solar system, and molecules in chemistry. For skills, a useful conceptualization is an information-flow model, which considers how information of various kinds is used in producing and learning a skilled action. The first portions of the text build this model, first considering how the sensory information that enters the system through the receptors is processed, transformed, and stored. Then, to this is added how this sensory information leads to other processes associated with decision making and planning action. To the emerging conceptual model are then added features of the initiation of action as well as the activities involved while the action is unfolding, such as controlling muscular contractions and detecting and correcting errors; this is highly related to the performer's analysis of the sensations produced as a result of performing the action—processes related to feedback. In the second portion of the text, which deals with learning, the model provides an effective understanding of the processes that are, and are not, influenced by practice.

Summary

People regard skills as an important, fascinating aspect of life. Knowledge about skills has come from a variety of scientific disciplines and can be applied to many settings, such as sport, teaching, coaching, industry, and physical therapy.

Skill is usually defined as the capability to bring about some desired end result with maximum certainty and minimum time and energy. Many different components are involved; major categories are perceptual or sensory processes, decision-making, and movement output. Skills may be classified along numerous dimensions, such as open versus closed skills, and discrete, continuous, and serial skills. These classifications are important because the principles of skills and their learning often differ for different skill categories.

The text's particular organization of materials should facilitate an understanding of skills. After this introduction, the remainder of part I treats the principles of human skilled performance and the underlying processes, focusing on how the various parts of the motor system act to produce skilled actions. Part II examines how to modify these various processes by practice and motor learning. Understanding how all of these components can operate together is facilitated by a conceptual model of human performance that is developed throughout the text.

WEB STUDY GUIDE ACTIVITIES

The student web study guide, available at www.HumanKinetics.com/MotorLearningandPerformance, offers these activities to help you build and apply your knowledge of the concepts in this chapter.

Interactive Learning

Activity 1.1: Classify skills as discrete, serial, or continuous in nature by selecting the appropriate category for each of five examples.

Activity 1.2: Review the types of error measured in motor learning research by matching various error measures with their definitions.

Situation-Based Exercise

Activity 1.3: The situation-based exercise for this chapter applies the concepts in this chapter to your own experience by asking you to analyze a motor skill that you have learned in the past or are currently learning. You'll describe the skill as open or closed and as discrete, continuous, or serial and identify the goals of the skill and the factors that contribute to your success when performing it.

Check Your Understanding

1. Define a skill and indicate why each of the following terms is important to that definition.
   - Environmental goal
   - Maximum certainty
   - Minimum energy costs
   - Minimum time
2. Distinguish between open and closed skills and between discrete, serial, and continuous skills. Give one example of each.
3. List and describe three elements critical to almost any skill.
4. Define a theory and describe how scientists use theories to design experiments.

Apply Your Knowledge

1. List three motor skills that you have learned, either recently or when you were younger (e.g., swinging a baseball bat, tying your shoelaces, or playing a chord on the piano). Classify each of the skills you have listed, distinguishing between open and closed and between discrete, serial, and continuous skills. Are maximum certainty, minimum energy costs, and minimum time equally important for each of the tasks you have listed? Why or why not?

Suggestions for Further Reading

Historical reviews of motor skills research were conducted by Irion (1966), Adams (1987), and Schmidt and Lee (2011). The first edition of *Motor Control and Learning* (Schmidt, 1982) contains a chapter devoted to the scientific study of motor skills. Snyder and Abernethy (1992) devoted a chapter to the early stages of the career of Franklin Henry. Skills classification systems are reviewed in Poulton (1957), Gentile (1972), and Farrell (1975). See the reference list for these additional resources.

Draft. Not for Distribution.

PART I

Principles of Human Skilled Performance

Chapter 1 introduced just a few of the types of motor performance that fascinate us—from the powerful movements of elite athletes to virtuoso musical performances. We now begin a two-part exploration of such skilled motor performances. In part I, we emphasize the research-based principles of how such motor performances can occur. As we introduce the various concepts concerning motor performance, we "build" a conceptual model of human skilled performance throughout the first part of the book. This model contains and summarizes many of the major factors that underlie such performances and is useful as a guide for understanding how motor skills are performed. In part I, the focus is mainly on the factors that allow skilled motor performances to occur, without much reference to practice and learning of skills. After we explain the terminology and fundamental concepts of human performance in part I, we turn in part II to some of the principles governing how certain components outlined in part I are acquired with practice and experience.

Draft. Not for Distribution.

Processing Information and Making Decisions

The Mental Side of Human Performance

KEY TERMS

choice reaction time
foreperiod
Hick's Law
information-processing approach
long-term memory (LTM)
movement time (MT)
population stereotypes
reaction time (RT)
response time
short-term memory (STM)
short-term sensory store (STSS)
simple RT
spatial anticipation
temporal anticipation

CHAPTER OUTLINE

Information-Processing Approach
Reaction Time and Decision Making
Memory Systems
Summary

CHAPTER OBJECTIVES

Chapter 2 describes a conceptualization of how decisions are made in the performance of motor skills. This chapter will help you to understand

- the information-processing approach to understanding motor performance,
- the stages that occur during information processing,
- various factors that influence the speed of information processing,
- the role of anticipation in hastening the speed of responding, and
- memory systems and their roles in motor performance.

The batter was ready this time. The pitcher had just thrown three slow curveballs in a row. Although the batter had two strikes against him, he felt confident because he thought the next pitch would be a fastball, and he was prepared for it. As the pitch was coming toward him, he strode forward and began to swing the bat to meet the ball, but he soon realized this was another curve. He could not modify his swing in time, and the bat crossed the plate long before the ball arrived. The pitcher had beaten him again.

How did the batter's faulty anticipation interfere with his performance? What processes were required to amend the action? To what extent did the stress of the game interfere? Certainly a major concern for the skilled performer is the evaluation of information, leading to decision making about future action. But what information was the batter reflecting on while the pitch was coming toward the plate—the spin of the ball? its velocity? its location? the type, speed, and location of previous pitches? how fast to swing the bat? where to try to hit the ball? Processing all, or even some, of this information would surely have affected the batter's success in hitting the ball.

Without a doubt, one of the most important features of skilled performance is deciding what to do (and what not to do) in situations in which these decisions are needed quickly and predictably. After all, the most beautifully executed baseball throw to first base is ineffective if the throw should have been directed somewhere else instead. This chapter considers factors contributing to these decision-making capabilities, including processing environmental information, and some of the factors that contribute to the actual decision. We begin with a general approach for understanding how the motor system uses information, which will form the basis of the conceptual model of human performance.

The Information-Processing Approach

Researchers have found it useful to think of the human being as a processor of information very much like a computer. Information is presented to the human as input; various processing stages within the human motor system generate a series of operations on this information; and the eventual output is skilled movement. This simple **information-processing approach** is shown in figure 2.1.

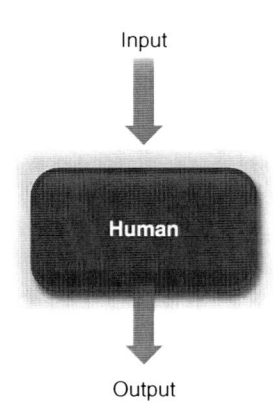

FIGURE 2.1 A simplified information-processing approach to thinking about human performance.

A major goal of researchers interested in the performance of motor skills is to understand the specific nature of the processes in the box labeled "Human" in figure 2.1. There are many ways to approach this problem; a particularly useful one assumes that there are separable information-processing stages through which the information must pass on the way from input to output. For our purposes, here are three of these stages:

- Stimulus identification
- Response selection
- Movement programming

This stage analysis of performance generally assumes that peripheral information enters the system and is processed in the first stage. When, and only when, this stage has completed its operations, the result is passed on to the second stage whose processing is completed, and then the Stage-2 result is passed to the third stage, and so on. A critical assumption is that the stages are nonoverlapping—meaning that all of the processing in a given stage is completed before the product of classification is passed to the next stage; that is, processing in two different stages cannot occur at the same time. This process finally results in an output—the action. What occurs in these stages of processing?

Stimulus Identification Stage

During this first stage the system's problem is to decide whether a stimulus has been presented and, if so, what it is. Thus, stimulus identification is primarily a sensory stage, analyzing environmental information from a variety of sources, such as vision, audition, touch, kinesthesis, and smell. The components, or separate dimensions of these stimuli, are thought to be "assembled" in this stage, such as the combination of edges and colors that form a representation of a car in traffic. Patterns of movement are also detected, such as whether other objects are moving, in what direction and how quickly they are moving, and so on, as would be necessary for driving a car in heavy traffic. The result of this stage is thought to be some representation of the stimulus, with this information being passed on to the next stage—response selection.

Response Selection Stage

The activities of the response selection stage begin after the stimulus identification stage provides information about the nature of the environmental stimulus. This stage has the task of deciding what response to make, given the nature of the situation and environment. In the driving example, the choice from available responses might be to overtake another vehicle, to slow the car, or to make an avoidance maneuver. Thus, this stage requires a kind of transition process between sensory input and movement output.

Movement Programming Stage

This final stage begins its processing upon receiving the decision about what movement to make as determined by the response selection stage. The movement programming stage has the task of organizing the motor system to make the desired movement. Before producing a movement, the system must ready the lower-level mechanisms in the brainstem and spinal cord for action, and it must retrieve and organize a motor program that will eventually control the movement. In the driving example, if the response-selection stage determined that a braking response was required, then the organization of the motor program responsible for executing a braking action would occur in the movement-programming stage.

Expanding the Conceptual Model

Figure 2.2 adds some detail to the simple notion of information processing described in figure 2.1 by including the stages of processing just described. This elaboration is the first revision of our conceptual model, which will be expanded throughout the text as we introduce more fundamental ideas of human performance.

Clearly, these stages are all included within the human information system and are not directly observable under usual circumstances. However, several laboratory methods allow scientists to learn about these stages. **Reaction time** (abbreviated **RT**) is one of the most important tools that researchers have used for many decades to learn about these stages. We will examine RT in much more detail to understand how information processing operates.

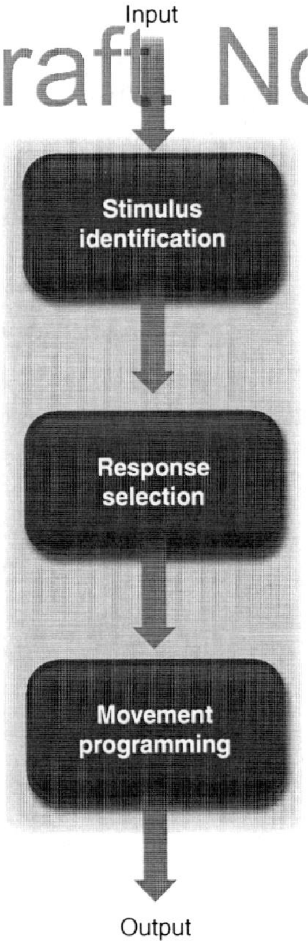

Reaction Time and Decision Making

An important performance measure indicating the speed and effectiveness of decision-making is the RT interval—the interval of time that elapses following a suddenly presented, often unanticipated stimulus until the *beginning* of the response. The concept and assessment of RT are important because it represents a part of some everyday events, such as braking rapidly in response to an unanticipated traffic event; responding to catch a glass that has been accidentally tipped over; and, in sport, in such events as sprint races, where an auditory tone serves as a stimulus to begin a race.

An old saying is that a picture is worth a thousand words. This is certainly borne out by the photo of a long-ago sprint race (figure 2.3) reprinted from Scripture (1905). The starter on the left side of the photo has already fired his gun, perhaps a couple of hundred or so milliseconds earlier, as you can see by the position of the smoke from the pistol rising above the starter. And yet the runners are all still in their ready positions, and are only now just beginning to move. The photo illustrates nicely the substantial delay involved in RT. Being able to minimize RT in such a situation is critical to getting the movement under way as rapidly as possible. Because RT is a fundamental component of many skills, it is not surprising that much research attention has been directed toward it.

But RT has important theoretical meaning as well, which is the major reason it has attracted so much research attention. However, sometimes there is confusion about what RT is and how it is measured. To review, researchers define the RT interval very carefully; it is the period of time beginning when the stimulus is first presented and ending when the movement response *starts*. Note

FIGURE 2.2 An expanded information-processing model, highlighting three critical processing stages in thinking about human performance.

Processing Information and Making Decisions

FIGURE 2.3 Illustration of the RT delay in a sprint start; the starting gun has been fired, yet the athletes are still on their marks because of the delay in processing the signal from the starting gun (the delay contained in the reaction-time interval)

that the RT interval does not include the time that is taken to complete the movement, as illustrated in figure 2.4. That period of time, from the end of RT until the completion of the movement, is typically called the "**movement time**" (or simply **MT**). Hence, terms like "brake RT" used to describe the time it takes a person to press the brake pedal in a car are technically incorrect, as the time taken to press the brake includes the time for the foot's movement from the accelerator to depress the brake, which occurs *after* the reaction interval. What many refer to as brake RT is actually the total of RT plus MT—what is called **response time**.

The RT interval is a measure of the accumulated durations of the three sequential and nonoverlapping stages of processing seen in figure 2.2. Any factor that increases the duration of one or more of these stages will thus lengthen RT. For this reason, scientists interested in information processing have used RT as a measure of the speeds of processing in these stages. Next is a discussion of how changes in RT can inform us about the stages of processing.

Factors That Influence Decision Making

There are many important factors that influence RT, ranging from the nature of the stimulus information presented to the nature of the movement required of the performer. Some of the more important factors related to human performance are considered in this section.

Number of Stimulus–Response Alternatives

Consider the following example involving driving a car. In light traffic, the number of possible emergency situations that require

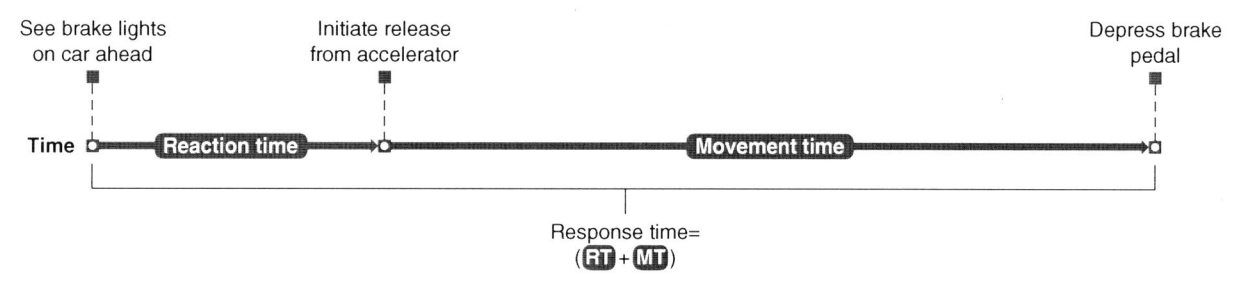

FIGURE 2.4 Measuring reaction time, movement time, and response time for pressing the brake pedal in a car.

Driving a car in traffic presents the driver with a wide range of possible stimuli and responses.

an evasive response is usually less than in heavy traffic. Unexpected events from multiple vehicles around you serve to amplify the possible trouble situations that could occur, compared to extremely light or no traffic. One of the most important factors influencing the time to start an action is the number of stimuli (each having its own response) that can possibly occur at any given time. Controlled laboratory experiments of this type generally involve several possible stimuli, such as lights, and several different responses from which the subject is to choose, such as pressing different keys depending on which stimulus light has been illuminated.

Figure 2.5 illustrates a typical experimental setup in which the stimulus array contains eight possible lights that could turn on and a response panel with eight corresponding response keys. Although all eight stimulus lights and response keys are seen in each version of the experiment, the researcher instructs the participant about the number of stimulus–response (S-R) alternatives from which to expect a stimulus (a light suddenly illuminated) on any given block of trials. For example, in figure 2.5c, the participant would know that any one of the middle four lights could be lit, which would require the response of pressing the assigned one of the corresponding keys. Note, however, that on any given trial, only one stimulus light will be illuminated so only one key needs to be pressed.

This is termed **choice reaction time**, in which the performer must choose one response from a subset of possible predetermined movements. Typically the performer receives a warning signal, followed by a **foreperiod** of unpredictable length (e.g., 2, 3, or 4 s, the order being randomly determined). When the reaction stimulus is suddenly presented, it is only then that the performer is informed about which button to press; RT is the time required to detect and recognize the stimulus and select and initiate the proper response.

Generally, as the number of possible S-R alternatives increases, there is an increase in the time required to respond to any one of them. The fastest situation involves only one stimulus and one response, termed **simple RT**. Increased RT due to a greater number of S-R alternatives is of critical importance in understanding skilled performance, forming the basis of **Hick's Law** (see Focus on Research 2.2). The increase in RT is very large when the number of alternatives is increased from one to two. As seen in figure 2.6, RT might increase from about 190 ms with simple RT to more than 300 ms for a two-choice case—at least a 58% increase in the time required to process the stimulus information into the response! As the number of choices becomes larger, adding extra choices still increases RT, but the increases become smaller and smaller (e.g., the increase from 9 to 10 choices might be only 20 ms, or about 2% or 3%). Even this small amount of delay can be critical in determining success in many situations.

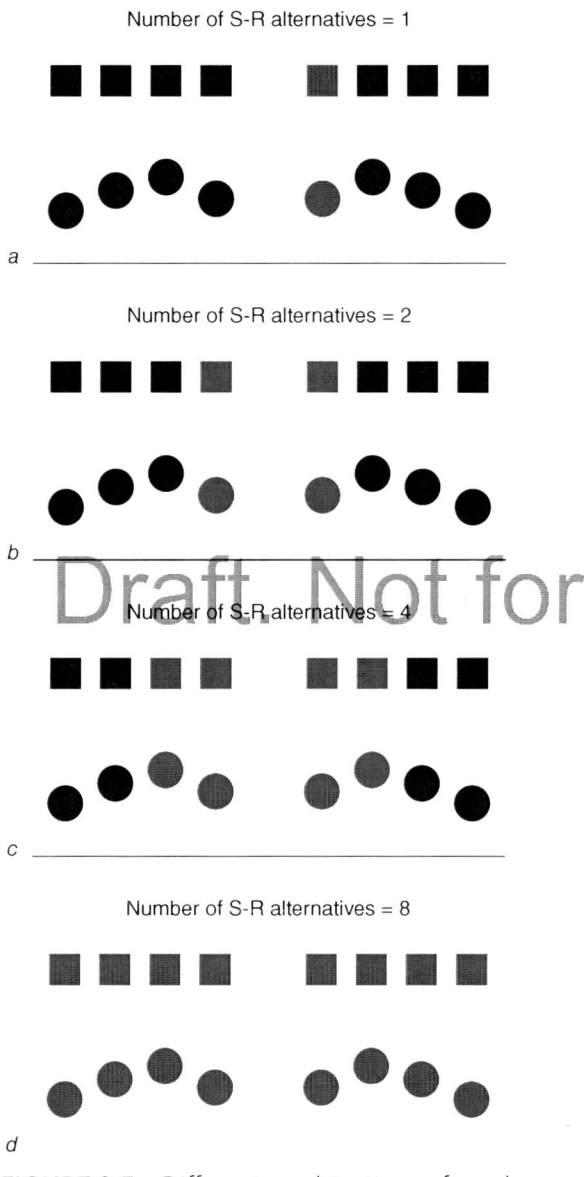

FIGURE 2.5 Different combinations of number of stimulus–response alternatives. The boxes represent potential visual stimuli; the circles represent the keys to press in response to these stimuli. Red colors represent the S-R events that are possible; black colors represent nonstimuli and nonresponse keys.

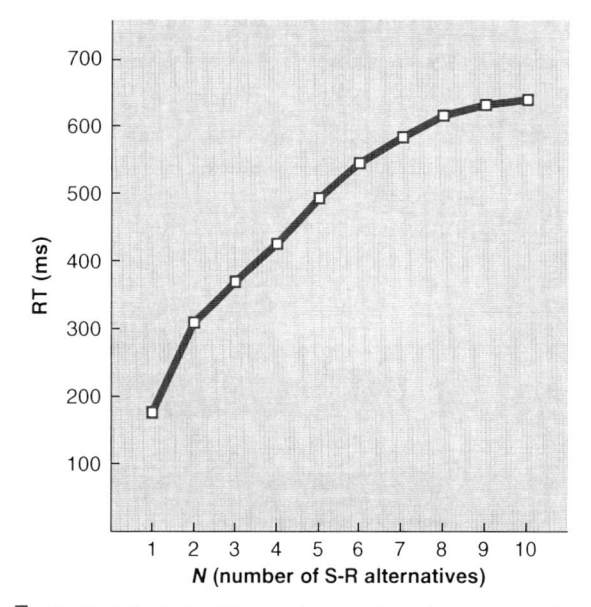

FIGURE 2.6 The relationship between the number of possible stimulus–response (S-R) alternatives and reaction time.

Reprinted by permission from Schmidt and Lee 2011; Data from Merkel 1885.

Focus on RESEARCH 2.1

Donders' Stages of Processing

Determining the durations of mental activities goes back many years, and one of the first experiments involving humans was undertaken by Dutch physician F.C. Donders in 1868. Donders' "additive-factors" logic was that insight into the durations of the various stages could be understood by adding, or subtracting, the time taken for specific task requirements. Have a look at the illustrations in figure 2.5. The illustration in figure 2.5a represents the simplest situation—the participant's task is to press the response key as rapidly as possible when the stimulus above it appears. No other stimulus will appear and no other response will be required—the task is merely to respond as quickly as possible in this situation. According to Donders, such a task (which he called an A-type, or what is now called simple RT) requires only the process of "stimulus detection," as the performer knows the response to make before the stimulus comes on.

Contrast this task with another in which the participant is required to respond to the signal, as in figure 2.5a, with a rapid key press. However, in this task (a C-type, currently called a "go/no-go reaction"), one of the other stimuli will appear at times. The participant's task is to *not respond* with a button press in these trials, but to respond only when the specified stimulus appears. Donders reasoned that this task also required stimulus detection, as in the A-type task. But, in addition, this task requires that the participant perform a "stimulus identification" process—identifying that the stimulus was the specified one before responding. Hence the difference in RTs between the two tasks supposedly required the additional stage of stimulus identification.

Lastly, Donders considered a third type of task—a B-type task (currently called a choice-RT task)—that required subjects to respond to one of the alternative stimuli with an appropriate key press as shown in figure 2.5, b through d. This task is similar to the C-type task in that the stimulus must be detected and identified. But, in addition, the B-task requires that the subject respond by selecting the appropriate key to press. Thus, compared to the C-task, the additional RT required to complete a B-response is caused by the insertion of a "response selection" stage of processing.

Requirements of Donders' Three Task Types

Type	Stimulus detection	Stimulus identification	Response selection
A-type reaction	Yes	No	No
C-type reaction	Yes	Yes	No
B-type reaction	Yes	Yes	Yes

It may be of interest that when one of us (RAS) was on a sabbatical leave in Utrecht, The Netherlands, Donders' laboratory building was located on F.C.-Dondersstraat (in English, F.C. Donders Street), which was directly on RAS's bicycle commute to the lab where he was working.

Exploring Further

1. According to Donders' logic, if the A-type RT was 150 ms, the B-type RT was 240 ms, and the C-type RT was 180 ms, what would be the durations of the stimulus identification and response selection stages?
2. Donders was one of the first to explore the contents and workings of the stages of information processing by rearranging task conditions to be able to add or subtract specific processing requirements systematically. The approach is not without problems, however. Critically examine the following assumptions of this method:
   a. That processing stages are serially arranged, with no overlaps in time
   b. That, as compared to the A-reaction, the C-type reaction task requires only the additional stage of stimulus recognition, and no others; an analogous assumption involves the B- and C-tasks and the response selection stage

   To what extent do you think that these assumptions are correct?

Focus on RESEARCH 2.2

Hick's Law

Over a century ago, Merkel (1885, cited by Woodworth, 1938) asked subjects in a choice-RT experiment to press a reaction key when one of up to 10 possible stimuli was presented. The stimuli were the Arabic numerals 1 through 5 and the Roman numerals I through V. Each stimulus was paired with one finger or thumb and response key. For example, the possible stimuli on a set of trials might be 2, 3, and V (a three-choice case), and the subjects were to respond with either the right index, right middle, or left thumb if and when the associated stimulus was presented. Merkel varied the number of possible stimulus–response alternatives in different sets of trials. (It is important to remember that only one of the N possible stimuli is ever presented on a given trial.)

Merkel's results are shown in figure 2.6, where choice RT is plotted as a function of the number of S-R alternatives. You can see that as the number of alternatives was increased there was a sharp rise in RT (roughly 120 ms; see figure 2.6) from $N = 1$ to $N = 2$; this rise becomes smaller as the number of alternatives is increased toward 10 (from $N = 9$ to $N = 10$, where choice RT increases roughly 3 ms; see figure 2.6).

Much later Hick (1952), and independently Hyman (1953), discovered that the relationship between choice RT and the logarithm to the base 2 of the number (N) of S-R alternatives abbreviated $Log_2(N)$ was linear (see figure 2.7). The $Log_2(N)$ is the power to which the base 2 must be raised to equal N. For example, the logarithm to the base 2 of 8 is 3 abbreviated $Log_2(8) = 3$, because the base 2 raised to the third power (2^3) = 8. This relationship has become known as Hick's Law, and it holds for a wide variety of situations using different kinds of subjects, different movements, and different kinds of stimulus materials. It is one of the most important laws of human performance.

> *continued*

> *continued*

The relationship implies that choice RT increases a constant amount every time the number of stimulus–response alternatives (*N*) is *doubled* (e.g., from *N* = 2 to *N* = 4, where the Log$_2$(*N*) is 1 or 2, respectively; or from *N* = 8 to *N* = 16, where the Log$_2$(*N*) = 3 and 4, respectively). This led to an important interpretation of Hick's Law: Because the amount of information needed to resolve the uncertainty among *N* possible choices is Log$_2$(*N*), Hick's Law says that choice RT is linearly related to the *amount of information* that must be processed to resolve the uncertainty about the various possible stimulus–response alternatives. Doubling the amount of information to be processed by doubling *N* therefore increases choice RT by a constant amount (the duration required to respond to one of the alternatives); that is, this operation (doubling *N*) increases choice RT by a constant amount. This constant amount is the slope of the log relation known as Hick's Law.

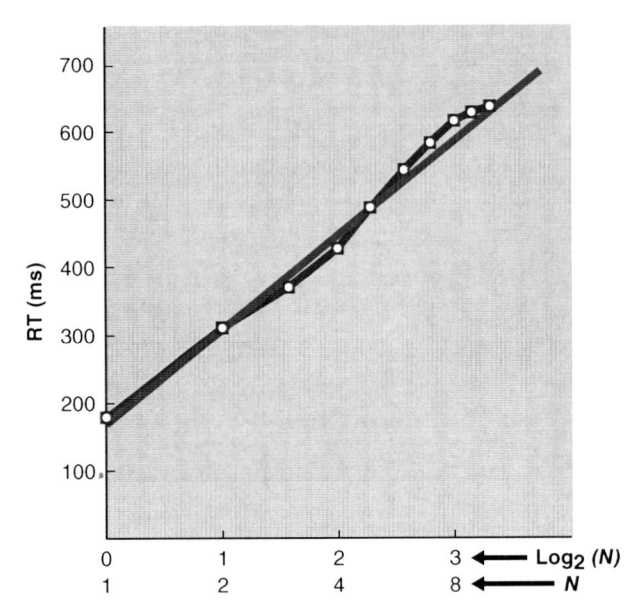

FIGURE 2.7 Hick's Law: The relation between RT and number of S-R alternatives (*N*) is replotted using Merkel's data from figure 2.6, with RT as a function of Log$_2$(*N*).

Reprinted by permission from Schmidt and Lee 2011; Data from Merkel 1885.

Exploring Further

1. How does the concept of "uncertainty" relate to amount of information in Hick's law?
2. Name two factors that would be expected to influence the magnitude of the slope (b) of Hick's Law, and describe how variations in these factors would be predicted to increase or decrease the slope.

Stimulus–Response Compatibility

An important determinant of choice RT is S-R compatibility, usually defined as the extent to which the stimulus and the response it evokes are connected in a "natural" way. Turning the handlebars of a bicycle to the right to move in that direction is an example of S-R compatibility because the movement of the handlebars and the change in the intended direction are the same—that is, they are said to be directionally compatible. Imagine how difficult it would be to require a movement of the handlebars to the left in order to turn right. Perhaps that explains some of the reason that steering a sailboat is trickier than steering a bicycle—the sailor needs to move the tiller to the left in order to change the heading of the boat to the right.

Figure 2.8 illustrates two types of S-R spatial compatibility "mappings." The ensemble of stimuli and responses in illustration in 2.8*a* is the more compatible of the two because either of the stimulus lights calls for the participant to respond in the same direction and on the same side of the body. In the example in 2.8*b*, however, the right light calls for the left hand to be moved and the left light calls for the right hand. The spatial mapping of the stimuli and required response is not nearly so spatially direct and unambiguous; this situation is said to be "S-R incompatible."

It is well established that for a given number of S-R alternatives, increasing S-R compatibility decreases choice RT. This is thought to be the effect of the relative "difficulty" of information processing in the response selection stage, where the more natural linkages between compatible stimuli and responses lead to faster resolution of uncertainty and thus to shorter choice RTs. The general rules regarding the number of possible stimuli and choice RT still apply to compatible S-R arrangements, however.

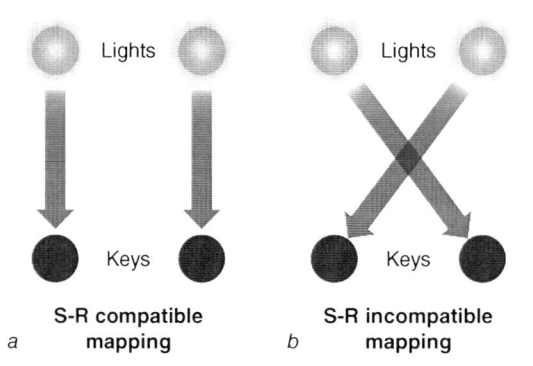

FIGURE 2.8 The relationship between the two stimuli and the two responses is more spatially "S-R compatible" in the array on the left (a) than in the array on the right (b).

Reprinted by permission from Schmidt and Lee 2011.

Population Stereotypes

There are many types of S-R compatibility other than just spatial mapping. For example, we tend to turn dials clockwise in order to increase the loudness of an auditory source or the speed of a fan. In North America we move a light-switch upward to turn the light on; in Europe, this relationship is reversed. However, in these cases it is more difficult to argue that the mapping of the stimulus and response represents a naturally existing

Learned associations such as flipping a switch down to turn off a light are often performed without awareness until our expectations are violated.

relationship, and not a purely arbitrary one. Instead, the likely association is a learned one—we sometimes act habitually due to specific cultural learning, referred to as **population stereotypes**.

Some colors represent common population stereotypes. Red is often associated with stop or danger, green with go or safety. Traffic lights exploit this relationship, as do many other lights in our environment. The small LEDs (light-emitting diodes) on our coffee machines are red while the coffee is being brewed, and they turn to green when the coffee is ready to drink. Once again, however, we tend not to pay attention to these stereotypes in our day-to-day activities unless the expected relationship is violated.

Amount of Practice

Highly practiced performers can overcome the disadvantages of low S-R compatibility, such as the highly experienced racing sailor who doesn't even have to think to move the tiller to the right when the boat needs to turn left. Research shows that two major factors affecting choice RT are (a) the nature or the amount of practice or both, and (b) stimulus–response compatibility. For a given number of stimulus–response alternatives, the higher the level of practice, generally the shorter

Focus on
APPLICATION 2.1

Light Switches

Stimulus–response (S-R) compatibility and population stereotypes are a very large part of our daily existence. We usually take notice of them only in situations in which unexpected issues arise. One common example occurs when you walk into a room and flip a switch to turn on a light or a bank of lights. In North American culture (but not in some other parts of the world), we turn lights on by flipping the light switch *up*; moving it *down* turns the lights off. We act accordingly when we enter a room and tend not to give the action a moment's thought. However, a light switch that has been installed upside down will bring the issue to our conscious attention.

A similar issue occurs with respect to the spatial organization of switches in relation to the spatial locations of the lights in the room that they control. Suppose you enter a room that has a light near to you, one in the middle of the room, and one in the far corner of the room, controlled by three switches on a switch panel located on the wall near the door you use to enter the room. Which switch would you flip to turn the middle light on? A panel that has been "compatibly mapped" will have the nearest switch control the nearest light, the middle switch control the light in the middle of the room, and so on. But how often have you been tricked into turning on the wrong light because of an incompatible light-to-switch mapping? Once again, the issue mainly comes to our attention when the unexpected occurs.

The examples could go on and on. Why is the brake pedal always to the left of the accelerator pedal in cars? Why does the CD system in your car have larger numbers assigned to later tracks on a CD? Why does your car always increase its speed when the accelerator is pushed down? In all of these examples, the designer who came up with the very first automobile accelerator pedal, a CD numbering system, or steering wheel logic could have done it either way. Now, however, we all have had sufficient benefit of experience with a particular organization that has become a *population stereotype*. Imagine the bother and wasted movements—or, indeed, the dangerousness—of the system designed with some other stimulus–response relationship.

the RT will be. Overall, practice reduces the steepness of the increase in RT as the number of stimulus–response alternatives increases. This means that there is only a small effect of practice on simple RT but there are very large effects of practice on choice RT. With extremely large amounts of practice, very high-level performers can produce reactions that approach automatic processing; these reactions are very fast and are slowed little, if at all, as the number of S-R alternatives is increased further.

This fits well with practical experience. To a beginning driver, the connection between the presentation of a red light to stop and the response of pressing the brake pedal is very clumsy. However, after thousands of hours of driving practice, the link between the red light and the brake pedal becomes extremely natural, leading almost automatically to the movement.

Anticipation to Minimize Delays

One fundamental way performers cope with long RT delays is to anticipate. Typically, a highly skilled performer predicts what is going to happen in the environment and when it will occur, and then can perform various information-processing activities in advance of the stimulus. The defensive lineman in American football predicts that the offensive team will try a running play, so he anticipates this and moves quickly to stop the play for a big loss. An experienced long-haul truck driver knows that many car drivers do not understand the stopping distance of an 18-wheeled vehicle and makes an evasive lane change to avoid a slow-moving car and a potential accident.

Highly skilled people know what stimuli are likely to be presented, where they will appear, and when they will occur, so these people can predict the required actions to take. Armed with this information, a performer can organize movements in advance, completing some or all of the information-processing activities usually conducted during the response selection or movement programming stage. This allows the performer to initiate the movement much earlier or at a time consonant with the movements of the environment, as in predicting where and when a pitched ball will arrive at the

Practice can overcome the processing delays caused by low stimulus-response compatibility. For example, a skilled sailor knows to move the tiller the opposite direction the boat needs to turn.

plate so that it can be struck effectively with a well-timed bat swing. Because of these capabilities to anticipate, skilled performers seem to behave almost as if they had "all the time they need," without being rushed to respond to stimuli using the reaction-time processes previously discussed.

Types of Anticipation

Anticipation can occur in different ways. Two closely related concepts are event anticipation and **spatial anticipation**. For example, two important shots in badminton are the "clear" and "drop" shots. The clear shot is high and long and sends the opponent to the back of the court. The drop shot is intended to land only just on the other side of the net, which brings the opponent to the front of the court. Anticipation, in badminton, involves predicting the type of shot your opponent will hit and being in the correct position to return the shot when it is hit. In other situations, it might be obvious what is going to occur and where, but there might be uncertainty about when it will occur, as in anticipating the snap of the ball in American football. This is usually called **temporal anticipation**. Although there is a strong advantage in knowing when some event will occur, not being able to predict *what* will occur prevents the performer from organizing the movement completely in advance.

Benefits of Anticipation

If the defensive lineman in American football can predict what play will be run (event

---

Focus on
APPLICATION 2.2

Strategies for Anticipating

The effective gains made when players anticipate correctly, coupled with the large losses when players anticipate incorrectly, produce important strategic elements in many rapid sport activities. One strategy is to do everything to prevent your opponent from anticipating correctly. A way to do this is to be as unpredictable as possible in deciding where and when certain actions are made so that the opponent cannot anticipate effectively. The opponent who anticipates incorrectly too often will be forced to switch to a strategy of merely reacting, which is clearly slower and less effective than anticipating.

An important principle for many rapid sport events is to organize your strategies so that your opponent must react to you using the slow, cumbersome reaction-time methods mentioned earlier. On the other hand, the opponent who can anticipate correctly has a strong advantage. The key is making your movements unpredictable, forcing your opponent to react rather than predict.

Another important strategy is to allow your opponent to anticipate but then to make the movement essentially "opposite to" the one anticipated. A racquetball player moves (and with the proper body language) as if to make a soft "dink shot" near the front wall, causing the opponent to move forward quickly. Then, as part of the plan, the anticipated dink suddenly turns out to be a hard, passing shot that has the opponent badly out of position. Such a strategy is a large part of almost every rapid sport. It is dependent on the fact that if you can lure your opponent into anticipation, you have the advantage because of the large costs of false anticipation—that is, taking the opponent out of the optimal position or requiring the opponent to generate an entirely new action.

anticipation), as well as when the ball snap will occur (temporal anticipation), he can initiate his movement simultaneously with the snap of the ball. In many respects, a correct anticipation will result in the processing lag equivalent to a "RT" equal to 0 ms and he can start the action simultaneously with the signal, or even before it in certain circumstances, and it is likely to be very effective. Effective anticipation is not always easy because it requires the performer to have a great deal of knowledge about the opponent's tendencies in various circumstances.

Several factors affect the capability to predict effectively. One is the regularity of the events. For example, if our racquetball opponent always serves the ball to our (weak) backhand side, we can predict this event and counter it in various ways. Clearly, the capability to anticipate would be minimized if three or four different serves were randomly used instead. Similarly, if the American football quarterback always has the ball snapped on the second of two rhythmical verbal signals, the defensive team can anticipate the critical event and be highly prepared for it. Varying the timing of the snap signals keeps the defensive team from anticipating temporally, yet still allows the quarterback's offensive teammates to anticipate both temporally and spatially (as they have learned in the huddle what is to be done and when). The goals here are for the offensive team to respond as a single unit to the snap count and to allow

Focus on
RESEARCH 2.3

Assessing Anticipation Skills

What skills separate an expert from a novice? Most would agree that an expert batter in baseball or cricket possesses motor skills that are more accurate, less variable, and generally more efficient than those of a lesser-skilled batter. The expert's motor skills are simply "better" and more finely tuned. For some skills, however, and most importantly for open skills, researchers have shown that experts also have a large advantage in perceptual anticipation (anticipating the movements of objects in the outside world). How do the researchers know this?

One of the frequently used experimental techniques is to show edited video clips of athletes in action and to ask the viewer to make certain predictions. For example, a video of a baseball pitcher might be edited such that a certain body part (e.g., the pitching arm) has been blocked from the viewer's vision. Presumably, editing out a body part that is critical to determining what type of pitch is being thrown (e.g., a fastball or a curveball) would interfere with such an anticipation *only if* the athlete were using that perceptual information. Another method of video editing is to freeze the display at certain time points in the action. Presumably, a more skilled viewer would be able to pick up more information in an earlier frozen frame than a less-skilled viewer. The idea that underlies both of these "occlusion" edit methods is to discover what types of information are being used by more highly skilled performers, and how much earlier in time this information is useful for making anticipatory judgments.

Exploring Further

1. What is an eye tracker and how is this equipment used to assess the "quiet-eye" effect?
2. What are point-light displays and how are they used in research to assess biological motion?

the defensive team no capability to anticipate. This provides the offense the greatest relative advantage.

Costs of Anticipation

There are several strong advantages to anticipation; but, as with most strategies for trying to gain an advantage, it comes with risks. The primary disadvantage occurs when the anticipated action is not what actually happens. In American football again, if the defensive lineman anticipates that the snap will occur on the second sound but the quarterback takes the snap on the third sound, the lineman could move too early, incurring a penalty for his team. In a similar way, when anticipating that an opponent will hit the ball to the left side of the court, a tennis player will move in that direction before the shot is hit, but is at risk of losing the point if the shot is actually hit to the right. Clearly, anticipating correctly can result in many benefits, but the costs of anticipating incorrectly can be disastrous.

Earlier, we discussed the idea that anticipating allows various information-processing activities to take place in advance so they do not have to occur after the reaction stimulus is presented. Suppose that a performer has gone

A skilled defensive lineman may be able to anticipate the timing of the snap and the play about to be run, reducing his effective reaction time to near zero.

through these preparatory processes but now the events in the environment change. The information processing "costs" in this case are actually magnified. First the performer must inhibit, or unprepare, the already prepared (falsely anticipated) action, and this process will require time to complete. Then the correct action must be prepared and initiated, which extends the processing delay even further. Thus, while a correct anticipation might reduce the lag period to essentially 0 ms, an incorrect anticipation will require more processing activities, and longer delay, compared to a response to a neutral or unanticipated event.

An additional problem occurs if the incorrect anticipation has resulted in a movement, as you have seen many times in sport events. As before, the performer still has the problem of inhibiting the incorrect action and preparing the correct one. But there can be an additional problem: The inappropriate action might be in the incorrect direction, taking the person farther from the best location and producing a biomechanical disadvantage because of her wrong direction. This makes the corrective action even more difficult, "costly," and time-consuming to overcome.

Memory Systems

We change tacks here slightly to discuss an important concept in thinking about skills, namely memory, which is usually seen simply as the storage of the results of the various information-processing activities discussed so far. The various types of memory and their characteristics will be useful later during the discussion of several aspects of human performance. First we consider three distinct memory systems involved in movement control: short-term sensory store, short-term memory, and long-term memory.

Short-Term Sensory Store

The briefest of all memories, the **short-term sensory store (STSS)**, is thought to retain information for a very short period of time. We rely on this memory store during almost all of our daily activities whenever we see, hear, or feel things. For example, after spotting the milk container in the refrigerator, we use that brief visual memory to reach for it as we then shift the eyes to a search for something else. Visual information is taken in by the eyes and acoustic information by the ears; and the aftereffects of movements are represented briefly as anticipated information. How long does it last? Early research by Sperling (1960) suggested that visual information may last no more than about 1 s in STSS. The basic idea is that STSS is responsible for storing vast amounts of sensory information only long enough for some of it to be abstracted and further processed (in short-term memory, STM). The STSS is not considered to be sustained by attention—it is simply a brief "holding cell" for sensory information.

Short-Term Memory

Short-term memory (STM), which researchers sometimes call "working memory," is a temporary holding place for information, such as a phone number given to you verbally. Unless we repeat the item we all know that this phone number will be lost from memory in a short period of time (probably within a few minutes at most). Information requires *rehearsal* as the process by which we keep from losing information from STM. Repeating the phone number over and over to yourself, either silently or out loud, is a process of rehearsing the information and thereby keeping it available in STM.

For example, subjects in a study by Peterson and Peterson (1959) were presented with verbal information (a three-letter trigram), and were prevented from saying it over and over again by having them count backward by 3's from a two digit specified number. Within about 10 s, the probability of recalling the trigram successfully was less than .20 and it was below .10 after about 20 s. Thus, verbal information (eight items) in STM is retained longer than in STSS but was still in lost quite rapidly when not given sustained attention.

A study similar to Peterson and Peterson's, but using motor skills, was conducted by Adams and Dijkstra (1966) to study the STM of movement information. Blindfolded subjects moved a slide on a trackway from a start position to a mechanical stop and tried to repeat this movement (with the stop removed) after various periods of time. The results of the Adams–Dijkstra study are presented in figure 2.9. In this experiment, memory loss is represented by increases in error over time. As in the Peterson and Peterson study, rapid forgetting occurred during the first 20 s of the retention period, with further decreases occurring over the next 60 s. This evidence suggests that information can be retained for a period of time that is much longer than STSS but is subject to forgetting if not given sustained attention.

Long-Term Memory

Long-term memory (LTM) contains very well-learned information that has been collected over a lifetime. Experiments show that LTM must be essentially limitless in capacity, as indicated by the vast amount of information that can be stored for very long periods of time. Such information might never be forgotten: You never seem to forget how to ride a bicycle or throw a ball, even after many decades of no practice. Even an apparent loss of information from memory, such as someone's name or your old phone number, may just be due to a temporary inaccessibility of the stored information. For example, you might recognize a person's name if someone else mentions it—suggesting that the memory was there but that retrieval of it posed a problem. The items stored in LTM are thought to be very abstract, with information coded by elaborate connections to other stored information and by imagery, sounds, smells, and the like, which neuroscientists are slowly beginning to understand more completely.

Essentially, a vast amount of information can be stored in LTM by processing in STM (rehearsal, connecting the information to other information, and so on), so LTM storage is generally effortful. To say that someone has learned something means that information was processed in some way from STM to LTM. This also applies to movement skills, with motor programs for action (discussed in chapter 5) stored in LTM for later execution. For many motor skills, particularly continuous ones such as riding a bicycle or swimming, evidence and common experience suggest almost perfect retention after years, even decades, without intervening practice; this is quite contrary to the forgetting seen with well-learned verbal and cognitive skills (e.g., foreign language vocabulary). However, discrete skills, such as throwing or gymnastics stunts, are more easily forgotten. More on retention is presented in chapter 9.

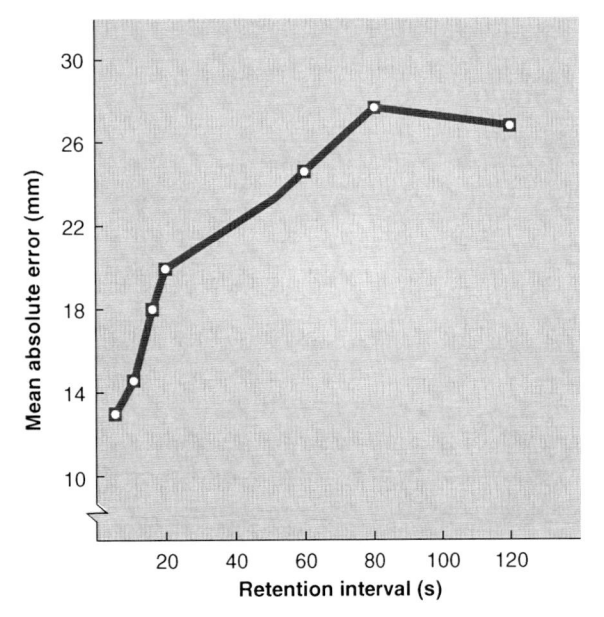

FIGURE 2.9 Error in recall of a blind positioning movement increases rapidly over different retention interval lengths (from Adams & Dijkstra, 1966).

Reprinted by permission from Adams and Dijkstra 1966.

Summary

The human motor system can be thought of as a processor of information—for motor skills, information is received from the various sense organs, is processed through various stages, and is output as movements. The system has three main stages: a stimulus identification stage, which detects the nature of environmental information; a response selection stage, which resolves uncertainty about what action should be made; and a movement programming stage, which organizes the motor system for action. Reaction time is an important measure of information-processing speed. Its duration greatly increases with more stimulus–response alternatives (described by Hick's Law), by the "naturalness" of the relationship between stimuli and their associated movements (stimulus–response compatibility), and by anticipation of the upcoming events. Three memory systems are described: a brief store (STSS) holds sensory information for a few seconds at most; a short-term memory (STM) that is capable of holding about eight items of information for longer periods of time; but these items last only as long as can be maintained by attention (about 30 seconds without attention); and a long-term memory (LTM), which is capable of holding information in permanent store for years.

WEB STUDY GUIDE ACTIVITIES

The student web study guide, available at www.HumanKinetics.com/MotorLearningandPerformance, offers these activities to help you build and apply your knowledge of the concepts in this chapter.

Interactive Learning

Activity 2.1: Arrange the stages of information processing in the correct order.

Activity 2.2: Answer a series of multiple-choice questions that will help you learn to describe the characteristics of each of the three stages of information processing.

Activity 2.3: Review the memory systems by matching each with its functions and characteristics.

Activity 2.4: Label a figure from the text in order to review and conceptualize the stages of information processing.

Situation-Based Exercise

Activity 2.5: The situation-based exercise for this chapter prompts you to use the stages of information processing to analyze a motor skill you are familiar with. You will describe some of the processing activities that would take place in each stage of the information processing model for this task and identify a factor that might influence decision making or reaction time for this skill.

Check Your Understanding

1. Describe the information-processing activities that might occur in the stimulus identification, response selection, and movement programming stages for a hockey goalie in a game and for a kayaker navigating a set of rapids.

2. Describe and provide an example of when spatial anticipation is important to a sport outcome, and describe and provide an example of when temporal anticipation is important to a sport outcome.

3. Provide an example of stimulus-response compatibility and an example of stimulus-response incompatibility that you have encountered today.

4. Three memory systems are involved in the learning process. The short-term sensory store (STSS)'s major role is to store large amounts of sensory information before processing by the short-term memory (STM), which is a temporary holding place for information, which can remain in STM through rehearsal. Information in the STM can be processed in order for it to be stored in long-term memory (LTM). This processing from STM to LTM can be described as learning. Explain how each of the three memory systems (STSS, STM, and LTM) is involved in learning a new dance routine. Provide examples of specific information that would be processed.

5. Anticipation can play a role in many sport contexts. One activity where the success or failure of anticipation can be particularly clear is racket sports, where players must anticipate the next shot of the opponent. Discuss how anticipation in a game of squash can be both beneficial and harmful, depending on the situation. What factors can affect the outcome of anticipation?

Suggestions for Further Reading

Many good references can be found on the information-processing approach in psychology, including work by Lachman, Lachman, and Butterfield (1979) and Sternberg (1989). Marteniuk (1976) applied this approach to thinking about motor-skills research. Welford's (1980) book on reaction times provides a good overview of the various applications of this method. Rasmussen (1986) discusses many applications of information processing. And Adams' (1976) book remains an excellent source for discussions of memory, with particular relevance to motor skills. See the reference list for these additional sources.

3

Attention and Performance
Limitations on Information Processing

KEY TERMS

arousal
attention
automatic processing
choking
cocktail-party effect
double stimulation paradigm
external focus of attention
hypervigilance
inattention blindness
internal focus of attention
inverted-U principle
looked-but-failed-to-see accidents
movement programming
perceptual narrowing
probe-task technique
psychological refractory period (PRP)
response selection
stimulus identification
stimulus-onset asynchrony (SOA)
sustained attention
unintended acceleration

CHAPTER OUTLINE

What Is Attention?
Limitations in Stimulus Identification
Limitations in Response Selection
Limitations in Movement Programming
Decision Making Under Stress
Summary

CHAPTER OBJECTIVES

Chapter 3 describes the role of attention as a limiting factor in human performance. This chapter will help you to understand

- attention and its various properties and definitions,
- attention as a limitation in the capacity to process information,
- attention as a limitation in the capability to perform actions, and
- performance under conditions of increased stress.

The task of driving to the store illustrates why the topic of attention is so complex. Consider the following:

- You are driving to the supermarket, but unfortunately, you forgot your shopping list, which was on the refrigerator door, and you are trying to reconstruct what might have been on it—eggs, milk, peanut butter, hmm, no, not milk, I bought some yesterday . . .
- You receive a phone call. It's your roommate, and she asks you to pick up some pasta for dinner, as well as some green peppers.
- There's an intersection ahead; the light has been green for quite a while and may turn to amber at any moment, so better be ready . . .
- The temperature is pretty warm today; maybe some air conditioning is needed. Which of these controls do I use?
- What was it that my roommate asked me to get? Think hard, I'll remember—pasta and . . . green onions, yeah, that's it.
- There's an amber light; do I have time to make a safe stop, or should I accelerate through the intersection?

And on it goes. In a very short time this scenario has illustrated the nature of the concept of attention and factors that influence it. Attention appears to be limited in that only a certain amount of information-processing capacity seems to exist. If it is overloaded, much information can be missed. Also, attention appears to be serial in that it seems to focus first on one thing, then on another; only with great difficulty (if at all) can we focus attention on two things at the same time. Sometimes attention is directed to external sensory events (what other drivers are doing). Sometimes it is focused on internal mental operations (trying to remember the items on the shopping list). And sometimes it is focused on internal sensory information (sensations from the muscles and the joints). In addition, there are the difficulties in doing two tasks at the same time, such as talking on the cell phone while driving. Attention is many different things (see also William James' quote in Focus on Application 3.1).

Focus on
APPLICATION 3.1

William James on Attention

Consider the following statement, made over a century ago by the famous psychologist William James (1890):

> Everyone knows what **attention** is. It is the taking possession by the mind, in clear and vivid form, of one out of what seem several simultaneously possible objects or trains of thought. Focalization, concentration of consciousness, is of its essence. It implies withdrawal from some things in order to deal effectively with others. (pp. 403-404)

Despite his questionable comment that "everyone knows what attention is," James goes on to reveal the complexity of the topic. In this statement James suggests that attention takes on at least three different roles. First, James says that attention involves "taking possession by the mind . . . of one out of . . . several . . . trains of thought." By this statement, James suggests that attention involves a process of *selection* in which the individual is juggling several ongoing lines of thinking, each competing for current resources (or consciousness). Second, he states that attention involves "focalization . . . of consciousness." This is a subtle, but important, difference from the first idea. Attention involves an active, *directive* process of current thinking, presumably one that is dynamic—that changes with the changing needs of the performer. And last, James suggests that attention requires "withdrawal from some things in order to deal effectively with others." Here, James is again implying something subtly different—that there is a limit to the *amount* of attention that can be allocated. The performer must be able to shift the amount of attention allocation as changes occur in the demands of the task.

As we will discuss in this chapter, James' intuitions and descriptions about attention were quite accurate.

What Is Attention?

All of the preceding examples represent different uses of attention. But what *is* attention? In our view, **attention** is a resource (or "pool" of slightly different resources) that is available and that can be used for various purposes. In many respects, attention is like a bank account, which contains financial resources that allow us to perform activities of daily living. The ways in which these attentional resources are allocated define how we *use* attention.

A way to think of attention is related to the limitations in doing two things at the same time. Psychologists have approached the limitations in information processing by first trying to understand the separate requirements of tasks that interfere with each other. The idea has been that, if two tasks interfere with each other, then they both demand some access to the limited capacity to process information; that is, they both require attention. Figure 3.1 illustrates this idea. Both circles represent the total capacity that is available to be allocated. In the bank account example, this would be the total of all of the money that we have available. Figure 3.1 illustrates how the fixed amount of attention (capacity resource) must be divided between a "main" task and some secondary task. When the main task is relatively "simple" and does not require very much attention, as depicted in figure 3.1*a*, then more attentional capacity remains for other tasks.

This notion has strong implications for understanding skilled performance. In many

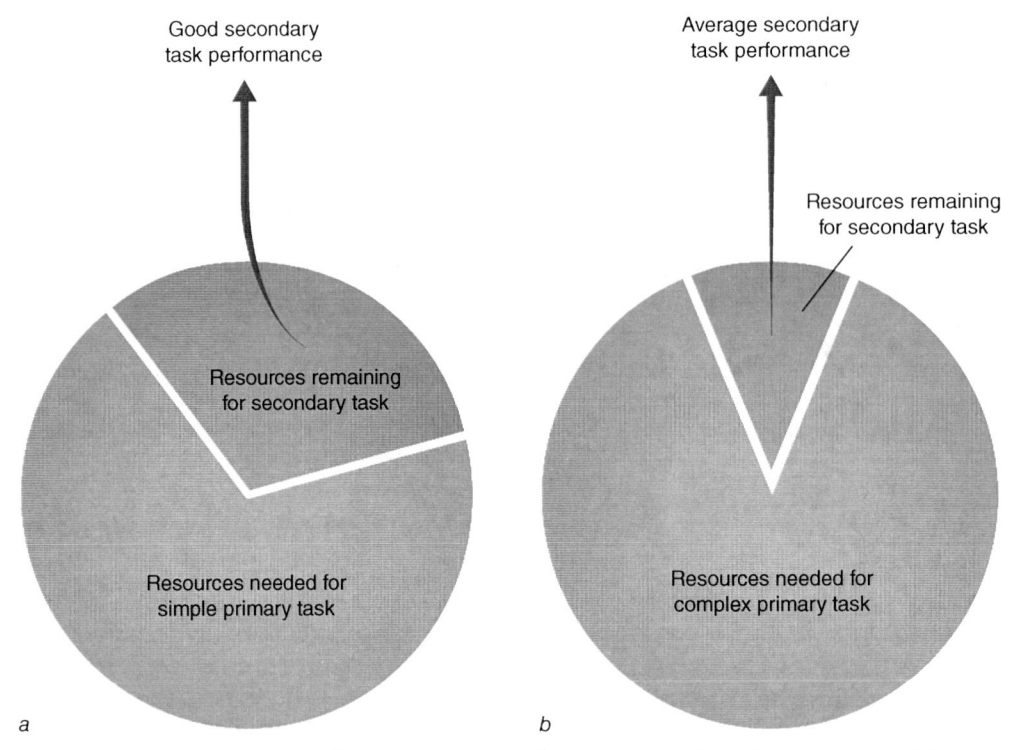

FIGURE 3.1 Attention remaining for a secondary task is reduced when the primary task is more complex (b) compared to when the primary task is simple (a).

Based on Posner and Keele 1969.

skills, there is an overwhelming amount of information that could be processed, some of it relevant to performance (e.g., what other drivers are doing, as in the earlier example) and some of it irrelevant to performance (e.g., the song that is playing on the radio). The performer's problem is how to cope with this potential overload. The performer must learn what to attend to and when, and must shift attention skillfully between events in the environment, monitoring and correcting her own actions, planning future actions, and doing many other processes that compete for the limited resources of attentional capacity.

The following sections turn to the question of when and under what conditions tasks interfere with each other. One way to understand the kinds of multiple-task interference involves the stages of information processing described in chapter 2—**stimulus identification**, **response selection**, and **movement programming** (see figure 2.2). It is useful to ask whether, within each stage, there is interference between two processes competing for the available capacity. There is evidence that some processing can occur "in parallel" (that is, without attention) in the stimulus identification stage, but that much less parallel processing occurs in the response selection stage. Finally, considerable interference often exists among tasks in the movement programming stage.

Limitations in Stimulus Identification

Some evidence suggests that information processing in the peripheral, sensory stages of the information-processing model can be done in parallel. With parallel processing, two or more streams of information can enter the system at the same time and can be processed together without interfering with each other. For other tasks, however, the capacity of information exceeds the limits of attention, requiring that we *switch* attention between competing sources. Still other research reveals that **sustained attention** tends to wane after extended periods of information processing. These influences on

Parallel Processing

Information from different aspects of the visual display, such as the color and the shape of objects, can apparently be processed together without interference. Evidence for parallel processing in stimulus identification comes from an analysis of the Stroop effect (Stroop, 1935; MacLeod, 1991). Imagine that you are a research subject, asked to respond as quickly as possible by naming the color of the ink in which words are printed, as in figure 3.2. In some cases, the words printed have no semantic relationship to the colors in which they are printed, as in list *a*. In other cases, as in list *b*, the ink colors compete with the names of the words themselves. The Stroop effect is the tendency for the set of stimuli on the right to require longer completion times to name the colors than those on the left. Evidence suggests that the color of the ink and the word that the ink spells are initially processed together and in parallel. The interference is caused later on by the two stimuli competing for different responses.

There is also considerable parallel processing of the sensory signals from the muscles and joints associated with posture and locomotion, and people seem to handle these together and without much awareness. The idea is that, considering the processes occurring in the stimulus identification stage, some sensory information can be processed in parallel and without much interference—that is, without attention.

Cherry (1953) developed the "dichotic listening" task to investigate these ideas. Subjects wore headphones, such that separate streams of information were directed to each ear; they were told to pay attention to one channel and to disregard the other. After a short period of time the subjects removed the headphones and were asked to repeat the information that had been presented to the "attended" ear. Unexpectedly, they were also asked to reveal what had been presented in the "unattended" ear. Subjects were largely unable to remember the information from the unattended ear, although they could identify some "surface features" of the message, such as the speaker's gender and loudness of the voice.

Cherry (1953) called this the **cocktail party effect**, and it represents another example of parallel processing. The effect is this: Imagine yourself in a large room at a party, in which many groups of people are engaged in conversations. There is considerable noise surrounding the conversation in which you are engaged—loud music, other conversations, and so on—yet you can still engage in a conversation successfully, effectively shutting out the background noise. But not all information is blocked. You can be engaged in an ongoing conversation and suddenly hear your name being spoken in a conversation in which you are not involved at all. Even though you have effectively "shut out" that background "noise," some of it must have been processed in parallel in the stimulus identification stage in order that you could hear your own name. The cocktail-party effect illustrates that even some "unattended" features of sensory processing are processed in parallel with other "attended" information in the very early stages of sensory processing.

a	b
HOUSE	BLUE
PENCIL	BLACK
HORSE	ORANGE
WATCH	GREEN
RIVER	YELLOW
LETTER	RED

FIGURE 3.2 The Stroop effect. Time yourself while naming the colors of the words printed in each list.

Inattention Blindness

The previous section illustrates how stimulus information can be processed in parallel, even despite efforts to block it out. And yet, sometimes a very simple, goal-directed visual search, such as looking for a specific entrance or building number, seems to absorb our attention, making us "blind" to other things. Some remarkable findings by several research groups have shown that we can miss seemingly obvious features in our environment when we are engaged in attentive visual search. For example, research participants in Simons and Chabris' (1999) study watched a video of six people who passed basketballs among themselves while all players were constantly in motion. Three players on one "team" were dressed in jeans and black t-shirts, and three in jeans and white t-shirts were on the other "team." Each team passed their ball only to players on their own team. The experimental subjects watched a video of this activity; their only task was to count the number of passes made by the team dressed in white. You can view the experimental setup at www.youtube.com/watch?v=vJG698U2Mvo.

After the 30-s video ended, the experimenter asked the participants for the answer to the number of passes made, and followed this by asking if they had seen anything unusual. Only about half of all subjects tested responded by saying that they had seen someone dressed in a gorilla suit walk through the group of players and pound his chest (gorilla style) about halfway through the video. Remarkably, the other half did not report seeing the "gorilla," even though it had been in plain view (see figure 3.3). When the video was replayed to them, these subjects were shocked at having missed the obvious "gorilla."

This phenomenon, which has been given the label "inattention blindness," was originally discovered by Neisser and Becklen (1975), who used a similar task, but with a woman with a parasol instead of a person in a gorilla suit. The effect has been studied vigorously since the Neisser–Becklen findings were published.

Missing the rather obvious "gorilla" is likely to occur only under a restricted set of circumstances, however—when the viewer is engaged in a specific search task. Watching

FIGURE 3.3 The inattention-blindness effect. Subjects (observers of the video) counted the number of basketball passes made among the subjects in white t-shirts. Later, about half of these subjects did not recall seeing the "gorilla" walk through the middle of the group.

Reprinted by permission from Simons and Chabis 1999.

the video under no specific search instructions, or being asked to count the passes made by the team in black t-shirts, produced very few cases of this "inattention blindness" (Simons & Chabris, 1999). Watching the video a second time, or thinking that something unexpected might occur, also eliminates the effect. Furley and colleagues (2010) found that highly skilled basketball players were also less likely to miss the "gorilla" than were low-skilled players.

Despite these limitations in the inattention-blindness effect, findings reveal that it is not restricted to watching videos but can be demonstrated in action events. Other "field" research studies reveal that people who are engaged in attention-demanding tasks are likely to miss quite obvious things such as a change in a person to whom they are giving directions (Simons & Levin, 1998) or a person on a unicycle dressed in a clown suit on a university campus (Hyman et al., 2010). In fact, a number of automobile accidents seem linked to this phenomenon. These have been given the label **"looked-but-failed-to-see" accidents**; here, even though there is evidence that the driver looked, he still drove into the path of a pedestrian, bicycle, or another vehicle, causing an accident (Brown, 2005; Langham et al., 2002); the driver simply did not "see" the other object coming, even though he "looked" at it.

Inattention blindness explains why we momentarily fail to recognize a friend we happen to encounter while looking for someone else in a crowd. Our search has been directed toward a person with specific visual characteristics, and we become temporally oblivious to people who don't match those search criteria. Magicians and pickpocket thieves use essentially the same concept. A focus by the "victim" on one specific detail, especially if attention has been directed there by the magician or thief, causes the victim to be "blind" to the other person's intentions (Stephen et al., 2008).

Sustained Attention

World War II generated a push in research on sustained attention in order to better understand the limits of radar operators who were on the lookout for enemy aircraft. Mackworth (1948), who was a leader in this research, devised a task in which subjects would watch the pointer of a clock-like apparatus jumping second by second. But, occasionally, after long, irregular (unpredictable) intervals, the pointer would jump by 2 s. Detection of these latter jumps was found to be reliable for the first 30 min of work but declined dramatically thereafter. These were termed "vigilance decrements," or decreases in vigilance.

A number of factors are known to affect vigilance, or sustained attention; these include the operator's motivation, arousal, and, of course, fatigue (clearly related to the accumulated amount of time in performing the task). Environmental factors, such as temperature and noise, are also known to affect sustained attention (see Davies & Parasuraman, 1982, for more). After a period of time, the task of concentrating on a single target of our attention becomes a progressively more difficult chore.

These effects are quite obvious on a daily basis, as they influence many occupations in which vigilance is a necessity. For example, consider the task of working as a security agent at a busy airport. Before people can board their aircraft, they must go through a series of security checks, which includes an X-ray scan of their carry-on luggage. Each X-rayed piece of luggage must undergo a visual search by a human operator, who looks for the presence of objects that are not permitted on board (figure 3.4). The obvious

FIGURE 3.4 An airport security guard is required to sustain effort over long periods of time.

ones (guns, knives) should be relatively easy to spot. But the problems faced by the security agent include trying to decide whether something that looks like a banned object is actually one or not, which slows the checkpoint process. Experiments on visual search tasks reveal that the number and similarity of distracting objects play an important role in the success of the search. The agent's task is made even more difficult by the fact that finding banned objects is (thankfully) a rare occurrence—so sustained attention to the task is of primary concern (Wolfe et al., 2005).

Limitations in Response Selection

Interference between tasks is never more obvious than when the performer must perform two actions simultaneously, with each task requiring mental operations, such as answering a telephone call while pouring water into a coffee maker. Both activities are thought to be done during response selection because they require that choices be made among several possible alternative responses—which hands to use to pour the water and pick up the telephone, which ear to listen with, monitoring the water so as to not spill any and to not pour too much, and so on. These activities are governed by *controlled processing*, which is thought to be (a) slow; (b) attention demanding, with interference caused by competing processing; (c) serially organized, with a given processing task coming before or after other processing tasks; and (d) volitional, easily halted or avoided altogether. Relatively effortful, controlled processing is a very large part of conscious information-processing activities, involving mental operations among relatively poorly learned, or even completely novel, activities. Having to perform two information-processing tasks together can completely disrupt both tasks.

A separate, very different kind of information processing seems to occur in highly practiced people. Some years ago, Peter Vidmar, a 1984 Olympic silver medalist in gymnastics, claimed that before mounting the apparatus, he paid attention just to the first move in his routine—the mount; the remainder of the elements occurred more or less "automatically," that is, without requiring attention (Vidmar, 1984). These later elements required only minor adjustments while being run off, allowing Vidmar to focus on such higher-order aspects of his routine as style and form. It is as if much of the information processing necessary in this complex gymnastics routine was fundamentally different from controlled processing, not requiring very much attention. This way of dealing with information, **automatic processing**, is (a) fast; (b) not attention demanding, in that such processes do not generate (very much) interference with other tasks; (c) organized in parallel, occurring together with other processing tasks; and (d) involuntary, often unavoidable.

Automatic information processing is thought to be the result of an enormous amount of practice. Your capability to quickly recognize collections of letters as the words you are reading now has come from years of practice. Many years ago, Bryan and Harter (1897, 1899) conducted studies of telegraph operators, whose job it was to identify (receive) and send Morse code—which is composed of varying periods of brief noise (called dots and dashes) that combine to define letters and numbers. Bryan and Harter found that telegraph operators focused on individual letters at the earliest stage of learning but that as they gained proficiency, they processed Morse code as combinations of letters, then later as whole words, and even in phrases.

The effectiveness of automatic processing has strong implications not only for many everyday tasks (like reading) but also for high-level performance skills. If a task is performed automatically, many important information-processing activities can be produced not only quickly but in parallel with other, simultaneous tasks and without disrupting performance. It is as if certain stages (e.g., response selection) are bypassed altogether.

Costs and Benefits of Automaticity

Automatic performances, whose benefits are nearly obvious, are related to processing information in parallel, quickly, and without interference from other processing tasks. For example, after much practice, high-level volleyball players can read their opponents' movement patterns automatically to mean that the ball will be spiked from, say, their left side (e.g., see Allard & Burnett, 1985). But what if, after consistently producing a pattern leading to a play to the left, the opposing team uses the same pattern leading to a play to the right? The defenders' automatic processing of the pattern would lead to a quick decision and a movement to counter the *expected* play, a response that would be hopeless as far as combating the actual play is concerned.

Clearly, then, automaticity can have drawbacks, as well as benefits. Although very fast processing is effective when the environment is stable and predictable, it can lead to terrible errors when the environment (or an opponent) changes the action at the last moment. Thus, automaticity seems most effective in closed skills, where the environment is relatively predictable. With open skills, so many more patterns are possible that the performer

Automaticity allows highly skilled athletes to process information about their opponents' movements quickly and respond.

must develop an automatic response to each of them; this is generally possible only after many years of experience.

Developing Automaticity

How do people develop the capability to process information automatically? Practice, and lots of it, is a very important ingredient, so you should not expect to see automaticity develop quickly. Practicing for automaticity is generally most effective under a "consistent-mapping" condition, where the response generated is related *consistently* to a particular stimulus pattern. For example, the response to a red light during driving is always to bring the vehicle to a stop. This is in contrast to a "varied-mapping" condition, where a given stimulus sometimes leads to one response and sometimes to another response (Schneider & Shiffrin, 1977). An example is the incredible variety of button layouts on different brands of TV remote-control units, where a given function (changing the channel) requires pressing different buttons depending on the brand. The diversity of such "varied-mapping" conditions makes automatic processing almost impossible to achieve, and such tasks require considerable controlled processing to avoid making errors.

Response Selection and Distracted Driving

Distracted driving is an excellent example involving attention's limited capacity. But an important question is: Does distracted driving affect the response selection stage or the movement programming stage? Laws passed in many U.S. states and other countries have banned the use of handheld cell phones during driving. Why? The assumption is that the hand operation of a cell phone interferes with the operation of a motor vehicle; this argument lays the blame for the cell phone–driving dual-task deficit as a movement programming limitation. But the research suggests otherwise, and is quite conclusive that hands-free and handheld phones are about equally problematic in exceeding the attentional capacity limits of the driver. The source of the problem lies in the capacity demanded by the phone *conversation*, and not whether the driver is holding on to, looking at, or manipulating the phone (e.g., Strayer & Johnston, 2001). The physical actions involved in manipulating the cell phone do not add significantly to the attention demands required in carrying on a conversation while driving (see Ishigami & Klein, 2009, for an important review of this research). The discussion in Focus on Research 3.1 provides more information about the methods used to understand the attention demands of distracted driving.

Remember, though, that using a cell phone at the same time as performing other activities can be just as dangerous as talking (or texting) and driving. For example, in an observational study, Thompson and colleagues (2013) found that people who texted or talked on a cell phone while they crossed a busy intersection walked about 20% slower than nondistracted pedestrians. The texting pedestrians were also more likely than nondistracted pedestrians to fail to look both ways for oncoming traffic before entering the intersection.

Limitations in Movement Programming

As you'll recall from chapter 2, the movement programming stage is the third in the sequence of information-processing stages. Here, after the performer has perceived what the environment will allow, and after having chosen a response that meets those demands, the performer must still organize the motor system in order to actually execute the action. In this stage, the performer must make critical adjustments that occur at various levels (e.g., in the limbs, muscles, and spinal cord). These adjustments take time, of course. A good example is the action of a fencer, who must preprogram a movement despite having to execute the movement in the face of a potentially changing environment. In the following example the programmed action is somewhat complicated, involving a move toward the center shoulder and then followed by a sudden change in the action.

Focus on RESEARCH 3.1

Distracted-Driving Research

Researchers have used varying approaches to understand the effects of various distractions, such as speaking on a cell phone, on the control of a vehicle. The obvious problem with doing the most logical type of research—using drivers in real traffic situations—is that it brings other drivers, the research participants, and sometimes the experimenters themselves into potentially dangerous situations, which is unethical. So, researchers have devised different methods to assess the attentional cost of performing various tasks while driving.

A statistical approach to the specific problem of cell phone use during driving uses call records of individuals who were involved in an accident. The findings of one study using this method revealed that the likelihood of being involved in a car accident increased by 400% when a driver was talking on a cell phone (Redelmeier & Tibshirani, 1997). These authors also found that the increase in accident rate while talking on a cell phone during driving is about the same as for driving with a .08% blood alcohol (which is the legal definition of driving under the influence [DUI] of alcohol in some states and countries).

The most common type of experiment involves humans performing in driving simulators in laboratory environments. Some simulators provide extremely realistic driving environments, enabling researchers to have control over the "traffic conditions" and varying distractions without endangering anyone.

A few experimenters have gone further to create an outdoor environment, using an actual car and a simulated driving environment in an otherwise safe area such as a large empty parking lot. In fact, one of the very first studies of its kind was performed over 40 years ago, and the authors suggested back then that mobile phones and automobile drivers were a dangerous mix (Brown, Tickner, & Simmons, 1969).

Of course, each method has advantages and disadvantages. Call records involve actual data about calls that have occurred. But, the co-occurrence of an accident and a call as shown in records says very little about the state of the individual during the call. Simulators provide the researcher with excellent control of mental workloads, ongoing distractions, the timing of critical events, and the measurement of behaviors. But these are all simulations of a driving environment, not the real thing. Outdoor environments, in actual cars but with simulated driving conditions, also have the advantage of good experimenter control of events, but, again, without the reality of an actual driving experience in real traffic. In the end, the information provided by all types of research activities together provides researchers with the best answers to these critical questions about distracted driving.

Exploring Further

1. How might the nature of a particular cell phone conversation affect a person's capacity to attend to the task of driving?
2. Do you think that a driver having a discussion with an in-car passenger would have the same effects on driving as the driver talking on the cell phone? Why or why not?

A fencer moves the foil toward the opponent's shoulder but then quickly alters the direction and contacts the waist instead. Responding to the first move, the fake, seems to have interfered with the opponent's speed of responding to the second move, and the point is lost. The delay in responding suggests strong interference between activities in the later stages of information processing. Specifically, the delay occurs because of interference to the movement programming stage, which has the task of organizing the motor system to make the desired movement.

Much of this view comes from considerable research evidence using the so-called "**double-stimulation paradigm**," where the subject is required to respond, with separate responses, to each of two stimuli presented very closely together in time (see Focus on Research 3.2). This paradigm is in many ways analogous to the problem facing the fencer's opponent, who must respond to one move and then another in rapid succession. The delays in responding occur because of the interference that arises in programming the first and second movements as rapidly as possible.

Psychological Refractory Period

The delay in responding to the second of two closely spaced stimuli is termed the psychological refractory period (PRP). An important question concerns how soon a person can switch from (a) making a goal-directed response to one stimulus to (b) making a different goal-directed response to a different stimulus. The motor system processes the first stimulus and generates the first response. Then, if the experimenter presents the second stimulus during the time the system is processing the first stimulus and its response, the onset of the second response can be delayed considerably (the PRP effect).

One explanation for the PRP is that there is a kind of "bottleneck" in the movement programming stage, and that this stage can organize and initiate only one action at a time, as diagrammed in figure 3.6. Any other action must wait until the stage has finished initiating the first. This delay is largest when the time between stimuli (SOA) is short, because at this time the movement programming stage has just begun to generate the first response; this response must be emitted before the stage can begin to generate the second response. As the SOA increases, more of the first response will have been prepared by the time the second stimulus is presented, so there is less delay before the movement programming stage is cleared.

One more finding is of interest here. When the SOA is very short, say less than 40 ms, the motor system responds to the second stimulus in a very different way. The system responds to the first and second stimulus as if they were one, which produces both

Focus on
RESEARCH 3.2

The Double-Stimulation Paradigm

Research on the **psychological refractory period (PRP)** uses the "double-stimulation paradigm," in which the subject is asked, for example, to respond to a tone (Stimulus$_1$) by lifting the right hand from a key as quickly as possible. A very short time following the tone a light (Stimulus$_2$) might appear; the subject is to respond by lifting the left hand from a key as quickly as possible. The separation between the onsets of the two stimuli, called the **stimulus-onset asynchrony (SOA)**, might range from zero to a few hundred milliseconds. Researchers are usually interested in reaction time (RT) to the second stimulus (RT$_2$) as a function of the SOA. (See the paradigm timeline shown in figure 3.5a.)

FIGURE 3.5 The double-stimulation paradigm (a) and results from experiment by Davis (1988) (b), showing that RT_2 is lengthened greatly at the shortest SOAs.
Reprinted by permission from Schmidt and Lee 2011; Data from Davis 1959.

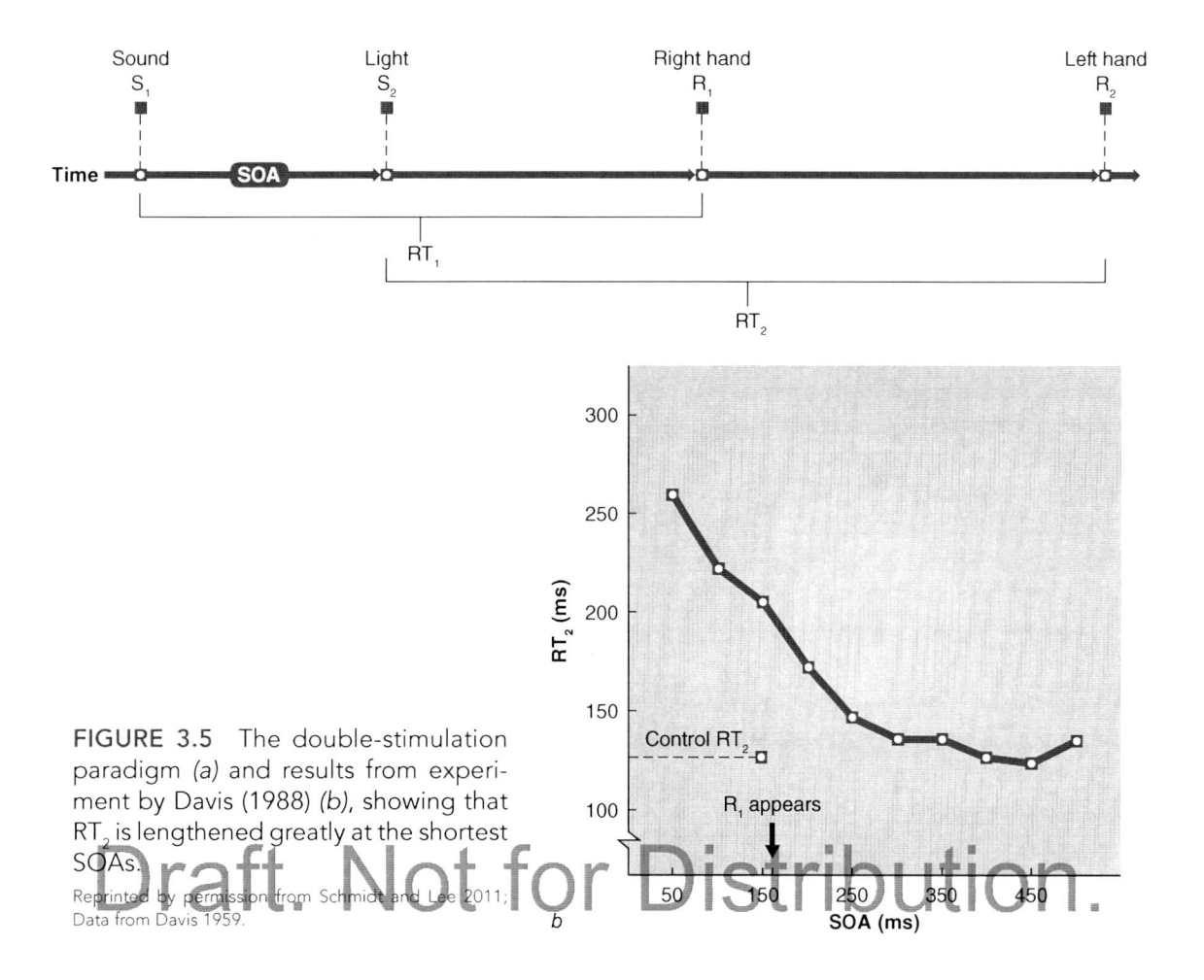

The general findings from one study using this paradigm are graphed in figure 3.5b, where RT_2 is plotted as a function of the SOA. The horizontal line (labeled RT_2) is the value of RT_2 when the first stimulus is not presented at all; it represents the "usual" (without interference) RT to this stimulus using this response. Depending on the length of the SOA, there is a marked delay in the RT_2 while the first stimulus is being processed. When the SOA is about 50 ms, the delay is very large, and it can more than double the value of RT_2, as compared to its control value. As the SOA lengthens, the delay in RT_2 decreases, but there is still some delay in producing RT_2 even with SOAs of 200 ms or more. The single-channel hypothesis (Welford, 1952), which was originally proposed to account for effects like these, argues that the processing of the first stimulus and response completely blocks the processing of the second stimulus and response until such time that the processing of the first stimulus and response has been completed. More recent thinking about data such as these holds that the major delay in RT_2 arises from interference between the movement programming stages of these actions.

Exploring Further

1. Why is the most important comparison in this paradigm the RT to the second of two closely spaced stimuli rather than to the response to the first stimulus?
2. How would the magnitude of the PRP effect be expected to change depending on the number of choices involved in responding to the first stimulus?

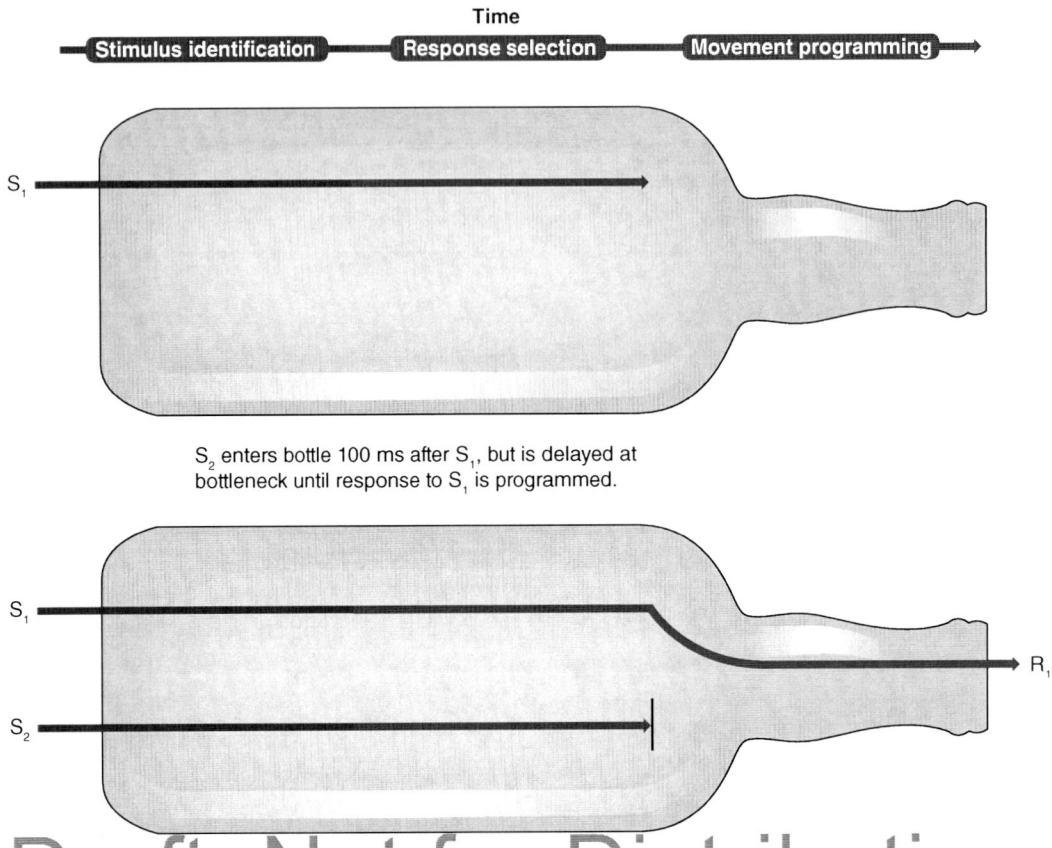

FIGURE 3.6 An information-processing bottleneck in the movement programming stage occurs when two stimuli (S_1 and S_2) are presented 100 ms apart. In (a), the first stimulus enters the information-processing system. In (b), the second stimulus is introduced, but it is delayed at the bottleneck while the first response is programmed. This is similar to what happens in response to a fake in rapid sports.

responses simultaneously. In this phenomenon, termed *grouping*, the early processing stages presumably detect both stimuli as a single event and organize a single, more complicated action in which both limbs respond simultaneously.

The phenomenon of psychological refractoriness just discussed accounts for many of the underlying processes in faking. In basketball, for example, the player taking the shot preprograms a single, relatively complex action that involves a move to begin a shot, a delay to withhold it, and then the actual shot—all done in rapid succession The shooter's movement is organized as a single unit and is prepared as any other movement would be in the movement programming stage. However, the defensive player sees only the first part of this action; this can be thought of as the first stimulus (S_1) in the double-stimulation paradigm, and it triggers the response to block the shot, which does not occur until later. The processing of the first stimulus leads to large delays in responding to the new information that the shot has been withheld, that it is a fake (as indicated by the fact that the second stimulus, S_2, the actual shot, is now being made). The result is that the first response (movement to block) cannot be withheld, and it occurs essentially as originally planned. This creates a very large delay in initiating a second, corrective response to block the actual shot, which is made at about the same time that the defensive player is dropping back to the floor after "taking the fake." This all makes the shot very easy for the offensive player and makes the defensive player look a little foolish at the same time.

Some principles of faking emerge from research on psychological refractoriness.

First, the fake—the first response—should be realistic, distinct, and clear, so the defensive player treats it as an actual shot. Second, for the effective fake, the single programmed action that contains both the fake and the actual shot is planned so as to separate the fake (stimulus 1) and the actual shot (stimulus 2) sufficiently to generate a relatively large delay for the response to stimulus 2. From the data in figure 3.7, for the fake to be maximally effective, this separation is somewhere around 60 to 100 ms. If this separation is too short, the defensive player can ignore the fake and respond instead to the actual shot (grouping). If the separation is too long, the defender will respond to the second stimulus with an essentially normal RT, and the shooter will have lost the advantage of the fake.

The Probe-Task Technique

Some researchers have used a different approach to studying the attention demanded during the movement programming stage, called the probe-task technique. Here, the researcher would have the subject perform one task (called the primary task; it could be either discrete or continuous in nature). At some strategic point in the performance of the primary task, the researcher would probe (or test) the attention demanded in the main task by presenting a secondary task, usually a discrete stimulus, such as tone or light (the probe stimulus). Now, the subject's additional task would be to respond to the stimulus as rapidly as possible with either a manual (e.g., a key press) or a vocal (e.g., saying "stop") response, and RT would measure the delay in responding to the probe. With this strategy, the researcher would use the RT to the probe as a measure of the attention demanded by the primary task; a more attention-demanding primary task would result in slower responses to the probe stimulus signal than would a primary task that demanded less attention.

An example of how this technique is used in research is the work of Posner and Keele (1969). In their study, subjects were asked to make a rapid, visually-guided aiming movement using a lever, through 135° of rotation to a target. Subjects made these movements to either large or small targets—the idea being that smaller targets might require more of the attentional capacity due the increased precision requirements of aiming. The probe technique was used to assess attention demands at various points during the movement—either before movement initiation, at the point of movement initiation, or at various later points. Trials that assessed RT were also conducted in a control condition, in which no aiming movement was made.

The results of the Posner and Keele study are presented in figure 3.7. There are several things of interest here. First, the control-RT value (represented as the solid line across the figure near 260 ms), was considerably less than the probe RTs for any of the other data points in the graph. This was interpreted as indicating that all parts of the aiming movements required some attention, since RT was elevated relative to the no-movement (control) condition. Second, the "bowed" nature of both the small-target and large-target curves in the graph suggests that attention demands were not evenly distributed throughout the movement. The elevated probe RTs at positions representing the beginning (0° position) and end (135° position) of the movement suggested that these were more attention-demanding parts of the movement than were the middle positions (i.e., the 15°, 45°, 75°, and 105° positions). Lastly, the probe RT for the small-target curve was generally larger than for the large-target curve, indicating that movements with greater precision requirements are more attention demanding than movements with less precise requirements. These secondary-task probe techniques are not without their limitations and problems, however. As we will see later (in chapter 6), producing two movements at the same time introduces special coordination challenges to the processing system. If the movements are compatible (e.g., keeping a rhythm beat with two hands, as in drumming), then two limbs can be coordinated in such a way that there is no detriment to performance (e.g., Helmuth & Ivry, 1996). A problem arises when two or more separate actions have distinct and

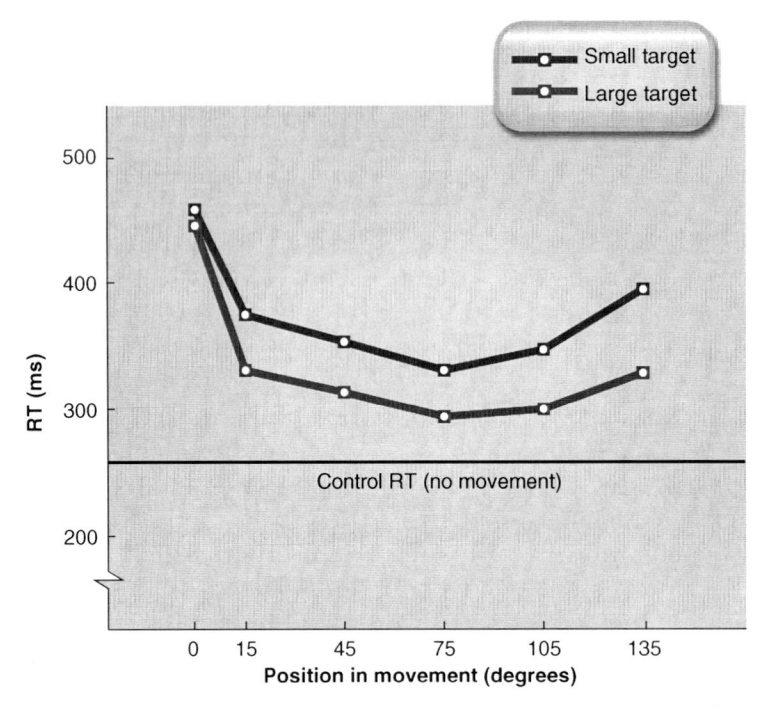

FIGURE 3.7 The attention demands as measured by probe RT at various points during the visually-guided pointing movement to either a small or large target. The straight line denotes average RT to the probe stimulus when no pointing movement is being made.

Reprinted by permission from Posner and Keele 1969.

incompatible *spatial* or *temporal* requirements. For example, one limb might be required to produce one spatial action while another produces a different action—such as rubbing your stomach and patting your head at the same time. Polyrhythms, in which one limb produces a faster beat than the other limb (e.g., 4:3 rhythms), are an example of a challenging task because of the incompatible timing requirements.

The problem for the probe technique is that responding manually to a probe can produce specific interference effects (over and above those associated with attention) with a manual primary task (McLeod, 1980). In McLeod's study, this occurred because the nature of the manual response to the probe was incompatible with the movement required for the primary task. Thus, attention demands assessed by the delay in probe RT were "contaminated" by the competition between movement requirements. McLeod (1980) found that much less competition occurred between a primary limb task and a vocal probe response, for example, and provided a less contaminated assessment of attention demand. This sort of idea prompted the notion of "pools" of attention, where a given pool would be related to vocal responses, and another pool would be related to motor responses. We will have much more to say about moving two limbs at the same time when we discuss coordination in chapter 6.

Focus of Attention During Action

A relatively recent research interest regarding the movement programming stage concerns a performer's recommended *focus* of attention. Would the performer be better off directing his focus to an *internal* source, for example by monitoring the ongoing movement, or would attention be directed more effectively at an *external* target, such as an object to be struck or the intended effect that the action will have on the environment? Considerable research conducted by Wulf and her colleagues suggests that, in almost all situations, an **external focus of attention** results in more

Producing two movements at the same time introduces a greater challenge if the movements are incompatible, as when a drummer plays a faster beat with one hand than with the other.

skilled performance than an **internal focus of attention**. These studies have revealed very impressive benefits to performance, seen in a wide variety of laboratory and sport tasks, and for children, adults, and healthy older adults (see Wulf, 2007, for a review).

One aspect of this research that remains to be clarified is this: At what skill level would an external focus would be preferred to an internal focus? Perhaps these internal-focus instructions benefit individuals who are just beginners, with an external focus preferred for those who have attained perhaps even just a minimal proficiency (e.g., Beilock et al., 2002; Perkins-Ceccato, Passmore, & Lee, 2003). We will return to the issue of focus of attention when we consider the process of learning in chapter 9.

Another feature to consider about this research is that these effects occur when one is focused on internal or external targets *during* skill execution. For example, an expert gymnast might go through a number of internal *and* external thoughts during a preperformance preparation. But, when it comes time to perform the movement, the research suggests that an external focus will produce the most skilled results. And, as we discuss later in this chapter, the consequences for an expert of reverting to an internal focus during movement execution can be disastrous, and may explain a large proportion of the famous cases of athletes and musicians who "choked" under pressure (Beilock, 2010). Skilled athletes who routinely perform with an external focus of attention sometimes shift their focus under pressure to movement production (perhaps thinking about how to perform the movement, or how the movement will feel when it is performed). This shift in attentional focus can reduce performance quality, leading to further internalized focus and a heightened anxiety. This downward spiral is one cause of **choking**.

Decision Making Under Stress

Arousal, the level of excitement produced under stress, is a common aspect of skill performance situations. This is certainly true of many athletic events, where the pressure to win and the threat of losing, as well as crowd influences, are important sources of emotional arousal for players. The level of arousal imposed by a situation is an important determinant of performance, particularly if the performance is dependent on the speed and accuracy of decision making.

Inverted-U Principle

One can think of arousal as the level of excitement or activation generated in the central nervous system. For example, low levels of arousal are associated with sleep-like states, and high levels are associated with the agitated and extremely alert states found in life-threatening situations. The influences of arousal level on performance have been studied for many years. The **inverted-U principle** (or, the Yerkes-Dodson, [1908] law) represents an early view of the relationship between arousal and performance. The idea is that increasing the arousal level generally enhances performance, but only to a point. Performance quality peaks at some intermediate value of arousal, and performance actually deteriorates as the arousal level rises further—hence the inverted-U function.

Support for the application of the inverted-U principle to human motor performance was provided in a study by Weinberg and Ragan (1978). The task involved throwing balls at a target, and levels of stress were induced by (falsely) comparing subjects' performances to those of other subjects like them (junior high school boys). In the "high-stress" condition, 90% of this "comparison" group supposedly performed more accurately than the test subjects did. The authors assumed, with good justification we think, that junior high school boys would find this sort of information feedback to be arousing or stressful. The moderate- and low-stress groups were told that 60% and 30%, respectively, of the comparison group had scored more accurately than they had. When the subjects performed the task again, following these stress-inducing false statements, their performances conformed well to the predictions of the inverted-U principle, as shown in figure 3.8.

The inverted-U principle might be surprising to many who deal with sport and coaching, because it is generally believed that the higher the level of motivation or arousal, the more effective the performance will be. Coaches often spend a great deal of time before games attempting to raise the team's arousal level, and we hear sportscasters argue that a team's performance was poor because the players were not "psyched up" enough for the contest. Yet this general view is contradicted by experimental evidence: A high level of arousal is effective only to

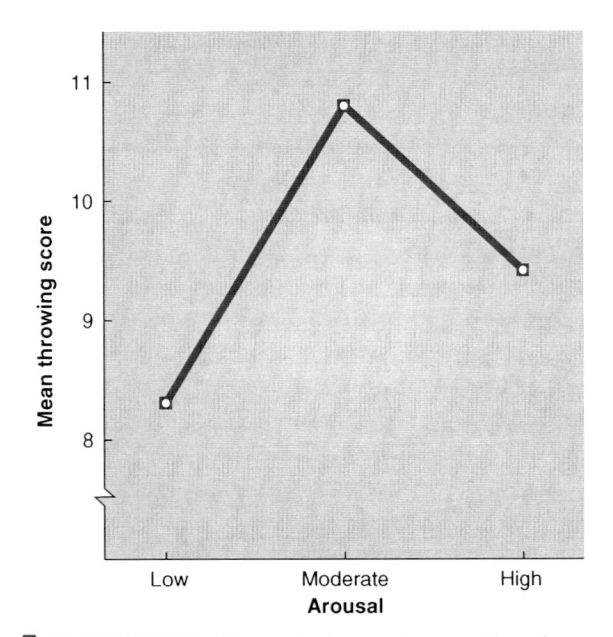

FIGURE 3.8 Stress-inducing instructions have effects on performance that are consistent with the predictions of the inverted-U principle (from Weinberg & Ragan, 1978).

Reprinted by permission from Schmidt and Lee 2011; Data from Weinberg and Ragan 1978.

a point, whereas further raising the arousal level actually damages performance.

Variations of the Inverted-U Principle

Over the years, the general shape of the inverted U has been a good guideline for thinking about the relationship between arousal and performance. However, it is probably best not to put too much faith in the "symmetrical" shape of this U-function. As shown in figure 3.9, more recent evidence and theorizing have suggested that task differences, as well as individual differences in the subject's "excitability," can result in changes to the shapes of the curve, with optimal performance occurring at either the lower or higher ends of the arousal continuum.

Consider the three hypothetical curves illustrated in figure 3.9. The red curve labeled "A" shows a steep rise in performance at relatively low levels of arousal, with performance peaking and then beginning to decline even before a moderate level in arousal. Such a curve might represent the shape of the arousal–performance function for a particularly complex task, perhaps requiring fine motor control (threading a needle) or cognition (playing chess), or for an individual who functions best under calm conditions. In contrast, the green curve labeled "C" could represent the arousal–performance function for a very simple task, perhaps requiring great amounts of force with very little cognition (e.g., powerlifting) or for a person who thrives under pressure. The point here is that the simple inverted U (the blue curve labeled "B" in figure 3.9) might best represent many other tasks that have medium levels of complexity, cognitive involvement, and so on. These principles have been recognized and studied in the fields of sport and exercise psychology, where the general problem has been to understand the effects of stress and arousal on performance, and to examine how arousal-regulation procedures can be used to manage arousal levels before performance (e.g., Weinberg & Gould, 2011).

Perceptual Narrowing

One important change in information processing that occurs with high arousal is **perceptual narrowing**—the tendency for the perceptual field to shrink under stress. (This phenomenon is sometimes known as "tunnel vision," in which the world seems to be viewed as through a pipe such that the entire focus is on central vision. It has also been referred to as "weapon focus," in which the panicked victim of an armed robbery cannot identify the robber because her attention had been riveted on the gun.) For

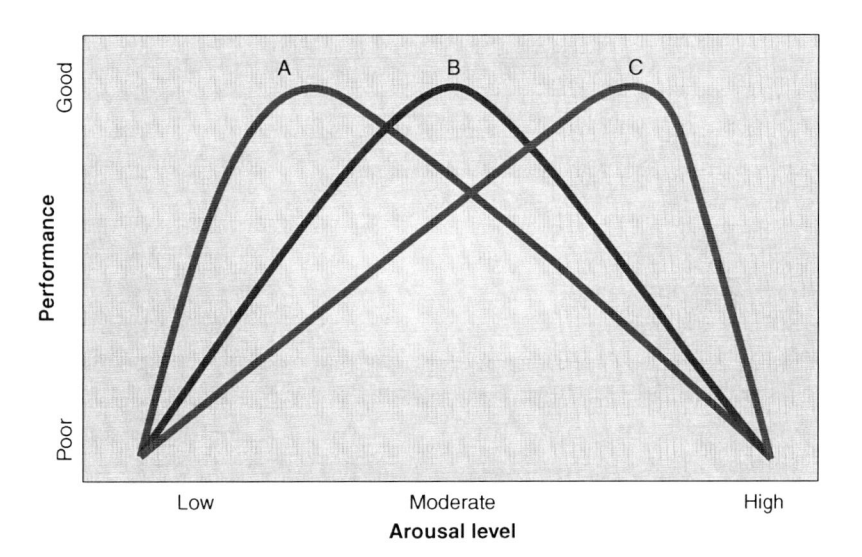

FIGURE 3.9 Variations to the inverted-U principle.

Focus on
APPLICATION 3.2

Automotive Panic

It was a fairly normal morning—the 35-year-old teacher reported that she had just dropped her son at day care before heading to school. She stopped for coffee at the local drive-through and moved the transmission lever from Drive to Neutral in order to reach for her purse. After putting the cup in the coffee holder, she intended to put her foot on the brake while she changed the transmission from Neutral back to Drive. Suddenly, the car lurched forward and gathered speed. Pressing harder on the brake pedal seemed only to make the car go faster. Thinking that the brakes had failed, the teacher pressed harder still, and this time the pedal went all the way to the floor. The car sailed across the parking lot, wildly out of control, with the driver in a complete panic state, before crashing into a parked vehicle on the other side of the street. The air bags engaged, and fortunately nobody was seriously hurt. It was only then, as the motor continued to race with the wheels still squealing, that the woman realized her mistake—she had pressed the accelerator instead of the brake.

This story illustrates a number of important issues about motor control that we will return to later in the book: how we guide movements in the absence of visual feedback; how movement selection errors can occur without our detection; how and when we make error corrections; and lastly, and most important for our present discussion, the fact that normal modes of information processing can cease to operate when we are in a heightened state of panic, sometimes called **hypervigilance**.

As you reflect on this story, there are a number of easy solutions to the situation that come to mind. Turning off the ignition, moving the transmission into Neutral, and removing the foot from the pedal would have all solved the problem. But in these cases of **unintended acceleration**, a phenomenon that occurs far too commonly, none of these corrective actions are typically made (Schmidt, 1989). Instead, it is usually some external agent, such as a tree, wall, or another vehicle, that brings the car to a halt.

Hypervigilance occurs at the very highest levels of arousal. In cases of unintended acceleration, the driver seems to "freeze" at the wheel, in terms of both normal movement control and information-processing activities. In a hypervigilant state, decision making is severely limited, resulting in an inability to produce "creative" actions (e.g., switching off the ignition key) and an ineffective performance generally. Fortunately, hypervigilant states are relatively rare. But when they do occur, the fate of the individual is almost completely turned over to the "fight-or-flight" functioning of a panicked information-processing system.

---

example, consider how vision changes for the novice in the relatively stressful sport of deep sea diving. Weltman and Egstrom (1966), for example, presented reaction stimuli in various peripheral locations to diving students who had been asked to perform a simple motor task. On land, where the diver can operate under a low level of arousal, the range of possible stimulus sources to which the subject can respond is relatively wide, representing most of the visual field. However, at the bottom of a swimming pool, and especially on the ocean floor, where arousal would be thought to increase, the visual field becomes more narrowly and intensely focused; systematically fewer peripheral stimuli are detected, with increased focus on the expected or important aspects of the task and increased focus on those sources of information most pertinent to or expected in the task (located in central vision). This is an important mechanism because it allows the person to devote more attention to those stimulus-sources that are immediately most likely and relevant. Perceptual narrowing is not limited to vision but apparently occurs with each of the senses in an analogous way.

Easterbrook's (1959) cue-utilization hypothesis also helps to explain the inverted-U principle. When the arousal level is low and the perceptual field is relatively wide, the performer has access to, and uses, a wide range of cues, only a few of which are relevant to effective performance, so performance is suboptimal. As the arousal level rises and the attentional focus narrows onto the most relevant cues, more and more of the irrelevant cues are excluded, so proficiency increases because the performer is responding to mostly relevant cues. When further arousal increases, though, the increased perceptual narrowing means missing even some of the relevant cues, so performance begins to suffer, particularly where the cues are not highly expected. The optimal level of arousal is presumably one in which the narrowed attentional focus excludes many irrelevant cues yet allows most of the relevant cues to be detected.

Choking Under Pressure

One of the most dramatic occasions in high-profile sporting events occurs when an individual or team, seemingly on the way to certain victory, does the unimagined thing, plays sloppily, and loses. Relatively recent examples of team collapses include the 2011 Boston Red Sox and Atlanta Braves baseball teams, both of which blew large leads in September and failed to make the playoffs. Rory McIlroy provided an individual example in the 2011 Masters golf tournament when he shot 7 over par on the back nine in a Sunday collapse. Everyone can probably recall events like this, and there is no shortage of examples in every sport, it seems.

What defines a "choke"? And, more importantly, why does it occur and how can it be avoided? By most accounts, *choking under pressure* is more than simply a failed performance in an important situation. Not even the very best basketball players would be expected to make every foul shot or every jump shot at the final buzzer, with the game on the line. Instead, the term "choking under pressure" is reserved for situations in which performers change their normal routine or fail to adapt to a changing situation, resulting in the failed performance. The reasons for a choke have as much to do with information-processing errors as they do with errors in motor performance.

Attentional control theory (Eysenck et al., 2007) suggests that increased levels of anxiety tend to reduce "controlled" selective attention activities of the performer and increase the attention to certain potentially lifesaving cues. This shift in attentional control results in an increased competition for resources, which has a devastating effect on processing efficiency and ultimately leads to degraded performance and the choke.

In contrast, researchers such as Beilock (2010) suggest that choking under pressure occurs when there is a change in one's *attentional focus*. As the pressure builds to perform well in a critical situation, athletes who choke often shift from performing in an overlearned, automatic type of attentional (external) focus to a more conscious, controlled (internal) focus of attention. This shift in attention is tantamount to moving to a type of control typical of skills in the very early stages of practice.

Summary

A good way to think about attention is to imagine a "pool" of resources such that, if the information-processing activities from a given task exceed the resources available, performance of this task and perhaps a second task attempted at that the same time will suffer. Under a limited set of circumstances, processing can be done "in parallel"; that is, performance on two tasks can be done together, without interference. As in common cocktail-party circumstances in which we can ignore the conversations around us, focusing on a conversation with a given person can occur until, for example, your name is spoken in a nearby conversation. Other findings tend to agree; information about the ink color of a word and the meaning of the word appear to be processed in parallel; but there is considerable interference involving selection of the action (the Stroop test). People can become "blind" to certain stimuli if attention is directed strongly elsewhere, for example failing to perceive the "gorilla" in plain sight when subjects' attention was directed strongly to another target. This appears to be related to a class of motor vehicle crashes in which one driver *looked but failed to see* (that is, to perceive) an oncoming vehicle. On the other hand, many highly practiced tasks tend to be performed without any attention; this is difficult to achieve without extensive practice under the proper conditions. While we might appear to be able to drive a car without any attention, studies of drivers attempting to drive and converse on a cell phone at the same time shows that this is a dangerous combination. The biggest attentional limitation of all appears to be in the movement programming stage. The so-called psychological refractory period (PRP) provides the evidence. The overall viewpoint appears to be that, while we may be able under certain circumstances to respond without attention in the stimulus identification and response selection stages, only one action can be programmed at a time during the movement programming stage.

WEB STUDY GUIDE ACTIVITIES

The student web study guide, available at www.HumanKinetics.com/MotorLearningandPerformance, offers these activities to help you build and apply your knowledge of the concepts in this chapter.

Interactive Learning

Activity 3.1: Review the concepts associated with limitations in attention by matching related terms to their definitions.

Activity 3.2: Indicate whether each in a list of descriptions applies to controlled processing or automatic processing.

Activity 3.3: Using a figure from the text, explore how the inverted-U relationship between arousal and performance varies by situation and person.

Situation-Based Exercise

Activity 3.4: The situation-based exercise for this chapter prompts you to choose an activity and analyze the attentional demands of three performance situations within that activity. You will also examine how stress might affect decision making during this activity.

Check Your Understanding

1. Both parallel and serial processing can occur during the stimulus identification stage of information processing. Provide examples of the types of information that might be processed in parallel and in serial as a rock climber decides which move to make next.
2. Explain how a fake in wheelchair basketball illustrates a strong interference between activities in the movement programming stage of information processing.
3. Regarding attention, explain why a lifeguard at a crowded pool may find it more difficult to perform his job as he nears the end of his shift. What factors influence his ability to sustain attention? Suggest two policies that a pool could put in place to make sustained attention easier for lifeguards.

Apply Your Knowledge

1. The way information is processed during the response selection stage of information processing can be very different between a novice and an expert performing the same task. Describe the differing types of processing, highlighting the key features of each. How is task interference related to each type of processing? How might a person performing a waltz perform differently as a novice and as an expert?
2. When mountain biking, some cyclists who have no trouble riding along a straight trail have difficulty performing the identical task (riding in a straight line) on a bridge that is the same width (or wider) than the trail, resulting in a less smooth performance or even a fall. What role might focus of attention play in this phenomenon? How could the inverted-U principle be used to help explain why a bridge over a ravine may make the task of riding in a straight line more difficult?

Suggestions for Further Reading

Many books and review articles about attention and human performance have been written. The works by Wickens and McCarley (2008), Chun, Golomb, and Turk-Browne (2011), and Kahneman (2011) are excellent recent resources. Wulf's (2007) book on attentional focus is of special relevance to motor performance and learning. The Chabris and Simons (2010) book discusses **inattention blindness** and other fascinating attention-related issues. Davies and Parasuraman (1982) discuss sustained attention in much detail. Weinberg and Gould (2011) discuss arousal, stress, and other topics of particular importance in sport and exercise psychology. Beilock's (2010) book on choking is also a fascinating read. See the reference list for these additional resources.

Draft. Not for Distribution.

4

Sensory Contributions to Skilled Performance

Feedback Processing in Motor Control

KEY TERMS

blindsight
closed-loop control system
comparator
cutaneous receptor
dorsal stream
exteroception
feedforward
Golgi tendon organs
joint receptors
M1
M2
M3
muscle spindle
optical array
optical flow
proprioception
quiet-eye effect
tau
ventral stream
vestibular apparatus

CHAPTER OUTLINE

Sources of Sensory Information
Processing Sensory Information
Principles of Visual Control
Audition and Motor Control
Summary

CHAPTER OBJECTIVES

Chapter 4 describes the roles of sensory feedback in human motor control. This chapter will help you to understand

- the types of sensory information available for motor control,
- motor control as a closed-loop processing system,
- how feedback and feedforward information work in the conceptual model, and
- the roles of vision in motor control.

Success in skilled performance often depends on how effectively the performer detects, perceives, and uses relevant sensory information. Frequently, the winner of a contest is the one who has detected a pattern of action in an opponent most quickly, as in many sports and games. Success can also be measured by the correct detection of errors in one's own body movements and positions, which provides a basis for subsequent movement (or positional) modifications, as in dance or gymnastics. A surgeon requires skilled touch (haptic) perception to detect an abnormal growth during a physical exam of a patient. Consequently, considerable emphasis is directed toward improving the skill with which performers detect and process *sensory information* because these improvements can lead to large gains in performance.

Sources of Sensory Information

Information for skilled performance arises from a number of sources, and can be categorized into two major types. One type comes from the environment and is termed *exteroceptive* (the prefix "extero-" means that the information is provided from outside the body). The other type of sensory information is termed *proprioceptive* (the prefix "proprio-" means that the information arises from within the body). **Exteroception** provides information to the processing system about the state of the environment in which one's body exists, and **proprioception** provides information about the state of the body itself. These sources of information are types of *inherent (or intrinsic) feedback*. The term "feedback" is used for situations in which, during a movement, sensations arise *because* the body is moving, which produces information that is "fed back" to the performer. For example, when we move from one place to another, information is available from the contracting muscles, and there are changes in what we see while moving. Proprioceptive feedback is sometimes also referred to as "movement-produced feedback."

For feedback to be "inherent" means that the information is directly available to the performer and is available "naturally" through the senses. A major distinction is made later in the book when we discuss the provision of *augmented* feedback—information about which the performer is not "normally" aware; this is "extra" information provided by an external source. An example is a video that shows a person performing a skill.

Exteroception

The most prominent of the exteroceptive information sources, of course, is *vision.* Seeing serves the important function of defining the physical structure of the environment, such as the edge of a stairway or the presence of an object blocking one's path, thus providing a basis for anticipating upcoming events. Vision also provides information about the movement of objects in the environment in relation to your own movements—such as the flight path of a ball while you are running to catch it—which can be used to make certain predictive judgments about the movement direction to take. Another function of vision is to detect your own movement within the (stable) environment, such as your path toward an external object and how much time will elapse before you arrive.

The second major kind of exteroceptive information comes from hearing, or *audition.* Although audition is not as obviously involved in motor skills as vision, there are many activities that depend heavily on well-developed auditory skills; one obvious example is the sounds of a musical instrument you are playing. However, audition is important for many other skills too, such as using the sounds of the sailboat's hull moving through the water as cues to boat speed, the sound of a power tool as a skilled carpenter cuts through different materials, or the sounds of an engine as an auto mechanic adjusts a carburetor.

Proprioception

The second major type of information is from the body's movement, usually termed proprioception. This term refers to the sense of movements of joints, tensions in muscles, and so on, giving information about the state of the body parts in relation to each other and relative to the environment. Several important receptors provide this information.

The **vestibular apparatus** in the inner ear provides signals related to movements, one's orientation (e.g., upside down), or both, in one's environment. These structures are sensitive to acceleration of the head and are positioned to detect the head's orientation with respect to gravity. It is not surprising that these structures are strongly implicated in posture and balance.

Several other structures provide information about what the limbs are doing. Receptors in the capsule surrounding each of the joints, called the **joint receptors**, give information about extreme positions of the joints. Embedded within the belly of the skeletal muscle are **muscle spindles**, oriented in parallel with the muscle fibers. Because muscles change lengths when the joints they span are moved, the muscle spindle lengths are changed as well; this is thought to provide indirect information about joint position and other aspects of the movement. Near the junction between the skeletal muscle and its tendon lie the **Golgi tendon organs**, which are very sensitive to the level of force in the various parts of the muscle to which they are attached. Finally, in most skin areas are **cutaneous receptors**, including several kinds of specialized detectors of pressure, temperature, touch, and so on. The cutaneous receptors are critical for the haptic sense, the sense of touch.

None of these receptors respond to just one physical characteristic, however. The signal from a particular source, for example the muscle spindles, provides ambiguous information about joint position because the receptor can be affected by several other physical stimuli (movement velocity, muscle tension, and the orientation with respect to gravity) at the same time. For this reason, the central nervous system is thought to use a complex combination of the inputs from these various receptors as a basis for body awareness.

Because of the multiple, complex receptors involved, perception of a movement's trajectory can be affected by how the movement is produced. There may be a difference depending on whether the movement was a normal, active action or a passive, guided action, as when an instructor or therapist moves a patient through a movement. The perception of the proper trajectory of an arm movement, for example, can be quite different if the movement is guided by a therapist, compared to being actively generated by the patient. Also, many guidance techniques, such as artificially manipulating the learner's movements during an action (creating the arm stroke in swimming, spotting in gymnastics), can affect the proprioceptive sensations generated markedly. These techniques can be useful at the beginning stages of learning, but because they distort the proprioceptive sensations (and for other reasons that we will discuss later), they could easily be overused in instructional or therapeutic situations. We will return to the concept of guidance later on, when we discuss learning.

However, such alterations in proprioception can be used in a positive way too, as when they are exploited by human factors engineers in the design of equipment. Adding spring resistance to a car's steering system adds "feel," which can make the car easier to control and more pleasant to drive. Perhaps for a similar reason, experienced typists prefer keyboards that provide some haptic feedback (Asundi & Odell, 2011), which provides the satisfying auditory "click," indicating to the operator that the key has been pressed successfully. Supplying aircraft instrument knobs of different shapes and locations for different functions makes confusion among them less likely by associating distinct proprioceptive sensations with each knob.

There are many different sources of sensory information for motor control, varying not only in terms of where the information is detected but also in terms of how it is processed and used. Even so, the next sections

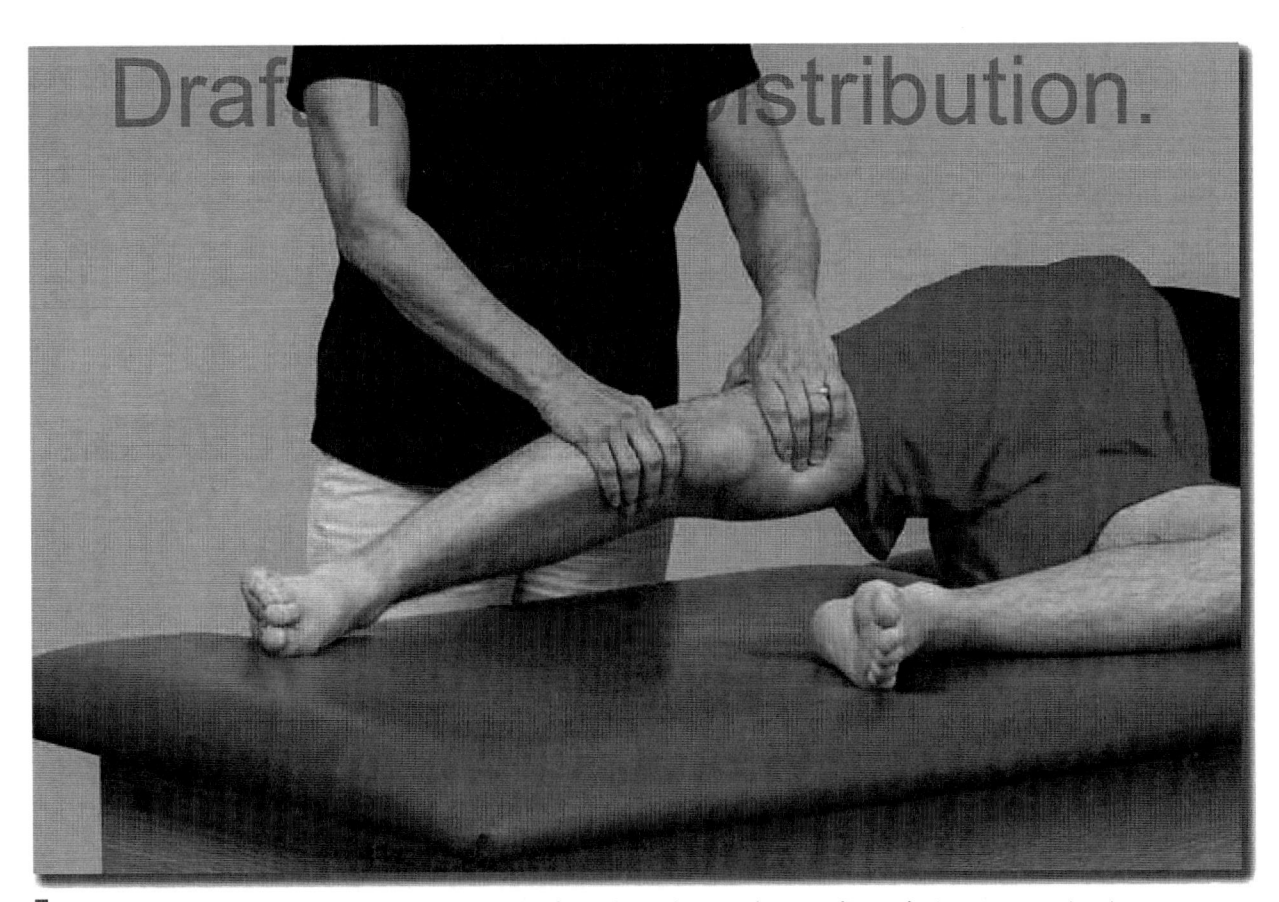

A physician or therapist relies on the sense of touch to detect abnormalities during an examination.

consider this variety of sensations as a single group, focusing on the common ways the central nervous system processes this information for skilled performance.

Processing Sensory Information

One important way to think about how sensory information is processed during movement is by analogy to closed-loop control systems, a class of mechanisms used in many applications in everyday life. Figure 4.1 provides an example of a simple closed-loop system.

Closed-Loop Control Systems

The simple **closed-loop control system** illustrated in figure 4.1 can be started in a number of ways; but one common way occurs when you input a desired state or system goal, such as the desired temperature in your house in the winter. Sensory information about the system's output (the room's actual temperature) is measured by a thermometer and is compared to the expected temperature. Any difference between the expected and actual temperature represents an *error* (e.g., the temperature is too low); this error information is transmitted to an executive to decide what action to take to eliminate or reduce the error. The executive sends a command to an effector, in this case turning on the furnace, which carries out the action. This action raises the room temperature until the actual state equals the expected state (where the error in temperature is now zero); this information is sent to the executive, and the executive sends a new instruction to switch off the heat production. This process continues indefinitely, maintaining the temperature near the desired value throughout the day. This kind of system is termed "closed loop" because the loop from the executive to the effector and back to the executive again is completely "closed" by sensory information, or feedback, forming a "loop" that supports the mechanism in regulating the system to achieve a particular goal.

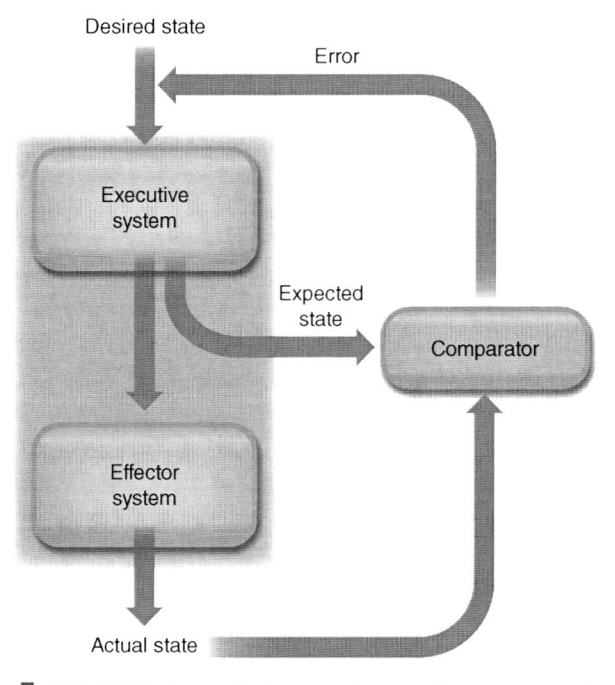

The same general processes operate in human performance, as in reaching to pick up a cup. Visual information about the hand's position relative to the cup represents the feedback. Differences between the hand's distance and the desired distance are sensed as errors. An executive determines a correction, modifying the effector system to bring the hand into the proper location. Of course, in more complicated skills, feedback consists of a collection of different kinds of sensory information arising from a variety of receptors both within and outside the body. Each kind of information is compared to a corresponding reference level, and the errors are then processed by the executive level in the system.

All closed-loop control systems have four distinct parts:

1. An executive for decision making about errors
2. An effector system for carrying out the decisions

FIGURE 4.1 A basic closed-loop control system.

3. A reference of correctness against which the feedback is compared to define an error
4. An error signal, which is the information acted on by the executive

Closed-Loop Control in the Conceptual Model

These closed-loop processes fit within the expanded conceptual model for movement control as shown in figure 4.2. This is simply an expansion of the conceptual model of human performance presented in chapter 2, which introduces the stages of information processing (see figure 2.2). However, now are added the notions of closed-loop control seen in figure 4.1 to achieve a more complete system that complements our discussion of human motor performance.

This conceptual model is useful for understanding the processes involved not only in relatively slow movements (e.g., slow positioning of a limb in physical therapy) where compensations can be made during the action, but also in relatively fast movements (e.g., swinging an ax) where the correction of the error must wait until the movements have been completed.

The executive system consists of the decision-making processes discussed in chapter 2—the stimulus identification, response selection, and movement programming stages. The executive then sends commands to an effector system consisting of several parts. One is the motor program, which produces commands for lower centers in the spinal cord, which finally result in the contraction of muscles and the movement of joints. At the same time, information is specified to define the sensory qualities of the correct movement, such as the "feel" of an effective ax swing. This information represents the performer's *anticipated sensory feedback,* that is, the sensations that should be generated if the movement is performed correctly. An example is the state of the thermostat when it is set to, say, 70°; incoming feedback from the room's air temperature (the *actual* feedback) is then compared to the *anticipated* feedback (70°, indicated by the thermostat's state) and an error is computed, which is then delivered to the executive. As such, the information that specifies that the thermostat should be anticipating a temperature of 70° is often termed *feedforward* information. The term **feedforward** is used to distinguish it from feed*back,* or the sensory qualities of the action itself. Feedforward information represents *anticipated* sensory consequences of the movement that *should* be received if the movement is correct, so that the error would now be zero.

The output (the movement) results in proprioceptive and exteroceptive feedback information, collectively termed movement-produced feedback. When muscles contract, the system receives feedback about forces as well as about the pressures exerted on objects in contact with the skin. Contracting muscles cause movement, and, as a result, feedback from moving joints and the changes in body position with respect to gravity. Finally, movements usually produce alterations in the environment, which are sensed by the receptors for vision and audition, generating yet more feedback. These movement-produced stimuli, whose nature is critically dependent on the production of a particular action by the performer, are compared against their anticipated states in the **comparator**. The computed difference represents error, which is returned to the executive. This process refines and maintains the performer's behavior, holding errors at acceptably low levels.

Notice that the stages of processing are critically important in the closed-loop model in figure 4.2. Every time an action's feedback goes to the executive for correction, it must go through the stages of processing. The various stages of processing are all subject to the mechanisms of attention, as discussed in chapter 3. However, this is not the only way in which feedback can be used, and we discuss various lower-level, reflex-like loops later in the chapter.

The closed-loop model in figure 4.2 is useful for understanding the maintenance of a particular state, as is necessary to perform many long-duration activities. For example,

Sensory Contributions to Skilled Performance

simply maintaining posture, where the goal is a natural, upright position, requires feedback. Various learned postures might be controlled in the same way, such as positioning the body in a handstand on the still rings in gymnastics. Also, most movement skills involving the various limbs require an accurate, stable posture as a "platform." Without this stable

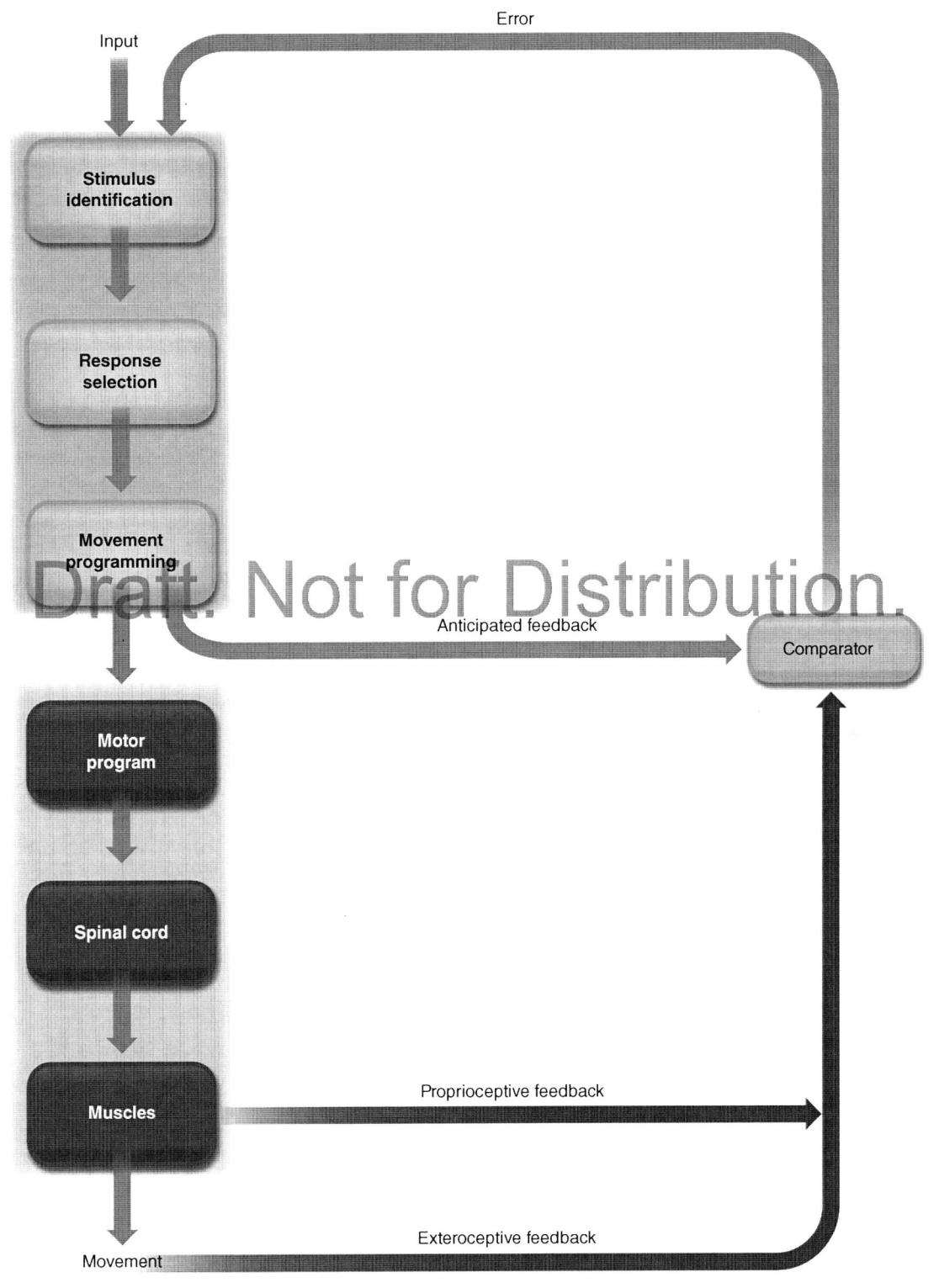

FIGURE 4.2 Expanded conceptual model with the addition of closed-loop components.

base, the movement, such as throwing darts or shooting a pistol, would be inconsistent. The comparator is thought to define and maintain the desired relative positions of the various limbs as well as the general orientation in space.

Other tasks are far more dynamic. For instance, in a continuous *tracking* skill, a performer must follow some constantly varying track by moving a control. Steering a car is a classic example, where movements of the steering wheel result from visually detected errors in the car's position on the road. There are countless other examples, as this class of activity is one of the most frequently represented in real-world functioning.

Without a doubt, closed-loop control models such as that shown in figure 4.2 are the most effective for understanding these kinds of behavior. Thus, understanding how such a model operates provides considerable insight into human performance and allows many important applications. Understanding the model's limitations for movement control is also important, as discussed next.

Limitations of Closed-Loop Control

The inclusion of the stages of information processing in the system, as depicted in figure 4.2, illustrates the flexibility in move-

---

Focus on
APPLICATION 4.1

Error Correction in Batting

In swinging the bat at a pitched baseball, the performer first evaluates the environmental situation and then selects a movement to meet the perceived demands. The stages of processing select a program and ready it for initiation. Once the movement is started, the response execution processes carry out that movement more or less as planned. Provided that the environment remains in the same state as it was when the movement was organized, the movement should be effective in meeting the environmental demand, so the bat should hit the ball.

But what if something in the environment suddenly changes? For example, if the ball curves unexpectedly, now the batter wants to swing at a different location or perhaps stop the swing altogether. The conceptual model enables an estimate of how much time would be required for this kind of information to influence an ongoing movement. Such information must pass through the stages of processing, therefore requiring several hundred milliseconds before the first modification in the movement can occur.

While these modification processes are occurring, the movement is still being carried out as originally planned. Therefore, the initial parts of the first movement occur before the batter can initiate the correction to stop or change the action. One of two common occurrences in baseball is observed if the batter detects the curving ball too late: (a) The original movement is carried out almost completely, resulting in a hopeless miss, or (b) the batter tries to stop ("check") the swing, but is too late to stop its momentum from carrying the bat across the plate. However, one of two other common occurrences in baseball is observed if the batter is successful in modifying the original plan: The batter either adjusts the swing and makes contact with the ball or stops the swing before the bat crosses the plate.

ment control, allowing various strategies and options and altering the nature of the movement produced, depending on the particular circumstances. However, these stages of processing represent a big disadvantage at the same speed—they are slow, especially when there is high demand for processing time, resources, or both, as in many complex actions (discussed in chapter 3). The following sections describe cases in which the closed-loop model is less effective for guiding movement.

Tracking Tasks

One important generalization arising from chapters 2 and 3 was that the stages of information processing require considerable time. Hence the closed-loop system with these processes embedded in it should be slow as well. The stages of processing are critical components in reaction-time (RT) situations, where presenting a stimulus requires various processes leading to a movement. The closed-loop model can be regarded in the same way, but the stimulus in this instance is the error that drives the executive, and the movement is the correction selected by the executive. Numerous studies of tracking suggest that the system can produce separate responses (that is, corrections) at a maximum rate of about three per second. This is about the rate that would be expected if the system were using RT processes as a critical component, reacting to errors by making corrections.

In the conceptual model presented in figure 4.2, each correction is based on a collection of information about the errors that have occurred over the past few hundred milliseconds. This error is processed in the stimulus identification stage; a movement correction is chosen in the response selection stage; and the correction is organized and initiated in the movement programming stage. Therefore, tracking tasks that involve more than three changes in direction per second are typically performed very poorly. What makes a fumbled football difficult to retrieve is the frequently unpredictable nature of the bounces it takes. For this reason, closed-loop control processes are most relevant to tasks that are relatively slow or have a long duration in time.

Rapid, Discrete Tasks

A feedback-based view of movement control fails to account adequately for movement production in skills that are very quick, such as the ballistic actions in sport skills (e.g., throwing and kicking) and pressing a key during texting. As a general rule with the most rapid human actions, the performer initiates a fully planned movement to achieve the goal. If later sensory information indicates that this movement will be incorrect and thus should be stopped or radically altered, this information is processed relatively slowly and sluggishly, so the first few hundred milliseconds of the original movement occur more or less without modification. As you will see later in this chapter, though, sensory information plays an increasingly important and effective role as the movement is made more slowly.

This sluggishness of feedback processing has implications for controlling the moment-to-moment adjustments in very rapid movements (say, movements less than 300 ms or so), such as typing a text message or plucking the strings of a banjo in a bluegrass song. According to the conceptual model, feedback arising from the rapid movement would not have enough time to be processed before the movement was completed. The feedback thus would not influence the fine, moment-to-moment control. More than any other observation, this sluggishness of feedback control has led scientists to believe that most rapid movements must be organized (or, as is usually said, programmed) in advance. In this view, the moment-to-moment control is included as part of the preorganized program and is not dependent on the relatively slow processes associated with feedback (this idea is discussed more fully in chapter 5). Feedback can also act reflexively to modify movements far more quickly than indicated by the basic closed-loop model presented in Figure 4.2. This aspect of feedback control is discussed next.

Proprioceptive Closed-Loop Control

To this point, only one kind of closed-loop processes has been considered: conscious, voluntary control of actions by sensory information. But there are other ways in which sensory information is involved in movement control, especially considering the many kinds of corrections, modifications, and subtle changes in skills that occur automatically (without conscious awareness).

There are a number of reflexive mechanisms that operate below our level of consciousness. One of the most well known of these is the so-called knee-jerk reflex. If one sits on a table with knee bent and lower leg freely hanging and then a small tap is applied to the patellar tendon (usually with a small rubber hammer, as done by a neurologist), the response to the tap is a brief contraction of the quadriceps muscle (on the thigh) and a small extension (straightening) of the knee. The time from the tap until the quadriceps is activated is only 30 to 50 ms. This reflexive response occurs without any active, voluntary control and occurs far too quickly to have come via the stages of information processing.

Here is what happens. In this seated position, a tap to the patellar tendon, which attaches the kneecap (patella) to the tibia of the lower leg, applies a brief downward movement of the kneecap. Then, because the kneecap is attached to the quadriceps muscle, which (together with the muscle spindles in the quadriceps) is stretched a small amount, too, the muscle spindles respond by sending a signal to the spinal cord via afferent (sensory) neurons. These neurons synapse (connect) with efferent (motor) neurons that lead back to the same muscle that was stretched (here, the quadriceps), causing a brief contraction. This occurs very quickly, and involuntarily, in part because the afferent and efferent neurons travel a relatively short distance and are connected by a single synapse. Hence, this reflex has been termed the *monosynaptic stretch reflex*. Nearly every skeletal muscle in the body can display this reflex, operating in the same general way.

Take a look at figure 4.3, which is another expansion of our conceptual model. Within the "effector" box (motor program–spinal cord–muscles), we have added a feedback loop (the so-called M1 loop) from the muscle to the spinal cord and back to the same muscle. This loop is an important component of the monosynaptic stretch reflex. This feedback loop is at a relatively low level in the spinal cord, so the responses do not involve conscious, voluntary control and reflect stereotyped, involuntary, usually very rapid responses to stimuli.

Now suppose that you are a subject in a simple experiment. You are standing, and your task is to hold one of your elbows at a right angle to support a moderate load on your hand, such as a book. You have a dial in front of you to indicate the height of the book, and you are instructed to hold the book at some target position. Suddenly, without your being able to anticipate it, the experimenter adds another book to the load. Your hand begins to drop, but after a delay you compensate for the added load and bring your hand up to the target position again. In all likelihood, your response was nearly immediate and involuntary, but this time more than one reflex was involved. The monosynaptic reflex just described was responsible for an initial, very brief, response to the added load. However, bringing the hand back to the target position likely involved one or more additional reflexes.

The slightly slower (50-80 ms latency) response occurrs because the stretched biceps muscle delivered a signal (via afferent neurons from the muscle spindles) to the spinal cord. Here, though, this signal is also sent up the spinal cord, and these neurons synapse with several higher-level neurons. Then, the signal is sent back down the pathway in the spinal cord where it synapses with the motor neurons leading to the biceps muscle, causing a second burst of biceps activity. This second burst of activity (labeled M2 in figure 4.3) is stronger and more sustained than the first one (the monosynaptic, M1, response), but it arrives with a slightly greater delay (50-80 ms) because the signal had to travel farther and because several synapses were involved. The

Sensory Contributions to Skilled Performance

M2 loop in figure 4.3 goes from the muscle to higher levels in the CNS. Together, these monosynaptic (M1) and multisynaptic (**M2**) reflexes are just two of the many types of reflexive mechanisms by which actions can be modified quickly (and automatically), leading toward goal achievement in a closed-loop manner.

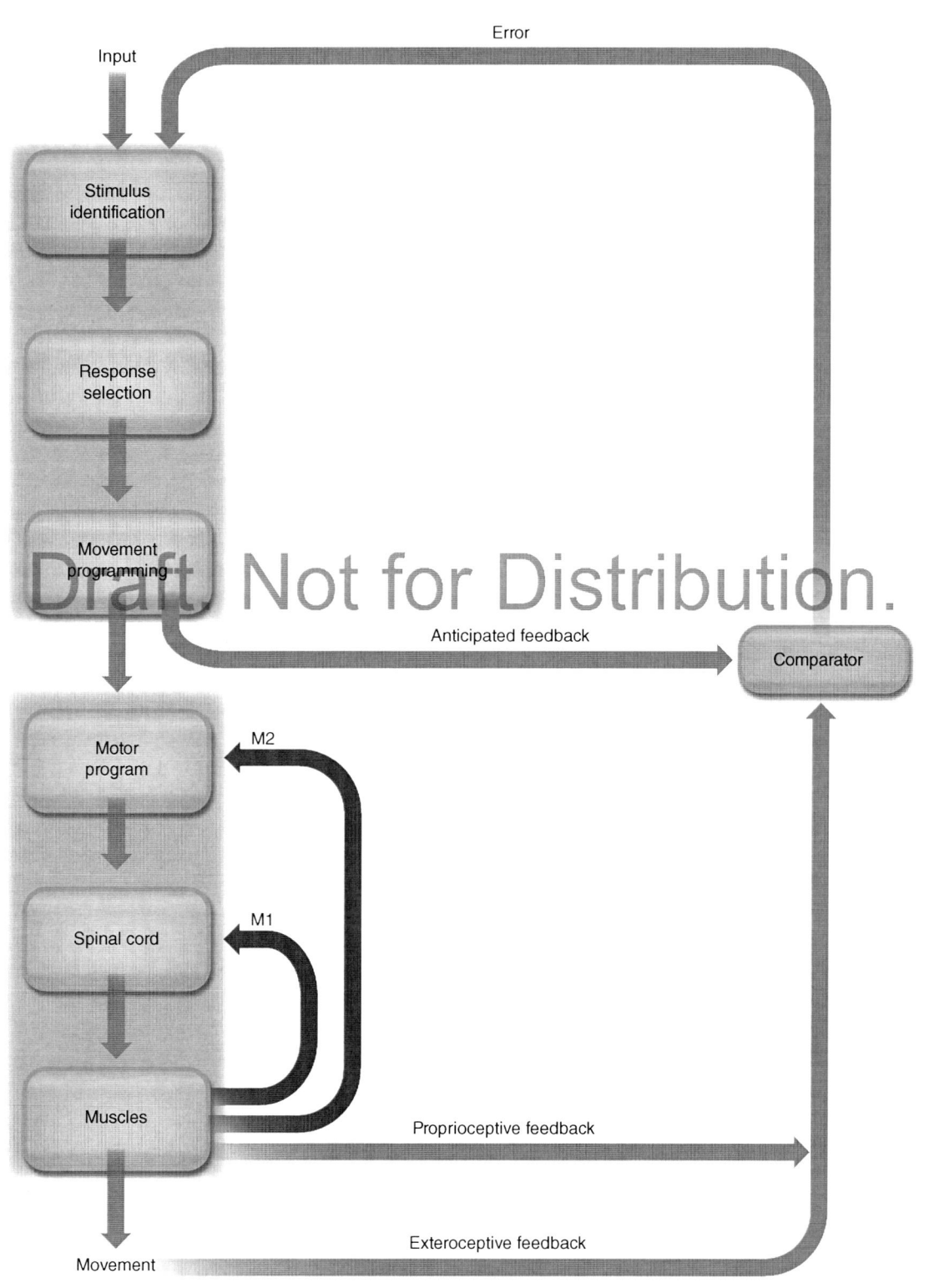

FIGURE 4.3 Conceptual model with the addition of M1 and M2 loops.

Principles of Visual Control

Vision seems to operate somewhat differently than the proprioceptive reflexes we have just seen. Vision, of course, has a very important role in everyday activities, and people deprived of vision have a relatively difficult time functioning in our visually dominated world. But vision also appears to operate somewhat differently from the other senses in the support of skills. For these reasons, vision deserves a place of its own in this chapter.

Two Visual Systems

Over the past 40 years or so, it has become increasingly clear that two essentially separate visual systems underlie human functioning, rather than just one. Visual information is delivered from the retina of the eye along two separate processing streams to different places in the brain, and there is good evidence that these two different pathways of information are used differently in the control of behavior.

These two systems, illustrated in figure 4.4, are called the **dorsal stream** and the **ventral stream** because of their anatomical distinctions (Ungerleider & Mishkin, 1982; note that they have also been referred to as the ambient and focal systems, respectively). Visual information in both streams travels first from the retina of the eye to the primary visual cortex. However, at that point it is thought that visual information processing becomes specialized. Information useful for the identification of an object is sent to the inferotemporal cortex via the ventral stream. Information that is used specifically for the control of movement within the visual environment is sent to the posterior parietal cortex via the dorsal stream.

The ventral stream is specialized for conscious identification of objects that lie primarily in the center of the visual field. Its major function seems to be providing answers to the general question "What is it?" Hence we use this system to look at and identify something, such as the words on this page you are reading now. This system contributes to conscious perception of objects and is severely degraded by dim lighting conditions, as you know from your attempts to read or do fine handwork without adequate light. The dorsal stream is believed to be specialized for movement control. Distinct from the ventral stream, which is sensitive only to events in central vision, dorsal vision involves the entire visual field, central and peripheral. Dorsal vision operates nonconsciously, contributing to the fine control of movements without our awareness (see

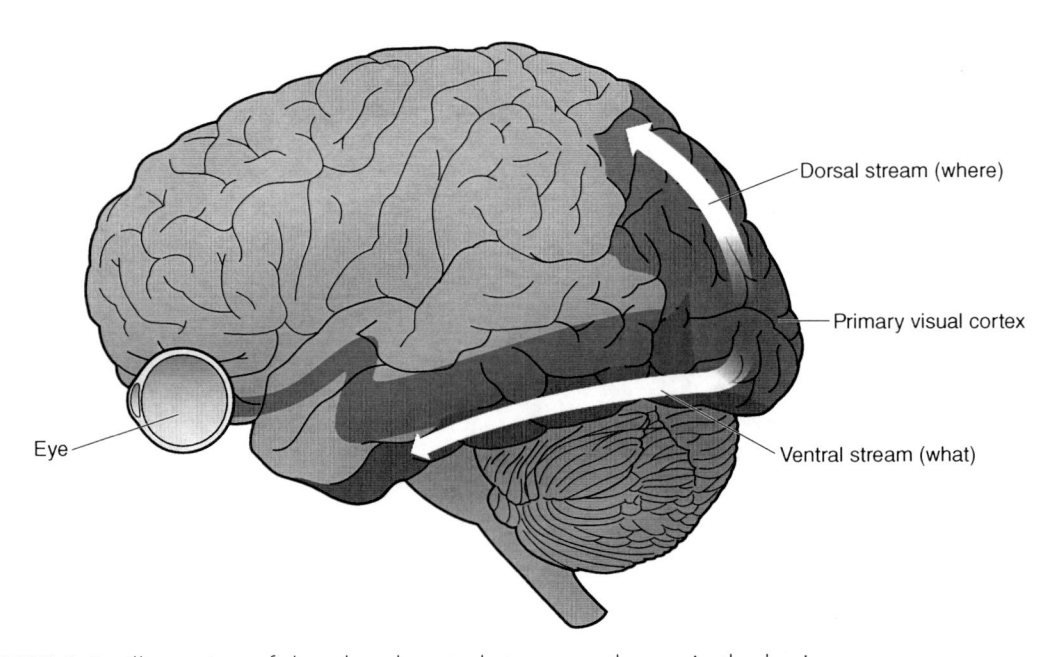

FIGURE 4.4 Illustration of dorsal and ventral stream pathways in the brain.

Focus on
RESEARCH 4.1

"Blindsight" Reveals Dorsal and Ventral Stream Processing

The term "blindsight" might at first sound self-contradictory, but this curious phenomenon led many to the discovery of the dorsal (ambient) visual system. Blindsight is usually defined a medical condition in which the person can respond to visual stimuli without consciously perceiving them. According to Weiskrantz (2007), the idea originally stemmed from work on the visual cortex of monkeys, where it was demonstrated that the animal, although technically "blind," could still respond to various kinds of visual stimuli. Later studies demonstrated the phenomenon in humans as well (e.g., by Humphrey, 1974; Weiskrantz et al., 1974).

Perhaps the most startling, and most convincing, evidence came from the study of two human neurological patients, TN and DB (the patients' initials; de Gelder et al., 2008; Weiskrantz et al., 1974). TN had had two successive strokes, causing major neurological damage in his visual cortex, which rendered him "blind" in both eyes by all traditional measures of vision. After considerable study, researchers took TN to a hallway, asking him to walk down the hallway without his usual cane. Unbeknownst to TN, researchers had placed several objects in the hall around which he would have to negotiate. To the researchers' obvious amazement and delight, TN avoided them all, even pressing himself against the wall to avoid a trash can. Patient DB, whose occipital cortex had been removed surgically because of a tumor, was also "blind" according to traditional measures of vision. Researchers used forced-choice tests, in which DB was asked to guess where, between two locations in front of him, an object had been placed. His guesses were considerably more accurate than chance, even though he could not "see" the objects. He was also sensitive to long or short temporal object presentation intervals, to color, to contrast, to motion, and to the onset and offset of the target's presence. Very clearly, both of these subjects were "seeing" objects that they were not consciously aware of.

These findings eventually were interpreted to mean that we possess two visual systems: a ventral (also called "focal") system with access to consciousness (which DB and TN had lost completely) and a dorsal system that does not have access to consciousness (which was intact in TN and DB). (The anatomical pathways for these systems are illustrated in figure 4.4.) The blindsight phenomenon demonstrates clearly that we can respond to objects in our environment unconsciously, guided by visual information of which we are completely unaware.

Bridgeman and colleagues (1981) provided some of the strongest evidence for the role of a dorsal system for movement control. Subjects sat in a darkened room in front of a screen on which was projected a rectangle (like a picture frame) with a spot of light inside it. Without the subject's awareness, the frame was moved back and forth slightly a few degrees, with the dot remaining in a fixed position on the screen inside the moving frame. Under these conditions, the subject reliably experienced the illusion that the dot was moving back and forth within the frame, rather than the reverse, which was actually the case. In terms of the notion of two visual systems, the ventral system (the one with access to consciousness) has been "deceived," judging that the dot was moving when it was actually stationary.

Next, Bridgeman and collaborators attempted to manipulate the dorsal system. The subjects were instructed that if the frame and dot were suddenly turned off, leaving the room in total darkness, they were to point a lever to the last position of the dot

> *continued*

> *continued*

as quickly as possible. Of course, the subject's *conscious* perception was that the dot was moving back and forth. So, if the ventral system were being used in controlling the hand, the pointing movements should vary from right to left as well, in coordination with the (consciously) perceived "movements" of the dot. To the contrary, when the lights were turned off, the subjects pointed to where the dot actually was, not to where they perceived it to be. The interpretation was that the visual information for the localization of the dot was being used by the nonconscious dorsal system, and this system was not deceived by the movements of the frame. This evidence supports the existence of two separate visual systems: the ventral system for consciousness biased by the frame movements, and the dorsal system for movement control, which was not biased by the frame movements.

Exploring Further

1. Patients with *optic ataxia* and *visual agnosia* have been the focus of study by neurophysiologists. With what information have these patients provided to researchers regard to the distinction between ventral and dorsal visual streams?
2. What other types of visual illusions have been used in research to separate dorsal and ventral stream processing?

Focus on Research 4.1). Clearly, one reason it is difficult to recognize the existence of dorsal vision is that it is nonconscious. Its function is to provide answers to the questions "Where is it?" or perhaps "Where am I relative to it?"

Visual Control of Movement Skills

How is visual information used for movement control, and what factors determine its effectiveness? It is useful to divide this discussion into separate parts, particularly because it deals with the separate roles of the dorsal and ventral systems.

Despite the characterization of ventral vision as a system for object identification, it would be wrong to conclude that it has no role in movement control. Ventral vision has access to consciousness, so it is processed through the information-processing stages discussed in chapter 2, leading to action in much the same way as any other information source. In the conceptual model in figure 4.3, vision can be seen as just another source of information arising from action, so its only access to the loop would be through the stages of information processing. In one sense, this is obvious. You can look at and consciously identify an oncoming car, which would then lead to the decision to try to avoid it. Ventral vision is critically involved here, and failures to identify objects properly can lead to serious errors. This is particularly important in night driving, when the ventral system's accuracy (visual acuity) is degraded considerably.

Before realizing there could be a dorsal system for movement control, scientists believed that a conscious ventral system was the only way visual information could influence action. In this outdated view, a baseball batter watching a pitch come toward the plate relied only on the relatively slow processes in the information-processing stages to detect the ball's flight pattern and to initiate changes in movement control. This idea was supported by numerous experiments that seemed to show that visual control of action (ventral stream processing) was particularly slow and cumbersome. However, recent information about the dorsal visual system, together with the ideas about optical-flow processes in vision, has markedly changed our understanding of visual information processing for action.

Dorsal Stream Movement Control

James J. Gibson (e.g., Gibson, 1966) altered radically the way scientists theorized about the visual control of movement. A particularly important concept promoted by Gibson was that of optical-flow patterns, and how this information was used by the ambient visual system to control body movement (such as balance) and to provide information about the timing of events, such as the time to close a gap between the performer and an object.

For example, riding a bicycle along a busy path or street requires rapid processing of many sources of visual information. The cyclist needs be aware of traffic signs and signals, pedestrians crossing the street, cars turning away and into the oncoming path, and, of course, the dreaded opening of the driver's door of a parked car. As the cyclist looks into this textured environment, each visible feature reflects rays of light, which enter the eyes at specific angles; collectively, this is called the **optical array**. Because the cyclist is moving, each object in the environment shifts its position relative to the cyclist continuously, causing a change in the information provided by the optical array. This change in information is termed **optical flow** and can be thought of as a "flow of light" across the retina. The important point is that optical flow provides numerous important kinds of information about the cyclist's movement through the environment, such as

- time before a collision between the cyclist and an object,
- direction of movement relative to objects in the environment,
- movement of environmental objects relative to the cyclist,
- stability and balance of the cyclist, and
- velocity of movement through the environment.

Time-to-Contact Information Figure 4.5 presents an example of how the optical array picks up information about an object first seen in the distance (say 25 m [meters] away—object A), then at a closer distance (15 m away—object B), then at a very close distance (5 m—object C). The angle of light given from the edges of the object at distance A is very small (α_1); it increases slightly as it gets 10 m closer (α_2), and then it expands at a much more rapid rate over the next 10 m (α_3).

The pattern of optical flow from an oncoming object, such as parked car, indicates the time remaining until the object reaches the plane of the eye (Lee & Young, 1985). The retinal image of an approaching object expands as the object approaches, and it expands more quickly as the object approaches more quickly. These changes in optical flow are picked up by the dorsal system, providing information about object distance and time

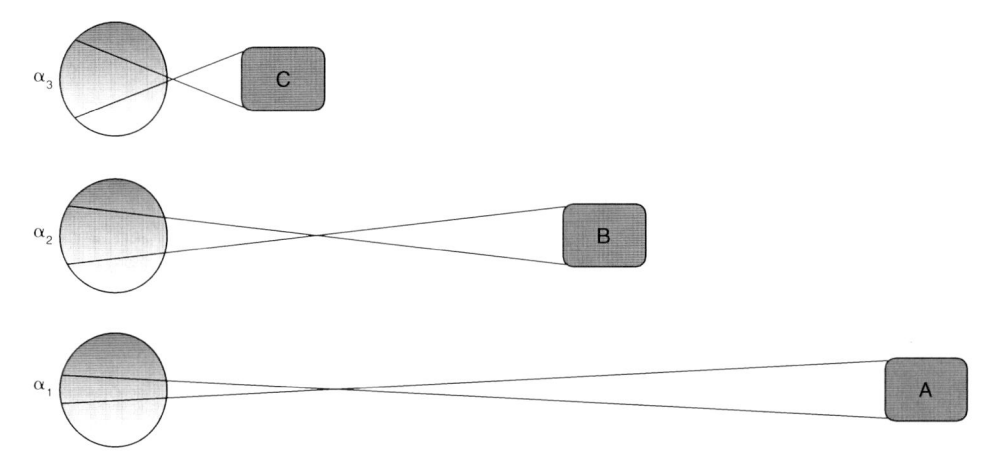

FIGURE 4.5 Objects A, B, and C are traveling at the same velocity in the right-to-left direction toward an eye (gray circles). The sizes of the object's optical image on the rear of the eye (the retina) at different distances are α_1, α_2, and α_3. Notice that when the object travels from A to B, the size of the retinal image changes at a slower rate than it does for the same distance covered from B to C. These changes in optical flow are picked up by the dorsal system, providing information about object distance and time until the object will contact the plane of the eye.

until the object will contact the plane of the eye. This time-to-contact is abbreviated with the Greek letter tau (τ). The optical variable **tau (τ)**, which is defined as the retinal image size divided by the image's rate of change in size, turns out to be proportional to the time remaining until contact. Thus, τ is derived from optical-flow information and used by the dorsal stream to specify time-to-contact with the object. This timing information is critical in interceptive actions involving coincident timing, such as striking or catching a ball, driving, or preparing the body for entry into the water during a dive.

Direction of Movement of Objects One can run through a forest, avoiding trees successfully, by using optical-flow information about the relative rates of change in the visual angles of the trees. Assume that the objects shown in figure 4.6 are trees. For tree A, the angles of light from the left and right edges expand at the same rate from both sides, indicating that the eye is traveling directly toward tree A and will collide with it. For tree B, on the other hand, the angles of light from the right side are expanding systematically more slowly than those from the left side. This indicates that the eye will pass to the right of the tree.

Balance Maintaining balance has traditionally been the domain of proprioceptive information in detecting sway and loss of stability. For example, when the body sways forward, the ankle joint is moved and the associated musculature is stretched, producing movement signals from the muscle spindles and other proprioceptors. Also, receptors in the inner ear are sensitive to movements of the head, providing information about body sway and balance.

However, vision also plays a key role in balance control. Look straight ahead at an object on the wall. Without shifting your direction of gaze, move your head slightly forward and backward and pay attention to the changes in visual information. You will probably notice that the objects in peripheral vision seem to sweep rapidly back and forth and that these

As a mountain biker navigates the trail, she processes a continuously changing stream of visual information about the environment.

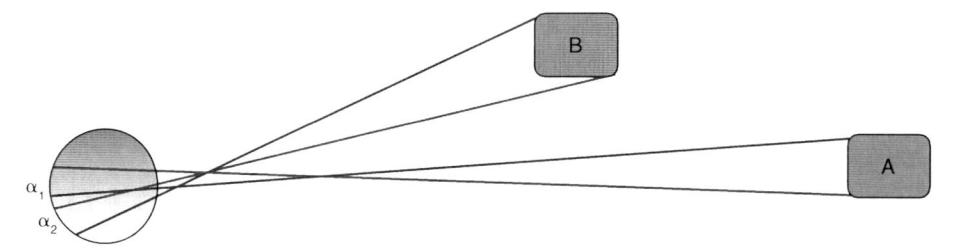

Sensory Contributions to Skilled Performance

FIGURE 4.6 The observer, represented here by an eye, is heading toward objects A and B, in our example, trees in the forest. The ambient system detects that the rays of light from both sides of tree A are expanding at about the same rate, whereas the light rays from the left side of tree B are expanding more quickly than are those from the right side. This indicates that, if the observer doesn't change course she will collide with Tree A and pass to right of Tree B.

changes are dependent on your head movement. Could this peripheral information serve for balance control?

Lee and Aronson (1974) have shown that balance is strongly affected by varying the visual information, suggesting that the optical-flow variables in peripheral vision are critical to balance. In their experiment, the subject stands in a special, small room surrounded by walls suspended from a very high ceiling, such that that the walls do not quite touch the floor. The walls can be moved, with the floor kept still, to influence only the optical-flow information. Moving the walls slightly away causes the subject to sway slightly forward, and moving the walls closer causes the subject to sway backward. With a little child, an away movement of the walls can cause the subject to stumble forward, and a toward movement of the walls can cause a rather ungraceful plop into a sitting position (see figure 4.7).

Moving the wall toward the person generates optical-flow information that ordinarily means the head is moving forward; that is, that the person is out of balance and falling forward. The automatic postural compensation is to sway backward. Such visually-based compensations are far faster than can be explained by conscious processing in the ventral system, with latencies of about 100 ms (Nashner & Berthoz, 1978). These experiments suggest that optical-flow information and the dorsal system are critically involved in controlling normal balancing activities.

This role of vision in balance control has strong implications for learned postures as well. In performing a handstand on the

FIGURE 4.7 David N. Lee's moving room apparatus. Moving the walls forward (away from the camera) makes the young subject sway forward, and moving the wall backward causes the subject to "plop" into a sitting position. This evidence suggests that vision is critical for balance. (Lee is second from the left in this photo).

Reprinted by permission from Lee and Aronson 1974.

still rings, where it is important to remain as motionless as possible, the visual system can signal very small changes in posture, providing a basis for tiny corrections to hold the posture steady.

Ventral Stream Movement Control

The ventral stream provides information about the "what" in motor control. An expert baseball batter knows that different types of pitches have different spins—rotations of the ball that help the batter to predict a pitch's trajectory. A dental assistant not only must know the difference between the appearance of a sickle probe and a periodontal probe, but also needs to be able to identify each with an associated verbal label when called upon. Thus, the ventral stream usually needs information presented in well-lit visual conditions in order to identify object information, which then can be used for conscious, decision-making processes for action.

Vision and Movement Planning Object identification, via the ventral stream, plays a crucial role in movement planning before the initiation of an action. For example, have a look at the objects in figure 4.8 and think about which grip you would use to pick up each object. For the beer glass (object a), a full-hand grip is needed. A four-finger grip

FIGURE 4.8 The ventral stream identifies the visual properties of an object for the purpose of advance grip planning of objects *a* through *c*. However, the visual properties of objects do not tell the whole story—intentions about what action will be performed with an object also determine which grip to use. For example, think about how you would grip object *d* if you were planning to write with it, and compare that to how you would grip object *d* if you planned to use it to puncture a balloon.

is needed for the beer mug (object b), but a thumb-and-finger grip is appropriate for the teacup (object c). The pen (object d) is usually picked up with a precision grip if the performer intends to use it to write something. However, if the performer intends to use the pen as a tool, say, to puncture a balloon, then a power grip would be used. Thus, information provided by the ventral stream is combined with the action goal for further processing in the movement planning stages.

Processing Visual Feedback Earlier, we mentioned that visual information can be used very rapidly (<100 ms) to make adjustments in the control of movement. In other situations however, visually based corrections involve the relatively slow stages of information processing; and one line of the research has been to identify how much time is needed to conduct this processing activity.

Following the initial attempts by Woodworth (1899), a unique strategy was devised by Keele and Posner (1968) to measure the time to process visual feedback. The subject's goal was to complete an aimed hand movement to a target with minimal spatial and temporal error. The target distance was 15 cm, and there were four target goal MTs (150, 250, 350, and 450 ms). Thus, the movements were completed in times that ranged from very rapid (150 ms goal, but they were actually completed in 185-190 ms) to fairly slow (450 ms). Subjects were given verbal feedback about their MTs after each trial to help them to move in the proper MT. A critically important feature of the research design was that subjects completed some of the trials in the dark—the ambient lights were suddenly extinguished on a randomly-selected 50% of the trials just at the initiation of the movement. The prediction was simple: If visual feedback was used to guide the movement onto the target, then having the ambient lights on should produce more accurate aims than when the ambient lights were off. But, if the movement was made too fast to *use* visual feedback, then no differences in accuracy would be expected.

Keele and Posner's results are presented in figure 4.9. The first thing to note is that, as the MTs became longer in time, the accuracy in hitting the target increased, but mainly so for the movements made with the lights on. It is important to note that the accuracies with the lights on versus lights off were identical for the fastest MT, and the curves diverged as movements became longer in time. These data suggest that the MT was approximately 190-250 ms and was the minimum time to use visual feedback in these actions. Thus, slower movements benefited from having the ambient lights on.

This evidence suggests that the minimum time required to use vision to improve accuracy in aimed movements is likely to be between 190 ms and 250 ms. If the vision offset is unexpected, as in Keele and Posner's task, the amount of time needed to process the visual feedback is roughly similar to that for *choice* RT. If availability of visual feedback can be predicted, then the processing time is reduced to that for *simple* RT (Elliott, Hansen, & Grierson, 2010).

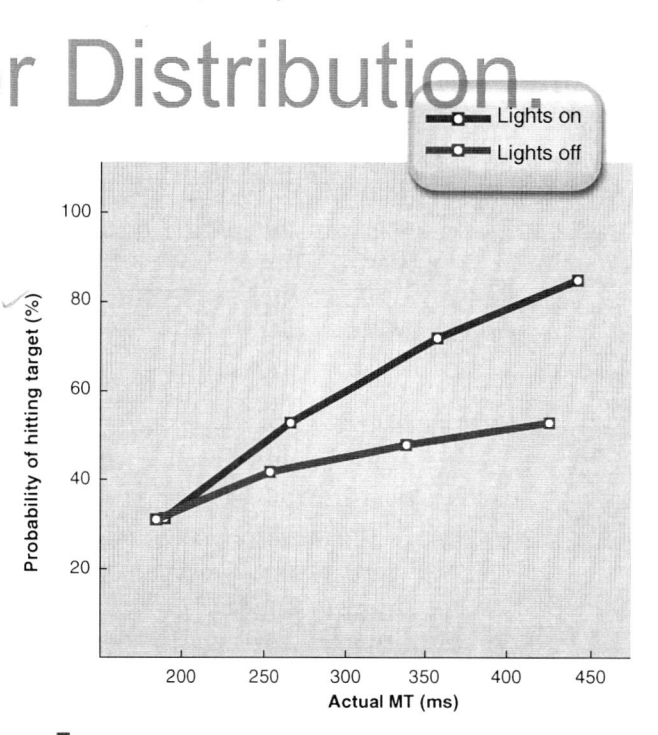

FIGURE 4.9 Movements completed in times less than 200 ms showed no improvement in accuracy with the ambient lights on (compared to lights off), but movements made in times longer than 250 ms did benefit from having the lights on.

Data from Keele and Posner 1968.

Focus on RESEARCH 4.2

Gaze Control

Eye-movement recording devices provide researchers with very precise measures of *gaze*—where a person is looking during an action or perceptual event. These studies have revealed that we voluntarily control gaze using two different types of eye movements: smooth-pursuit eye movements and discrete-saccadic movements.

The goal of smooth-pursuit movements is to keep the target of our gaze fixed on the fovea of the retina. The eyes fixate on an object that is either motionless or moving slowly, allowing the viewer to pick up precise detail. -yet movements, on the other hand, are characterized by brief fixations and rapid shifts to a different location in the visual environment. Information is picked up during the fixations, but not during the saccades between fixations. Saccadic shifts provide us with the capability to pick up information rapidly from a wide range of sources in our visual environment, for example as required when driving (looking out the front and side windows, checking the various mirrors, etc.).

Researchers have discovered something very interesting about the way highly skilled and less skilled athletes use vision just before the onset of action. Expert performers keep their eyes fixated for a longer period of time just before movement onset than do nonexperts. Moreover, individuals can improve their performance if they are trained to fixate their gaze for a longer period of time just before action. These findings have been replicated in many different types of activities (e.g., basketball free-throw shooting, target shooting, golf, juggling) and have been termed the "quiet-eye" effect (see Vickers, 2007, for a good review).

However, there remains considerable uncertainty regarding the mechanism(s) responsible for these effects. One hypothesis is that a prolonged gaze period might stabilize the perceptual system, facilitating movement processes dependent on them. Another view is that this period of inactivity provides an opportunity to shift attentional resources to an optimal-control focus. Although many other possible reasons cannot be excluded at this time, the generality of the "quiet-eye" effect suggests that these mechanisms probably arise with skill development. Clearly, there is much more research to be conducted on this topic.

Exploring Further

1. What are rods and cones of the eye, and what specific information do they contribute to vision?
2. What is the difference between looking and seeing? How does the activity known as Parkour reveal that what traceurs and traceuses see is different from what the rest of us see?

Vision in the Conceptual Model

The distinction between dorsal- and ventral-stream visual processing has obvious implications for our conceptual model as presented in figure 4.3. Although ventral-stream processing would still occur as suggested in the model (through the slow processing stages, in the "outer loop"), dorsal-stream processing would be expected to be unconscious—perhaps almost reflex-like. Because dorsal-stream processing is nonconscious, relatively fast, and inflexible, it is fed back to relatively low levels in the central nervous system, considerably "downstream" from the processes that select and initiate movement but "upstream"

Sensory Contributions to Skilled Performance

from the muscles and the spinal cord. Thus, dorsal vision can be thought of as operating at intermediate levels of the system to make minor adjustments in already programmed actions, such as compensation for head movement in the golf swing and alterations in posture to maintain balance on the still rings. For this reason, we have added a feedback loop from the resulting movement to the level of the motor program in figure 4.10.

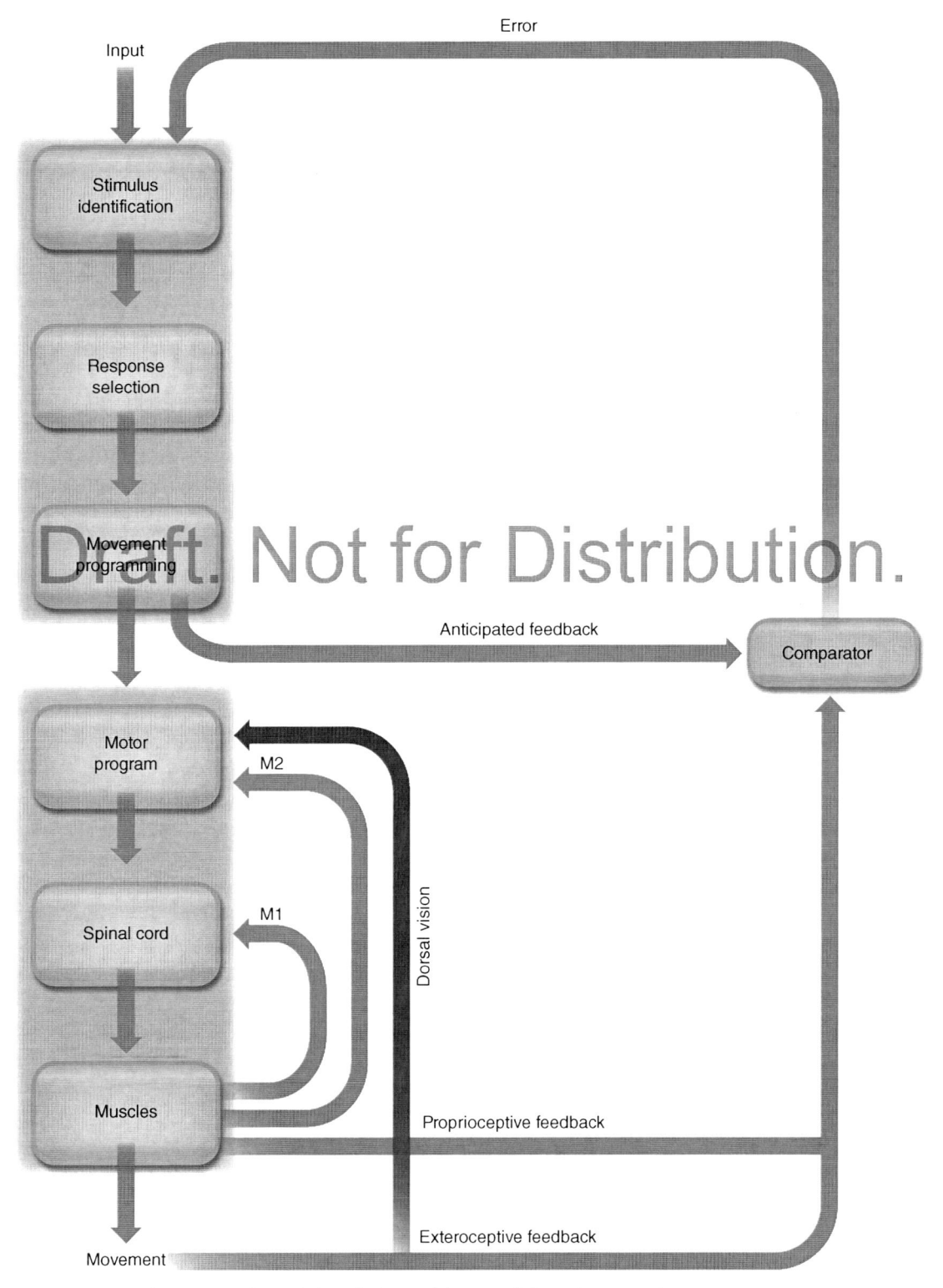

FIGURE 4.10 Conceptual model with the addition of dorsal stream loop.

Focus on
APPLICATION 4.2

Visibility in Nighttime Car–Truck Accidents

A not uncommon motor vehicle accident occurs at nighttime—the driver of a car going at the posted speed limit runs into the back of a vehicle that is stopped or moving very slowly (perhaps a truck on a hill). The driver of the car had no trouble seeing the taillights on the back of the parked or slowly moving vehicle. Rather, the problem was that the driver did not know what the lights were "doing." What could be going on here?

On a clear night, the driver can probably see the taillights from quite a long distance away (perhaps a mile or so). Presumably, the rate of visual expansion (in this case, the lights appearing to move farther apart) of the optical flow on the retina provides information that the vehicle ahead is stopped (or going very slowly), instead of going at the same speed as the car. But the problem is illustrated quite clearly in figure 4.11 (from Ayres et al., 1995)—the rate of expansion is so small (smaller than the threshold for detecting any expansion—0.2 degrees/second, see the horizontal line in figure 4.11). This means that the following driver cannot perceive the expansion until the car is about 400 ft (about 133 m) from the object, where it is just possible to detect that the optical array is expanding. The problem is that 400 ft is very close to the distance over which a car at 60 mph (about 95 kph) can be brought to a complete stop—and this is under ideal (i.e., dry, good visibility) conditions. Therefore, the following driver does not perceive that the truck is moving from more slowly than he is until it is almost too late. Unless the following driver is extremely alert, the car can easily strike the slow-moving truck.

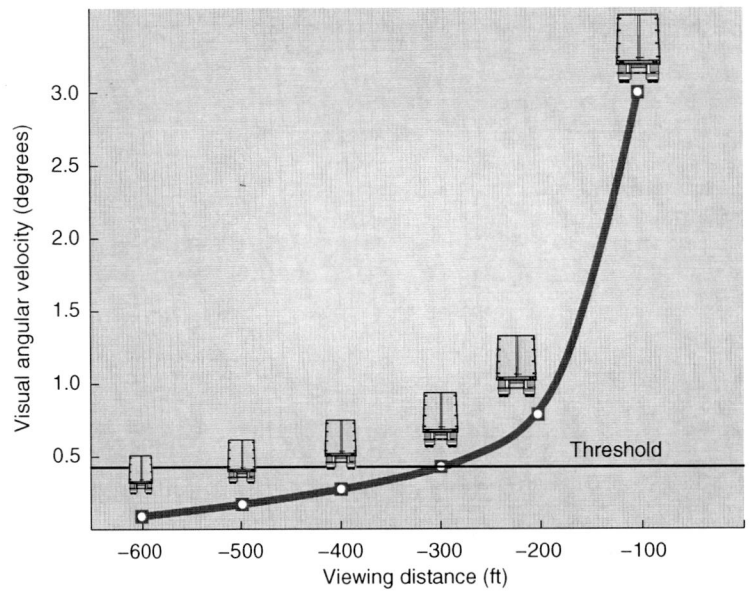

FIGURE 4.11 The rate of visual expansion of a car at 60mph (about 95 kph) approaching a slow-moving truck remains below threshold until the truck is approximately 400 ft (about 133 m) away.

Reprinted by permission from Ayres, Schmidt et al. 1995.

Another issue is that, at a very far distance away, the visibility of taillights does not necessarily indicate to the driver that what she is approaching is actually a truck. It could be lights on two separate objects, such as road signs (spaced apart by a small distance), or two motorcycle taillights, or something other than a vehicle. Some proponents of vehicle safety have advocated placing additional retro-reflective material on trucks to make them more visible or conspicuous. But this really does not reduce the visual perception problem raised here, because the rate of visual expansion of the retro-reflective material is essentially the same as that of the lights. Therefore, when you are 500 ft (about 150 m) from the truck, you have the same problem of not being able to identify what the object is doing, speed-wise.

Audition and Motor Control

Perhaps one of the more understudied areas of research is the role of auditory feedback in movement. Yet we know that it can have profound effects on motor control. For example, a speaker who talks into a microphone at a large concert hall and hears his voice projected from the sound system at the very back of the hall will experience a delay in hearing the auditory feedback of his voice. Such delays are well known to increase timing errors and slowed rates of speaking and to disrupt other forms of movement, such as playing a musical instrument (Pfordresher & Dalla Bella, 2011). Ironically, delayed auditory feedback is sometimes effective in the treatment of stuttering, perhaps because it causes individuals to slow their speech (Lawrence & Barclay, 1998).

Auditory feedback plays other roles in performance as well. An outfielder in baseball might be fooled into predicting that a line drive seen leaving a batter's bat will go over her head. In fact, the sound of the bat–ball contact correctly indicated that it was a softly hit ball requiring the outfielder to run in, rather than back. Here the visual information distorted the correct information provided by sound (see Gray, 2009, for more). The overshadowing of audition by vision is also illustrated in the McGurk effect, discussed in Focus on Application 4.3.

The question of how auditory feedback is processed in movement control remains largely unanswered, although we suspect that

■ A skilled carpenter may use the sound of a saw cutting through wood as a source of information.

information is processed as outlined in our conceptual model in figure 4.10, with both anticipatory (feedforward) and actual feedback mechanisms serving important roles in movement. Clearly, much research remains to be done in this area.

Focus on
APPLICATION 4.3
When Vision Degrades Performance

In chapter 3 we discussed the various properties of attention. Directing one's attention toward a specific external source is considered an important mechanism, and vision can provide information critical for effective performance. However, performers often find that visual control dominates the other senses and that visual information leads to an unavoidable capture of attention. In fact, many believe that vision tends to dominate all other sources for our attention, and this dominance does not always produce positive outcomes. In many activities, performers have a choice of the modes of control they use, such as the race car driver or pilot who can monitor the sounds of the engine or kinesthetic information from the "seat-of-the-pants" as opposed to the visual information provided by numerous cockpit gauges or information seen through the windscreen. And sometimes this nonvisual information is more reliable than the information provided by vision.

Visual information is obviously very important in many situations, but in other situations an overreliance on vision can result in ineffective performance. A good example comes from sailboat racing, which is very rich in visual information about the aerodynamic shapes of the sails and the way the wind is flowing over them. This visual information can yield relatively good performance. However, focusing on vision is ignoring other forms of information, such as the sounds the boat makes as it goes through the water, the action and position of the hull felt by the "seat of the pants," and forces on the tiller, all of which provide additional useful information about speed—but only if the person at the helm is attending to them. Some racing sailors have used blindfolded training methods to learn to decrease their reliance on vision and share the attentional resources among other internal targets (senses) to optimize performance. The idea is that when vision is prevented for a long time, the sailors develop sensitivity to the less dominant sources of information.

Visual illusions provide a powerful demonstration of visual dominance effects. In the *size–weight illusion,* for example, two opaque containers, one much larger than the other, are filled with amounts of sand so that they are of identical weights. The subject is asked to lift both and judge which one is heavier. Vision (and experience) tells us that the larger container is usually heavier than the smaller one, and when proprioception fails to confirm that, we naturally conclude the opposite—that the *smaller* container must have more weight in it than the larger container. Here, visual information is overriding proprioception.

The McGurk effect reveals a vision–audition interaction. For example, a subject is asked to watch and listen to a video of someone speaking a word over and over again (e.g., "blow"). If you close your eyes and listen to the audio portion of the video it is obvious that the person is saying "blow." But the video is actually of someone mouthing the word "flow" over and over again, with "blow" being given on the audio. Most people who watch the video and also listen to the audio report that the person is saying "flow," even though what is actually heard is "blow." And sometimes people even report something completely different than either "flow" or "blow." Here, vision is distorting the (true) information provided by audition.

This McGurk effect and the size–weight illusion are just two examples of how visual dominance tends to overshadow the contributions made by the other senses.

Summary

The effectiveness with which a performer processes various forms of sensory information often determines overall performance level. Sensory signals from the environment are usually termed exteroceptive information, whereas those from the body are termed proprioceptive information. For human performance it is useful to think of these signals as operating in a closed-loop control system, which contains an executive for decision making, an effector for carrying out the actions, feedback about the state of the environment, and a comparator to contrast the environmental state with the system's goal.

In the conceptual model of human performance, closed-loop control is added to the stages of information processing discussed in previous chapters. This model is particularly effective for understanding how slower actions as well as tracking tasks are performed. To the conceptual model are then added several reflex-like processes that account for corrections without involving the information-processing stages. In moving from the M1, M2, and M3 (or voluntary reaction time), these responses show systematically increased flexibility and increased latency. Finally, vision is considered as a special case of closed-loop control. Two visual streams are introduced, a dorsal stream for motor control and a ventral stream for object identification, and the role of the dorsal stream in balance and in producing and correcting actions is considered. These sensory systems are then integrated into the conceptual model, which helps to show how these various sensory events can support or modify skilled actions and under what conditions they operate.

WEB STUDY GUIDE ACTIVITIES

The student web study guide, available at www.HumanKinetics.com/MotorLearningandPerformance, offers these activities to help you build and apply your knowledge of the concepts in this chapter.

Interactive Learning

Activity 4.1: Identify the roles of the sensory organs involved in proprioception by matching each structure with its description.

Activity 4.2: Answer a series of multiple-choice questions that will help you learn to describe the characteristics of each of the components of a closed-loop control system.

Activity 4.3: Indicate whether each in a list of descriptions applies to the dorsal or ventral visual processing stream.

Activity 4.4: Label the conceptual model of motor control to review its stages, including closed-loop control pathways and visual stream information.

Situation-Based Exercise

Activity 4.5: The situation-based exercise for this chapter prompts you to choose an activity, identify sources of proprioceptive and exteroceptive information during the activity, and evaluate which sources of information are useful to the performer. You will also apply the concept of closed-loop control to the activity.

Check Your Understanding

1. Name the four distinct parts of a closed-loop control system. Describe how each of these parts might function for a child stacking toy blocks.
2. Explain how the pattern of optical flow can inform an outfielder attempting to catch a fly ball about when and where the ball will reach the height of the fielder's glove.
3. How does ventral-stream movement control play a role in movement planning when opening various doors throughout your day?

Apply Your Knowledge

1. Several sources of sensory information are available to a skier as she makes her way down an alpine ski run. Describe and provide examples of exteroceptive and proprioceptive information that she might receive during her run, and indicate why this information is important for movement.
2. How closed-loop control processes are used (if at all) is dependent on the task that is performed. Contrast the role played by closed-loop control processes for casting a fishing line and tracing a clothing pattern onto fabric. Would this role change if either of the tasks were sped up?

Suggestions for Further Reading

An overview of closed-loop control of movement is provided by Ghez and Krakauer (2000), with specific roles assigned to spinal reflexes presented by Pearson and Gordon (2000). Elliott and Khan (2010) edited an excellent book that provides many contributions regarding the various roles of vision in motor control. The contributions of ventral- and dorsal-stream processing are debated in Norman (2002). And a more comprehensive discussion of the various topics presented in this chapter can be found in chapter 5 of Schmidt and Lee (2011). See the reference list for these additional resources.

5

Motor Programs
Motor Control of Brief Actions

KEY TERMS

central pattern generator (CPG)
deafferentation
generalized motor program (GMP)
invariant features
motor program
novelty problem
open-loop control
parameterized
parameters
reflex-reversal phenomenon
relative timing
sensory neuropathy
startle RT
storage problem
surface feature

CHAPTER OUTLINE

Motor Program Theory
Evidence for Motor Programs
Motor Programs and the Conceptual Model
Problems in Motor Program Theory: Novelty and Storage
Generalized Motor Program Theory
Summary

CHAPTER OBJECTIVES

Chapter 5 describes how motor programs are used in the control of movement. This chapter will help you to understand

- motor control as an open-loop system and the role of motor programs,
- experimental evidence for motor programs,
- limitations and problems in the simple motor program concept, and
- generalized motor programs and evidence for this expanded concept.

Watching a guitarist pluck a series of notes with blazing speed, or a pianist run trills up and down the keyboard, reminds us that in many skills, a number of separate actions can appear in very quick sequence. Yet these separate actions are produced while maintaining a specific rhythm to the sequence that leaves the impression of a single, fluid, coordinated motion. How does the skilled musician produce so many movements so quickly? What controls them, and how are they combined to form a whole? The skilled musician gives us the impression that these quick movements might be organized in advance and run off without much feedback control.

This chapter investigates the idea of open-loop control, introducing the concept of the motor program as responsible for this kind of movement control. Then the various feedback pathways discussed in the previous chapter are examined as to their interaction with motor programs, giving a more complete picture of the interplay of central and peripheral contributions to movements. The chapter also focuses on the concept of a **generalized motor program (GMP)**, which can account for the common observation that movements can be varied along certain dimensions—for example, playing the guitar or piano sequence slower or faster (or louder or softer) without sacrificing their underlying structure (i.e., the rhythm).

In many actions, particularly quick ones produced in stable and predictable environments (e.g., springboard diving, hammering), most people would assume that a performer somehow plans the movement in advance and then triggers it, allowing the action to run its course without much modification or awareness of the individual elements. Also, the performer does not seem to have much conscious control over the movement once it's triggered into action; the movement just seems to "take care of itself." Perhaps this is obvious. Certainly you cannot have direct, conscious control of the thousands of individual muscle contractions and joint movements—all the *degrees of freedom* that must be coordinated as the skilled action is unfolding. There is simply too much going on for the limited-capacity attentional mechanisms (which we have discussed in chapters 3 and 4) to control any one of them individually.

If these individual contractions are not controlled directly by processes of which you are aware, how then *are* they controlled and regulated? In many ways, this question is one of the most fundamental to the field of motor behavior because it goes to the heart of how biological systems of all kinds control their actions. This chapter focuses on the ways the central nervous system is organized functionally before and during an action and how this organization contributes to the control of the unfolding movement. As such, this chapter is a close companion to chapter 4, which considered the ways sensory information contributes to movement production. This chapter adds the idea of centrally organized commands that sensory information may modify somewhat. First, though, comes the important concept of a **motor program**, which is the *prestructured set of movement commands that defines and shapes the movement*.

Motor Program Theory

The concept of the motor program, which is central to this entire chapter, is based on a kind of control mechanism that is in some ways the opposite of the closed-loop system discussed throughout chapter 4. This type of functional organization is called **open-loop control**.

Open-Loop Control

The basic open-loop system is illustrated in figure 5.1, and consists essentially of two parts: an executive and an effector. This open-loop structure has two of the main features used in closed-loop control (figure 4.1), but missing are feedback and comparator mechanisms for determining system errors. Open-loop control begins with input about the desired state being given to the executive (or decision-making) level, whose task it is to define what action needs to be taken. The executive then passes instructions to the effector level, which is responsible for carrying out these instructions. Once the actions are completed, the system's job is over until the executive is activated again. Of course, without feedback, the open-loop system is not sensitive to whether or not the actions generated in the environment were effective in meeting the goal; and since feedback is not present, modifications to the action cannot be made while the action is in progress.

This kind of control system can be observed in many different real-world mechanisms. For example, an open-loop system is used in most traffic signals, where it sequences the timing of the red, yellow, and green lights that control the traffic flow. If an accident should happen at that intersection, the open-loop system continues to sequence the lights as if nothing were wrong, even though the standard pattern would be ineffective in handling this new, unexpected traffic flow problem. Thus, the open-loop system is effective as long as things go as expected, but it is inflexible in the face of unpredicted changes.

A microwave oven is another example of an open-loop system. The user places a frozen entree in the oven and programs it to defrost for 5 min, and then cooks on high

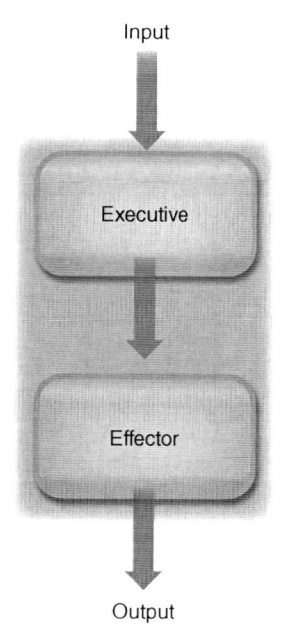

FIGURE 5.1 A basic open-loop system.

power for another 2 min. Here, the program tells the machine what operations to do at each step and specifies the timing of each operation. Although some microwave ovens are sensitive to the temperature of the item being cooked, many are not, and these latter machines follow the instructions without any regard for whether they will result in the desired state (an entree that is ready to eat).

Generally, the characteristics of a purely open-loop control system can be summarized as follows:

- Advance instructions specify the operations to be done, their sequencing, and their timing.
- Once the program has been initiated, the system executes the instructions, essentially without modification.
- There is no capability to detect or to correct errors because feedback is not involved.
- Open-loop systems are most effective in stable, predictable environments in which the need for modification of commands is low.

Motor Programs as Open-Loop Systems

Many movements—especially ones that are rapid, brief, and forceful, such as kicking and key pressing—seem to be controlled in an open-loop fashion, without much conscious control once the movement is under way. The performer in these tasks does not have time to process information about movement errors and must plan the movement in its entirety before movement initiation. This is quite different from the style of control discussed in the previous chapter, where the movements were slower (or longer in time) and were largely based on feedback processes of various kinds.

Open-loop control seems especially important when the environmental situation is predictable and stable. Under these circumstances, human movements appear to be carried out without much possibility of, or need for, modification. This general idea was popularized more than a century ago by the psychologist William James (1891) and has remained as one of the most important ways to understand movement control.

Consider a goal such as hitting a pitched baseball. The executive level, which consists of the decision-making stages of the system defined in chapter 2, evaluates the environment in the stimulus identification stage, processing such information as the speed and direction of the ball. The decision about whether or not to swing is made in the response selection stage. Then, the movement is programmed and initiated in the movement programming stage, in which details about the swing's speed, trajectory, and timing are determined.

Control is then passed to the effector level for movement execution. The selected motor program now carries out the swing by delivering commands to the spinal cord, which eventually directs the operations of the skeletal system involved in the swing. This movement then influences the outcome—resulting in the desired movement (hitting the ball squarely) or not (e.g., missing the ball, popping the ball up).

Although the decision-making stages determine what program to initiate and have some role in the eventual form of the movement (e.g., its speed and trajectory), movement execution is not actually controlled by the conscious decision-making stages. Therefore, the movement is carried out by a system that is not under direct conscious control. On this view, the motor program is the agent determining which muscles are to contract, in what order, when, and for how long (timing).

Practice, which leads to learning skilled actions, is thought of as "building" new, more stable, more precise, or longer-operating motor programs (or some combination of these). Initially a program might be capable only of controlling a short string of actions. With practice, however, the program becomes more elaborate, capable of controlling longer and longer strings of behavior, perhaps even modulating various reflexive activities that support the overall movement goal. These programs are then stored in long-term memory and must be retrieved and prepared for initiation during the response programming stage.

Open-Loop Control in the Conceptual Model

How does this concept of open-loop control and the motor program fit with the conceptual model of human performance? Figure 5.2 shows the conceptual model developed in chapter 4 (figure 4.10), now with the portions highlighted (light-green shading) that comprise the open-loop components. The conceptual model can here be thought of as an open-loop control system with feedback added (the parts not shaded) to produce corrections through the other loops discussed previously. This more complete conceptual model has two basic ways of operating, depending on the task. If the movement is very slow or of long duration (e.g., threading a needle), the control is dominated by the feedback processes. If the movement is very fast or brief (e.g., a punch or kick), then the open-loop portions tend to dominate. In most tasks, motor behavior is not either open or closed loop alone but a complex blend of the two.

For very fast and or brief actions, the theory of motor programs is useful because it gives a set of ideas and a vocabulary to talk about a functional organization of the motor system. If a given movement is said to be "a programmed action," it appears to be organized in advance, triggered more or less as a whole, and carried out without much modification from sensory feedback. This language describes a style of motor control with *central* movement organization, where movement details are determined by the central nervous system and are then sent to the muscles, rather than controlled by peripheral processes involving feedback. Of course, both styles of control are possible, depending on the nature of the task, the time involved, and other factors.

Evidence for Motor Programs

A number of separate lines of evidence converge to support the existence of motor program control. This evidence comes from some rather diverse areas of research: (a) studies of reaction time in humans; (b) experiments on animals and case studies involving animals and humans in which feedback has been removed; (c) the impact on performance when movement is unexpectedly blocked; (d) the analysis of behaviors when humans attempt to stop or change an action; and (e) studies of movements initiated by startling stimuli.

Reaction-Time Evidence

Studies of the effects of information processing on reaction time (RT) were discussed in some detail in chapter 2. Recall from that chapter that, in general, RT was slowed when more information needed to be processed (e.g., Hick's Law), when processing was not "natural" (e.g., in S-R incompatible situations), and so on. Generally, RT was influenced mainly by the slowness of the stimulus identification and response selection stages. In this section we review evidence that RT is also influenced by the factors affecting the movement programming stage.

Response Complexity Effects

Subjects in RT experiments are typically asked to respond to a stimulus by initiating and carrying out a predetermined movement as quickly as possible (as discussed in chapter 2). Duration of the RT delay is measured as the interval from the presentation of the stimulus until the movement begins, so any added time for the movement itself does not contribute directly to RT. However, beginning with the work of Henry and Rogers (1960; see Focus on Research 5.1), many experimenters have shown that RT is affected by several features of the movement *to be performed*, presumably by influencing the complexity (and duration) of the movement programming stage.

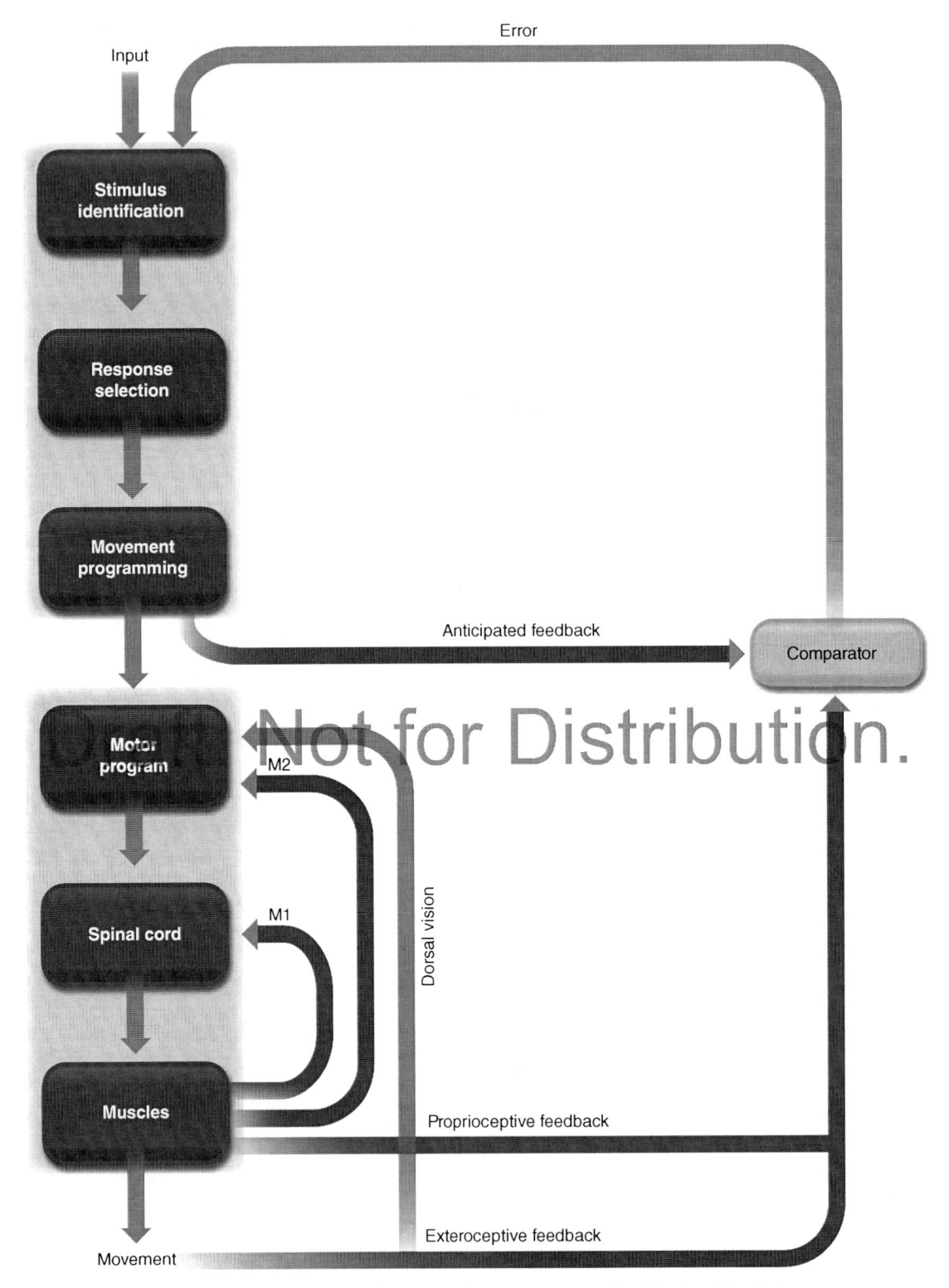

FIGURE 5.2 Conceptual model with the open-loop processes highlighted in light green.

Focus on
RESEARCH 5.1

The Henry–Rogers Experiment

One of Franklin Henry's many important contributions was a paper that he and Donald Rogers published in 1960. The experiment was simple, as many important experiments are. Subjects responded as quickly as possible to a stimulus by making one of three movements that were prepared in advance. Only one of these movements would be required for a long string of trials, so this was essentially a simple-RT paradigm (see chapter 2). The movements, designed to be different in complexity, were (a) a simple finger lift, (b) a simple finger lift plus a reach to slap a suspended ball, and (c) a movement requiring a simple finger lift followed by several reversals in direction to targets (see Fischman, Christina, & Anson, 2008, for details).

The seated subject would begin with his finger on the release key (labeled as "D" in Figure 5.3). For the most complex action, the subject would respond to the stimulus lights by lifting his finger from the release key, reaching forward to slap the first tennis ball, moving down to push the button on the base (E), then, finally, reaching forward and upwards to slap the second tennis ball; for the movement of intermediate complexity, the subject responded to the stimulus lights by lifting his finger off the release key, and then reaching to slap the first tennis ball; for the simplest movement, the subject only had to lift his finger off the release key. Each of these actions was to be done as quickly as possible.

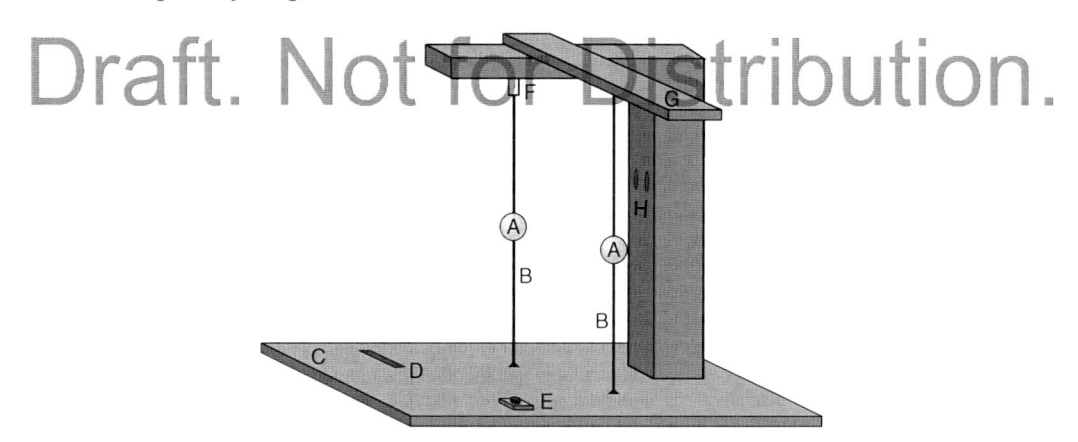

FIGURE 5.3 Apparatus used by subjects in the Henry and Rogers (1960) experiment. Relevant parts are: A = tennis balls; B = release key; C = push button; D = stimulus lights.
Reprinted from Howell 1953.

Henry and Rogers measured the RT to *initiate* each of these actions—the interval from the presentation of the stimulus until the beginning of the required movement. (Remember that the RT does not include the time to complete the movement itself.) They found that the time to initiate the movement increased with added movement complexity. The finger-lift movement (a) had an RT of 150 ms; the grasping movement (b) had an RT of 195 ms; and the movement with two reversals in direction (c) had an RT of 208 ms.

> continued

> continued

Notice that in each case, the stimulus to signal the movement (processed during the stimulus identification stage) and the number of movement choices (processed during the response selection stage) remained constant across the different conditions. Thus, because the only factor that varied was the complexity of the movement, the interpretation was that the elevated RTs were somehow caused by increased time for movement programming to occur before the action. This notion has had profound effects on the understanding of movement organization processes and has led to many further research efforts to study these processes more systematically (reviewed in Christina, 1992). Most importantly, these data support the idea that rapid movement is organized in advance, which is consistent with the motor program concept.

Exploring Further

1. Analyze the differences in actions required for the three movements in the Henry and Rogers study. Describe at least three differences in the movements' requirements that might have led to increases in the complexity of the motor program.
2. What additional changes could be made to the action requirements of the most complex movement (C) that might be expected to increase movement programming time?

Henry and Rogers (1960) found that simple RT was elevated with increases in the complexity of the movement to be performed *after* the response was initiated. This, plus much more research on this important finding since the publication of Henry and Rogers' work, has produced the following set of findings (Klapp, 1996):

- RT increases when additional elements in a series are added to the action (e.g., a unidirectional forward stroke in table tennis would likely be initiated with a shorter RT than a backswing plus a forward stroke).
- RT increases when more limbs must be coordinated (e.g., a one-handed piano chord would be initiated with a shorter RT than a two-handed chord).
- RT increases when the duration of the movement becomes longer (e.g., a 100 ms bat swing would be initiated with a shorter RT than a 300 ms bat swing).

The interpretation is that when the to-be-produced movement is more "complex" in any of these ways (number of elements, number of limbs involved, the overall duration of the action), RT is longer because more time is required to organize the motor system before the initiation of the action. This prior organization occurs, as discussed in chapter 2, in the movement programming stage. The effect on RT of the nature of the to-be-performed movement provides evidence that at least some of the action is organized in advance, just as a motor program theory would expect.

Startled Reactions

In the previous section we discussed the idea that RT becomes longer with increases in the "complexity" of the to-be-performed movement. Here, we focus on research showing that RT can be dramatically shortened under certain conditions.

We have all been in situations in which a completely unexpected event, such as a very loud noise or very bright light, caused a severe reaction—we were *startled*. The response is often accompanied by contractions in the muscles of the face and neck and protective movements of the upper limbs. A very interesting property of the startle response (RT) is that these movements are initiated much faster than can be accounted for by voluntary responses to a stimulus.

An innovative series of studies involved the **startle RT** as a paradigm to reveal insights about movement programming. In these studies (reviewed in Carlsen et al., 2011; Valls-Solé, Kumru, & Kofler, 2008), the subject is typically asked to prepare to make a rapid, forceful, sometimes complex response to a moderately intense stimulus (auditory or visual). Occasionally, the stimulus is accompanied by an extremely loud acoustic signal (e.g., 130 decibels [dB]; by comparison, the sound of a chainsaw is about 110 dB).The loud acoustic signal usually produces the typical startle indicators (clenched neck and jaw muscles, among other reactions). However, what also happens is that the prepared movement is produced normally, but with an RT that may be up to 100 ms shorter than on the control trials without the loud stimulus. The pattern of the actions remained unchanged.

These findings fit quite well into the motor program concept. The idea here is that the executive has prepared a motor program in advance of the stimulus to respond, which is normally released by a voluntary, internal "go" signal from the executive to the effectors. The startle RT has the effect of hastening the release of this signal, by means of either speeding up the executive's processing time or perhaps even bypassing the executive altogether. The research is unclear at this point as to exactly *why* the same movement is initiated much faster on startled trials than on normal, unstartled trials, but the role of the motor program in carrying out the response is clearly implicated.

Deafferentation Experiments

In chapter 4, we mentioned that information from the muscles, the joints, and the skin are collected together in sensory nerves, which enter the spinal cord at various levels. A surgical technique termed **deafferentation** involves cutting (via surgery) an animal's afferent nerve bundle where it enters the cord, so the central nervous system no longer can receive information from some portion of the periphery. The motor pathways are not affected by this procedure as information about motor activity passes through the (uncut) ventral (front) side of the cord. Sensory information from an entire limb, or even from several limbs, can be eliminated by this procedure.

What are experimental animals capable of doing when deprived of feedback from the limbs? Films of monkeys with deafferented upper limbs reveal that they are still able to climb around, playfully chase each other, groom, and feed themselves essentially normally. It is indeed difficult to recognize that these animals have a total loss of sensory information from the upper limbs (Taub, 1976; Taub & Berman, 1968). The monkeys are impaired in some ways, however; they have difficulty in fine finger control, as in picking up a pea or manipulating small objects. On balance, though, it is remarkable how little impaired these animals are in most activities.

If the movement is quick enough, the motor program controls the entire action; the movement is carried out as though the performer were deprived of feedback. The capability to move quickly thus gives additional support to the idea that some central program handles the movement control, at least until feedback from the movement can begin to have an effect.

Case studies of humans also support this general conclusion. Lashley (1917) found that a patient with a gunshot wound to the back, who was without sensory feedback information from the legs, could still position his knee at a specified angle without feedback. And individuals who have lost much of their sensory feedback (so-called **sensory neuropathy** patients) are able to perform quite well in their environments as long as visual information is available (Blouin et al., 1996).

These studies show that sensory information from the moving limb is certainly not absolutely critical for movement production, and it is clear that many movements can occur nearly normally without it. This evidence suggests that theories of movement control must be generally incorrect if they *require* sensory information from the responding limb. Because feedback-based theories cannot account for these actions, many theorists have argued that the movements must be organized centrally via motor programs and carried out in an open-loop way, not critically dependent on feedback (e.g., Keele, 1968). In this sense, the deafferentation evidence supports the idea that movements can be organized centrally in motor programs.

Central Pattern Generator

The idea of motor programs is similar to that of the **central pattern generator (CPG)**, which was developed to explain certain features of locomotion in animals, such as swimming in fish, chewing in hamsters, and slithering in snakes (Grillner, 1975). A genetically defined central organization is established in the brainstem or the spinal cord. When this organization is initiated by a triggering stimulus from the brain, sometimes called a *command neuron*, it produces rhythmic, oscillating commands to the musculature as if it were defining a sequence of right–left–right activities, such as might serve as the basis of locomotion. These commands occur even if the sensory nerves are cut (deafferented), suggesting that the organization is truly central in origin.

An example of a simple network that could account for the alternating flexor–extensor patterns in locomotion is shown in figure 5.4. Here, the input trigger activates neuron 1, which activates the flexors as well as neuron 2. Then neuron 3 is activated, which activates the extensors. Neuron 4 is then activated, which activates neuron 1 again, and the process continues. This is, of course, far too simple to account for all of the events in locomotion, but it shows how a collection of single neurons could be connected to each other in the spinal cord to produce an alternating pattern.

The notion of the CPG is almost identical to that of the motor program. The main difference is that the motor program involves learned activities that are centrally controlled (such as kicking and throwing), whereas the CPG involves more genetically-defined activities, such as locomotion, chewing, and breathing. In any case, there is good evidence that many genetically defined activities are controlled by CPGs (Zehr, 2005).

Inhibiting Actions

Another line of evidence to support motor program control can be found in experiments in which subjects are required to inhibit or stop a movement after having initiated the

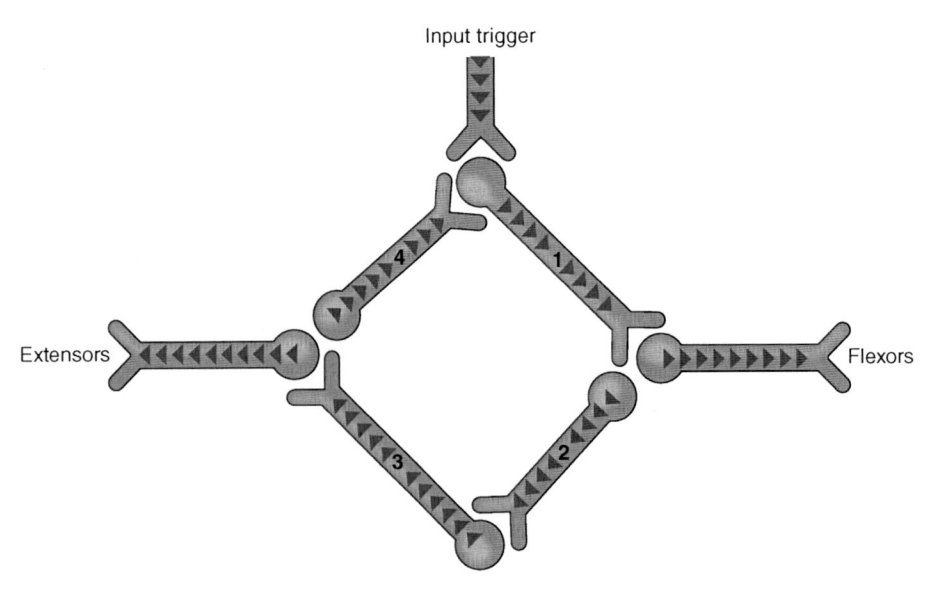

FIGURE 5.4 A simplified illustration of a central pattern generator.
Reprinted by permission from Schmidt and Lee 2011.

Motor Programs

> The concept of a central pattern generator is used to describe simple, genetically-defined activities such as walking, whereas motor program theory applies to learned skills such as riding a bicycle.

process of making the action. This is the kind of activity that one sees quite frequently in baseball batting (see Focus on Application 5.1 on checked swings). The question asked by researchers concerns the "point of no return"—at what point after starting the processing stages that lead to a movement is one committed to making, or at least starting, the action? In other words, at what point is the signal released to send the motor program to the muscles?

The "stop-signal" paradigm is the method most frequently used to study action inhibition, and an early contribution to this research was provided by Slater-Hammel (1960), described in detail in Focus on Research 5.2. The findings of this study, which involved a very simple finger lift off a key (presumably with little biomechanical delay), suggested that the point of no return occurred about 150 to 170 ms before the time when the movement was initiated. An action such as a baseball swing has a much longer

> ### Focus on
> ### APPLICATION 5.1
>
> ### Checked Swings in Baseball
>
> The bat swing in baseball is a good example of a motor program in action. The typical swing consists of a coordinated action involving a step with the lead foot toward the oncoming ball, followed by a rapid rotation of the trunk and shoulders, propelling the bat with a large angular velocity and minimum overall movement time. There is good reason to believe that the step and swing are part of a single motor program, initiated by good batters on almost every pitch; but parts of this swing can be *inhibited* before a full execution on many of those pitches. How do batters do this, and how successful are they at doing it?
>
> The physics of baseball tell us that there is very little time available for a major league batter to hit a baseball. For pitches in the range of 85 to 95 mph (137 to 153 kph), the ball takes less than a half second (500 ms) to reach the hitting zone after being released from the pitcher's hand. The batter typically prepares for the pitch and may initiate the step before the pitcher has actually released the ball. And at some point along the way, usually before the ball reaches the midpoint in its flight toward the plate, the batter must decide whether to proceed with the swing (including where to aim the bat for its intended collision with the ball) or inhibit its execution. The result is four different types of batter responses (Gray, 2009):
>
> 1. The batter successfully inhibits the motor program, and the swing is never initiated.
> 2. The batter starts the swing but inhibits the completion of the motor program, resulting in the bat stopping before it crosses the plate (which defines it as a "nonswing").
> 3. The batter starts the swing but fails to inhibit the motor program in time, resulting in a slowed velocity of the bat as it crosses the plate (resulting in a "completed swing," according to the rules of baseball).
> 4. The batter starts and completes the motor program without attempting to inhibit the swing—a classic example of a completed swing.

movement completion time than the finger lift used by Slater-Hammel. Nevertheless, considerable evidence suggests that a motor program is released that is responsible for initiating the action in tasks like this and that serves to carry out the entire action unless a second stop-signal program is initiated in time to arrest its completion (Verbruggen & Logan, 2008).

Muscle Response Patterns

The final line of evidence supporting motor program control comes from experiments in which patterns of muscle activity are examined when a performer is instructed to make a brief limb action (moving a lever in the extension direction from one position to another). Figure 5.6 shows integrated electromyogram (EMG) tracings from a quick elbow extension movement (Wadman et al., 1979). In the normal movement (red traces), first there is a burst of the agonist (here, the triceps) muscle; then the triceps turns off and the antagonist muscle (the biceps) is activated to decelerate the limb; and finally the agonist comes on again near the end to stabilize the limb at the target area. This triple-burst (agonist–antagonist–agonist) pattern is typical of quick movements of this kind.

Focus on RESEARCH 5.2

Initiating a Motor Program

Not so long ago, races like the 100 m sprint were timed by hand, with a stopwatch. The timing judge started her stopwatch when she saw the smoke of the starter's pistol and stopped it when the runners crossed the finish line. But, let's consider *how* she stopped her stopwatch. If she stopped it when she saw the runner cross the line, then the clock would actually be stopped a short time later, because completing her action would be delayed by two factors: (1) the amount of time required to send the motor instructions to the hand holding the watch and (2) the biomechanical delays in pushing the button.

Our interest, of course, is the first concern—how long does it take to send the motor instructions? To answer this question, Arthur Slater-Hammel (1960) conducted an experiment that was similar to the example of the timing judge just presented. Subjects held a finger on a key while watching an analog timer moving at one revolution per second; lifting off the key brought the sweep hand to an instantaneous stop. Subjects were instructed to lift their finger from the key such that the clock hand would stop at exactly the point marked 800, or roughly at the 10 o-clock position on the clock (800 refers to a lapse of 800 ms after the start from the 12:00 position; see figure 5.5a). Note that in order to do this task accurately, they would need to initiate the action at some point before the clock hand actually reached the 800 position (just as the timing judge would need to initiate the action of stopping her timer before the sprinter crossed the finish line).

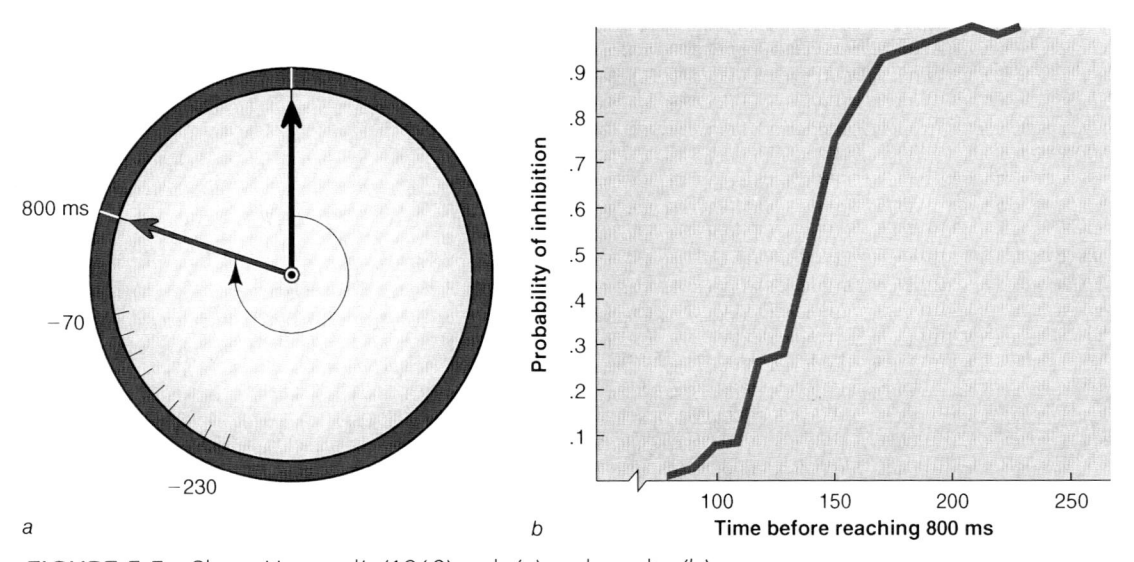

FIGURE 5.5 Slater-Hammel's (1960) task *(a)* and results *(b)*.
Reprinted by permission from Schmidt and Lee 2011. Part b data from Slater-Hammel 1960.

An important aspect of the Slater-Hammel study was the insertion of special (probe) trials that occurred rarely and unpredictably. On these probe trials the experimenter would stop the clock hand at various locations before it reached 800. If this happened, the subjects' job was simply to keep their finger on the key; thus, the probe

> *continued*

> *continued*

trials required an *inhibition* of the normal task of lifting the finger to stop the sweep hand. The rationale was simple—if the motor program had not yet been sent to the muscles when the sweep hand stopped, then the subject should be able to inhibit the finger lift successfully. But there would be little chance of changing such a short, ballistic action if the sweep hand stopped after the motor program to lift the finger that had already been sent.

Slater-Hammel plotted the probability of inhibiting the action successfully as a function of the time interval between 800 and where the clock hand had stopped. The data are shown in figure 5.5*b*. When the interval before the intended finger lift was relatively large (greater than 210 ms), stopping the clock hand resulted in inhibiting the movement successfully almost all the time. However, as this interval decreased, the subjects would lift the finger more and more often, to the point that when the clock hand stopped at −700 (100 ms before the 800 position), the subject could almost never inhibit the movement. Generally, when the clock hand was stopped about 150 to 170 ms before the intended finger lift, the subject could inhibit the movement successfully about half the time. This finding can be interpreted to mean that the internal "go" signal is issued about 150 to 170 ms before the intended action. This "go" signal is a trigger for action, after which the movement occurs even though new information indicates that the movement should be inhibited.

Exploring Further

1. Slater-Hammel's estimate of the time required to anticipate the sweep hand's arrival at the 800 position is complicated by the fact that subjects had a +26 ms constant error (CE) on the normal trials. What are the implications of this positively biased CE?
2. How could this stop-signal paradigm be adapted to examine the time required to make anticipatory actions in sport tasks such as batting a baseball?

Occasionally, and quite unexpectedly, on some trials the lever was blocked mechanically by the experimenter so that no movement was possible. Figure 5.6 also shows what happens to the EMG patterning on these blocked trials (blue lines). Even though the limb does not move at all, there is a similar pattern of muscular organization, with the onset of the agonist and the antagonist occurring at about the same times as when the movement was not blocked. Later, after about 120 ms or so, there is a slight modification of the patterning, probably caused by the reflex activities (e.g., stretch reflexes) discussed in chapter 4. But the most important findings are that the antagonist (biceps) muscle even contracted at all when the movement was blocked and that it contracted at the same time as in the normal movements.

The feedback from the blocked limb must have been massively disrupted, yet the EMG patterning was essentially normal for 100 ms or so. Therefore, these data contradict theories arguing that feedback from the moving limb (during the action) acts as a signal (a trigger) to activate the antagonist muscle contraction at the proper time. Rather, these findings support the motor program idea that the movement activities are organized in advance and run off unmodified sensory information for 100 to 120 ms, at least until the first reflexive activities can become involved.

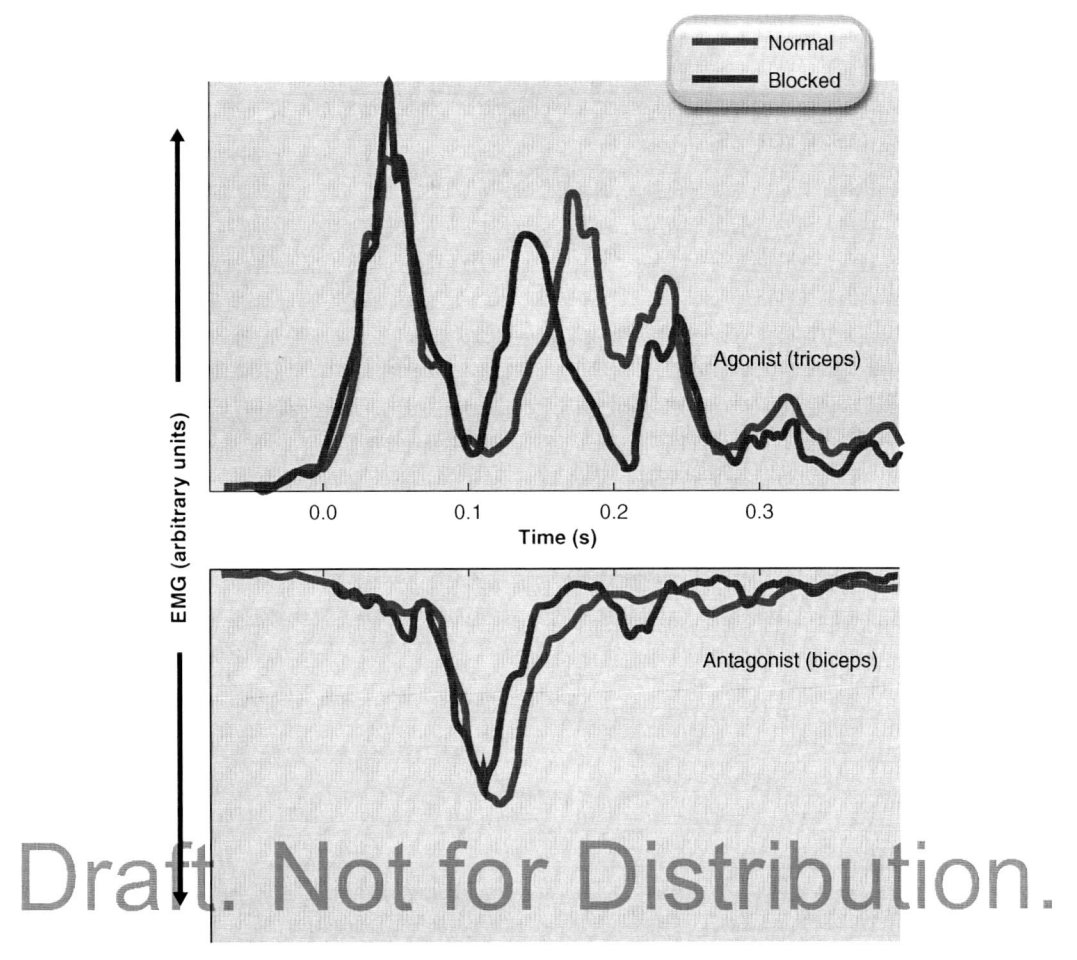

FIGURE 5.6 Electromyographic results from agonist (upper traces) and antagonist (lower traces) muscles when the subject actually produced the movement (normal trials— red lines) and when the movement was blocked by a mechanical perturbation (blocked trials—blue lines).

Reprinted by permission from Wadman 1979.

Motor Programs and the Conceptual Model

Motor programs are a critical part of the conceptual model seen in figure 5.2, operating within the system, sometimes in conjunction with feedback, to produce flexible skilled actions. The open-loop part of these actions provides the organization, or pattern, that the feedback processes can later modify if necessary. The following are some of the major roles of these open-loop organizations:

- To define and issue the commands to musculature that determine when, how forcefully, and for how long muscles are to contract and which ones are to contract
- To organize the many degrees of freedom of the muscles and joints into a single unit
- To specify and initiate preliminary postural adjustments necessary to support the upcoming action
- To modulate the many reflex pathways to ensure that the movement goal is achieved

In the following sections we see research examples of how motor programs use anticipatory and feedback information to regulate movement control.

Anticipatory Adjustments

Imagine that you are standing with your arms at your sides and an experimenter gives you a command to raise an arm quickly to point straight ahead. What will be the first detectable EMG (muscular) activity associated with this movement? Most people would guess that the first contraction would be in the shoulder muscles that raise the arm. But, in fact, the EMG activity in these muscles occurs relatively late in the sequence. Rather, the first muscles to contract are in the lower back and legs, some 80 ms before the first muscle in that shoulder (Belen'kii, Gurfinkel, & Pal'tsev, 1967).

This order may sound strange, but it is really quite a "smart" way for the motor system to operate. Because the shoulder muscles are mechanically linked to the rest of the body, their contractions influence the positions of the segments connected to the arm—the shoulder and the back. That is, the movement of the arm affects posture. If no compensations in posture were first made, raising the arm would cause the trunk to flex, as well as to shift the center of gravity forward, causing a slight loss of balance. Therefore, rather than adjust for these effects *after* the arm movement, the motor system compensates before the movement through "knowing" what postural modifications will soon be needed.

There is good evidence that these preparatory postural adjustments are really just a part of the movement program for making the arm movement (W.A. Lee, 1980). When the arm movement is organized, the motor program contains instructions to adjust the posture in advance as well as the instructions to move the arm, so that the action is a coordinated whole. Thus, we should not think of the arm movement and the posture control as separate events; rather, these are simply different parts of an integrated action of raising the arm and maintaining posture and balance. Interestingly, these preparatory adjustments vanish when the performer leans against a support, because postural adjustments are not needed here.

Integration of Central and Feedback Control

Although it is clear that central organization of movements is a major source of motor control, it is also very clear (see chapter 4) that sensory information can modify these commands in several important ways, as seen in the conceptual model in figure 5.2. Thus, the question becomes how and under what conditions these commands from motor programs interact with sensory information to define the overall movement pattern. This is one of the most important research issues for understanding motor control.

Reflex-Reversal Phenomenon

In addition to the various classes of reflex mechanisms discussed in chapter 4 that can modify the originally programmed output (figure 4.10), another class of reflexive modulations exists that has very different effects on the movement behavior. Several experiments show how reflex responses are integrated with open-loop programmed control.

In one study, for example, the experimenter applies a light tactile stimulus to the top of a cat's foot while it is walking on a treadmill. If this stimulus is applied as the cat is just *placing* its foot on the surface of the treadmill (in preparation for load bearing), the response is to extend the leg slightly, as if to carry more load on that foot. This response has a latency of about 30 to 50 ms and is clearly nonconscious and automatic. If exactly the same stimulus is applied when the cat is just *lifting* the foot from the surface (in preparation for the swing phase), the response is very different. The leg flexes upward at the hip and the knee so the foot travels above the usual trajectory in the swing phase. Thus, the same stimulus has different (reversed) effects when it is presented at different locations in the step cycle.

These alterations in the reflex—reversing its effect from extension to flexion (or vice versa) depending on where in the step cycle the stimulus is applied—has been called the **reflex-reversal phenomenon** (Forssberg, Grillner, & Rossignol, 1975). It challenges our usual conceptualizations of a reflex, which is typically defined as an automatic, stereotyped, unavoidable response to a given stimulus: Here the same stimulus has generated two different responses.

These variations in response must occur through interactions of sensory pathways and the ongoing movement program for locomotion (the CPG, discussed earlier). The CPG is responsible for many of the major events, such as muscle contractions and their timing, that occur in locomotion and other rhythmical activities. In addition, the CPGs are thought to be involved in the modulation of reflexes, enabling responses such as the reflex-reversal phenomenon. The logic is that the CPG determines whether and when certain reflex pathways can be activated in the action, as illustrated in figure 5.7a and b. During the part of the action when the cat's foot is being lifted from the ground (swing phase), the CPG inhibits the extension reflex and enables the flexion reflex (i.e., allows it to be activated, Figure 5.7a). If the stimulus occurs, it is routed to the flexion musculature, not to the extension musculature. When the foot is being placed on the walking surface, the CPG inhibits the flexion reflex and enables the extension reflex (Figure 5.7b). It does this all over again on the next step cycle.

Finally, notice that if no stimulus occurs at all, there is no reflex activity, and the CPG carries out the action "normally" without the contribution of either reflex.

Movement Flexibility

There is much more to be learned about these complex reflex responses, but they undoubtedly play an important role in the flexibility and control of skills. The cat's reflexes are probably organized to have an important survival role. Receiving a tactile stimulus on the top of the foot while it is swinging forward probably means that the foot has struck some object and that the cat will trip if the foot is not lifted quickly over the object. However, if the stimulus is received during the beginning of stance, flexing the leg would cause the animal to fall because it is swinging the opposite leg at this time. These can be thought of as temporary reflexes in that they exist only in the context of performing a particular part of a particular action, ensuring that the goal is achieved even if a disturbance is encountered. Analogous findings have been produced in speech, where slight, unexpected "tugs" on the lower lip during the production of a sound cause rapid, reflexive modulation, with the actual responses critically dependent on the particular sound being attempted (Abbs, Gracco, & Cole, 1984; Kelso et al., 1984). The critical goal for the motor system in such situations seems to be to ensure that the intended action

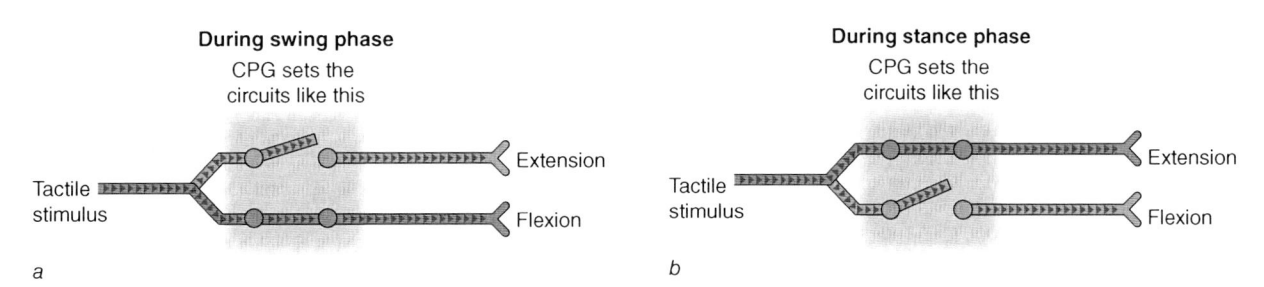

FIGURE 5.7 Role of CPGs in reflex reversals. In (a), the application of a tactile stimulus at the start of the swing phase of a CPG results in movement flexion; in (b), the application of the same tactile stimulus at the start of the stance phase of a CPG results in movement extension. The effect of the stimulus has been reversed.

is generated and that the environmental goal (in this case, the desired speech sound) is achieved.

This adaptable feature of a movement program provides considerable flexibility in its operation. The movement can be carried out as programmed if nothing goes wrong. If something does go wrong, then appropriate reflexes are allowed to participate in the movement to ensure that the goal is met.

Problems in Motor Program Theory: The Novelty and Storage Problems

Open-loop control occurs primarily to allow the motor system to organize an entire, usually rapid, action without having to rely on the relatively slow information processing involved in a closed-loop control mode. Several processes must be handled by this prior organization. At a minimum, the following must be specified in the programming process in order to generate skilled movements:

- The particular muscles that are to participate in the action
- The order in which these muscles are to be involved
- The forces of the muscle contractions
- The **relative timing** and sequencing among these contractions
- The duration of each contraction

Most theories of motor programs assume that a movement is organized in advance by the establishment of a neural mechanism, or network, that contains time and event information. A kind of movement "script" specifies certain essential details of the action as it runs off in time. Therefore, scientists speak of "running" a motor program, which is clearly analogous to the processes involved in running computer programs.

However, motor program theory, at least as developed so far in this chapter, does not account for several important aspects of movement behavior. Perhaps the most severe limitations of motor program theory are (1) the failure to account for how novel movements are produced in the first place, and (2) lack of the efficiency that would be required to store the massive number of motor programs that would be required in order to move.

This capability for producing novel actions raises problems for the simple motor program theory as we have developed it to this point in the chapter. On this view, a given movement is represented by a program stored in long-term memory. Therefore, each variation in a tennis stroke, for example, associated with variations in the height and speed of the ball, the position of the opponent, the distance to the net, and so on, would need a unique and separate program stored in memory because the instructions for the musculature would be different for each variation. Extending this view further suggests that we would need literally a countless number of motor programs stored in memory just in order to play tennis. Adding to this the number of movements possible in all other activities, the result would be an absurdly large number of programs stored in long-term memory. This leads to what has been called the **storage problem** (Schmidt, 1975), which concerns how all of these separate programs could be stored in memory.

There is also the **novelty problem**. For example, when I am playing tennis, no two strokes, strictly speaking, are the same. That is, every stroke requires a very slight difference in the amount of contraction of the participating muscles. In this sense, then, every stroke I hit is 'novel', implying that the system would need a separate program for every shot. If motor programs that are stored in memory are responsible for all such rapid movements, then how could something essentially novel be performed with elegance and skill without violating the storage problem mentioned earlier? The simple motor program theory, as presented here to this point, is at a loss to explain the performance of such novel actions.

To summarize, these observations raise two problems for understanding everyday movement behavior:

1. How (or where) do humans store the nearly countless number of motor programs needed for future use the storage problem?
2. How do performers produce truly novel behavior such as performing a variant of a tennis swing that you have never performed previously? The program for such an action cannot be represented in an already stored motor program: the novelty problem.

Many years ago the British psychologist Sir Fredrick Bartlett (1932), in writing about tennis, said this: "When I make the stroke, I do not . . . produce something absolutely new, and I never repeat something old" (p. 202). What did he mean? The first part of his statement means that, even though a movement is in some sense novel, it is never totally brand-new. Each of his ground strokes resembles his other ground strokes, possessing his own style of hitting a tennis ball. The second part of Bartlett's statement conveys the idea that every movement is novel in that it has never been performed *exactly* that way before.

The novelty and storage problems for motor program theory discussed in the previous section, and indeed, in explaining Bartlett's keen insight regarding the tennis stroke, motivated a search for alternative ways to understand motor control. There was a desire to keep the appealing parts of motor program theory, but to modify them to solve the storage and novelty problems. The idea that emerged was that movement programs can be *generalized* (Schmidt, 1975). This generalized motor program (GMP) consists of a stored pattern, as before. The generalized program stored in memory is thought to be modulated at the time of movement execution, allowing the action to be adjusted to meet the current environmental demands.

Generalized Motor Program Theory

The quote from Bartlett captures the essence of GMP theory: Some features of the tennis stroke remain the same from shot to shot, and some features of the stroke are changed each time. According to GMP theory, what remains the same reflects the **invariant features** of a motor program—those features that make the pattern appear the same, time after time. Invariant features are the reason our unique writing style appears the same regardless of whether we are using a pen to write in a notebook, a marker to write large enough on a whiteboard for everyone in a large class to read, or our toe to write something in the beach sand at Marina del Rey.

The aspect that allows changes from stroke to stroke (in Bartlett's quote) is represented in GMP theory as the relatively superficial, or **surface features** of the movement. If the pattern represents the invariant features of your writing style, then modifying what are called parameters determines how it is executed, representing its surface features. Writing something slow or fast, large or small, on paper or in the sand, and with a pen or a toe, represents how the GMP is executed at any one time. The word *parameter* comes from mathematics, and represents numerical values in an equation which do not change the *form* of the equation. For example, in a linear equation, whose general form is Y = a + bX, the values a and b are parameters—Y and X are related to each other in the same way for any values of a and b. The unique performance that occurs when certain parameters are changed does not alter the invariant characteristics of the GMP—the parameters change only how the GMP is *expressed* at any given time.

In GMP theory, movements are thought to be produced as follows. As determined via sensory information processed in the stimulus identification stage, a GMP for, say, throwing (as opposed to kicking) is chosen during the response selection stage. This GMP is then retrieved from long-term memory, much the same as you retrieve your friend's telephone number from memory. During the movement programming stage, the motor program is prepared for initiation, or **parameterized**.

One of the necessary processes here is to define *how* to execute this program. Which limb to use, how fast to throw, which direction to throw, and how far to throw must be decided based on the environmental information available just before action. These decisions result in the assignment (probably in the response selection stage) of movement parameters—characteristics that define the nature of the program's execution without influencing the invariant characteristics (that determine its form) of the GMP. Parameters include the speed of movement, its amplitude (overall size), and the limb used. Once the parameters have been selected and assigned to the program, the movement can be initiated and carried out with this particular set of surface features.

According to GMP theory, the key variables to consider are what constitute the invariant features of the GMP and what the parameters, or surface features, are. These important issues are discussed in the next sections.

Invariant Features of a GMP

To begin to discover the nature of GMP representations, we need to know what features of the flexible movement patterns remain invariant, or constant, as the more surface features (such as movement speed, movement amplitude, and forces) are altered. When movement time is altered, for example, almost every other aspect of the movement changes too: The forces and durations of contractions, the speed of the limbs, and the distances the limbs travel all can change markedly as the movement speeds up.

Generalized motor program theory suggests that the motor program for signing your name retains its invariant features, no matter what you are writing on.

However, what if some aspects of these movements could be shown to remain constant even though just about everything else was changing? If such a value could be found, scientists argued, it might indicate something fundamental about the structure of the GMP that serves as a basis for all of these movements, thus providing evidence for how motor programs are organized or represented in long-term memory. Such a constant value is termed an *invariance*, and the most important invariance concerns the temporal structuring of the pattern (or the pattern's "rhythm").

Relative Timing

Rhythm, or relative timing, is a fundamental feature of many of our daily activities. Of course, rhythm is critically important in such activities as music and dance. But timing is also a key feature of many sporting activities (such as the golf swing) and work activities (e.g., typing, hammering). There is strong evidence to suggest that relative time is an invariant feature of the GMP. An example is the evidence provided in the Armstrong (1970) study, discussed in Focus on Research 5.3.

The graph in figure 5.8 shows a sample trial in which one of Armstrong's (1970) subjects produced a pattern from memory that was made too quickly (red trace, overall time about 3.2 s rather than the goal movement [blue trace], to be done in about 4.0 s). But compare the red movement pattern with the blue goal pattern in this figure—you will notice that the *whole movement* appeared to speed up as a unit. That is, each of the peaks (movement reversals) occurred sooner and sooner in real time, but occurred at about the same time relative to the overall time of the pattern; hence the term *relative time* is used to refer to the constant occurrence of these peaks (see Gentner, 1987, or Schmidt & Lee, 2011, for more on these issues).

Relative timing is the fundamental temporal structure of a movement pattern that is independent of its overall speed or amplitude. Relative timing represents the movement's fundamental "deep structure," as opposed to the "surface" features seen in the easily modified alterations in movement

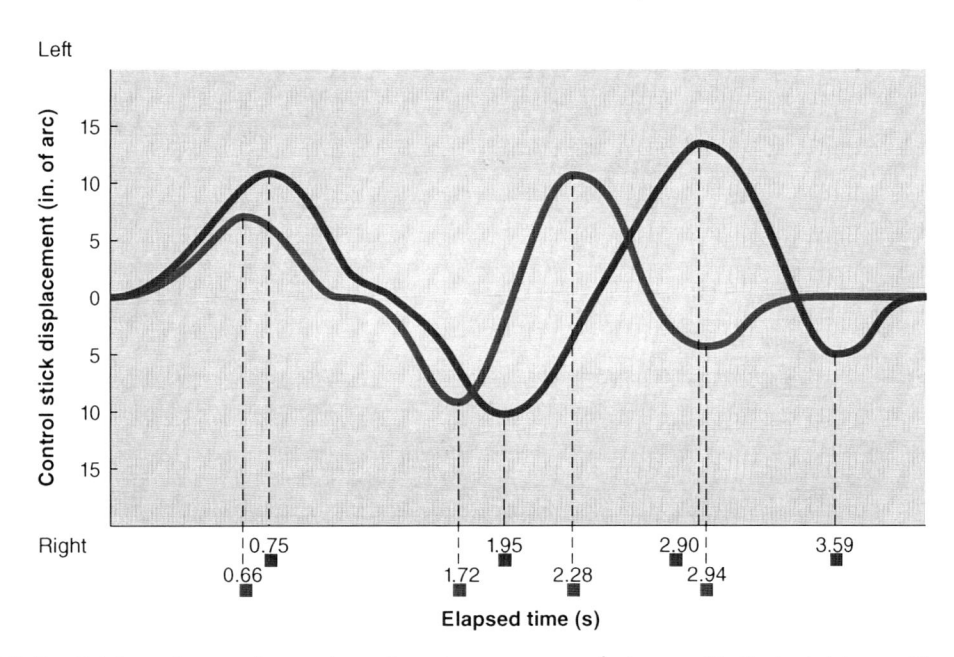

FIGURE 5.8 Subjects learned to make a timed movement of a lever with their right arm. The goal movement pattern is depicted by the blue line. The trace in red represents a trial in which the entire movement is made too rapidly; the error in the timing of the reversals increases as the movement unfolds, which is what would happen if the red trace were simply a speeded-up version of the blue trace.

Adapted by permission from Armstrong 1970.

time. This deep temporal organization in movements seems to be invariant, even when the actions are produced at different speeds or amplitudes.

More specifically, relative timing refers to the set of ratios of the durations of several intervals within the movement, as illustrated in figure 5.9. Consider two hypothetical throwing movements, with movement 1 being performed with a shorter movement time than movement 2. Imagine that you measure and record the EMGs from three of the important muscles involved in each action (in principle, nearly any feature of the movement could be measured). If you measure several of these contraction durations, you can define relative timing by a set of ratios, each of which is the duration of a part of the action divided by the total duration. For example, in movement 1, the ratios b/a = .40, c/a = .30, and d/a = .60 can be calculated from the figure. This pattern of ratios is characteristic of this throwing movement, describing its temporal structure relatively accurately.

This set of ratios (the relative timing) stays the same for movement 2 (even though the duration of movement 2 is longer), because the values of b/a, c/a, and d/a are the same as in movement 1. When this set of ratios is constant in two different movements, we say that the relative timing was invariant. Notice that movement 2 seems to be simply an elongated (horizontally "stretched") version of movement 1, with all of the temporal events

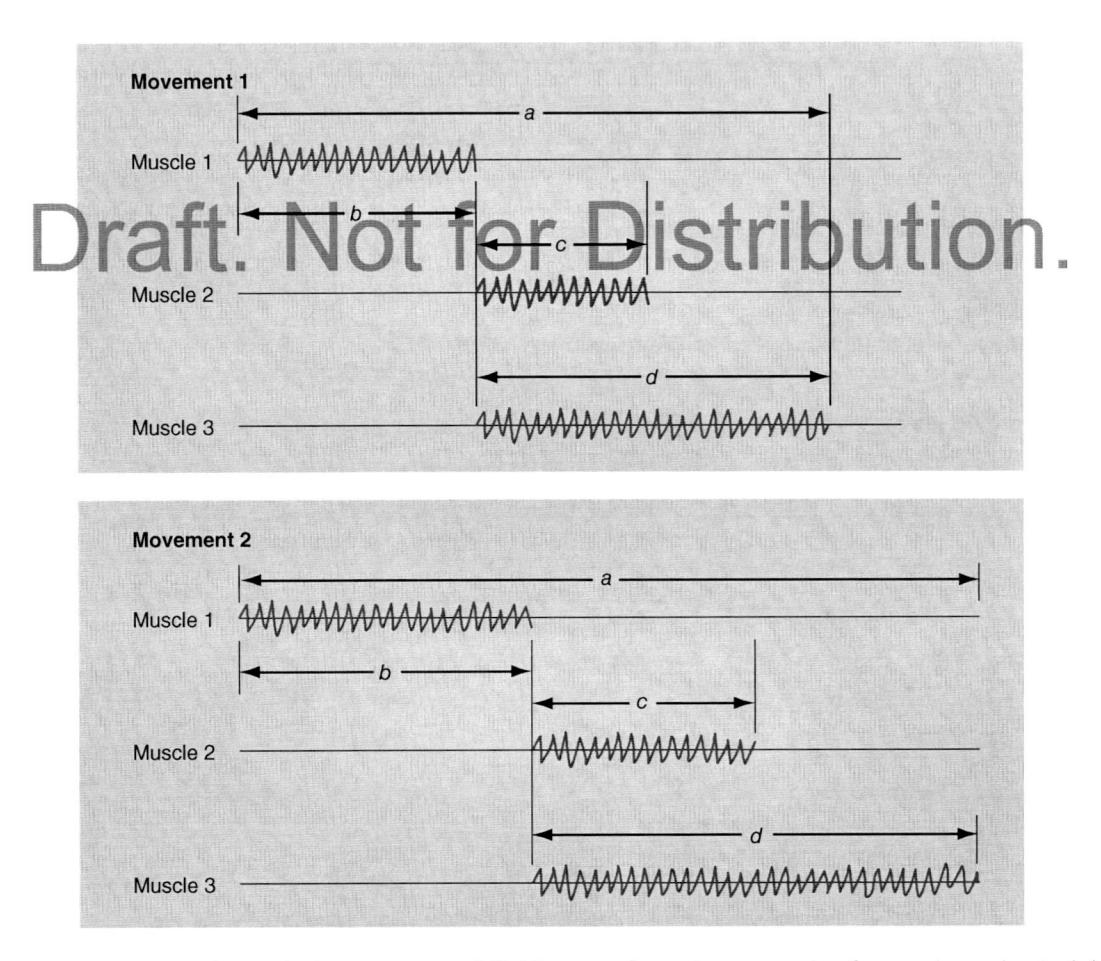

FIGURE 5.9 Hypothetical relative timing of EMG traces from three muscles for two hypothetical throwing movements. The relative-time ratios are computed by dividing the muscle EMG durations (i.e., b, c, and d) for each muscle (i.e., 1, 2, and 3) by the overall movement time (i.e., a).

Reprinted by permission from Schmidt and Lee 2011.

Focus on RESEARCH 5.3

Invariances and Parameters

An important contribution to the development of the GMP theory was made by Armstrong (1970) in analyzing the patterns of movements that subjects made in one of his experiments. In Armstrong's experiment, learners attempted to move a lever (figure 5.8) from side to side in such a way that a pattern of movement at the elbow joint (defined in space and time) occurred, as depicted by the blue line in figure 5.8. This goal movement (blue line) had four major reversals in direction, each of which was to be produced at a particular time in the action, with the total movement occupying about 4 s.

Armstrong noticed that when the learner made the first reversal movement too quickly (red trace), the *whole* movement was also done too quickly. Notice that the red line's first peak (at reversal) was just a little early (at .66 rather than at .75). The discrepancy between the actual and goal reversal times increased roughly proportionally as the movement progressed (1.72 vs. 1.95; 2.28 vs. 2.90; and 2.94 vs. 3.59). This gives the impression that every aspect of the movement pattern was produced essentially correctly but that the entire pattern was simply run off too quickly.

Armstrong's findings provided an early impetus to the development of the idea that the motor program can be generalized (Schmidt, 1975). Here, the program controlled the relative timing of the movement reversals. When an early reversal appeared sooner or later than the goal time, then all of the subsequent reversals sped up or slowed proportionally.

Exploring Further

1. In Armstrong's figure (figure 5.8), sketch a graph of how you predict an action with a 4.5 s overall movement time would look if the subject had preserved the same relative-timing structure.
2. Suppose Armstrong's subjects had performed the pattern again, one month after the original sessions of practice. Which do you think would be remembered better, the overall timing or the relative-time structure of the pattern? Give reasons for your answer.

---

occurring systematically more slowly. This will always be found when relative timing is invariant. According to the GMP theory, movement 2 was produced with a slower timing parameter than movement 1, so the whole movement was slowed down as a unit but its relative timing was preserved.

One of the important principles of movement control is that, when a brief, rapid movement is changed in terms of the speed of the action (a fast vs. a slow throw), the size of the action (making your signature large or small), or the trajectory of the action (throwing overarm vs. sidearm), these alterations seem to be made with an invariant relative timing. Relative timing is invariant across several different kinds of "surface" modifications, so the form of the movement is preserved even though the superficial features of it may change. There is some controversy about whether relative timing is perfectly invariant (Gentner, 1987; Heuer, 1988), but there can be no doubt that relative timing is at least approximately invariant.

Classes of Movements

You can think of an activity like throwing as a class consisting of a nearly infinite number of particular movements (e.g., throwing overarm, throwing rapidly). The theory holds that the entire class is represented by a single GMP, with a specific, rigidly defined relative-timing structure. This program can have parameters in several dimensions (e.g., movement time, amplitude), making possible an essentially limitless number of combinations of specific throwing movements, each of which contains the same relative timing.

Locomotion represents another class of movements that could be considered to be controlled by a GMP. However, the research by Shapiro and colleagues suggests that, in fact, there are at least two separate GMPs for gait, each with unique relative timings—one for walking and another for running. Note, however, that we can speed up and slow down either the walking or running gait selectively without having to abandon the GMP (see Focus on Research 5.4).

Focus on RESEARCH 5.4

Relative Timing in Locomotion

Shapiro and collaborators (1981) studied the shifts in relative timing in locomotion. They filmed people on a treadmill at speeds ranging from 3 to 12 kph and measured the durations of various phases of the step cycle as the movement speed increased. The step cycle can be separated into four parts, as shown in figure 5.10 a. For the right leg, the interval between the heel strike at the left until the leg has finished yielding (flexing) under the body's load is termed extension phase 2 (or E2), and the interval from maximum flexion until toe-off is E3; together, E2 and E3 make up the stance phase. The interval from toe-off until maximum knee flexion is termed the flexion phase (F), and the interval from maximum flexion to heel strike is E1; together F and E1 make up the swing phase.

The locomotion data shown in Figure 5.10b are expressed as the proportions of the step cycle occupied by each of the four phases; the duration of each phase is divided by the total step-cycle time. When the treadmill speed ranged from 3 to 6 kph, all subjects walked, each with a particular pattern of relative timing. About half of the step cycle was occupied by E3; about 10% of it was occupied by F and E2 each, with about 28% occupied by E1. Notice that as speed increased from 3 to 6 kph, there was almost no shift in the relative timing for any of the parts of the step cycle. When the speed was increased to 8 kph, however, where now all subjects were running, we see that the relative-timing pattern was completely different. Now E1 had the largest percentage of the step cycle (32%), and E2 had the smallest (15%). E3, which had the largest proportion of the step cycle in walking, was now intermediate, at about 28%. But notice that as the running speed increased from 8 to 12 kph, there again was a tendency for these proportions to remain nearly invariant.

The interpretation is that there are two GMPs operating here—one for walking and one for running. Each has its own pattern of relative timing and is quite different from the other. When the treadmill speed increases for walking, the parameter values are changed, which speeds up the movement with the same program while maintaining the relative timing. At about 7 kph, a critical speed is reached, and the subject abruptly shifts to a running program; the relative timing of this activity is maintained nearly perfectly as running speed is increased further.

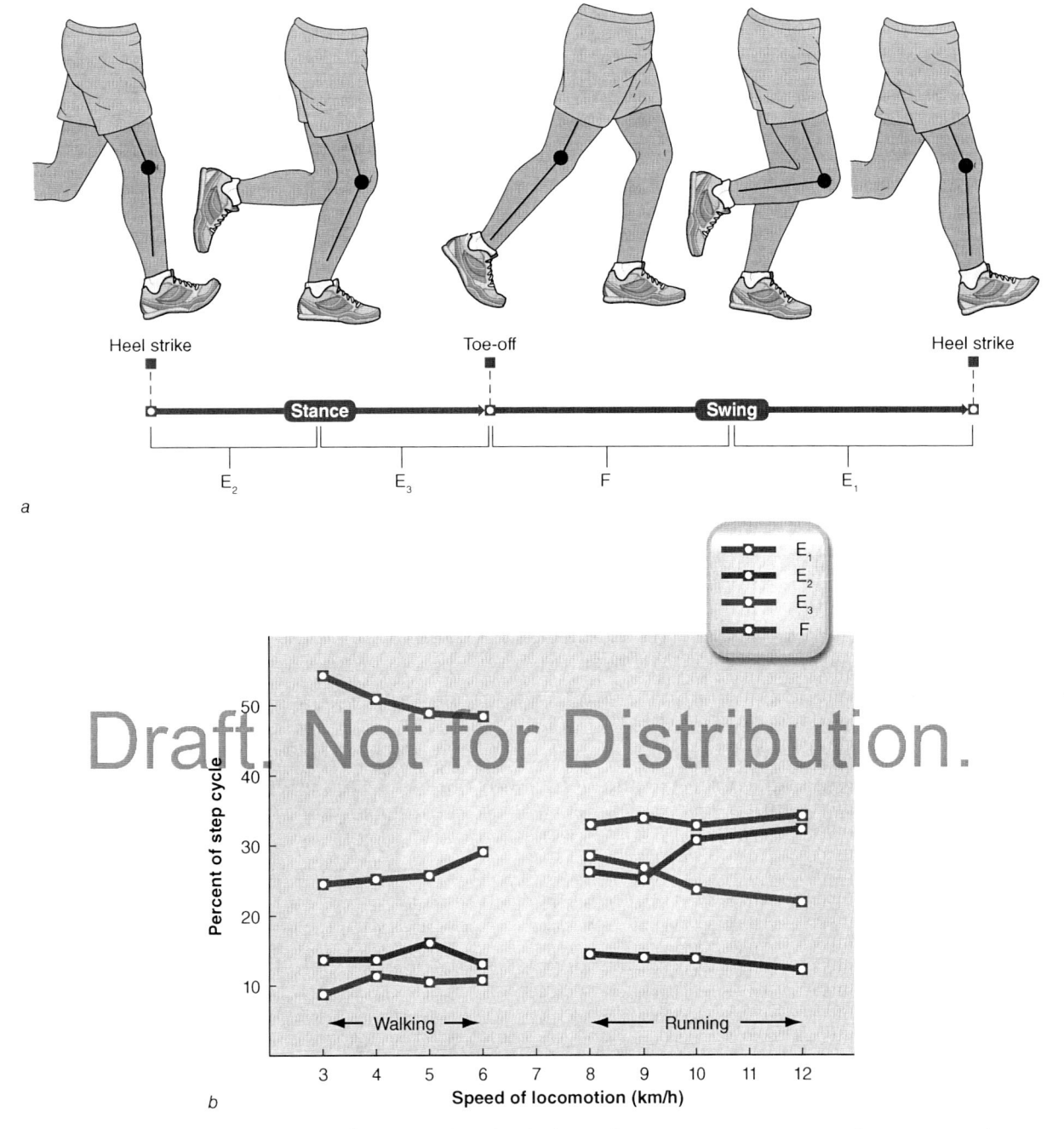

FIGURE 5.10 One cycle of gait can be divided into four parts, representing the swing and stance portions (a). These four parts of the step cycle occupy relatively consistent relative timing within walking and running speeds, but change between gaits (b).

Reprinted by permission from Shapiro et al. 1981.

Exploring Further

1. Suppose that Shapiro and colleagues had found that a single GMP controlled *both* the walking and running gaits. How would the graph in figure 5.10*b* have appeared if the findings had supported this alternative hypothetical result?
2. Another gait that humans sometimes use is skipping. Given the findings of Shapiro and colleagues, how would the various parts of the step cycle appear during skipping slowly versus quickly?

Note that the relative timing actually produced by a performer can be thought of as a kind of *fingerprint* unique to a particular movement class. This pattern can be used to identify which of several motor programs has been executed (Schneider & Schmidt, 1995; Young & Schmidt, 1990). Focus on Application 5.2 provides more examples of how our GMPs reflect other kinds of biological "fingerprints."

Focus on APPLICATION 5.2

Relative-Timing Fingerprints

Identity fraud has represented a major threat to security for years. Forging someone's signature on a check and hacking into an account with someone's password are just two methods used by fraudsters to get illegal access to wealth and information. However, the invariant features of one's GMP provide an important tool to combat the problem.

A person's signature is usually considered unique and different from anyone else's signature. Forging the spatial characteristics of a signature is not a very difficult task. All the forger needs to do is obtain the target signature, compare the illegal and legal signatures, and continue to practice by making improvements on the imperfections until a realistic forgery is very difficult to distinguish from the original. A password that is typed into an account on a computer is even easier to forge if the fraudster knows the characters to enter. All that is needed is to enter the correct sequence, and access is granted. However, relative timing is the missing ingredient in both cases of fraudulent information.

Suppose, for example, that when you signed your name, the spatial *and* temporal recordings of each of the various loops and cursives in producing the letters, as well as the timing of your "t" crossings and "i" dottings and so on, were compared to a data bank in which a large number of your previous signatures had been stored. According to GMP theory, the invariant characteristics of your signature would be repeated regardless of the tool you used to sign your name (e.g., familiar or unfamiliar pen), the surface on which you wrote it (e.g., paper or digital tablet), or the size of the writing. Moreover, the fraudster who had access only to the spatial characteristics of your signature would be completely at a loss to replicate its relative timing.

Typing your password also has a relative-timing characteristic that is uniquely yours, especially for those such as the authors of this book who are not trained typists. We each have our own unique style of typing—which letters are typically contacted with which fingers, how long each key is held down (dwell time), and the transition times that usually occur between particular letters. Once again, a data bank of previous executions of our passwords would give rise to a range of overall timings of these dwell and transition times, from which a relative-timing "profile" could be derived and to which the fraudster would not have access.

Fortunately for us, these methods of using digital knowledge of our GMPs are now a reality. A Google search of terms such as "keystroke dynamics" reveals a large number of articles about the theory and technology underlying this security advance, as well as information about a growing number of security firms that are developing the industry. In many ways you can think of your signature and passwords as relative-timing "fingerprints" that are unique to you.

Motor Programs

Parameters Added to the GMP

In the previous section we discussed some of the features of movement that remain the same from one time to the next—the invariant features of the GMP. According to the theory, surface features need to be specified each time a movement is performed. That is, the GMP needs to be parameterized before it can be executed. What are some of these parameters?

Movement Time

Both the Armstrong study (Focus on Research 5.3) and the study by Shapiro and collaborators (Focus on Research 5.4) provided strong evidence that overall movement time could be varied without affecting the relative timing of the GMP. In Armstrong's study, the subject who accidentally sped up the movement pattern still retained that same timing of reversals in the movement. And the subjects in the

The relative timing of a person's motor program for typing a name or password has the potential to serve as verification of identity

study by Shapiro and colleagues could vary speeds of walking and running without disrupting the relative timing of the step cycle. This also agrees with the common experience that we seem to have no trouble speeding up and slowing down a given movement, such as throwing a ball at various speeds, or writing more slowly or more quickly. These findings indicate that, when movement time is changed, the new movement preserves the essential temporal-pattern features of the old movement. Therefore, both movements are represented by a common underlying temporal (and sequential) pattern that can be run off at different speeds. Therefore, overall movement time is a parameter of the GMP.

Movement Amplitude

The amplitude of movements can also be modulated easily in a way that is much like varying the time. For example, you can write your signature either on a check or five times larger on a blackboard, and in each case the signature is clearly "yours" (Lashley, 1942; Merton, 1972). Making this size change seems almost trivially easy.

The handwriting phenomenon was studied more formally by Hollerbach (1978), who had subjects write the word "hell" in different sizes. He measured the accelerations of the pen (or, alternatively, the forces delivered to the pen) during the production of the words. These accelerations are graphed in figure 5.11. When the trace moves upward, this indicates acceleration (force) away from the body; a downward trace indicates acceleration toward the body. Of course, when the word is written larger, the overall magnitude of the accelerations produced must be larger, seen as the uniformly larger amplitudes for the larger word. But what is of most interest is that the temporal patterns of acceleration over time are almost identical for the two words, with the accelerations having similar modulations in upward and downward fluctuations.

This leads to an observation similar to the one just made about movement time. It is easy to increase the amplitude of the movements by uniformly increasing the accelerations (forces) that are applied, while preserving their temporal patterning. Therefore, the same word is written with different ampli-

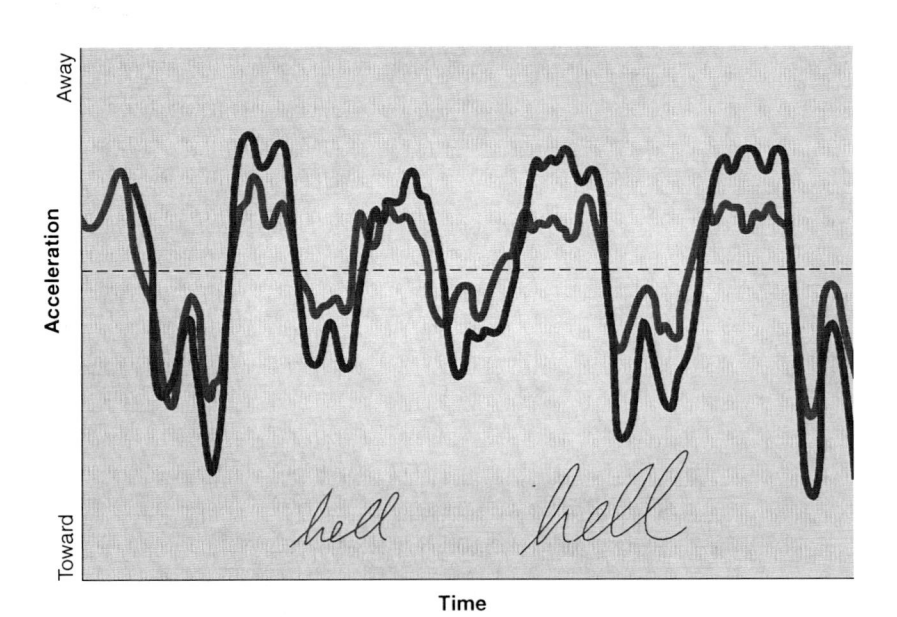

FIGURE 5.11 Acceleration-time tracings of two instances of writing the word "hell," once in small script (red) and again in larger script (blue). Although the amplitudes (which are proportional to the forces exerted on the pen) for the two traces are markedly different, the temporal organization of the patterning remains nearly the same in the two instances.

Adapted by permission from Hollerbach 1978.

Motor Programs

tudes can be based on a common underlying structure that can be run off with different forces to produce movements of different sizes. Therefore, overall amplitude of force is a parameter of the GMP.

Effectors

A performer can also modulate a movement by using a different limb – and, hence, different muscles – to produce the action. In the signature example, writing on a blackboard involves very different muscles and joints than writing on a check. In blackboard writing, the fingers are mainly fixed, and the writing is done with the muscles controlling the elbow and the shoulder. In check writing the elbow and the shoulder are mainly fixed, and the writing is done with the muscles controlling the fingers. Yet the writing patterns produced are essentially the same. This indicates that a given pattern can be produced even when the effectors – and the muscles that drive them – are different.

These phenomena were studied by Raibert (1977), who wrote the sentence "Able was I ere I saw Elba" (a palindrome, spelled the same way backward as forward) with different muscles. In figure 5.12, line A shows his writing with the right (dominant) hand, line B with the right arm with the wrist immobilized, and line C with the left hand. These patterns are very similar. Even more remarkable is that line D was written with the pen gripped in the teeth, and line E used the pen taped to the foot! There are obvious similarities among the writing styles, and it seems clear that the same person wrote each of them, yet the effector system was completely different for each.

This all indicates that changing the limb and effector system can preserve the essential features of the movement pattern relatively easily. There is some underlying temporal structure common to these actions, which can be run off with different effector systems while using the same GMP.

Summary of GMP Concepts

Some of these elements of the theory of GMPs can be summarized as follows:

- A GMP underlies a class of movements and is structured in memory with a rigidly defined temporal organization.
- This structure is characterized by its relative timing, which can be measured

a Able was I ere I saw Elba

b Able was I ere I saw Elba

c Able was I ere I saw Elba

d Able was I ere I saw Elba

e Able was I ere I saw Elba

FIGURE 5.12 Five samples of writing a palindrome by the same subject, using (A) the dominant hand, (B) the dominant hand with the wrist immobilized, (C) the nondominant hand, (D) with pen gripped by the teeth, and (E) with the pen taped between toes of the foot.

Reprinted by permission from Raibert 1977.

Focus on
APPLICATION 5.3

The Stereo System Analogy

A good analogy for GMPs involves the standard phonograph/stereo system, in which a turntable sends signals from a record into an amplifier, whose output is delivered to speakers. In this analogy, illustrated in the top portion of figure 5.13, the phonograph record itself is the GMP, and the speakers are the muscles and limbs. (Does anyone remember what a record is?) The record has all of the features of programs, such as information about the order of events (the guitar comes before the harmonica), the temporal structure among the events (i.e., the rhythm, or relative timing), and the relative amplitudes of the sounds (the first drumbeat is twice as loud as the second). This information is stored on the record, just as GMP theory says that the analogous information is stored in the program. Also, there are many different records to choose from, just as humans have many motor programs to choose from (e.g., throwing, jumping), each stored with different kinds of information.

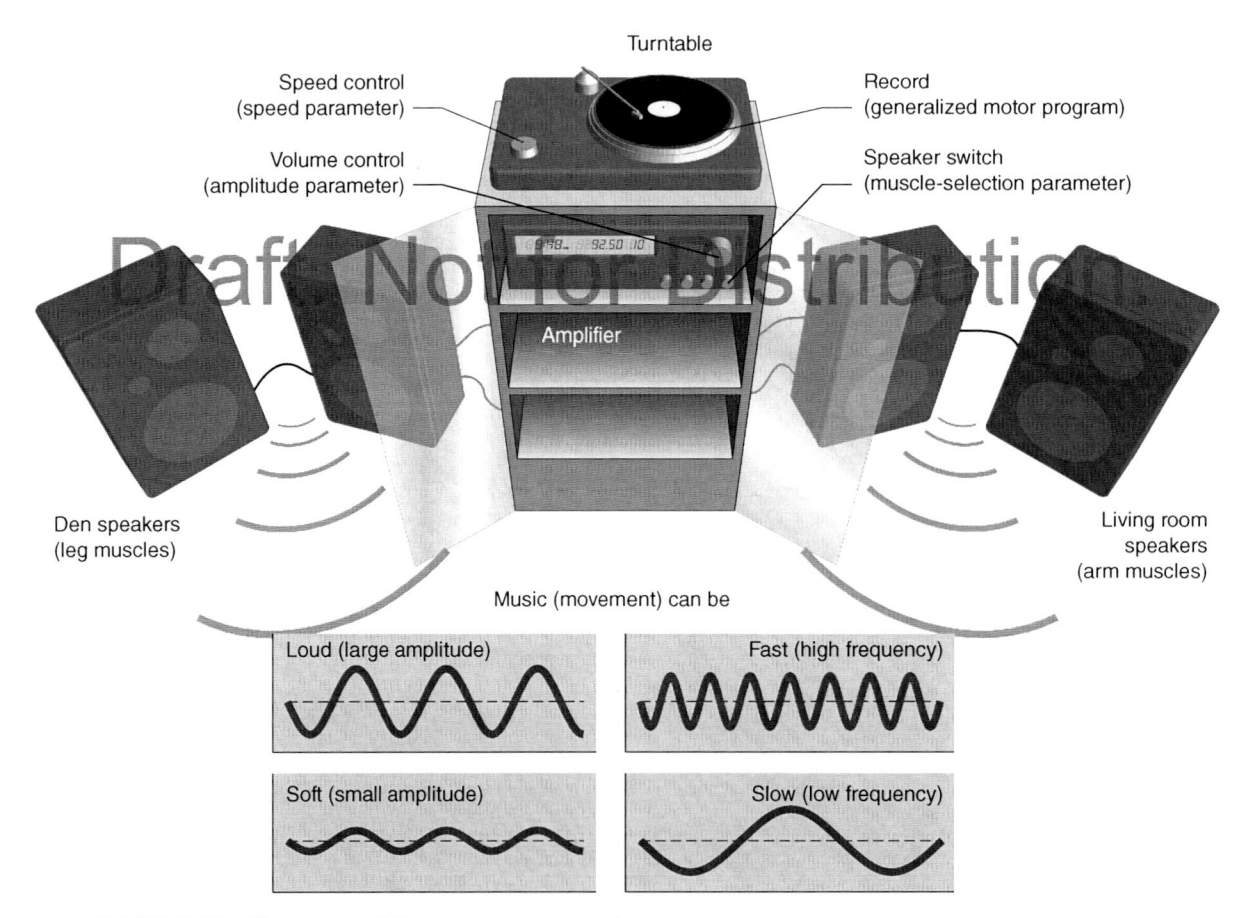

FIGURE 5.13 Illustration of the stereo system analogy.

Notice, though, that the record's output is not fixed (lower portion of figure 5.13): The speed of output can be changed if the speed of the turntable is increased. Yet relative timing (rhythm) is preserved even though the speed of the music is increased. You can change the amplitude of the output by raising the volume uniformly; this increases the amplitudes of all the features of the sounds. Also, you have a choice of which effectors to use: You can switch the output from a set of speakers in the den to a second set of speakers in the living room; this is analogous to hammering either with the left hand or with the right, or with a different hammer, still using the same pattern. Perhaps if you think of the theory of GMPs in concrete terms like a stereo system, you can understand most of the important features of the theory more easily. For example, when subjects in the study by Shapiro and colleagues switched from walking to running (Focus on Research 5.4), they first had to remove the walking "record" and replace it with a running "record." Then they had to parameterize it, like setting the volume, speed, and speaker controls. This analogy of the GMP and its parameters to the characteristics of a stereo system sometimes helps people to understand the basic idea.

---

by a set of ratios among the durations of various events in the movement.

- Variations in movement time, movement amplitude, and the limb used represent the movement's surface structure, achieved by executing the action with different parameters, whereas relative timing represents its deep, fundamental structure.
- Even though a movement may be carried out with different surface features (e.g., duration, amplitude), the relative timing remains invariant.
- Whereas surface features are very easy to alter by parameter adjustment, the deeper relative-timing structure is very difficult to alter.

A particularly good way to understand the invariant features of a GMP with certain added parameters is to consider movement as you would the various components of a stereo system (see Focus on Application 5.3).

We started this section on GMPs by expressing dissatisfaction with the simple motor program views as developed earlier in the chapter. Two issues were considered to be especially problematic: the storage problem and the novelty problem. The GMP theory provides solutions to both of these problems. For the storage problem, the theory holds that an infinite number of movements can be produced by a single GMP, so only one program needs to be stored for each class of movement rather than an infinite number. And for the novelty problem, the theory suggests that a second memory representation, a *schema*, is the theoretical structure responsible for supplying parameters needed at the time of movement execution. Note that, by using a parameter not used before, the person can produce a novel action. Much more will be said about schema development in later chapters. But, for now, think of the schema as a mechanism responsible for selecting the parameters for the chosen GMP.

Summary

In very brief actions, there is no time for the system to process feedback about errors and to correct them. The mechanism that controls this type of behavior is open loop, called the "motor program." This chapter is about motor programming activities. Considerable evidence supports the motor program idea: (a) Reaction time is longer for more complex movements; (b) complex movements can be elicited in their complete form by certain stimuli; (c) animals deprived of feedback information by deafferentation are capable of strong, relatively effective movements; (d) some cyclical movements in animals are controlled by inherited central pattern generators; and (e) a limb's electrical muscle activity patterns are unaffected for 100 to 120 ms when the limb is blocked by a mechanical perturbation.

Even though the motor program is responsible for the major events in the movement pattern, there is considerable interaction with sensory processes, such as the organization of various reflex processes to generate rapid corrections, making the movement flexible in the face of changing environmental demands. Finally, motor programs are thought to be generalized to account for a *class* of actions (such as throwing), and parameters must be supplied to define the way in which the pattern is to be executed (such as throwing either rapidly or slowly).

WEB STUDY GUIDE ACTIVITIES

The student web study guide, available at www.HumanKinetics.com/MotorLearningandPerformance, offers these activities to help you build and apply your knowledge of the concepts in this chapter.

Interactive Learning

Activity 5.1: Indicate whether each in a list of statements applies to simple motor program theory or general motor program theory.

Activity 5.2: Determine whether motor skills are controlled by open-loop or closed-loop processes, or a combination of both.

Activity 5.3: Review the conceptual model of motor control by identifying which elements are associated with open-loop processes and which are associated with closed-loop processes.

Situation-Based Exercise

Activity 5.4: The situation-based exercise for this chapter prompts you to choose a skill and identify components of the movement that a person would control using open-loop and closed-loop processing as well as situations in which both types of control would be important.

Check Your Understanding

1. Name the two distinct parts of an open-loop control system. How does an open-loop control system differ from a closed-loop control system? Describe how each part of an open-loop control system might function for a child tossing toy blocks into a bin.

2. Research evidence for the existence of motor program control comes from diverse research areas. List the four types of research evidence and discuss how two of these areas provide evidence for movements being planned in advance.

3. Though there were appealing parts of motor program theory, a desire to modify motor program theory to solve the storage and novelty problems arose. What idea emerged from this desire? How does it help to explain novel movements? How does it deal with the storage problem?

Apply Your Knowledge

1. A student is packing her lunch for school. List three movements (or components of movements) involved in packing a lunch that would be controlled using open-loop processes and three that would be controlled using closed-loop processes. Choose one of the open-loop controlled movements

and describe a parameter of the generalized motor program that the student could modify.
2. A woodworker is building a piece of furniture that includes large, small, simple, and complex pieces. Describe two GMPs that may be used in building the furniture, and discuss two parameters that the woodworker might need to modify throughout the project for each GMP.

Suggestions for Further Reading

Keele (1968) has provided a historical review of the motor program concept. Selverston (2010) reviews CPGs in invertebrate models. The effects of response complexity on RT are reviewed by Christina (1992). More on the startle RT paradigm can be found in Carlsen et al. (2011). Schmidt introduces the concept of GMPs (1975) and later provided reviews of the evidence for them (1985). A more thorough treatment of all of the issues discussed in this chapter can be found in chapter 6 of Schmidt and Lee (2011). See the reference list for these additional resources.

Draft. Not for Distribution.

6

Principles of Speed, Accuracy, and Coordination

Controlling and Timing Movements

KEY TERMS

amplitude
anti-phase
effective target width (W_e)
Fitts' Law
index of difficulty
in-phase
self-organization
speed–accuracy trade-off
width

CHAPTER OUTLINE

Speed–Accuracy Trade-Offs
Sources of Error in Rapid Movements
Exceptions to the Speed–Accuracy Trade-Off
Analyzing a Rapid Movement: Baseball Batting
Accuracy in Coordinated Actions
Summary

CHAPTER OBJECTIVES

Chapter 6 describes various principles and laws of simple and coordinated actions. This chapter will help you to understand

- the speed–accuracy trade-off in simple aiming movements,
- logarithmic and linear relationships between speed and accuracy,
- the relationship between timing accuracy and movement time, and
- principles of bimanual timing and the role of self-organizing principles.

The construction worker is pounding nails into the shingles of a new roof when she notices a storm approaching. She quickens her pace, but in so doing, she notices that her aims are missing the nail more and more often—something that occurs rarely when she is working at her normal pace. Why is this happening? How does working at a faster pace and swinging her hammer with more force contribute to more frequent misses?

This chapter addresses questions such as these about movement control. Some of the most fundamental principles of movement production—analogous to the simple laws of physics—are shown to govern the relationship between movement speed, distance, and accuracy. Along the way, we reveal some of the underlying causes of errors in movements and discuss ways to minimize these errors. These laws of movement production are considered first as they apply in the control of relatively simple movements; later in the chapter we discuss some of the ideas related to more complex, coordinated actions.

The first several sections of this chapter deal with the laws or principles of simple movements, describing fundamental relationships such as how the time required for a movement changes as the distance to be moved increases, and how accuracy is affected by movement speed. These basic principles form the foundation of much knowledge about movements. One of the most fundamental principles concerns the relationships among the speed of a movement, its amplitude, and the resulting accuracy.

Speed–Accuracy Trade-Offs

Everybody knows that when you do things too quickly, you tend to do them with less accuracy or effectiveness. The old English saying "Haste makes waste" is evidence that this idea has been prevalent for many centuries. Woodworth (1899) studied these phenomena early in the history of motor skills research, showing that the accuracy of line-drawing movements decreased as their length and speed were increased. A major contribution to our understanding of this problem was provided in 1954 by the psychologist Paul Fitts, who described for the first time a mathematical principle of speed and accuracy that has come to be known as Fitts' Law.

Fitts' Law

Fitts used a paradigm in which the subject tapped alternately between two target plates as quickly as possible. The separation between the targets (A, or movement **amplitude**) and the width of the targets (W, or target **width**) could be varied in different combinations (see figure 6.1). The movement time (MT) taken to complete these rapid taps increased systematically with either increases in the movement amplitude (due to a larger distance between the targets) or decreases in the target width (due to a smaller target-landing area). These relationships were combined into a formal mathematical statement that is now known as Fitts' Law (see Focus on Research 6.1).

Fitts' Law states that MT is constant whenever the ratio of the movement amplitude (A) to target width (W) remains constant. So, very long movements to wide targets require about the same time as very short movements to narrow targets. In addition, Fitts found that the MT increased as the ratio of A to W increased by either making A larger, making W smaller, or both. He combined these various effects into a single equation:

$$MT = a + b\,[\mathrm{Log}_2(2A/W)]$$

where a and b are constants (the y-intercept and slope, respectively) and A and W are defined as before. The relationships between A, W, and MT are plotted in figure 6.2 for one of Fitts' data sets. The term $\mathrm{Log}_2(2A/W)$ is referred to as the **index of difficulty** (abbreviated ID), which seems to define the "difficulty" of the various combinations of A and W. Therefore, Fitts' Law says that MT is linearly related to the $\mathrm{Log}_2(2A/W)$, or that MT

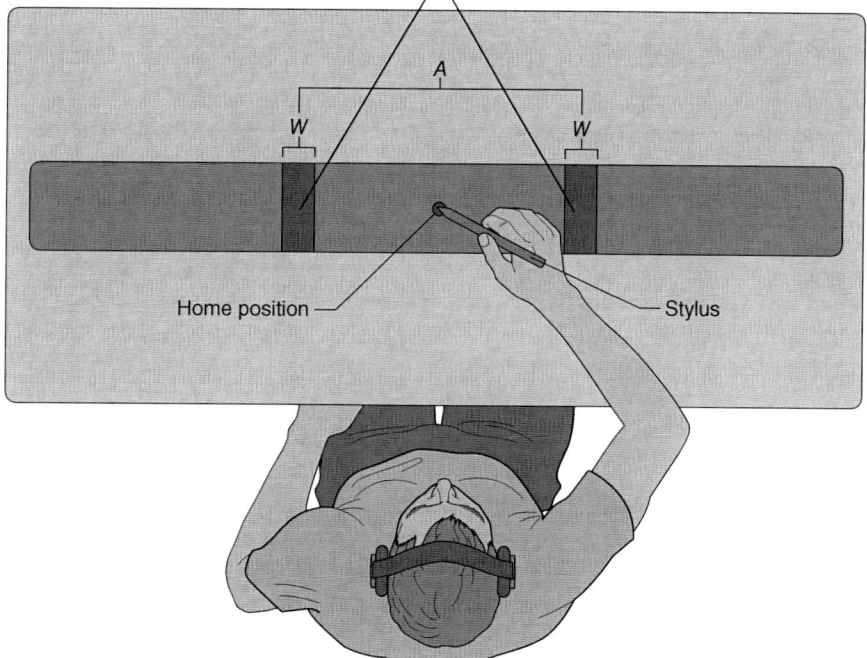

FIGURE 6.1 Illustration of a subject performing a Fitts tapping task. The subject taps between two targets of varying width (W) and with varying amplitude between them (A), attempting to move as rapidly as possible while minimizing the number of target misses.

Adapted from Fitts 1954.

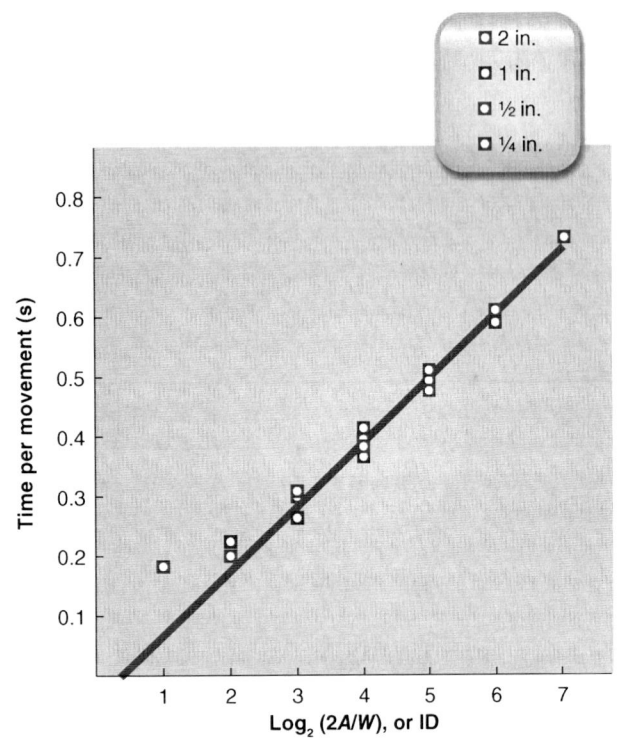

FIGURE 6.2 Variations in the target widths and amplitudes of single movements of a stylus to a target result in different indexes of difficulty (IDs). When plotted against MT, they result in a linear relationship that has come to be known as Fitts' Law.

Reprinted by permission from Schmidt and Lee 2011; Data from Fitts 1954.

is linearly related to the index of movement difficulty (ID).

An important point is that Fitts' Law describes the tendency for performers to trade speed for accuracy. In what has now become the "typical" Fitts tapping task, subjects are instructed explicitly to minimize the number of target misses. In other words, they are instructed to adjust movement time so that the errors are acceptably small. Thus, when the target size is increased, the accuracy requirements are relaxed and MTs are smaller than when narrow targets are used. This has led to the general notion of a **speed–accuracy trade-off**—the tendency for people to "give up" speed in order to trade speed off for acceptable levels of accuracy—as one of the most fundamental principles of movement behavior.

Fitts' Law, which describes MT as a function of the movement distance and the accuracy requirements of a task, has been found to hold under many different conditions (tapping underwater as well as in outer space), for many different classifications of people (children, older adults, individuals with neurological impairments), and for movements made by different body parts (hand-held, foot-held, and even head-mounted pointing devices) (see Schmidt & Lee, 2011; Plamondon & Alimi, 1997). Fitts' Law also applies in many tasks of everyday living (see Focus on Application 6.1).

The movements studied with the Fitts tapping task are almost certainly blends of programmed actions with feedback added near the end. That is, the performer generates a programmed initial segment of the action toward the target, processes feedback about the accuracy of this action during the movement, and initiates one (or sometimes more) feedback-based corrections to guide the limb to the target area (Keele, 1968). As discussed in chapter 4, such visual compensations are probably processed through the dorsal visual stream and might not be controlled consciously. Thus, Fitts' Law describes the effectiveness of the combined open- and closed-loop processes that operate in these common kinds of actions, where potentially all of the open- and closed-loop processes shown in the conceptual model in figure 4.10 are operating together.

Finally, it is reasonable to suspect that slower movements are more accurate, at least in part, because there is more time to detect errors and to make corrections (as discussed in chapter 4), and that movement time lengthens when the number of corrections to be made increases. In this way, the main reason MT increases with narrow target widths is that each correction takes a finite amount of time, and the times for multiple corrections each contribute to MT. Meyer and colleagues (1988) provided a formal model of processes involved in the speed–accuracy trade-off that extends our understanding of Fitts' principles.

Focus on RESEARCH 6.1

Fitts Tasks

In his most well-known experiment, Fitts (1954) asked subjects to make movements of a handheld stylus between two target plates. In this task, which is now typically known as the Fitts tapping task (see figure 6.1), the widths (W) of each target and the amplitude (A) between the targets were varied in different conditions, and the subject's goal was to alternately tap each target as quickly as possible while making as few errors as possible (usually less than 5% misses). The experimenter would measure the number of taps completed in, say, a 20 s trial, and then compute the average time per movement, or movement time (MT).

However, this typical Fitts task is not the only variation of reciprocal movements that has been studied in this type of rapid aiming paradigm. In fact, Fitts studied two lesser-known variants in his classic paper (Fitts, 1954). Figure 6.3 illustrates these tasks. In figure 6.3*a*, the subject's task was to move small metal discs with holes in the center (like carpenters' washers) from one peg to another. In figure 6.3*b* the task was to move small pegs (like the pegs used in the game of cribbage) from one hole to another. In both of these task variations, Fitts defined the ID in terms of the "clearance" between the target pegs and the washers (part *a*) or the diameter of the holes in the plate in relation to the diameter of the peg (part *b*). Defined in this manner, Fitts found that the same equation [$MT = a + b\,(ID)$] held well in accounting for the effects of the task parameters of movement speed.

FIGURE 6.3 Alternative reciprocal-movement tasks used by Fitts (1954). *(a)* Disc-transfer task; *(b)* pin-transfer task.
Adapted from Fitts 1954.

How do all of these experimental tasks converge to define Fitts' Law? The first part is easy—amplitude is the distance-covering portion of MT and is common to each task. The target size is more complicated. In the aiming task, this is essentially just target width. However, in the disc-transfer (figure 6.3*a*) and peg-transfer tasks (figure 6.3*b*), the target size is operationalized as the difference between sizes of the object and the target. For example, in the peg-transfer task, a large hole only represents an easy ID if the peg being transferred is relatively narrow. If the peg is wide, then the

> *continued*

> *continued*

task becomes more difficult because there is less tolerance for error. Thus, all three of these tasks converge nicely upon the central problem of the speed–accuracy trade-off—how the task parameters cause the subject to vary MT in order to make the end product of the aimed movement accurate.

Exploring Further

1. What would be the ID for a tapping task that had W = 4 and A = 16?
2. What changes in the foot's travel time from the accelerator to the brake pedal would you expect to see if you doubled the size of the brake pedal?

Focus on
APPLICATION 6.1

Fitts' Law in Everyday Actions

Fitts' Law has many obvious applications in sport, in the design of industrial workspaces, and in the organization of controls in automobiles, aircraft, and so on. One example, of which you might not be aware, is the design of keyboards and calculators. Have a look at the keyboard on your computer, cell phone, or other text input device. If the layout uses the principles consistent with Fitts' Law, you will notice that some keys are much larger than others (e.g., "Enter," "Backspace," and "Shift"). For example, the space bar on most keyboard layouts is much larger than any of the other keys. Having a larger key means that we can make the movements to frequently pressed keys ("Backspace" and "Enter" are others) very quickly without the risk of making an error. In other words, we can sacrifice a considerable amount of precision if we aim at a relatively large, as opposed to relatively small, key. This feature allows us to move very quickly to these often-pressed keys. What other keys on your keyboard are afforded the same "privilege"? Does your calculator or cell phone keyboard layout have similar advantages for one or more keys?

Navigating a cursor around a computer monitor also uses the principles of Fitts' Law, as noted in some pioneering work by Card, English, and Burr (1978). For example, the size of an icon affects the time to "acquire" it; icons that are increased in size as the cursor approaches them also influence MT and error, and the size and distance of pop-up menus have obvious implications for time and errors when we are aiming the cursor at them.

Some designs use Fitts' Law in the opposite way too. For example, the next time you navigate to a website with a pop-up advertisement that can be closed by clicking the "x" icon in one of the corners, note how small the "x" is and whether or not it is moving or stationary. Presumably, the longer it takes for you to get your cursor over the icon before clicking the mouse button, the longer the information on the screen will have been there for you to process it (perhaps unwillingly). In this way, the design purposely *reduces* the size of the target to make the user slow down. How many other applications can you think of in which the designer's intention is to make you move *more slowly* in order to be accurate?

Wishing to extend their ideas to tasks that are more typical and realistic, Fitts and Peterson (1964) used the same idea and variables as in the reciprocal-tapping task (figure 6.1), but used them with movements in which a single action was required from a starting position to a single target. These targets were located various distances (A) from the starting position and were of different sizes (W). As in the reciprocal paradigm, these single actions were to be done as rapidly as possible while maintaining an "acceptable" (to the experimenter) rate of error. The independent variables *A* and *W* and the dependent variable *MT* were related to each other in essentially the same way as they were in the reciprocal task. That is to say, the equation for Fitts' Law also applied to the single-movement paradigm, which increases our confidence that Fitts' Law is one of the truly fundamental laws of motor behavior.

In brief, Fitts' Law tells us the following:

- Movement time (MT) increases as the movement amplitude (A) increases.
- MT increases as the aiming accuracy requirement increases, that is, as target width (W) decreases.
- MT is essentially constant for a given ratio of movement amplitude (A) to target width (W).
- These principles are valid for a wide variety of conditions, subject variables, tasks or paradigms, and body parts used.

However, a number of other questions remained unanswered. What about movements that are completed in a *very* short period of time, where presumably no feedback is involved during the movement? How can MT depend on the number of corrections

How can Fitts' Law help to explain the varied sizes of keys on a keyboard?

when there isn't enough time to make even a single correction? Some of these questions are answered in the next section.

The Linear Speed–Accuracy Trade-Off

Suppose that you were to make a quick action to move your hand or an object, as in the example of swinging a hammer at the start of this chapter. How does your accuracy change as the time for the movement and the distance of the movement vary? Such factors have been studied in aiming movements, where the subject directs a handheld stylus from a starting position to a target, with MT and movement distance being varied experimentally. The subject is instructed to move with a given MT (e.g., 150 ms) and receives feedback after each movement to help maintain the proper MT. One set of results from this kind of task is shown in figure 6.4, where accuracy is expressed as the amount of "spread" or inconsistency of the movement end points about the target area. This measure, called **effective target width (W_e)**, is the standard deviation of the target end points. This measure is analogous to the target size that the subject "actually used" in making the action with the required MT. (Note that W_e is used here as a variant of Fitts' W.)

Notice from the legend in figure 6.4 that these movements are very fast, with all MTs of 200 ms or less. From the previous chapters, you would expect that such actions are controlled primarily by motor programming processes, with negligible feedback-based corrections. Even with these quick actions, as the movement distance increases, there is a gradual increase in the spread of the movements, that is, their inaccuracy around the target for each of the different MT conditions (e.g., compare the W_e for the 140 ms MT condition for the three different distances). Similarly, the inaccuracy of the movement increases as the MT is reduced at each of the distances (e.g., compare the W_e for the three MT conditions at the 30 cm distance). These two effects are more or less independent, as if the effects of increased distance can be added to the effect of reduced MT to produce aiming errors.

These effects of movement distance and MT suggest that open-loop processes necessary to produce the movement are also subject to the speed–accuracy trade-off. That is, the decreases in accuracy when MTs are short are not due simply to the fact that there is less time for feedback utilization; these effects of MT occur even in movements too brief to have any feedback modulations at all. Decreases in MT also seem to have effects on the consistency of the processes that generate the initial parts of the movement, that is, on the open-loop processes necessary to produce quick movements.

This is consistent with the ideas from Fitts' Law. In that situation, if the subject tries to make movements of a given distance too quickly, the result will be too many failures to hit the targets (which is unacceptable in terms of the experimenter's instructions that gen-

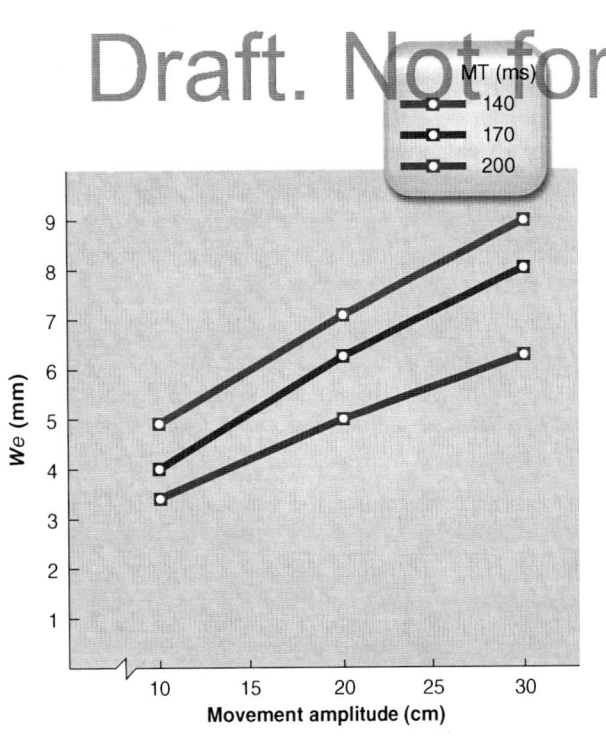

FIGURE 6.4 Variability of movement end points (defined as the standard deviation of the produced movement distances, or effective target width, W_e) in a rapid aiming task as a function of MT and distance.

Reprinted by permission from Schmidt et al. 1979.

erally demand errors on no more than about 5% of the movements). So, the subject must slow down to comply with the experimenter's instructions, decreasing the variability in the movements and hitting the target more often.

These separate effects of movement amplitude and MT can be combined into a single expression, more or less as done by Fitts. Research from the first author's lab showed that the amount of movement error (W_e) was linearly related to the movement's average velocity, that is, to the ratio A/MT (Schmidt et al., 1979). For example, in figure 6.5 the variability in hitting the target is plotted against the movement's average velocity (in centimeters per second, or cm/s), showing that, as the movement velocity increased, the aiming errors increased almost linearly as well. This principle, the *linear speed–accuracy trade-off*, suggests that, for various combinations of movement amplitude and MT that have a constant ratio (that is, a constant average velocity), the aiming errors are about the same. Thus, increases in movement distance and decreases in MT can be traded off with each other to maintain movement accuracy in these rapid tasks.

Sources of Error in Rapid Movements

Why do very rapid movements, in which there is little time for feedback processing and corrections, produce more errors as the movement distance increases or the MT decreases? The answer seems to lie with the processes that translate the motor program's output in the central nervous system into movements of the body part. Earlier sections showed that motor programs are responsible for determining the ordering of muscle contractions and the amounts of force that must be generated in the participating muscles. How might these sources of error contribute to movement inaccuracy?

It has been known for a long time that even if the performer attempts to produce the same force over and over on successive trials, the actual force produced will be somewhat inconsistent. This variability is thought to be caused by the relatively "noisy" (i.e., inconsistent) processes that convert central nervous system impulses into the activation of muscle motor units, which ultimately exert forces on bones, thus causing movements. Also, there is variability in the contractions generated by various reflex activities.

The presence of these "noisy" processes in the system means that the forces actually produced in a contraction are not exactly what were intended by the motor program level. This can also be seen in the phonograph record analogy presented in chapter 5, where noise can be introduced in several places in the stereo system, such as scratches on the record, noise inherent in the electronics and wires that run from the turntable, and quality of the speakers. These deviations from perfect *fidelity* in the stereo system make the sounds heard through the speakers slightly different than the sounds as originally recorded.

In movement control, these noisy processes are not constant; they change as the amount

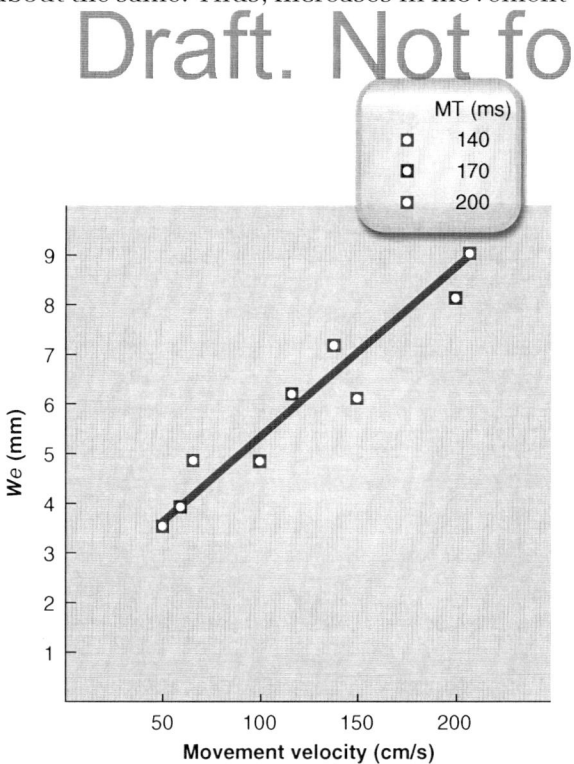

FIGURE 6.5 Variability of movement end points (W_e) in a rapid aiming task as a function of average movement velocity (A/MT).

Reprinted by permission from Schmidt et al. 1979.

of contraction force changes. This has been studied using tasks in which the subject is asked to produce brief ("ballistic") force applications to an apparatus handle; these force applications are such that the peak force produced on any contraction matches a (submaximal) goal force. Figure 6.6 has a typical set of results. Notice that as the contraction force increases, there is more variability in these forces, as if the noisy processes were becoming larger as well. In the figure, the variability in these forces (i.e., the within-subject standard deviation of the force productions), which is interpreted as the size of the noise component, is shown as a function of the size of the contraction, expressed as a percentage of the performer's maximum force. The noise component generally increases as the amount of force increases, up through about 70% of the subject's maximum. However, when the contractions are very large, approaching maximal values, the amount of force variability appears to level off again, with perhaps a slight decrease in the force variability in nearly maximal contractions (Sherwood, Schmidt, & Walter, 1988).

How does this information help in understanding error generation? To extend the example discussed at the beginning of the chapter, consider a movement like hammering a nail into a wall by swinging the hammer with the arms and hands. In such a movement, many muscles operate on the hands, arms, and upper torso to produce forces against the bones, which direct the hammer toward the nail. The direction of action of some of these muscles may happen to be lined up with the intended movement, but most of them are not; rather, the muscles are aligned at various angles to the action, as shown in figure 6.7. And, in many actions such as this, gravity acts as one of the contributing forces as well. To complete such an action perfectly, the various muscles must contract with just the right amounts of force, in coordination with each other, so that the *resultant* force is in line with the intended movement. Of course, if any of these forces is substantially in error, for example if the contraction of muscle 1 is too great, the movement's direction will be in error as well, with the movement missing the target.

Now, what happens when a given movement is made more rapidly? Of course, as the MT decreases, the forces exerted against the bones of the arm must increase. When these forces increase (up to about 70% of maximum), figure 6.6 shows that the "noisiness" of these forces increases as well. This has the effect of adding a slight error com-

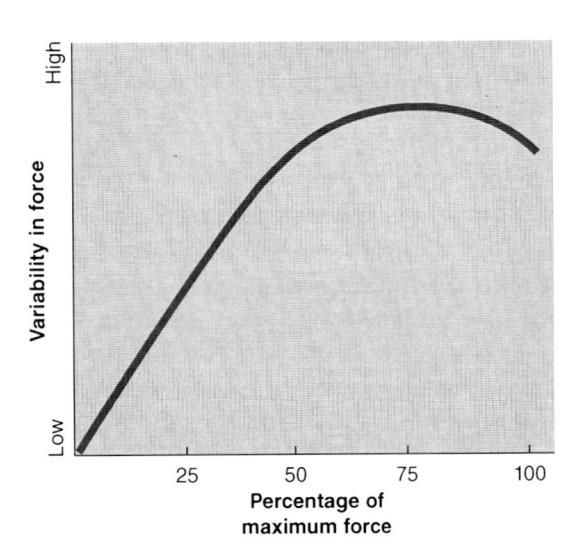

FIGURE 6.6 The relationship between the variability in force produced as a function of the percentage of maximum force used.

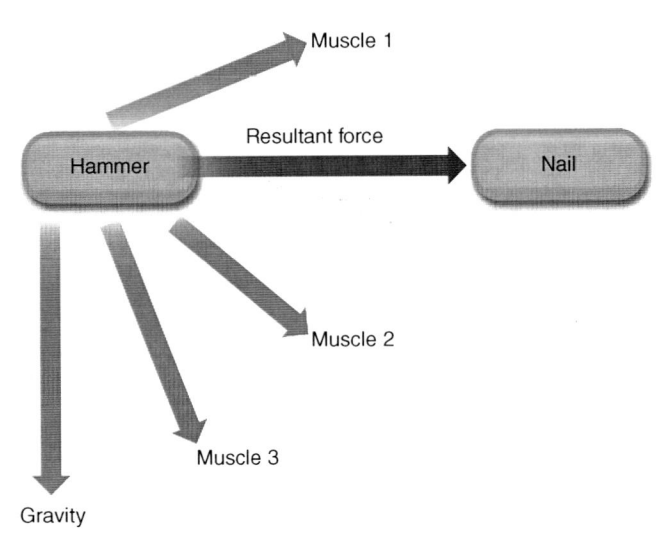

FIGURE 6.7 A hammer, swung at a nail on a vertical board by an arm and hand, is influenced by many forces.

ponent (with the variations in muscle force being independent) to the contraction of each of the involved muscles, causing them to contract slightly differently from how the movement program intended. If these forces are no longer perfectly coordinated with each other, the movement will tend to miss its target. Thus, the movement's inaccuracy increases as MT decreases, primarily because of the increased noise involved in the stronger muscle contractions.

In summary, this is why increasing the speed of a rapid movement contributes to its inaccuracy:

- The relative contraction forces of the various participating muscles are a major factor in determining the ultimate trajectory of the limb.
- The inconsistency in these forces increases with increased force.
- When MT decreases, more force is required.
- When amplitude increases, more force is required.
- More force generates more variability, which causes the movement to deviate from the intended trajectory, resulting in errors.

Exceptions to the Speed–Accuracy Trade-Off

As common as the speed–accuracy trade-off seems to be for movement behavior, there are a few situations in which it does not appear to hold, or at least in cases in which the principles are somewhat different from those indicated in the previous sections. These situations involve cases in which (a) extremely rapid and forceful actions are involved and (b) accuracy in timing is the action's critical feature.

Very Forceful Movements

Many human movements, especially those in sport, require extremely forceful contractions of muscles, leading to nearly maximal movement speeds, as in kicking a football or hitting a golf ball. Making the movement at near-maximal speed is often only a part of the problem because these actions often must be performed with great precision in space and time. As it turns out, alterations in movement speed affect these nearly maximal actions somewhat differently from many of the less forceful actions discussed so far.

Consider a rapid, horizontal, straight-arm movement in which a handheld pointer is aimed at a target as if it were a ball to be hit. What would happen to the spatial accuracy if the required MT decreased, so the movements would be closer and closer to the performer's maximal force capabilities? This is similar to your swinging of a hammer harder and harder, with the limit being your own force capabilities. As you might expect from the speed–accuracy trade-off principles, movements with shorter MTs are less spatially accurate, but only up to a point, as seen in figure 6.8. When the MT was reduced further,

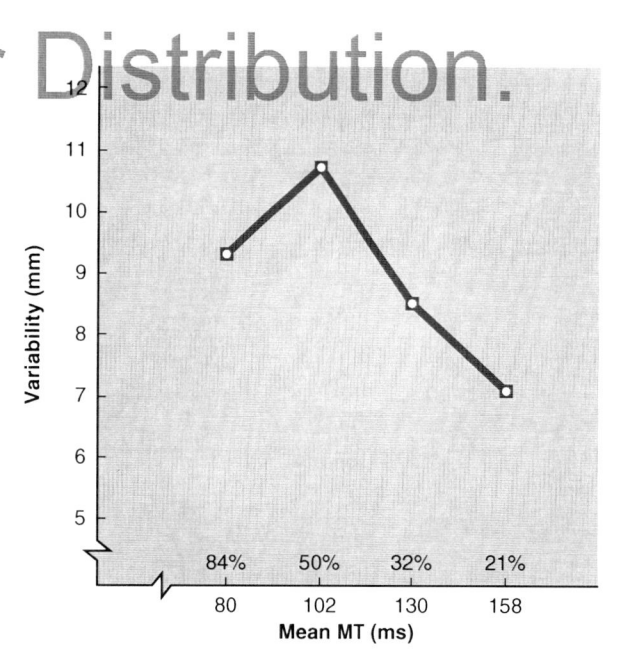

FIGURE 6.8 The effect of movement time (MT) on the positional variability in horizontal arm swing movements. The percentage values above the x-axis (corresponding to mean MTs) are the percentages of the subject's maximum force produced over those MTs. Thus, the movement becomes increasingly accurate with increasing MTs.

Reprinted by permission from Schmidt and Sherwood 1982.

from 102 to 80 ms, which increased the percentage of maximum force capability required to improve, but, from figure 6.8, decreasing the MT from 102 to 80 ms increased the percentage of maximum force form 50% to 84%. Also raising the percentage of maximum force from 50% to 84% decreased the variability in force (see figure 6.6). Thus, very rapid and very slow movements have the most spatial accuracy and the moderate-speed movements having the least accuracy. This set of data goes against the strict view of the speed–accuracy trade-off, in which faster movements are always less spatially accurate.

How can these movements be made so rapidly yet be so spatially accurate? These movements are very much like those illustrated in figure 6.7, where several muscles operate in coordination to determine the limb's trajectory. Also recall that, when the forces are very large, approaching maximum, the force-variability levels off and actually decreases slightly, as seen in figure 6.6 by the small downturn near the highest levels of

Very forceful movements performed at nearly maximal speed are an exception to the speed–accuracy trade-off.

force. Therefore, the nearly maximal movements in figure 6.8 are operating in a range where the forces are becoming *more consistent* with increases in force. This low force variability allows these very forceful actions to be very consistent spatially.

In summary, here's what results when a movement requires very high levels of muscular contractions (greater than about 70% of the subject's capabilities):

- Increasing speed by reducing MT can decrease spatial and timing error.
- Because a greater muscular force requirement increases accuracy, adding inertial load to the movement can decrease error, up to a point.
- An inverted-U relationship exists between spatial accuracy and force requirements, with least accuracy at moderate levels of force.

Movement Timing

In previous sections the concern was with situations in which spatial accuracy was the major goal, and we showed how this changes as movement velocity changes. However, for many skills the main goal is *temporal accuracy* (e.g., batting a baseball). In such skills a movement must be *timed* so that some part of it is produced at a particular moment (e.g., the bat must cross the plate at the same time the ball is there). The timing accuracy is critical to the success of the movement. For example, a perfectly struck chord on the guitar makes the most contribution to the music when it is timed just right.

Still other skills have both temporal and spatial goals, intermixed in complicated ways. Of course, batting a pitched baseball requires accuracy in terms of where to swing to meet the ball (spatial) as well as when to swing (temporal). But an important skill in batting demands that the performer be able to time the *duration* of the swing. Knowing or predicting the duration of the swing is critical in order for the batter to determine when to initiate the swing so the bat arrives over the plate coincident with the arrival of the ball.

So, being able to make a fast movement that occupies a specific amount of time is a critical factor in batting effectiveness.

In this section we are concerned with the temporal component of such skills, discussing the factors that affect timing accuracy. The temporal component can be isolated somewhat in the rapid task in which the performer makes a fast movement, whose goal is to produce a particular MT as accurately as possible. Timing accuracy is studied as a function of changes in the movement distance and the MT, as well as other variables. It turns out that skills with purely temporal goals seem to follow somewhat different principles than those having purely spatial goals (Schmidt et al., 1979).

What happens when subjects are asked to produce one of these movements of a given distance, but with the MT goal reduced from 300 ms to 150 ms? One might expect that because the velocity of the movement is larger, it would have more error, as was found in figures 6.4 and 6.5. Not so. Decreasing the MT has the effect of *decreasing* the timing error, making the movement more accurate in time, not less. This can be seen in figure 6.9, in which variability in timed actions

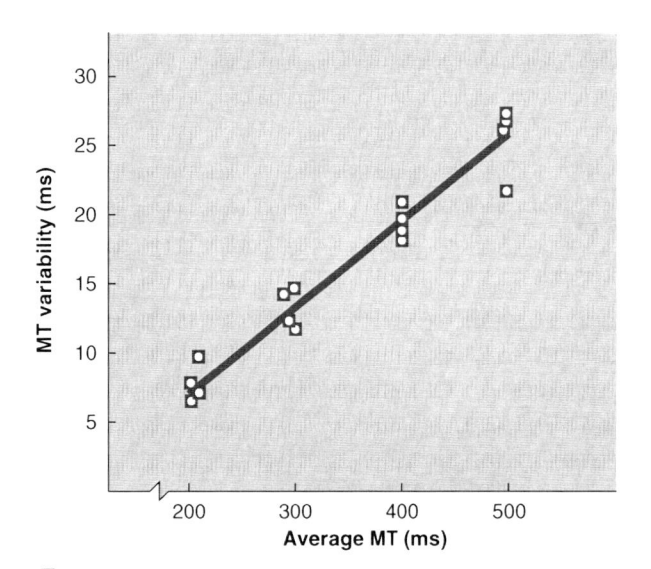

FIGURE 6.9 The effect of average MT duration on the variability of timing. As MT decreases (i.e., movements are made faster), the variability of timing decreases (i.e., becomes more stable).

Reprinted by permission from Schmidt and Lee 2011.

increases almost linearly with increases in goal MT; halving the goal MT (within limits) almost tends to halve the timing errors. An additional finding is that this relationship for MT and timing variability holds not only for discrete, single-action movements but also for repetitive movements (Wing & Kristofferson, 1973). Therefore, for skills in which timing error has to be reduced, the main factor is the MT, which is quite different from the situation for skills with spatial goals as demonstrated in figures 6.4 and 6.5 (see Schmidt et al., 1979).

These findings about timing errors are not as strange as they seem at first, as you will see if you do the following simple demonstration. Use the timer function on a cell phone or watch and, without looking at it, start and stop the timer in order to generate exactly 2 s. Do this 10 times in total and record the amount of error you make on each trial. Next do 10 trials of the task again, but this time try to generate 4 s. Compare the error measures generated from the 10 trials on the two tasks. You will likely find that the amount of error you make in estimating 2 s will be about half the amount of error for 4 s. Why? The system that generates these durations (including both the stopwatch and arm movement tasks) is "noisy" or variable, and the amount of this variability increases, or accumulates, as the duration of the event to be timed increases.

Analyzing a Rapid Movement: Baseball Batting

It may seem from the previous section that sometimes contradictory principles are involved in these rapid actions. To help in understanding, it will be useful to apply these principles to a familiar task like batting in baseball. This task requires several of the processes discussed so far, such as anticipation and timing, prediction of the ball's spatial trajectory and its arrival time at the coincidence point, and rapid movements that must be both forceful and accurate, so the principles can be applied to various parts of this action. To examine the effects of altering the MT of the swing of the bat, let's assume that some factors are held constant, such as the nature of the pitch and the situation in the game.

A few facts about the timelines involved in hitting a baseball are summarized in figure 6.10. In elite skill–level baseball, a 90 mph (145 kph) pitch requires about 460 ms to travel from the pitcher to the plate, and the MT of the swing of the bat is about 160 ms (Hubbard & Seng, 1954). Evidence presented earlier showed that the internal signal to trigger the swing occurs about 170 ms before the movement starts (Slater-Hammel, 1960; review figure 5.5b and Focus on Research 5.2). With these process durations combined, the signal to trigger the action must be given about 330 ms before the ball arrives at the plate—that is, 170 ms to prepare the swing plus 160 ms to carry it out. Therefore, the decision about whether or not to swing at the ball must be made well before the ball has traveled halfway to the plate, or after only 130 ms of ball travel. Although some late, visually-based corrections in the movement are possible, as discussed in chapter 4, the majority of the action must be planned in advance and initiated by the central nervous system some 330 ms before the ball arrives. Making decisions relative to the occurrence of these critical times plays a decisive role in a batter's success in hitting a pitched ball and also in making changes to an initial decision to swing (see Focus on Application 5.1 for more on checked swings).

An important consideration, given the previous discussion of speed and accuracy processes in the chapter, is this: What would happen if the batter could speed up the swing, say from 160 ms to 140 ms? The bat swing's MT could be made shorter through instructions or training to make the actual movement faster, through shortening the movement distance by reducing the backswing (a very slight effect), through using a lighter bat, or through changing the biomechanics of the movement in various ways. Reducing the bat swing MT

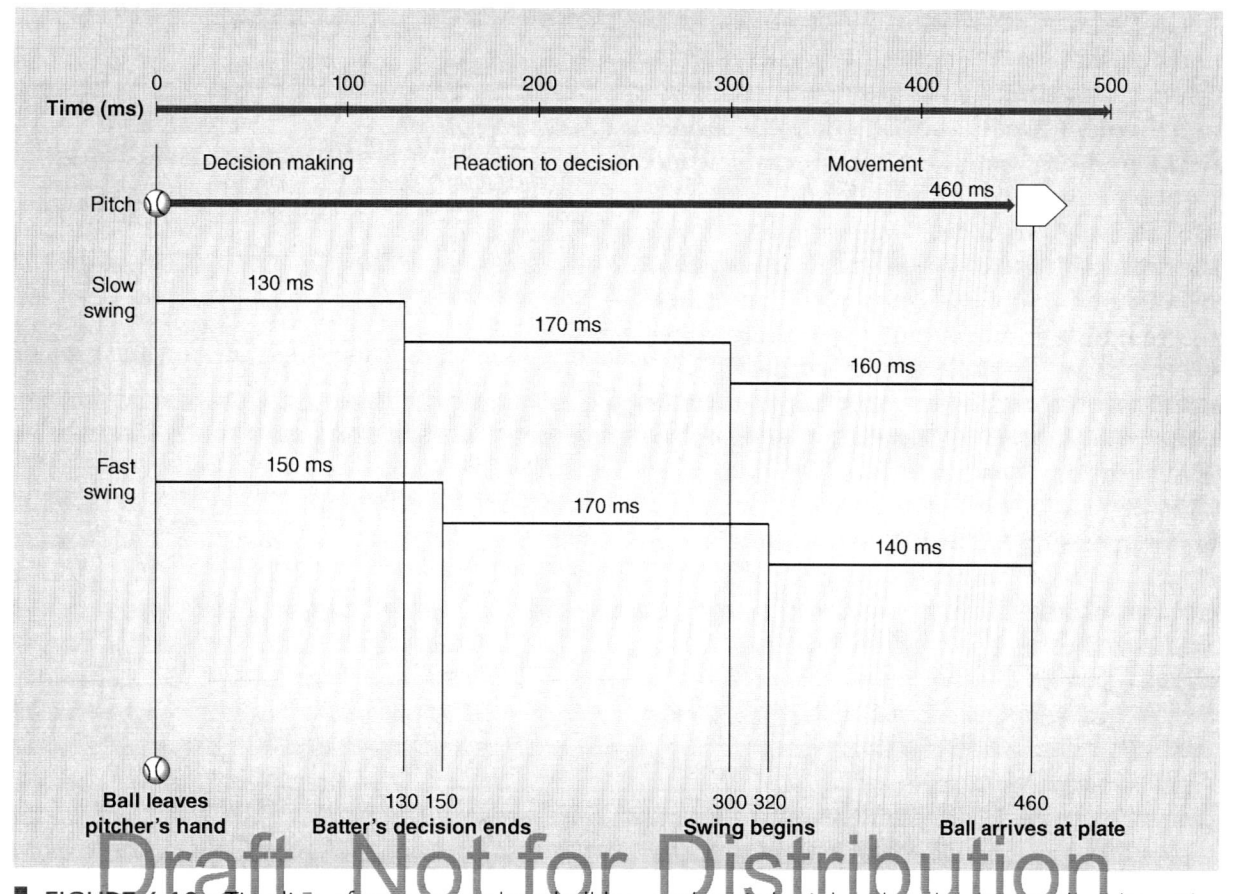

Principles of Speed, Accuracy, and Coordination

FIGURE 6.10 Timeline of events as a baseball leaves the pitcher's hand and arrives at the plate. The pitch is traveling at a velocity of 90 mph. A "fast" swing (140 ms) has 20 ms less MT than a slower swing (160 ms).

by 20 ms would affect several separate factors discussed in the previous few sections.

Visual Information Processing

Figure 6.10 shows that shortening the MT delays the beginning of the swing, hence the point at which the details of the action have to be specified, to a position several feet later in the ball's flight. This provides additional time for viewing the ball's trajectory and for determining time to contact, and should allow more accurate anticipation of where and when the ball will arrive. And this extra information comes at a point that is maximally useful—when the ball is closer to the batter—making these extra 20 ms of viewing time particularly beneficial. Therefore, shortening the MT provides more effective anticipation of the ball's trajectory.

Swing-Initiation Timing Accuracy

If the swing of the bat is speeded up, the decision about when to initiate the movement is made later and is more temporally accurate. In an experiment on a simulated batting task, shortening the MT stabilized the initiation time of the movement, as if the batter were more certain of when to start the swing (Schmidt, 1969). Starting the swing at a more stable time therefore translates into a more stable time for the movement end point at the plate, which yields greater movement timing accuracy.

Movement Timing Accuracy

One process the batter must go through in planning the swing is to estimate the duration of his *own* movement (Poulton [1974] termed

137

this "effector anticipation"). Therefore, the batter selects a MT, then initiates this action at such a time that the "middle" of the movement coincides with the arrival of the ball at the plate. If the actual MT is different from the one predicted, the "middle" of the movement will be too early or late, causing timing errors in hitting the ball. Because reduced MT increases movement timing consistency (figure 6.9), the movement's actual duration will be closer to the batter's estimate. This results in greater accuracy in hitting the ball, particularly in terms of the timing aspects (see also Schmidt, 1969).

Movement Spatial Accuracy

Making the movement faster also influences spatial accuracy, as discussed earlier. If the movement is already relatively slow, instructions to decrease the MT have a detrimental effect on accuracy in hitting the ball. However, most bat swing movements are already quite fast, near the performer's limits in producing force. Recall that when movements are very fast and forceful, reducing the MT tends to increase—not decrease—accuracy (figure 6.9), because the force variability decreases in this range with decreases in MT (figure 6.6). Therefore, reducing the MT when it is already quite short results in improved spatial accuracy, giving more frequent ball contact.

Ball Impact

Finally, of course, a faster swing gives more impact to the ball if it is hit—a critical factor in the particular game of baseball. Increasing the load by having a heavier bat can improve spatial accuracy (Schmidt & Sherwood, 1982) and would have only minimal negative effects on movement speed. Clearly, both added bat mass and a faster MT contribute to greater impact with the ball if and when it is hit.

Nearly every factor associated with decreased bat swing MT discussed here would be expected to influence the chances of hitting the ball. Perhaps understanding these factors makes it clearer why professional batters seem to swing nearly maximally.

Accuracy in Coordinated Actions

The previous section of this chapter presented various factors related to the speed and accuracy in making rapid, mainly single-limb, aiming movements. Much of this discussion focused on actions similar to the kind you might see in moving a finger or limb at a target (e.g., moving a computer mouse to point a cursor at an icon, or moving your foot from the accelerator to the brake pedal), or moving a single object with more than one limb (e.g., swinging a baseball bat to hit a ball, or swinging an ax to split a block of wood). The principles discussed already, such as Fitts' Law and the relationship between force and force variability, appear to describe speed–accuracy trade-offs well for these types of movements.

But, consider now what happens when we coordinate limbs not with the purpose of moving a single object (e.g., a bat or an ax), but rather with distinct goals for each limb. For example, a pianist often maintains a bass rhythm with the left hand while performing a lead with the right hand; the skill of knitting requires that two hands control the separate movements of two needles, interspersed by grasping and moving the thread according to a mental representation of the desired stitch; and a plumber welds a pipe fitting by holding a flaming torch in one hand while spreading a bead of solder over the joint with the other hand. Are these types of actions explained by the same principles as previously discussed, or are unique principles required to explain them?

Bimanual Aiming Tasks

Simultaneously performing two tasks that each require spatial precision combines two topics discussed in previous chapters. In chapter 4, we discussed closed-loop processes—if MT is sufficiently long, then endpoint precision is facilitated when we guide the limb visually toward the target. And, in chapter 3, we said that attention is limited to producing and controlling only one motor program at a time. Putting these two discussions together, then, how is the simultaneous, visually guided control of two separate limbs achieved when moving to separate targets? As we will see in the following sections, speed and accuracy becomes a much more complex issue when two or more limbs have distinct spatial goals.

Bimanual Fitts Task

The bimanual Fitts task is a simple variation of the single-limb task. A bimanual version of the continuous task (Fitts, 1954) was first used by Robinson and Kavinsky (1976), and a bimanual version of the discrete task (Fitts & Peterson, 1964) was introduced by Kelso, Southard, and Goodman (1979). In the bimanual version, both limbs could be assigned identical tasks, with either low (figure 6.11a) or high IDs (figure 6.11b). However, the limbs could also be assigned to different (incongruent) tasks, say one with a low ID and one with a high ID (figure 6.11c). According to Fitts' Law, MT is a function of the task parameters, width (W) and amplitude (A)—the MT for any particular task should be simply a function of its ID. Therefore, a strict prediction of Fitts' Law would be that each limb would arrive at its target in a MT that was consistent with that task's ID. For congruent tasks, MTs should be similar; for incongruent tasks, MT should be faster for the limb moving to the smaller ID.

The studies by Kelso and colleagues (1979) showed that these predictions did not hold true. For example, when paired with a limb moving to a high ID, the MT of the limb moving to a low-ID task was considerably slower than would be expected. The set of findings from this research is rather complex, but in general, the conclusion was that the explanatory power of Fitts' Law is reduced when separate and incongruent task demands are required of two limbs. This finding could be a result of an attempt by the executive to deal with an overloaded attentional demand by issuing a single motor program that controls both limbs.

Such a conclusion is supported by other bimanual research (Kelso, Putnam, & Goodman, 1983) in which one limb was to clear a physical barrier placed between the home position and the target. The barrier required the limb to be elevated in order to clear it.

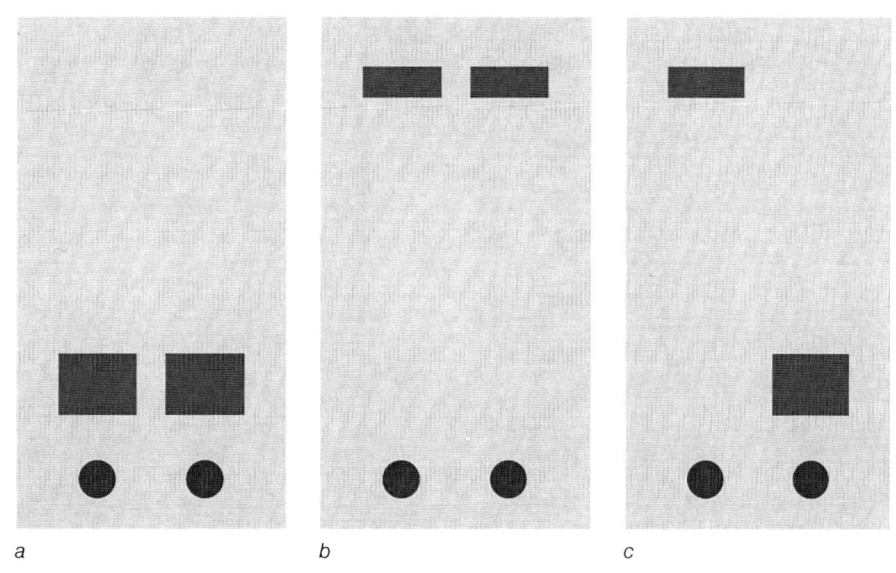

FIGURE 6.11 Three variants of the bimanual Fitts task: *(a)* Both limbs move to a low-ID task; *(b)* both limbs move to a high-ID task; and *(c)* incongruent limb-ID assignment, where the right hand performs a low-ID task and the left hand performs a high-ID task. Note that the blue-filled circles represent the starting points for each limb; red rectangles are the targets.

However, the limb without the barrier did not have to be lifted in this way. The latter limb, even though not physically required to do so, was lifted so as to match the barrier limb. Similar common kinematic evidence was found in tasks in which subjects had to reach and grasp two objects at different locations (Jackson, Jackson, & Kritikos, 1999). Together, these findings support a view in which the MT and kinematics for both limbs are not determined independently but rather by a joint command.

The Gamma–V Experiment

Try this simple experiment for yourself. With a pencil in your right hand, practice drawing small (2 in. [5 cm]) figures that represent the Greek letter gamma (γ). Draw the "γ" relatively quickly, without modification during its production. Start with the pencil against the edge of a ruler laid on the paper, and finish with the pencil against the ruler again. The figure must cross over near the center and have a rounded bottom. When you can do this effectively, use the other hand to draw regular "V"s. The procedure is the same except that now the figure must not cross over itself and must have a pointed bottom. Based on chapter 5, each figure is represented by its own motor program because the temporal structures for the two figures are different: down–up for the "V" and down–over–up for the "γ." Most people do not have any trouble producing these figures when each is drawn on its own.

Now try to produce these two figures together, using the same hands as before. You will find, as Bender (1987) did, that doing both tasks at the same time is very difficult, with results such as those shown in figure 6.12. Most performers show a strong tendency to make the same figure with both hands or at least to produce certain features of the different figures with both hands (e.g., a rounded bottom). Clearly, the fact that the subjects could produce these actions separately was evidence that there was a motor program for each of them. Even after considerable practice, most people cannot do this dual task effectively. This demonstration indicates that, with separate programs for producing a "V" and a "γ," these programs cannot be run off at the same time without considerable interference between the hands.

These findings, together with the results from Robinson and Kavinsky (1976) and Kelso and coauthors (1979, 1983) presented in the previous sections, can be interpreted to suggest that the motor system can produce only a single motor program at one time. This is an extension of the idea expressed earlier that the movement programming stage could organize (during reaction time [RT]) only a single action at a time. But now the focus is on the production of the movement itself, after the RT has been completed.

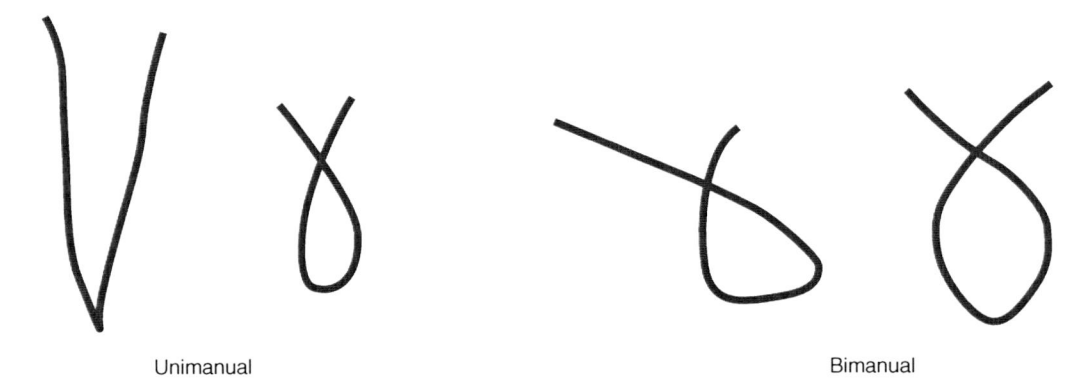

FIGURE 6.12 The gamma–V task. Subjects are asked to produce the capital letter "V" with the left hand and the Greek letter gamma ("γ") with the right hand. In unimanual trials only one letter is written at a time; in the bimanual trials both letters are written simultaneously.

Reprinted by permission from Bender 1987.

Focus on
APPLICATION 6.2

Coordination in Golf Putting

Almost every golf instructor contends that body sway during the golf putt is detrimental to accuracy—the golfer should keep the lower body, torso, and, most importantly, the head as still as possible and simply rotate the shoulders to move the putter and strike the ball. But, for a number of reasons, this is very difficult to do. For example, a putting study by Lee and coauthors (2008) showed that both novice and expert golfers moved their heads considerably during a putt. However, they did so in fundamentally different ways.

Figure 6.13 illustrates 60 putts taken by one of the novices (top) in the study and one of the experts (bottom). The red lines show the movement velocities of the head during a putt, and the blue lines trace the velocity profiles of the putter during the same time period. Note that although both the novices and experts moved their heads during each and every putt, they did so in fundamentally different ways—while the novice moved the head in the same direction as the movement of the putter, the expert moved the head in the *opposite* direction of the putter.

Regardless of the direction of head movement, have another look at both graphs. Do you notice some similarity between the two? The point at which the putter velocity traces reversed their direction in the graphs coincided generally with the reversal of the head velocity. We take this evidence as suggesting that the timing of the movements of both the putter and head are the result of the common motor program. The novices dealt with the "head problem" by moving it together with the motion of the putter; the experts dealt with the head problem by moving it in opposition to the putter motion.

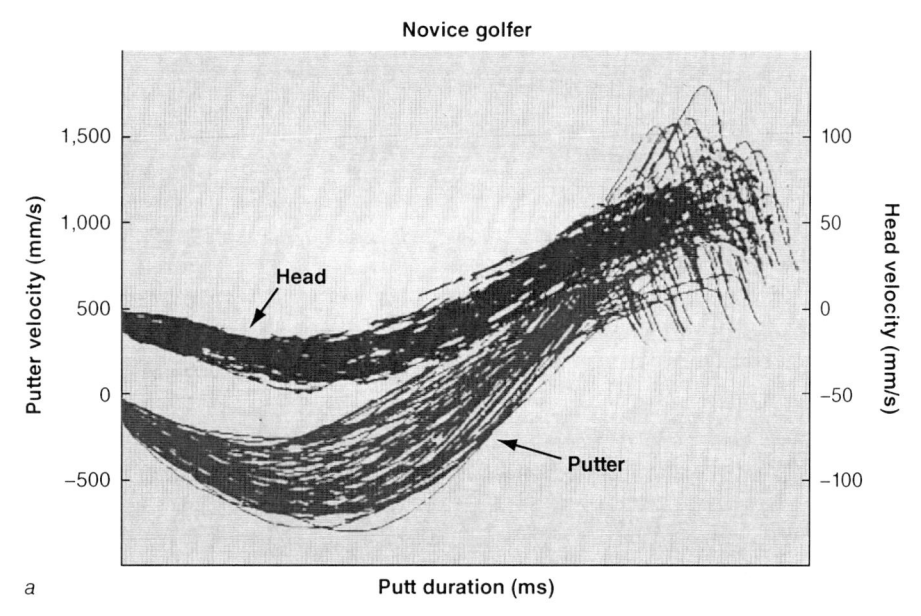

FIGURE 6.13 Velocity traces of 60 putts made by a novice golfer (*a*) and an expert golfer (*b*). Each line represents the kinematic timeline of one putt. Blue lines illustrate the velocity profiles of the head during the putt; red lines are the motions of the putter. It seems clear that both novices and experts moved their heads during the putt—but in opposite directions!

Reprinted by permission from Lee et al. 2008.

> *continued*

> *continued*

Expert golfer

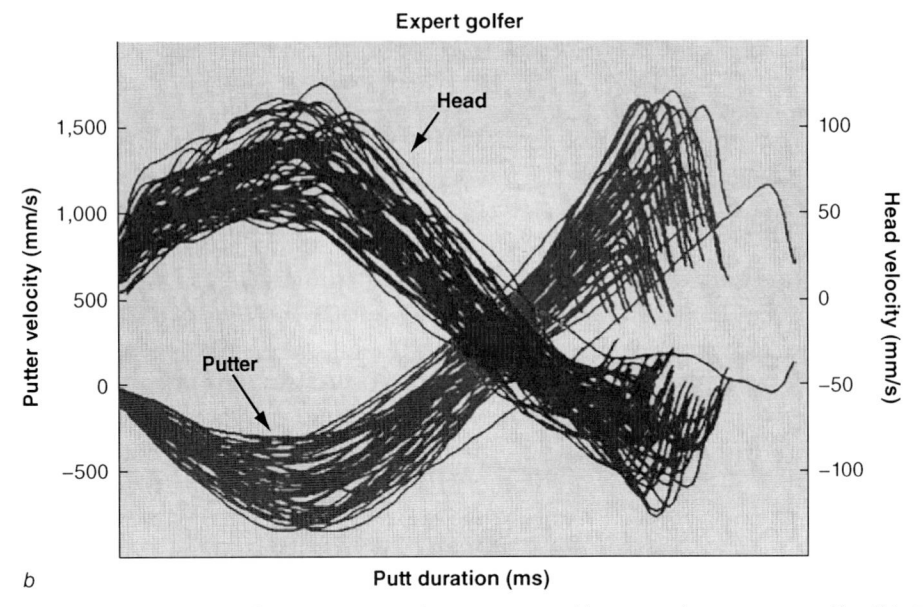

b

FIGURE 6.13 Velocity traces of 60 putts made by a novice golfer (*a*) and an expert golfer (*b*). Each line represents the kinematic timeline of one putt. Blue lines illustrate the velocity profiles of the head during the putt; red lines are the motions of the putter. It seems clear that both novices and experts moved their heads during the putt—but in opposite directions!

Reprinted by permission from Lee et al. 2008.

Complex Coordination Patterns

A more complex version of the gamma–V experiment by Heuer, Schmidt, and Ghodsian (1995) revealed more evidence for this single motor program view. In this experiment, subjects were given extensive practice in performing a single-reversal arm movement of a lever with the left arm (flexion, then extension), together with a double-reversal lever movement of the right arm (flexion, extension, flexion). Analysis of the movement kinematics revealed a tight coupling of the temporal occurrence of specific landmarks of each limb pattern, suggesting again that such a complex coordination was being governed by a single motor program. Also, subjects found it almost impossible to move one limb faster than the other if asked to do so. Moreover, the subjects were asked to do a probe-RT task, involving a foot response to a tone stimulus. Although these data are not included in the paper, the strong impression was that people could do the two-hand coordination task more or less automatically without interfering with the probe-RT task. This finding, plus the evidence of a strong *coupling* between the arms, provided more support for the idea that a common GMP can be applied to the control of both arms to control a coordinated, simultaneous action.

Continuous Bimanual Tasks

Controlling the continuous movement of two limbs, each with its own spatial or temporal goal (or both), represents a different problem for the motor control system. Because the movements are ongoing, the executive has the flexibility to use a common movement command to control the movements of both limbs (as discussed for discrete movements) or to switch attention rapidly between the executions of the two tasks.

Continuous Bimanual Timing

Try this simple example of a continuous bimanual task: Point your index fingers on

Analysis of the movements of novice and expert golfers during a putt showed different coordination patterns between head movement and putter movement.

both hands straight ahead of you, as if you were pointing two pistols at a target. Now start to wiggle both fingers. Most people spontaneously do this task by wiggling each finger toward their midline, then away, cycling back and forth using what researchers call an **in-phase** mode of coordination. Here, "in-phase" means that right-finger flexion (and any other feature, such as peak velocity, time of reversal-point arrival) and the corresponding left-finger flexion occur at the same time and are controlled by a common structure with relatively fixed timing. Considering the limitless ways in which one could choose to wiggle both fingers at the same time, why do most people choose this in-phase mode of coordination?

Two studies from Kelso's lab provide evidence for an answer. In one study (Kelso, Scholz, & Schöner, 1986), subjects were instructed to coordinate their fingers by starting in either an in-phase position, as just defined, or in an **anti-phase** position in which both fingers point to the right and then to the left, like the movements of windshield wipers on many cars. The movements started slowly and then were gradually sped up in tempo. Interestingly, the in-phase mode of coordination was maintained regardless of the tempo, but the anti-phase mode became highly variable. In another study, Kelso, Scholz, and Schöner (1988) asked subjects to start moving with one coordination pattern (either in-phase or anti-phase) and then to switch to the other mode as quickly as possible. The switching took longer to achieve and to stabilize when going from in-phase to anti-phase than it did from anti-phase to in-phase. Together, these two sets of findings suggest that in-phase was the more stable of the two coordination patterns—it was easier to switch into than away from and was more resistant to the effects of speed.

So, what is the importance of having stable coordination patterns, and to have one that is the most preferred? From one viewpoint, controlling the timing of two fingers as a *single* coordination pattern should reduce the attention demanded for control, compared to controlling them as two independent events (Temprado, 2004; see also Focus on Research 6.2, "Coordination as a Self-Organization Process"). In essence, rather than having distinct lines of control (including separate executive commands and feedback channels), the limbs are controlled as a single unit, which greatly reduces the role of the executive in issuing commands and evaluating feedback.

The advantage of having one pattern that is *preferred* (i.e., more stable) over all others probably provides us with one way to deal with the speed–accuracy trade-off (although this is described somewhat differently than in the discussion earlier in the chapter). Let's go back to the results of Kelso and colleagues (1986) once again. Recall that subjects performed rhythmic movements of the two index fingers and gradually increased their speed. Anti-phase accuracy and stability diminished with increasing speed but, surprisingly, only to a point. Kelso and colleagues had instructed their subjects to start with a specific pattern (either in-phase or anti-phase) but to go with whatever pattern felt more comfortable if coordination stability became threatened at higher speeds. Figure 6.14 illustrates their findings. The accuracy (figure 6.14a) and stability (figure 6.14b) measures of in-phase and anti-phase patterns are presented as a function of the cycling frequency. As noted earlier, increased speed caused the anti-phase pattern to lose accuracy and stability. But note that something curious happened, starting at around a frequency of 2.25 Hz (1 Hertz is the number of complete cycles per second): the anti-phase pattern (defined as 180° relative phase, blue line) switched to an in-phase pattern of coordination (figure 6.14a). Now

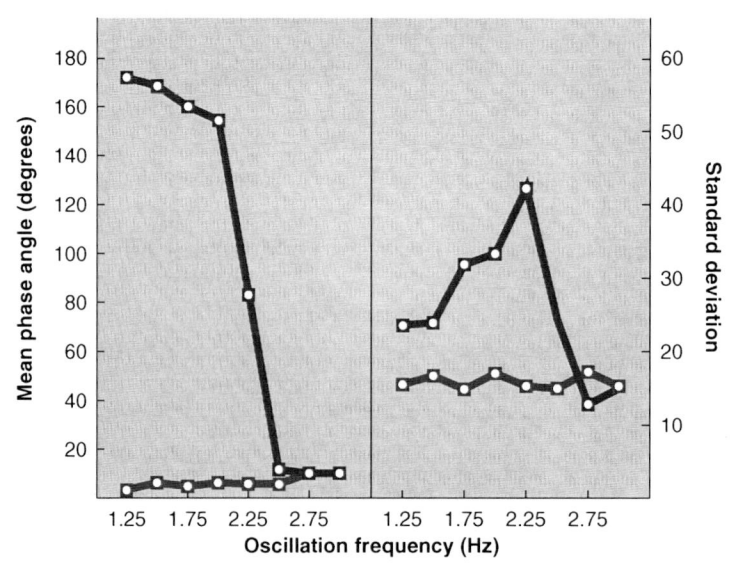

FIGURE 6.14 Mean relative phase (a) and standard deviations (b) for coordination patterns starting as in-phase (red) or anti-phase (blue), as a function of movement speed.

Reprinted by permissions from Kelso, Scholz, and Schöner 1986.

Focus on RESEARCH 6.2

Coordination as a Self-Organization Process

The notion of the motor program is not without its critics. Some of those with opposing views have offered an alternative that is generally termed the dynamical systems, or self-organizational perspective (Haken, Kelso, & Bunz, 1985; Kelso, 1995; Turvey, 1977) or simply, the dynamical perspective. These critics argue that the program notion assumes too much cognition, neural computation, and direct control by brain and spinal cord mechanisms, so that every movement must have an explicit representation stored in the central nervous system.

Investigators from the **self-organization** perspective hold that the regularities of movement patterns are not represented in programs but rather emerge naturally (that is, through physics) out of the complex interactions among many connected elements, or degrees of freedom. This is analogous to the ways in which many complex physical systems achieve organization and structure without having any central program or set of commands, such as the sudden transformation of still water to rolling patterns as it begins to boil and the organization among molecules to form crystals. Just as it would make little sense to postulate a central program for governing the patterns in boiling water, these researchers argue that it is incorrect to think that complex patterns of human motor activity are controlled by such programs. Kelso and Engstrøm (2005) provide a useful analogy here. Think of the motor program perspective as an orchestra whose actions are under the supervision of a conductor, and the self-organization perspective as a conductor-less orchestra.

A scientific debate about these issues has been continuing for several decades now. At best, what has emerged is an agreement to disagree. The two sides of the debate tend to study different tasks (e.g., rapid, discrete movements vs. ongoing, cyclical motions), so there is little basis on which compare theoretical predictions. In the end, it is likely that neither theoretical perspective will be correct in all aspects, which should lead to the development of new theories with stronger predictive powers. And this is a good thing, as such is the fate of a healthy science.

Exploring Further

1. Name two features of discrete tasks that make them more suitable than continuous tasks for motor program study.
2. Name two features of continuous tasks that make them more suitable than discrete tasks for self-organizational study.

---

look at the blue line at the corresponding point (2.25 Hz) in figure 6.14*b*—at the same time that the anti-phase pattern switched to in-phase, the stability of the pattern was reduced dramatically.

The Speed–Accuracy Trade-Off Reconsidered

The findings of Kelso and colleagues (1986) are very important, for they suggest that an alternative solution to the speed–accuracy trade-off is achieved in different types of tasks. In the first part of the chapter we noted that MT is slowed as task demands are increased in order to maintain accuracy (Fitts' Law). For very rapid (i.e., brief) movements, the linear speed–accuracy trade-off suggested that error increases steadily as MT decreases. The effect on timing was increased variability as MT became longer. However, the findings

The self-organization perspective views human movement as analogous to a conductor-less orchestra.

of Kelso and coworkers (1986) suggest that when performance accuracy (or stability) is threatened by increased speed, an alternative solution is that the motor system seeks out a different, more stable coordination pattern to take its place. In other words, accuracy does not continue to diminish with increasing speed; instead, the coordination pattern *changes* so that stability can be reestablished.

These findings are not peculiar to moving two fingers—we change from a walk to a run when the gait stability is pushed to the limit at high walking speeds (Diedrich & Warren, 1995). And many four-legged animals have three or more gaits from which to choose as the task demands change (Alexander, 2003). Why might solutions to the speed–accuracy trade-off change when movements become more complex?

Presumably, simultaneous movements of two limbs have more ways to be organized than do movements of a single limb. Having more degrees of freedom to organize, although burdensome from an organizational point of view, also provides more flexibility in how to solve the problem. When increases in speed result in decreased accuracy (more instability), the motor system is faced with at least three alternatives: (a) reduce the speed and maintain accuracy; (b) decrease inaccuracy and maintain speed; or (c) maintain the speed and change the movement pattern in order to reestablish stability.

Summary

The accuracy of rapid movements controlled by motor programs is influenced by speed and amplitude variations, and these actions display a typical speed–accuracy trade-off. Increases in speed (decreases in MT) usually degrade spatial accuracy unless the movements are very rapid and forceful. On the other hand, decreasing the MT usually enhances *timing* accuracy. These effects are caused by relatively noisy low-level processes in the spinal cord and the muscles that make the contractions differ slightly from those originally intended. Movements involving more than one limb are not controlled independently, but rather by a command structure that coordinates both actions simultaneously. The increased complexity of coordinating two movements also provides more flexibility, such that increases in speed result in changes to the coordination pattern in order to maintain stability.

WEB STUDY GUIDE ACTIVITIES

The student web study guide, available at www.HumanKinetics.com/MotorLearningandPerformance, offers these activities to help you build and apply your knowledge of the concepts in this chapter.

Interactive Learning

Activity 6.1: Review the equation for Fitts' Law by assembling the components of the equation in the correct order.

Activity 6.2: Answer a series of multiple-choice questions that will help you understand the speed–accuracy trade-off and exceptions to it.

Situation-Based Exercise

Activity 6.3: The situation-based exercise for this chapter prompts you to identify a skill that involves rapid movement and requires accuracy, then to explore how the speed–accuracy trade-off phenomenon applies to the skill you have chosen.

Check Your Understanding

1. Distinguish between temporal and spatial accuracy. Give an example of an activity (e.g., a game of tennis) where both might be important. Describe a situation where temporal accuracy is important and explain why this is so, and then do the same for a situation where spatial accuracy is important.

2. In words, explain what Fitts' Law tells us about motor control and speed–accuracy trade-offs.

3. Describe both a single-limb and a bimanual Fitts' task. Explain, in general terms, how findings using the bimanual Fitts' task were different than those using the single-limb task. What view (along with other findings) do these differences support?

Apply Your Knowledge

1. Your friend has come up with a silly competition: At the driving range you race to see who can go through a bucket of golf balls the fastest, while keeping score for accuracy in hitting a middle distance on the range. The winner is determined by a combined score of time and error (distance from the target). Discuss two strategies that you might use to win the competition.

147

Would your strategies change if the winner were determined by time and the combined distance of your shots? What if the competition got even sillier and the accuracy in timing between the shots mattered?

Suggestions for Further Reading

Woodworth's legacy on speed and accuracy research is presented by Elliott, Helson, and Chua (2001). Further details on sources of error in motor control for aiming movements have been reviewed by Meyer and colleagues (1988), who provide an elegant theory of these processes that applies to many different kinds of limb movement situations. And Meyer and coauthors (1990) have written an interesting and readable review of the history of thought about speed–accuracy trade-off effects. Wing (2002) provides a detailed account of timing variability from an information-processing viewpoint, which presents an interesting contrast to a self-organization view (see Kelso, 1995). See the reference list for these additional resources.

Individual Differences

How People Differ in Their Performance Capabilities

KEY TERMS

ability
correlation coefficient (*r*)
differential method
experimental method
general motor ability
individual differences
prediction
reference tests
relative-age effect
skill
specificity hypothesis
superability

CHAPTER OUTLINE

The Study of Individual Differences
Abilities Versus Skills
Is There a General Motor Ability?
Abilities and the Production of Skills
Prediction and Selection Based on Ability
Summary

CHAPTER OBJECTIVES

Chapter 7 describes research that considers why and how people differ in motor skills and abilities. This chapter will help you to understand

- the scientific approach to the study of individual differences,
- the nature of abilities and how they are distinguished from skills,
- two approaches to conceptualizing the "all-around athlete," and
- the difficulty in predicting future successes in motor performance.

To win the gold medal at the 2008 Summer Olympics, decathlete Bryan Clay had to achieve elite-level performances in the 100 meter sprint, long jump, shot put, high jump, 400 meter sprint, 110 meter hurdles, discus throw, pole vault, javelin throw, and the 1500 meter run. Many ascribe the title of "World's Greatest Athlete" to the winner of this event. But what makes one athlete skilled at so many disparate skills? Is there a single athletic ability relevant to all ten of these events, or are there ten skills independent of each other? This chapter will address how we can describe and understand the wide variability in people's motor performance capabilities.

This chapter changes tacks rather markedly, to deal with an area of psychology and motor behavior that, at least on the surface, appears to be very different from the motor skills topics we have discussed in the previous chapters. Previously, the focus was on the effects of certain variables on the motor behavior of people *in general*. This method is termed the **experimental method** because the methods typically involve conducting actual experiments (this is also the basis for the term "experimental psychology"). This experimental tradition is by far the more popular part of movement science. This experimental method typically treats people identically and tacitly assumes that all people behave in the same way when treated in the same way. In fact, differences between and among people are thought to be one of the sources of error, or "noise," in the experimental tradition; and a great deal of effort is usually devoted to eliminating or reducing these sources of variability in the experiment.

The Study of Individual Differences

A research area that diverges from the experimental method concerns the *differences between and among people* on some measure, frequently on measures of performance. This area, sometimes referred to as the **differential method**, is concerned with the fact that not all of us are the same, and, as we will see as the chapter unfolds, it focuses on the ways in which we are different from one another. This shifted interest implies rather different ways of thinking, different ways of doing research, even different ways of collecting data and analyzing them statistically; as a result, research in **individual differences** tends to look very different from experimental research. This subfield of psychology and of motor behavior is sometimes called individual differences; more formally, in psychology it is referred to as differential psychology. Consider the conceptual model presented in figure 5.2 as illustrating all the ways in which individual differences could occur. Essentially, every one of the processes we discussed in the earlier parts of the book is a candidate for having individual differences in its functioning.

It is interesting to note that the very aspects of the experimental method that are viewed as "noise" or "error" by the experimental tradition are, in many ways, precisely the topic of interest to the individual-differences researcher. The study of individual differences actually involves two, rather distinct emphases: the study of abilities and the study of **prediction**. These are discussed next.

Studying Abilities

The first of these emphases is the study of the fundamental, largely-genetically determined factors that cause us to be different from one another. A typical question might be, Why is so-and-so such a standout surgeon? One answer, on which we focus in the second part of the book, concerns practice and experience. That is, it is usually the case that the standout surgeon has devoted many hours to practicing her craft, and, of course, we all know that practice makes a large contribution to skilled performance.

But is that all there is to it? Can we really account for the differences among all of us by considering only practice? Most scientists, especially those who study individual differences, would answer this question with a resounding "No." One answer to these kinds of questions suggests that the surgeon inherited a certain fundamental capability that allows her to perform at a high level. If so, what is this capability, what is its nature, how do we discover what it is, and how do we measure it? Most scientists in the area of motor behavior would refer to this capability as an "ability." In this regard we offer the following definition of ability: An ability is a fundamental characteristic of different individuals that tends to underlie particular skills; ability is largely inherited genetically and is not modifiable by practice.

Studying Prediction

The second aspect of individual-differences research concerns what is called *prediction*. Here is a typical real-world example. In the car insurance industry we are charged rates that are dependent, at least in part, on the likelihood that we will have an automobile accident. For example, young male drivers (16-25 years), statistically at least, have more accidents than females; for this age range, this elevated accident rate (vs. that for older drivers) appears to be larger with younger drivers of both genders. Essentially, what the insurance company is doing is estimating the probability that you will have an accident based on your age, where you live, and your driving history in terms of citations and accidents, among other things. The insurance company knows that there is a relationship between certain fundamental features of the drivers (e.g., the driver's age, accident record) that are relatively strongly related to future accident propensity. All these features of the driver (such as driving experience, age) can be thought of as abilities. So, we could say that the insurance company is predicting your likelihood of an accident based on some measure of your abilities. Of course, the company cannot predict with 100% accuracy whether or not you will have an accident next year; but if you are in a younger age group, your chance of having an accident is somewhat larger than that of someone in an older age group.

The following photo shows three-time gold medalist Misty May Treanor returning a volleyball in the 2012 Olympic beach volleyball finals. Tallness is an obvious ability related

151

Misty May Treanor (here, right) has an ability (height) that has facilitated her development as a top-level beach volleyball player.

to beach volleyball; Misty and her volleyball partner (Keri Walsh Jennings, who is 6 ft 3 in, or 1.9 m) are quite tall, and the Misty–Keri team made good use of their height abilities in winning the gold medal in 2012.

Within the field of motor behavior, prediction is all around us. The gymnastics coach predicts who will not become a collegiate gymnast on the basis of, say, body configuration. People who are over 6 ft tall (1.8 m) and who weigh more than 210 lb (95 kg) are probably better suited for a different sport. Universities typically use various test measures as estimates of who among the applicants is most likely to succeed in their programs (e.g., the SAT test), and they then admit the most promising students. In another area, some dental schools use various "spatial abilities" tests as a means to screen applicants for admittance into their programs.

Defining Individual Differences

Here we define *individual differences* as stable, enduring differences among people in terms of some measurable characteristic (e.g., one's age) or perhaps performance of some task (e.g., one's reaction time in a certain situation). Two people can differ on a given performance in at least two different ways. First, if the test involves a very stable measure such as body weight, after a single measurement we might conclude that one person is really heavier than the other. Although the scales might have some small degree of variability, the *repeatability* of the measure is very good. This is an example of a measured characteristic that reveals a stable, enduring difference between two people.

A second difference between people, however, can also occur when no stable enduring difference is really present. For example, if one person rolls a strike in bowling on one attempt and another person rolls a gutter ball, it might not be wise to conclude immediately that the first person is a better bowler than the second person based on this one measurement. Why not? The answer is related to the fact that almost anything can happen on a particular performance attempt by chance alone, and individual differences must be based on *stable*, *enduring* differences. In the first case (weighing people on scales), you are relatively confident of stable, enduring differences in the measured trait, whereas in the second case you are not.

To summarize, individual differences in skills have these characteristics:

- Differences tend to be stable from attempt to attempt.
- Differences endure across time.
- Differences on a single measurement are often not sufficient to establish individual differences.

Abilities Versus Skills

It is useful to distinguish between the concepts of ability and skill. In common language, these words are used more or less interchangeably, as in "Buddy has good ability in [or skill at] _____." However, scientists generally define an **ability** as genetically determined and largely unmodifiable by practice or experience. An ability, therefore, can be thought of as a part of the basic "equipment" people inherit in order to perform various real-world tasks. **Skill**, on the other hand, refers to one's proficiency at a particular task, such as shooting a basketball. Skills, of course, can be modified by practice, are countless in number, and represent the person's potential to perform those particular activities. Thus, one could say "Eric has good visual ability," implying that he can generally see very well; but Eric has developed the specific skill of identifying patterns of motion in football through considerable practice, and this skill has Eric's visual ability as an underlying component. Differences between abilities and skills are summarized in table 7.1.

It is helpful to think of ability as a factor that sets limits on performance. The authors will never become linemen in professional football, regardless of how much time they devote to practice, because they do not have the proper body-configuration ability for this skill. People who are color-blind will never be effective in the skill of identifying and classifying wildflowers, and someone with weak "courage ability" (should this actually exist) should probably not be encouraged to join the circus as a tightrope walker. Thus, limitations in the requisite ability for a particular task are seen to limit the level of performance that a particular individual can eventually attain.

On the other hand, if a novice does not perform very well on a particular task, this might lead to the suspicion that he does not have the proper ability for the task. However, much of this deficit can often be made up through effective practice, as we discuss in the last section of this chapter. Notice that

TABLE 7.1 Some Important Distinctions Between Abilities and Skills

Abilities	Skills
Are inherited traits	Are developed with practice
Are stable and enduring	Are easily modified with practice
Number perhaps 50	Are essentially countless in number
Each underlies many different skills	Each depends on several abilities

even though measures of the skill would change with practice and learning, the ability underlying this skill would not change with practice (see the definition of ability presented earlier). It would be a mistake to make a firm and final judgment about someone's ability for a task when the person has reached only the novice level of proficiency. Several factors can change through practice to improve performance, as we will see later in the chapter.

Is There a General Motor Ability?

What does the term "all-around athlete" really mean? Most of us have known kids from school who starred on the football and basketball teams and who also won medals in track and field. And then there were those other kids—the all-around *non*athletes. They seemed to have no proficiency in motor skills whatsoever. How do we understand these apparent all-around athletes and nonathletes? Two hypotheses, quite different in their approach to answering this question, have been proposed and are discussed next (see also Focus on Application 7.1).

General Motor Ability Hypothesis

An outdated view, made popular in the first half of the 20th century, held that all motor performances are based on a single ability called **general motor ability**. On this view, the all-around athlete is one who possesses a strong *general* capability for skilled motor performance. Conversely, the "all-around *non*athlete" is the person who lacks a strong general motor ability and thus succeeds in essentially no skilled physical activities.

A similar concept of a generalized capability to *learn* new skills was also popular at the time; this concept was called *motor educability* by Brace (1927). Analogous to the idea of the intelligence quotient (IQ)—the innate capability to learn cognitive materials, generally—motor educability was thought to represent some general ability to *acquire* new motor skills. Early attempts to create tests that would measure motor educability were made by Brace (1927: the Brace Test) and McCloy (1934: the General Motor Capacity Test). These tests tended to use whole-body actions that purported to measure the general capability to *learn* athletic skills. Motor educability is not considered a viable concept today, for reasons that will become clear later.

Not surprisingly, the idea of a general motor ability shared many similarities with ideas popular in the early 20th century about the structure of other skills. This kind of thinking led to the idea of "general intelligence," which attempted to explain a person's supposed potential for cognitive activities in terms of an overall, unitary value—the IQ. Further, general cognitive ability (IQ) and general motor ability were thought to be relatively separate, with intelligence not contributing very much to movement skills and vice versa.

This general motor ability notion can be summarized as follows:

- A single, inherited motor ability is assumed.
- This ability presumably underlies all movement or motor tasks.
- A person with strong general motor ability should be good at all motor tasks.

Henry's Specificity Hypothesis

In the 1950s and 1960s, Franklin Henry (1958/1968; personal communication, University of California at Berkeley, 1965) examined a very important statistical prediction about general motor ability. He reasoned this way: Assume that a relatively large number of people are tested on each of two skills, A and B. Henry reasoned that if one person was an outstanding performer on skill A, then this person would be assumed to have a strong general motor ability. If so, this person should also score well on task B, which also depended on general motor ability. Conversely, if another person did not score well on skill A, at least part of the reason would

Focus on
APPLICATION 7.1

The Babe (Mildred "Babe" Zaharias)

If any single athlete were to be given the label "all-around athlete," it would certainly be Mildred "Babe" Zaharias. She played professional basketball, baseball, tennis, and bowling; she won two gold medals and one silver medal in track and field at the 1932 Summer Olympics; and she dominated women's golf at both the amateur and professional levels for two decades. In fact, Babe Zaharias was the first female to ever play in a Professional Golfers' Association event, 65 years before Annika Sorenstam gained notoriety for doing it at the Colonial tournament in 2003. The Babe would surely have continued to impress people with her athleticism had she not met her untimely death from cancer at the age of 45.

Mildred "Babe" Zaharias—greatest all-around athlete, ever.

But, what was it that made Babe Zaharias so special? One view is that she had one, very strong, all-around *ability* that was superior to most others' and that allowed her to perform many motor skills at a superior level. Another view is that she had many separate abilities that allowed her to develop certain specific skills at which she was highly proficient.

---

be that this person had a weak general motor ability, and this person would be expected to score relatively poorly on skill B also. In this way, skill A and skill B are *related* to each other, in that "good" scores on A go with "good" scores on B, and "poor" scores on A go with "poor" scores on B.

With this kind of relationship, if we were to plot skill A against skill B, as we have done in figure 7.1, where each dot represents a single subject measured on both tests A and B, these two tests should plot linearly with each other, which they tend to do in figure 7.1a. However, if skill A and skill B are not related to each other, then they should plot more or less as seen in figure 7.1b. One interpretation of these plots is that in figure 7.1a, skill A and skill B tend to be measures of the same thing, and the usual interpretation is that they are both measures of the same ability. In figure 7.1b, on the other hand, we would be forced to say that skill A and skill B are not measures of the same ability. This leads to the straightforward prediction that if general motor ability exists, with all skills being dependent on a single general motor ability, then all skills should show strong relationships among them, as in figure 7.1a.

155

Statistically, a scatter plot such as that in Figure 7.1a implies that the two skills are *correlated* with each other; that is, the statistical **correlation coefficient (r)** computed between these two tests should be close to +1, and far away from zero. The scatter plot illustrated in figure 7.1b implies a very low positive correlation between the two tests and an *r* value just slightly above zero. (See Focus on Research 7.1 for more on correlations.)

Correlations Among Various Skills

Scientists have examined both field and laboratory data to determine whether or not high correlations among motor skills could be found. There are numerous data sets in the literature, but one by Drowatzky and Zuccato (1967) makes the point particularly well. The authors examined six tests of balance typically found in the physical education literature. A large group of subjects was given all six tests, and the correlations between each pair of tests were computed (15 pairs in all). These values are shown in the correlation matrix in table 7.2, which contains the correlation of every test with every other test. The highest correlation in the entire matrix was between the tests named "bass stand" and "sideward stand" (*r* = .31). All of the other correlations were numerically lower than this, ranging from .03 to .26. Even the highest correlation of .31 means that there was only $.31^2 \times 100$ = 9.6% in common between these two tests; over 90% of the abilities underlying the two tests were different (i.e., 100% − 9.6% = 90.4% being different). Based on these data, it is impossible to argue that there was some single, underlying general motor ability that accounted for individual differences in all of these tests.

The argument for general motor ability is even weaker considering that the tests in this study were all tests of different ways of balancing. There seemed to be no general ability even to balance, with each test measuring some separate ability to control posture. Lotter (1960) obtained similar findings for correlations among tasks that purport to measure movement speed; the highest correlation between any two tasks was .36. In a study of 50 tests in the Armed Services Testing Program (Fleishman & Parker, 1962), the correlations among tasks were generally less than .50 (i.e., $.50^2 \times 100$ = 25% in common) unless the tests were practically identical to each other.

Henry based most of his thinking on numerous studies that examined correlations among skills, all of which showed patterns similar to that seen in table 7.2. In seeking additional evidence about specificity, though,

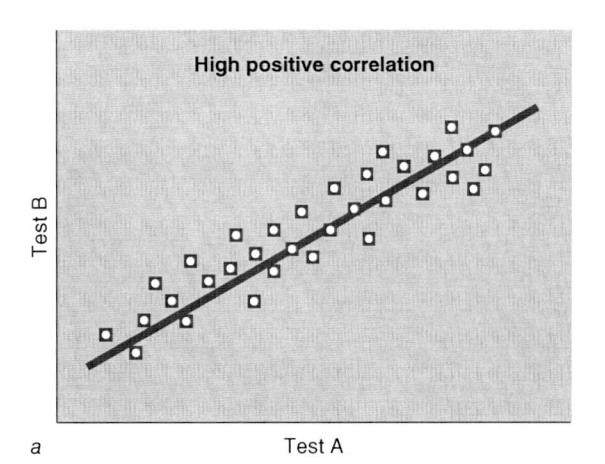

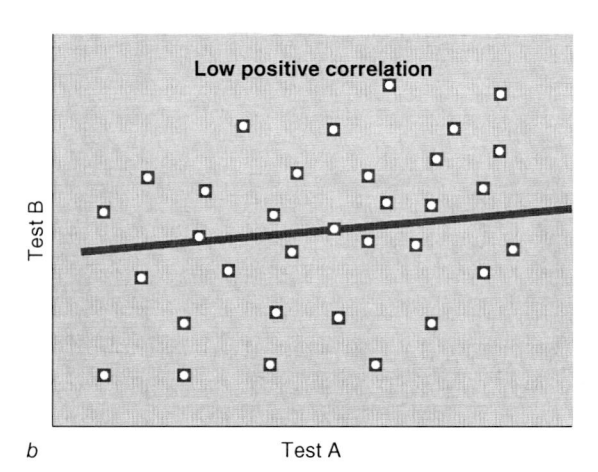

FIGURE 7.1 Scatter plot of two tests revealing a high positive correlation (*a*) and a very low positive correlation (*b*). Each dot in the figure represents the performance of one individual, plotting performance on one test against performance on the other test.

Focus on
RESEARCH 7.1

Correlation: The Statistic of Individual Differences

An important concept for understanding abilities is correlation, a statistic for measuring the strength of a relationship between two or more tests. Assume we administered two tests, A and B, to a large group of subjects (say, 100 people), such that each person has been measured on both tests. The goals are to determine whether the two tests are related to each other and whether they share any underlying features, such as abilities.

Figure 7.1 shows special graphs called *scatter plots*, with test A on one axis and test B on the other. Each subject's score is represented as a single dot on each of the two tests. If the dots tend to lie along a line, then we say that test A and test B are *related* to each other in that scores on one test are associated with scores on the other. In the case of figure 7.1a, this relationship is strong and positive: Those individuals with high scores on test A tend to be the same individuals with high scores on test B. The scatter plot in figure 7.1b shows only a small positive relationship: The scores on test A are virtually unrelated to those on test B. The direction of the relationship is given by the sign of the correlation coefficient.

The correlation can range in size from −1.0 to +1.0. The size of the correlation indicates the strength of the relationship, or how close the individual dots are to the best-fitting line passing through them. If the line is sloped negatively – downward to the right – then the sign of the correlation will be negative. If the dots are close to the line, as they are in figure 7.1a, the correlation is close to +1.0, indicating a very strong tendency for skill in A to be associated with skill in B ($r = +.90$). If the dots lie relatively far from the line, as they do in figure 7.1b, the correlation is closer to zero, indicating a relatively weak tendency for scores in A to be associated with scores in B ($r = +.15$). The strength of a relationship is estimated by the squared correlation coefficient multiplied by 100. Thus, the correlation of +.15 means that the two tests have $.15^2 = (.15 \times .15) \times 100$, or about 2% in common with each other. Note that the size of the correlation has nothing to do with its sign, because a strong correlation can be either positive or negative. Finally, a correlation of .00 indicates that the line of best fit is a horizontal line (a slope of 0), with the dots scattered about it in a random way. In such a case, tests A and B would not be related at all.

Correlations are used in studying abilities. If two tests are related to each other, then they have some underlying feature(s) in common. In the study of skills, these common features are assumed to be the abilities that underlie the two tests in question. If the correlation between two tests is large in value (e.g., ±.80), we conclude that there is at least one ability that underlies both tests. On the other hand, if the correlation is near zero, we conclude that there are no abilities underlying both tests; in other words, the abilities underlying one test are separate from those underlying the other.

Exploring Further

1. What would be the expected correlation value that would support a general, underlying ability for running fast (low time score) and jumping far (large distance score)?
2. What would be the expected correlation value for Henry's specificity view for the two skills in question 1?

TABLE 7.2 Correlations Among Six Tests of Balance

	Stork stand	Diver's stand	Stick stand	Sideward stand	Bass stand	Balance stand
Stork stand	–	.14	–.12	.26	.20	.03
Diver's stand	–	–	–.12	–.03	–.07	–.14
Stick stand	–	–	–	–.04	.22	–.19
Sideward stand	–	–	–	–	.31	.19
Bass stand	–	–	–	–	–	.18
Balance stand	–	–	–	–	–	–

Adapted by permission from Drowatzky and Zuccato 1967.

Henry (personal communication, University of California at Berkeley, 1964) once studied four different populations representing different sport groupings: basketball players, gymnasts, rifle shooters, and people who had never performed on any athletic team, ever. He compared these groups on four novel laboratory skills. If a general motor ability view were correct, then the athletes, who assumedly possessed strong general abilities, would be expected to outperform the nonathlete group on the laboratory skills. Henry found that all of the groups performed essentially similarly, which tended to support his **specificity hypothesis** view and provided even more evidence against the notion of general motor ability.

This large body of literature on correlations among skills is remarkably consistent in supporting the following conclusions:

- Correlations computed among different skills are generally very low.
- Even skills that appear to be quite similar usually correlate poorly.
- This overall lack of correlation among skills argues against the concept of a general motor ability.
- On the other hand, two skills with only minor differences (e.g., throwing 10 m for accuracy and throwing 15 m for accuracy) can correlate strongly.
- The data tell us that there are many abilities and not simply a single general motor ability.

Abilities and the Production of Skills

From the evidence just presented, scientists have been forced to conclude that a single, general motor ability simply does not exist. Such an idea cannot cope with the mass of correlational evidence like that seen in figure 7.2b. Alternatively, scientists have argued that there are many abilities, each with a relatively narrow group of tasks that it supports. This leaves many questions unanswered, such as how many abilities exist, what abilities might underlie some particular performance of interest, and how these abilities are organized with respect to each other.

In baseball, for example, we might suspect that running speed is one of the abilities that underlies, or supports, base running. There must be many such abilities useful in various human performance tasks, such as visual acuity and color vision, body configuration (height and build), numerical ability, reaction speed, manual dexterity, and kinesthetic sensitivity. But only some of these will be related to baseball. Of course, these various abilities are spread throughout the motor system. The individual-differences research in motor behavior is based on a wide variety of tasks, ranging from simple laboratory skills to relatively complex skills associated with flying an airplane. Although there is still much research to be done, at present we understand a great deal about the structure of human motor abilities.

Types of Motor Ability

Individual-differences researcher Edwin Fleishman (1964) conducted numerous investigations of abilities that underlie skills. Following is a brief list (there are many more abilities that are not listed here). For many years Fleishman employed a statistical technique called *factor analysis*, which uses as a starting point the correlations among skills (information analogous to that seen in table 7.2). This brief list gives the name of the ability (generated by Fleishman), a brief description of what it is thought to measure, and an example from real-world activities that might use this ability.

- *Reaction time.* Important in tasks with a single stimulus and a response to the stimulus, where speed of reaction is critical, as in simple reaction time. An example is a start in a running or swimming race.
- *Response orientation.* Involves quick choices among a number of alternative movements, more or less as in choice reaction time. An example is batting in baseball, where the nature of the pitch and thus the bat positioning are uncertain.
- *Speed of movement.* Underlies tasks in which the arm(s) must move quickly but without a reaction-time stimulus, the goal being simply to minimize movement time. An example is swinging a cricket bat.
- *Finger dexterity.* Involves tasks in which small objects are manipulated by the fingers and hands. An example is threading a needle.
- *Manual dexterity.* Underlies tasks in which relatively large objects are manipulated with the hands and arms. An example is dribbling a basketball.
- *Response integration.* Involved in tasks in which many sources of sensory information must be integrated to make an effective response. An example is playing quarterback in American football.
- *Physical proficiency abilities.* Fleishman (1964) also identified several abilities that do not have so much to do with skills but rather involve what he termed "physical proficiency." Here, nine additional abilities, such as dynamic strength, explosive strength, gross body coordination, and stamina (cardiovascular endurance), have been identified. There are probably many others: This group of tests can be best thought of as related to what is usually called physical fitness.

These ideas about abilities have serious implications for some of the most common beliefs held by coaches, sportscasters, and the public in general about the structure of movement ability. Consider often heard statements like "B.B. has good hands." What does that mean? For many people it usually means that, given the many different activities in which B.B. might participate, the use of his hands is generally effective. But examine the preceding list of abilities. Except for physical proficiency, *each* ability involves the hands in some way, either to move small or large objects, to move quickly to press a button, or to follow a moving target with a handheld apparatus. Yet each ability is independent of the others. Therefore, there must be no general "good hands" ability; rather, the abilities needed for a particular task depend on what the hands are asked to do.

Here's another example. We often hear something like "Jessie Mae is quick," the speaker meaning that Jessie Mae generally reacts, responds, and moves quickly whenever speedy actions are required. Yet the preceding list includes at least three separate abilities to act quickly: (a) reaction time (simple reaction time), where a single stimulus leads to a single response; (b) response orientation (choice reaction time), where one of many stimuli is presented, each of which requires its own speeded response; and (c) speed of movement (movement time), which measures the time of a movement produced without an initiating stimulus (i.e., not including reaction time). Subjectively, each of these abilities involves what we would

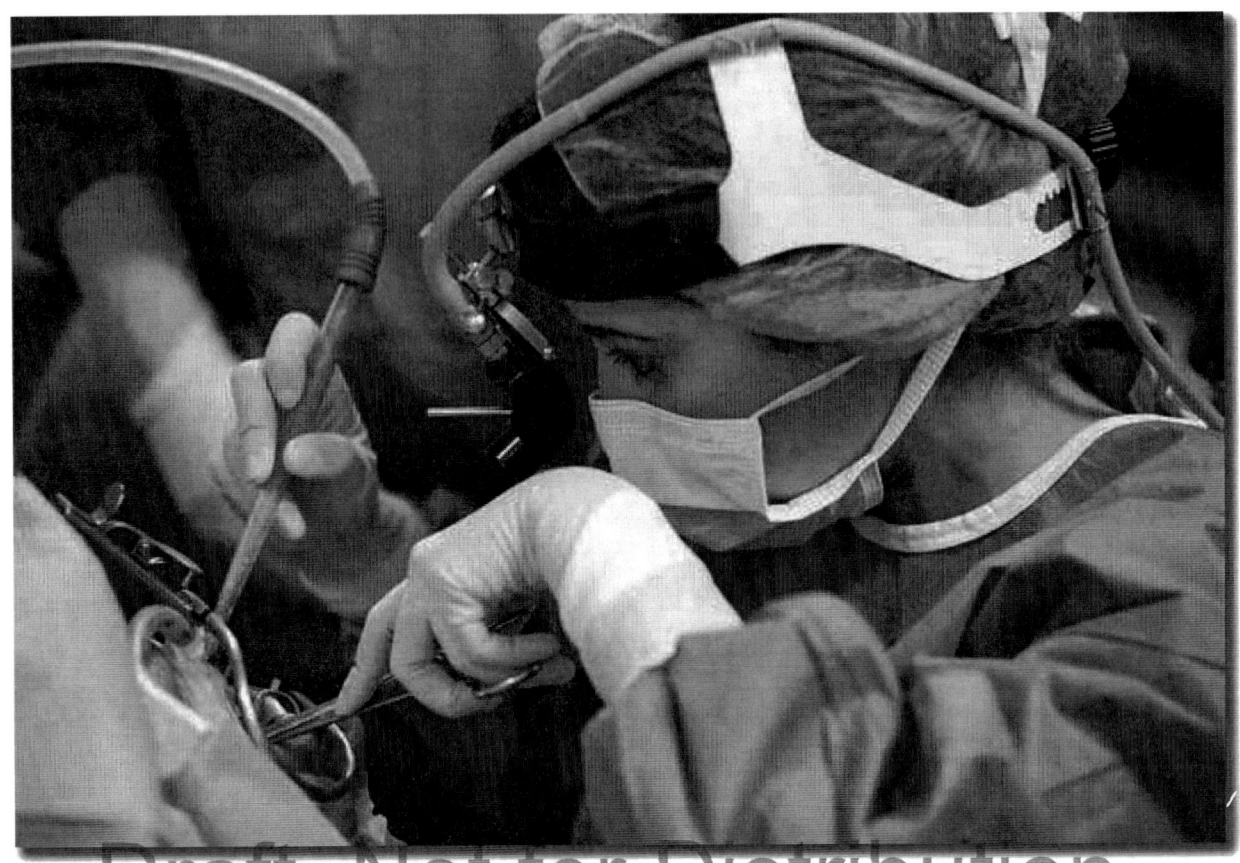

What types of motor ability would contribute to the success of an expert surgeon?

call "quickness." However, as in the situation with B.B's "good hands," these abilities are separate and independent, indicating that there are at least three ways to have the ability to be quick. Therefore, being quick depends on the particular circumstances under which speedy responses are required.

General Motor Ability Reconsidered

Looking collectively at the research on the different types of motor ability, there may be a very minor way in which a general motor ability hypothesis does make sense after all. While the correlations among skills are generally very low, they are not exactly zero, meaning that the tests correlate with each other to a very minor extent (as illustrated in figure 7.2). Thus, there may be a very weak general factor underlying most movement skills, giving a slight advantage to those individuals with such a strong ability. This is sometimes called a **superability**, to distinguish it from the earlier notion of general motor ability. In any case, such a superability must not be very strong, given that the correlations between skills are generally so low. Perhaps abilities for skills are similar to the abilities for intellectual activities: A weak general intellectual ability (IQ) is thought to underlie almost all cognitive functioning, but several specific abilities are far more important (e.g., numerical abilities and verbal abilities); something similar seems to be the case for motor skills.

Be careful, though, because this argument in no way makes correct the earlier notion that all movement capabilities are based on a single general motor ability. There is simply too much evidence against this view, and it has no place in our modern thinking about human motor abilities.

This section on abilities can be summarized with a diagram of how the important concepts of superability, abilities, and skills are related. Figure 7.2 shows just some of

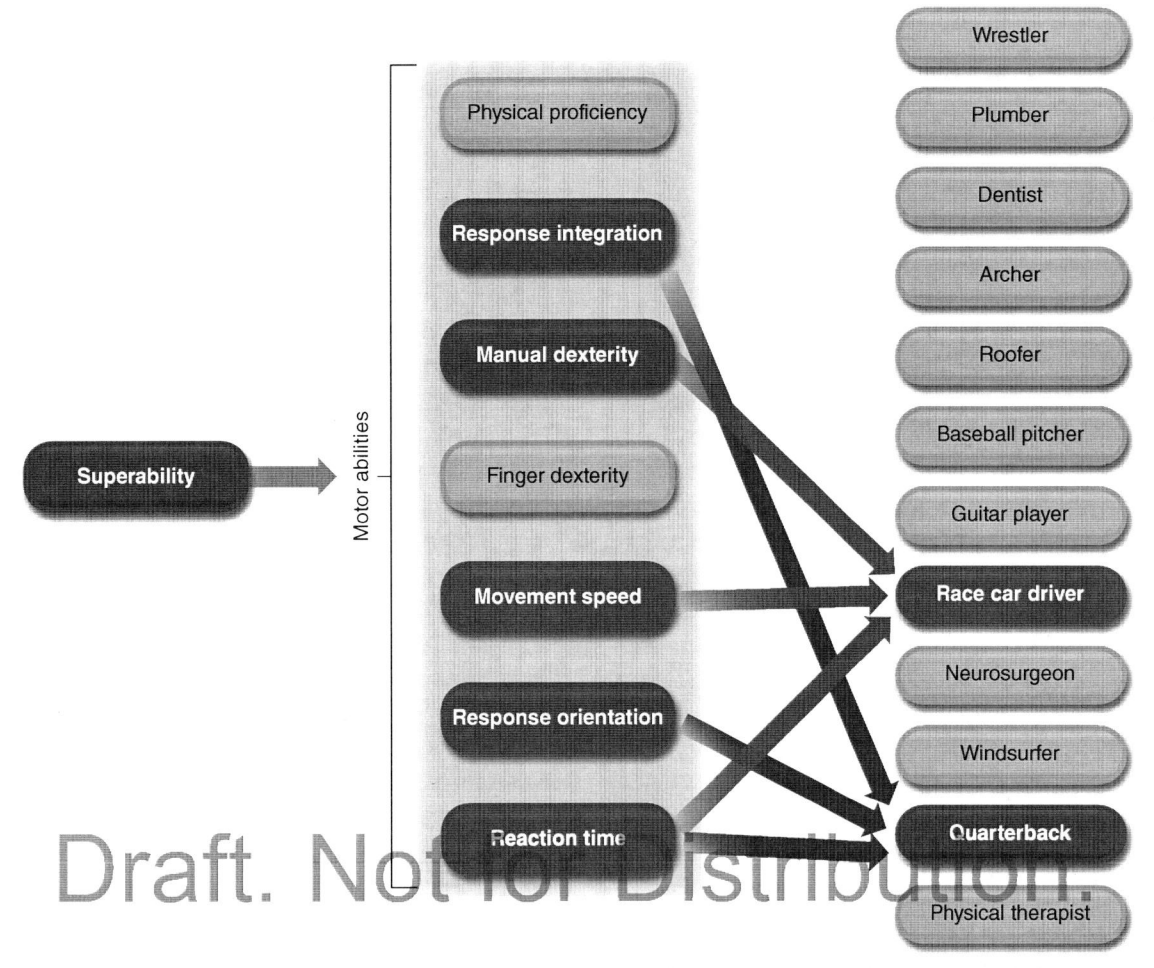

FIGURE 7.2 Link between a superability, various motor abilities, and selected movement skills. Every task is composed of a selection of abilities, and any given ability can contribute to a number of separate tasks.

the abilities and skills discussed so far. At the left of this structure is a superability, which contributes in a minor way to all the separate motor skills. Next would come 20 to 50 motor abilities (only 7 are shown), which provide the specific capabilities to perform these many skills.

There are several important features to notice here. A given skill, say that of the race car driver, is contributed to by a small number of the underlying abilities. We might imagine that movement speed, manual dexterity, and reaction time are represented in this skill, whereas other abilities (e.g., response orientation) might not be. This goes along with the view that particular skills are based on combinations of several underlying abilities. Also, different skills can use overlapping subsets of abilities. A successful quarterback's pattern of abilities is different from that of the race car driver; yet a few of the same abilities are used in both skills (e.g., possibly reaction time), whereas other abilities are not shared between the two (e.g., possibly finger dexterity). This is necessarily so because there are countless individual skills and only a relatively few abilities that can support them.

To summarize the involvement of abilities in the production of skills, the following conclusions can be stated:

- Any given skill has contributions from several of the fundamental motor abilities.
- Some of the abilities underlying a skill play very dominant roles, whereas others have relatively weak roles.

- Two different skills will have different patterns of underlying abilities.
- Two different skills can have a few abilities in common.

Abilities as a Basis for Skill Classification

In chapter 1, we classified skills as (a) open versus closed skills, (b) serial–continuous–discrete skills, and so on. The study of individual differences also leads us to identify the types of ability that underlie skills, which allows for additional skill classification. These classifications are important for practical application because they allow instructors to orient instruction and practice methods to particular task requirements, thereby facilitating performance and speeding up learning. Classifications help with instruction in several ways:

1. The principles of performance and learning are somewhat different for different classes of activities. Therefore, in order to apply those principles properly to the appropriate classification of action—not mixing principles intended for task type A when attempting to teach task type B, for which the principle might not apply, seems essential.
2. Second, knowing that a task has a strong cognitive component or has a particular emphasis on kinesthetic feel could influence the ways you instruct the learner during practice. You can orient instruction and practice methods to particular task requirements, thereby facilitating performance and speeding learning.
3. Finally, task analysis tells you the category in which the task you are teaching might lie so that you can adjust your advanced teaching methods accordingly.

Therefore, effective classification allows the instructor to ensure that the learning principles she is using are appropriate for the skill being taught, to give the learner more assistance with underlying features of the skill important for movement control, and to choose an individual for advanced training based on the match of abilities possessed by the person and involved in the task.

Classifications in terms of abilities can be made either casually or formally, with differing precision as a result. On a very casual level, you can simply produce an "educated guess" about the underlying abilities in a skill by asking yourself which actions seem to require which of the abilities. Alternatively, many have used the method whereby experts or coaches are asked about the fundamental structure of the task. Because expert performers, teachers, and coaches can be very sophisticated about skills, this kind of analysis has the potential for uncovering much useful information (e.g., Fleishman & Stephenson, 1970).

The disadvantage of this method is that, often, very highly proficient performers do not know how they do what they do. As you have learned, many processes in skills are nonconscious, such as the execution of motor programs and the detection of optical-flow patterns; thus, performers do not have good conscious access to them and can't tell you how they use them. A pertinent example comes from Polanyi (1958), who found that champion cyclists could not explain the principles of balancing on the bicycle, which of course was absolutely fundamental to their task. Also, the famous tennis player Bjorn Borg claimed that immediately before striking the ball in a forehand stroke, he would "roll" the racket "over the ball," which produced topspin on the ball so that it would drop more quickly after it crossed the net. Braden (personal communication, 1975) had an opportunity to observe Borg at Vic Braden Tennis College, where he made high-speed video recordings of Borg's forehand stroke. Braden learned that Borg did not rotate his racket immediately before ball contact. It was true that Borg struck the ball with the racket in a "rotated" orientation, presumably to aid topspin, but this rotation occurred quite early in his stroke—not immediately before striking the ball as Borg claimed. It is easy to imagine how a well-meaning tennis instructor who had assumed that Borg's characterization was correct might ask students to attempt to "roll the racket over the ball," just as Borg had said. There are many examples like this in the sport world. Much can be learned from champion performers, but you should be prepared not to believe everything they tell you.

Prediction and Selection Based on Ability

As indicated early in this chapter, a large part of the work on individual differences concerns prediction of performance or skill. We discussed the insurance company's attempt to predict the possibility that you will have a vehicle accident on the basis of certain of your characteristics, or abilities. In industry, a personnel director might want to predict which of several applicants for a job will be most successful at the job, not right now but after a year's training and experience. In sport, Ed Fleishman (personal communication, 1970) described the effort by the owner of the then–Kansas City Royals professional baseball team to develop a procedure whereby abilities found to be critical for adult baseball could be measured in relatively young (junior high school level) players. Knowing which of the younger players had the "right" abilities for adult baseball, the team's coaches could devote extra attention and practice time to those players possessing abilities related to adult-level baseball, of course with the idea of drafting them later.

There are several features common to all these examples. First, someone wants to know something about an individual's *future* performance capabilities at some "criterion skill"—the ultimate skill in which the person is interested. It would be simple to estimate who *at present* is a good performer, but it is another matter altogether to be able to predict who—after growth, maturation, or additional training—will become most skillful on the criterion test (see Fleishman & Hempel, 1955). Second, this prediction process requires knowing which abilities are important for the criterion task. The process could involve measurement of the abilities in already skilled employees in industry, or measuring abilities of accomplished athletes. Third, the process involves measurement (or at least some estimation) of the abilities seen in the applicants' present performance that would predict which of the candidates has the pattern of abilities that matches the criterion skill most completely.

Focus on
APPLICATION 7.2

Moneyball

The recent book and the movie made from it, both titled *Moneyball*, provide a realistic example of these ideas from professional baseball. In earlier times, the variables (measured on high school or college players) that were used to predict who could become professional ballplayers used rather obvious predictor variables, such as batting average and home runs hit. But one team, the Oakland Athletics, decided that these variables were not as important as some others, such as the number of times a player reached first base (by whatever means) and the number of ground-ball outs that a pitcher induced in a game. The book and movie set forth some of the successes of these attempts at predicting success in professional baseball. Changing methods appeared to have paid off for the Oakland team.

Focus on
RESEARCH 7.2

The Relative-Age Effect

Here is an interesting phenomenon. Assume that you are examining the statistics on high-level hockey players in Canada (i.e., those playing on Junior A or professional teams). These statistics, used mostly for promotional purposes, include such things as each player's height, weight, position played, hometown, and birthday. If you examine the birthdays of these players, you will find that hardly anyone on the team was born in the late months of the year, and most were born in January, February, and March. Why should it be the case that most high-level hockey players were born early in the year? Astrology?

Beginning with the research of Barnsley, Thompson, and Legault (1992), followed by many investigations since (reviewed by Cobley et al., 2009), there is a very compelling and reasonable explanation. (Malcolm Gladwell, author of several wonderful books, including *The Tipping Point* [2000] and *Outliers* [2008], also had some interesting ideas about the subject.)

Nearly everyone knows that in Canada, hockey is a very special and traditional sport. Seemingly, most kids would like to see themselves succeed at the highest level possible in hockey. As a result, Canadian hockey is structured so that many age-group teams are available for kids to join, starting at a very early age (as young as 5 years old). Typically, in the leagues in which they play, players are assigned to teams on the basis of calendar-year age groupings. The result is that a child playing on a 10-year-old team in the year 2014 would have been born sometime in the year 2004; if the child's birthday was early in 2005, then he would be directed to the 9-year-old team. Very similar methods are used for many different youth sports in many countries around the world.

This procedure creates a very interesting bias. For example, a child born on January 1, 2005, would play on the 9-year-old team, whereas a child born on December 31, 2004, would play on a team of 10-year-olds, even though these two children are only one day apart in age. We know, of course, that especially in young boys, a year of age (especially at 10 years old) makes a big difference in terms of maturation, body size, and so on; older boys (i.e., those with a birth date earlier in the calendar year) tend to be bigger, faster, and stronger, other things being equal. Naturally, coaches of these age-group teams focus most of their attention on the most effective players, setting the stage for a "rich-get-richer" phenomenon. The kids born early in the year are bigger, faster, and stronger on average than the kids born later in the year, so they receive more attention and more coaching. As a result they improve more than the kids born later in the year, which carries over to the next age-group team: Now they have an advantage because (a) they are still older than the kids born late in the year, and (b) they had the extra coaching and attention during the previous year because they were older—and so on, and so on.

This phenomenon has been labeled the "**relative-age effect**" because the players who are born early in a given year are "relatively older" than the players born late in that year, even though, by traditional methods, they may be the "same age". In a way, this argument goes against the idea that champion players are born with the "right" abilities; rather, this argument suggests that those players who were "lucky enough" to be born early in the year have an advantage over their late-in-the-year counterparts. This theme—that high-level skill performers were simply "fortunate" in various ways—occurs repeatedly in Gladwell's (2008) *Outliers*.

Exploring Further

1. Suppose sport teams in school were based on school-year birth dates rather than calendar-year birth dates. Which children (born in which months) would be the beneficiaries and losers in this "luck of the draw"?
2. Aside from hockey skills, name two motor skills that might be similarly affected by this relative-age effect and two motor skills that you might anticipate would be unaffected.

Therefore, attempts at prediction involve these components:

- Understanding the abilities that underlie the criterion task
- Estimating the strength of these abilities in applicants as indications of their future capabilities in the criterion task
- Estimating (or predicting) the potential (i.e., future) skill level on the criterion task based on present information about the applicants

If the individual's potential for eventual skilled performance at some task can be estimated, many advantages can be realized. Novices could be directed toward those activities for which they could become most suited. Of course, everyone could be trained for an extended time, and those people who succeed at the end of this training period could then simply be selected or hired. But training is generally expensive and time-consuming. Prediction provides a method for reducing the total amount of training time that must be used for a given task. Also, in this way, training can be more focused on the selected individuals. For those individuals not selected for a particular activity, training can be focused on other activities to which they are better suited. This is the rationale for the Olympic training and selection procedures used by many countries recently.

Patterns of Abilities Change With Practice

An important phenomenon to consider when attempting to predict skilled performance is that the pattern of abilities underlying a particular task changes with practice and experience. At one level this is obvious. For beginners, considerable cognitive activity is involved in deciding what to do; remembering what comes after what; and trying to figure out the instructions, rules, task scoring, and the like. With some experience, as one learns the intellectual parts of the task, these cognitive abilities are replaced by more motor abilities related to limb movement.

This general idea was shown in a study by Fleishman and Hempel (1955). They used what are called "**reference tests**," relatively well-understood tests from earlier studies (some of these are referred to earlier in the chapter) that are used to measure abilities of various kinds (e.g., reaction time, movement time, spatial relations). Fleishman and Hempel administered these reference tests to a group of subjects to identify each subject's level of various abilities. The subjects then practiced a complex visual discrimination reaction-time (RT) task. The task involved a series of four colored lights (two red and two green) arranged in a square pattern. Four horizontal toggle switches, which could be pushed or pulled, were used to respond to the lights, depending on a complex spatial relationship among the stimuli. The researchers entered the scores on the reference tests, along with the results of the discrimination RT test, into a factor analysis, which allowed them to measure how much of the performance on the discrimination RT test could be explained by each of the abilities measured by the reference tests. More importantly, these factor analyses allowed the researchers to determine how the relationship between task and the reference tests *changed as a function of practice on the discrimination task.*

First of all, note the large shaded area at the bottom of Figure 7.3 labeled "discrimination reaction time, specific." This line begins at about 20% (meaning that it is a moderately large contributor to performance); then it increases across practice to a value of approximately 40%—where it becomes the largest single contributor to performance. This can be interpreted as showing that the discrimination RT test becomes increasingly *specific* with practice, meaning that discrimination RT relies less and less on various reference tests as practice continues, or that discrimination RT correlates less and less with other tests, or both. In essence, discrimination RT becomes increasingly its "own task," without as much reliance on other abilities.

Second, notice that the contributions of the various reference tests also seem to change as practice continues. For example, the second panel up from the bottom of the graph in Figure 7.4 represents the contributions from the reference test "spatial relations." On the very first trial, "spatial relations" is by far the most important ability in this task, accounting for more variance (about 30%) than any of the other of the reference tests. But its contribution decreases markedly across practice, to the point that it contributes only about 5% to performance on the 15th trial. Notice also

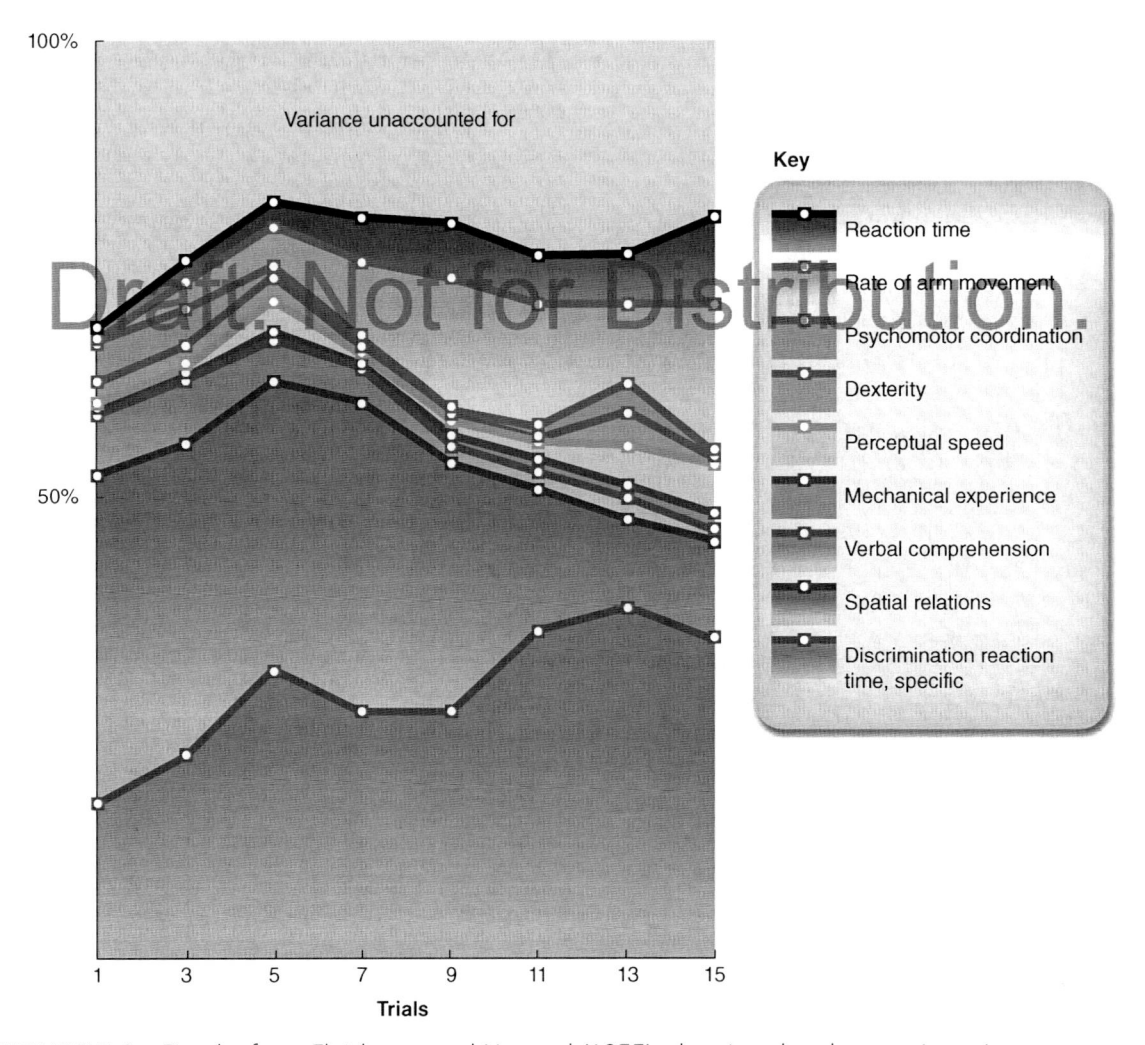

FIGURE 7.3 Results from Fleishman and Hempel (1955), showing the changes in variance accounted for by reference tests on a discrimination RT task as a function of practice.

Reprinted by permission from Fleishman and Hempel 1955.

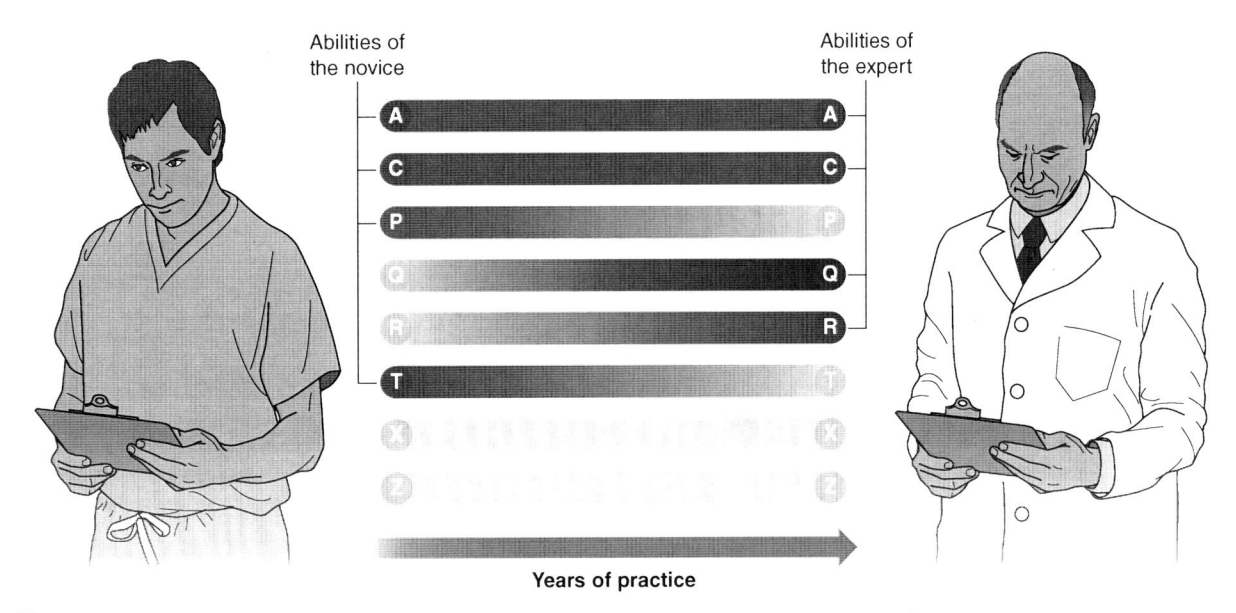

FIGURE 7.4 Changes in the underlying abilities as the learner progresses from novice to expert. Some abilities drop out and are replaced by others, whereas other abilities remain.

that the reference test "rate of movement" increases its contribution to discrimination RT at the same time. That is, the structure of this task seem to "change" with practice; performance seems to depend on (or be related to) different abilities at the start of practice as compared to the end of practice. That is, practice produced changes in the relative contributions of the various abilities – not changes in the abilities themselves.

Consider an activity such as surgery, and assume that it is known which abilities underlie this skill when performers are essentially novices. As seen in figure 7.4, when the person is a novice, this task is composed of hypothetical abilities A, C, T, and P (note the position of the darkened end of each bar). With additional training at this task, this pattern of abilities gradually changes, so the expert's pattern of abilities involves abilities A, C, Q, and R. Notice that two of the abilities, A and C, are present in both novice and expert performers. Other abilities, T and P, drop out to be replaced by abilities not represented earlier—Q and R. Perhaps abilities T and P were cognitive abilities, which dropped out as practice continued (e.g., see Fitts' stages of learning in chapter 9). Still other abilities, X and Z, are never represented in this skill, regardless of the skill level. Remember, abilities are genetically defined and not modifiable by practice. It is the use of, or the selection of, these abilities that changes with practice.

The difficulty is that, although an individual might have the proper abilities for novice performance (abilities A, C, T, and P in figure 7.4), this often is not the proper pattern of abilities required for expert performance (abilities A, C, Q, and R). Therefore, selecting people because they are good as novices—or because they have strong abilities in A, C, T, and P, which is the same thing—will capture only a part of the job of prediction. Most knowledge about abilities is based on relatively novice-level performances; and, unfortunately, little is known about the abilities that underlie very high-level performances, making the task of predicting them particularly difficult.

Performances in Early Practice

This shift of abilities with practice and experience can be a problem if you attempt to select performers on the basis of their performance in early practice. A common procedure is to invite a large group of youngsters to try out for

Running speed is one ability likely to influence success in base running. What other abilities would be important, for either a novice or expert base-runner?

a particular team or activity. After a relatively brief practice period of a few hours, those performers most skilled at these activities are invited to remain on the team, and the others are told that they will not be retained. You can perhaps see the difficulty with this procedure. Referring to figure 7.4 again, assume that the people who have succeeded at this early stage of practice are strong in abilities A, C, T, and P. These people, after extensive practice, may not be very well suited for high-level proficiency because they may not be strong in abilities Q and R.

The problem is even more serious than this. Consider an individual who has the proper abilities for *expert* performance (say, A, C, Q, and R, to use our current example). While this person does have the abilities to perform this skill at the end of practice, he does not have the proper abilities for *novice* performance; notice that if abilities T and P are not strong, there is the likelihood that he will not even be selected to remain with the team after the brief initial practice period. Because the abilities underlying a skill change with proficiency level, we stand a good chance of missing the "right" people if we base selection on performance at the novice level. The solution for this problem seems to be to allow as many performers as possible the opportunity to participate as long as possible, so the applicants can gradually move toward their own highest levels of proficiency. Then, by evaluating high levels of skill and stable, expert patterns of abilities, coaches and trainers can select more confidently.

How Effective Is Skill Prediction?

Prediction for future success sounds wonderful in principle, but there are several difficulties in actual practice. For example, in various attempts to predict success in activities such as military pilotry, subjects are measured on a large number of "predictor tests," which are presumably (as determined by prior factor analysis research—reference tests) measures of various underlying abilities. The relationship between this battery of predictor tests and the criterion task of pilotry is computed using a statistical technique called multiple regression. It is beyond our scope here to provide much discussion of multiple regression; we will just say that multiple regression procedures apply weights (indicating "importance in") to various predictor tests in such a way that the weighted sum of the predictor variables correlates maximally with the criterion.

These correlations (called multiple correlations, abbreviated R) are not usually very high in skills-prediction situations—perhaps .30 or .40; the *largest* of these correlations that we have seen reported in the literature was only .70 (Adams, 1953, 1956; Fleishman, 1956). Remember, with correlations, this means that only $.70^2 \times 100$ or 49% of the abilities underlying the criterion pilotry task are being measured by the test battery; the remaining abilities underlying pilotry are unknown. The situation is even more dismal in athletics because this problem has received almost no systematic study, whereas the prediction of pilotry has had much research support. The result is that prediction in sport situations is not very effective.

Why is effective prediction so difficult to achieve, even with tasks that have attracted strong research efforts? Several factors contribute to the problem.

Patterns of Abilities Are Not Generally Known

One difficulty is that the pattern of abilities underlying successful performance of various criterion tasks is generally not very well understood. Coaches and instructors usually have some general ideas about these abilities, of course, such as the abilities to be tall in basketball or large in football. Beyond this, though, determining the abilities for various sport activities is based mainly on guesswork. Related to this is the fact that even if the abilities were known, no one is certain how to measure them. Therefore, because the abilities underlying a given sport and performance are generally poorly understood and difficult to measure, there is little basis for effective prediction.

Many Abilities Underlie a Given Skill

Even if some of a particular criterion activity's abilities were understood and could be measured, there are probably many other abilities underlying this task. For example, if 15 of the 50 or so abilities must be measured to predict effectively, imagine the time and expense in measuring each ability in each of a large group of applicants. Of course, some success at prediction can be achieved using only one or two tests, but the advantage will be relatively small because of the many relevant abilities that are not considered.

Generally, the prediction of success in movement skills is not very effective in motor behavior for the following reasons:

▶ The underlying abilities in motor performances have not been studied systematically and are not well understood.
▶ The number of such underlying abilities is probably large, requiring that many abilities be measured.
▶ The pattern of relevant abilities shifts with practice and experience, making prediction of expert performances difficult.

Summary

There are many interesting aspects of individual differences among people and ways in which these variations can be understood. A critical concept is that of an ability, which is defined as a mainly genetically-defined, stable, enduring trait that underlies the performance of various tasks. An ability is distinguished from a skill, which is proficiency in some particular task. Henry's (and others') research tells us that the old concept of a general motor (or athletic) ability, with one ability thought to underlie all motor proficiency, is simply incorrect. Generally, the relationships (measured by correlations) between various skills are low, suggesting that there are many abilities, which are very specific to particular tasks. There appear to be many motor abilities—perhaps 50 or so, when they are all discovered—that should be able to account for motor performances.

The capability to predict performers' success in some future activity is a critical individual-difference consideration, and the success of prediction is based on the notion of abilities. However, even in the most thoroughly studied areas of motor performance, prediction is not very effective, probably because of the incomplete understanding of the fundamental abilities that underlie performance. This is particularly so in sport, where most areas have received little scientific study. Finally, the pattern of abilities for a particular skill changes with practice, requiring caution in attempts to predict a performer's ultimate success on the basis of performances in early practice.

WEB STUDY GUIDE ACTIVITIES

The student web study guide, available at www.HumanKinetics.com/MotorLearningandPerformance, offers these activities to help you build and apply your knowledge of the concepts in this chapter.

Interactive Learning

Activity 7.1: Explore the distinction between an ability and a skill by indicating which in a list of descriptions applies to each.

Activity 7.2: Test your understanding of the correlations between skills by interpreting three correlation graphs and matching them to the appropriate pair of skills.

Activity 7.3: Identify the relevant factors for predicting an individual's future performance capability for a specific skill.

Situation-Based Exercise

Activity 7.4: The situation-based exercise for this chapter prompts you to identify a sport or activity and analyze the abilities and skills that would affect its performance, as well as consider the issues that would arise when predicting who would be successful in the sport or activity.

Check Your Understanding

1. List three characteristics that individual differences in skills have. Can these be measured in a single test? If so, which test? If not, why not?
2. How were statistical correlations used to examine abilities? What did researchers find out about correlations among skills? What does this tell you about the concept of a general motor ability?
3. Describe three components involved in attempts at prediction of a future skill level on a criterion task. How effective is skill prediction in a sport setting?

Apply Your Knowledge

1. Explain the differences between an ability and a skill. How would you illustrate these differences to a friend who has told you that she would like to train quickness in her young field hockey team? What might you suggest to include in practice to improve on skills requiring speed?

2. What difficulties might a talent scout for a high-level swim team encounter when predicting which young children at a swim camp are likely to do well at an elite level? How might the abilities needed to perform well as a novice differ from those needed after several years of training?

Suggestions for Further Reading

Additional reading on early thinking about individual differences in motor control can be found in Henry (1958/1968); other treatments have been written by Fleishman (1957; Fleishman & Bartlett, 1969); and a short discussion is included in Adams' (1987) review. Ackerman has conducted much of the most recent research and theorizing in the area of individual differences (e.g., Ackerman, 2007). A general discussion of the history and nature of motor abilities can be found in Schmidt and Lee (2011, chapter 9). See the reference list for these additional resources.

Draft. Not for Distribution.

PART II

Principles of Skill Learning

Up to this point in the text, our focus has been on understanding some of the factors that underlie motor behavior: the principles of movement control. Most of the major variables that determine the quality of movement output have been introduced and discussed. In addition, we have developed a conceptual model of motor behavior. This model collects in one place most of the important factors that determine motor output and indicates their interactions, providing a relatively complete diagram representing how skills are controlled. This conceptual model is consistent with the research evidence; indeed, no process would have been included in the model unless the empirical data suggested that it should be included. By this point, then, you should have a reasonably good overall grasp of how skills are performed and what some of the limiting factors might be.

Now is the time to put this model to work to help with understanding how skills are acquired and improved with practice, as well as how the motor system can adapt itself after stroke or injury so that motor behavior is possible again. The concepts and terminology in part II should be familiar, as they are mainly the same as those used in part I. A major focus in part II is on the ways in which the components of the conceptual model can change with practice and experience, as well as the research-based principles that govern such changes. So, as in part I, a major emphasis is on research indicating how certain variations in practice contribute to the future capability for movement. As you will see, many of these variations of practice are available to the coach or instructor to use directly with learners; hence this discussion includes many ways in which practice can be varied in real-world settings to maximize learning. Another important idea concerns the notion of transfer of learning—the concept that practice on one variation of the task can carry over, or "transfer to," some different task. Hence, a major concern is how practice on simulators may, or may not, carry over well to some different task. Another related issue concerns the extent to which skills are retained over time so they can be helpful to the performer in the future. The practically-oriented reader should find this section of the text useful.

Draft. Not for Distribution.

Introduction to Motor Learning

Concepts and Methods in Research and Application

KEY TERMS

capability
learning curves
motor learning
performance curve
retention test
transfer of learning
transfer test

CHAPTER OUTLINE

Motor Learning Defined
How Is Motor Learning Measured?
Distinguishing Learning From Performance
Transfer of Learning
Summary

CHAPTER OBJECTIVES

Chapter 8 introduces the concept of motor learning and describes fundamental principles regarding how it is studied. This chapter will help you to understand

- a clear definition of motor learning and how it differs from motor performance,
- temporary and "relatively permanent" effects of practice variables,
- transfer designs and their importance in learning research, and
- the measurement of transfer of motor skills.

Imagine that you are an instructor in a two-day cardiopulmonary resuscitation (CPR) course, charged with teaching a set of skills to a group of adults. For grading, you want to measure skill levels at the end of the course, but are puzzled about how to do it. Would the best measure of skill take into account the students' levels of proficiency at the start of the class? Would you measure the amount learned at the end of a course, when fatigue might influence the measurements? Or would you measure skill at some time later, after the course has finished, by which time some forgetting might have occurred? What skills should you ask learners to perform as a test—the same as practiced earlier or slight variations of them? And under what conditions would the test be conducted—in the stress-free conditions in which the skills were taught, or in the heightened levels of excitement that would no doubt put the skills to the test in a real emergency, or something in between?

This chapter concerns motor skill learning, the remarkable set of processes through which practice and experience can generate large, nearly permanent gains in human performance. The initial focus is on understanding the concept of learning, establishing some basic ideas about how learning is defined and conceptualized. Then we turn to how, and with what standards, one can measure and evaluate the effectiveness of practice, both in laboratory and in practical settings with relevance to teaching. Finally is a discussion of transfer of learning, by which the skills acquired in one situation can be applied to another.

The capability to learn is critical to biological existence because it allows organisms to adapt to the particular features of their environments and to profit from experience. For humans, this learning is most critical of all. Think how it would be to go through life equipped only with the capability inherited at birth. Humans would be relatively simple beings indeed without the capability to talk, write, or read, and certainly without the capability to perform the complex movement skills seen in sport, music, or industry. Although learning occurs for all kinds of human performances—cognitive, verbal, interpersonal, and so on—the focus here is on the processes that underlie learning the cognitive and motor capabilities that lead to skills as defined earlier.

176

Learning seems to occur nearly continuously, almost as if everything you do today generates knowledge or capabilities that affect how you do other things tomorrow and beyond. However, this book takes a more restricted view of learning, in which the focus is on situations involving practice, that is, deliberate attempts to improve performance of a particular skill or action. Practice, of course, often takes place in classes or lessons, either in groups as might be seen in the CPR example provided earlier, or individually, as in private ski lessons or physical therapy sessions. Usually, but certainly not always, there is an instructor, therapist, or coach to guide this practice, to evaluate the learner's progress and give feedback about it, and to decide about future activities to maximize progress. This focus on practice with an instructor defines an important class of human activities and requires investigation of the many factors—such as the nature of instructions, evaluation, and scheduling—that collectively determine the effectiveness of practice.

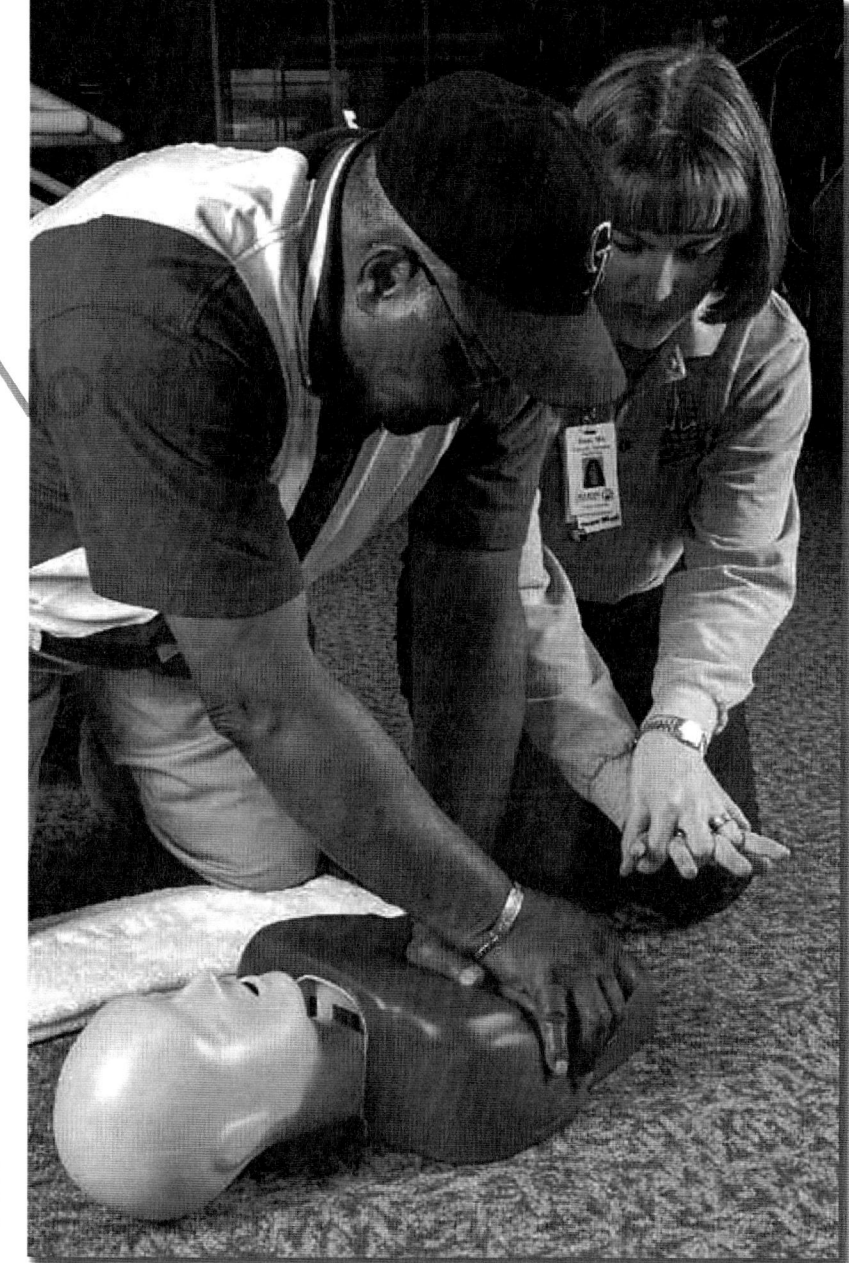

For students learning CPR, how can learning be structured so that the skill will transfer to real-world situations?

Instructors in charge of practice are in an important position to influence learning if they have a solid understanding of the fundamental processes underlying practice settings. A critical starting point is understanding the nature and definition of learning.

Motor Learning Defined

When a person practices, the obvious result is almost always an improved performance level, which can be measured in a number of ways, such as a lower golf score, reduced time to complete a simple surgical operation, or a larger number of roofing shingles nailed in a 20 min period. But there is more to learning than just improved performance. Psychologists have found it useful to define learning in terms of the gain in the underlying *capability* for skilled performance developed during practice, with the improved capability leading to improved performance.

But, be aware that improved performance does not, by itself, define learning. Rather, improved performance is an indication that learning *may* have occurred, which represents an important distinction. This idea can be formalized by a definition:

> **Motor learning** is a set of processes associated with practice or experience leading to relatively permanent gains in the capability for skilled performance.

There are several important aspects to this definition, which are discussed in the next sections.

Learning Affects Capability

The term "**capability**" for performance may seem odd, but it simply reflects the fact that any single performance may not reflect the skill level that underlies the performance. Just as the fastest runner does not always win the race, any performance may exceed or fall short of its theoretical true capability. So, we are interested in measuring the underlying capability (or capacity) for performance, being mindful that on any given occasion the learner might not for various reasons perform up to her capability.

Learning Results From Practice or Experience

Everyone knows there are many factors that improve the capability for skilled performance. However, learning is concerned with only some of these factors—those related to practice or experience. For example, the performance capabilities of children increase as they mature and grow. However, these growth factors are not evidence of learning because they are not related to practice. Similarly, gains in cardiovascular endurance or strength could occur in training programs, leading to more effective performance in activities like soccer; but these changes are not related to practice as considered here.

Learning Is Not Directly Observable, But Its Products Are

During practice there are many alterations to the central nervous system, which some refer to as "brain plasticity," where the term "plasticity" refers to a brain that is changeable under various conditions. Some of these alterations help establish relatively permanent changes in movement capability. These processes are generally not directly observable, though, so their existence must usually be inferred from the changes in performance they presumably support. It is useful to think of these changes as occurring to the fundamental decision-making and movement-control processes, discussed in the previous chapters, that are brought together in the conceptual model of human performance. Figure 8.1 shows the conceptual model again, this time highlighting some of the human performance processes thought to be influenced by practice.

Some examples of changes to these processes are (a) increased automaticity, together with speed and accuracy, in analyzing the environmental and movement feedback information (during stimulus identification); (b) improvements in the ways actions are

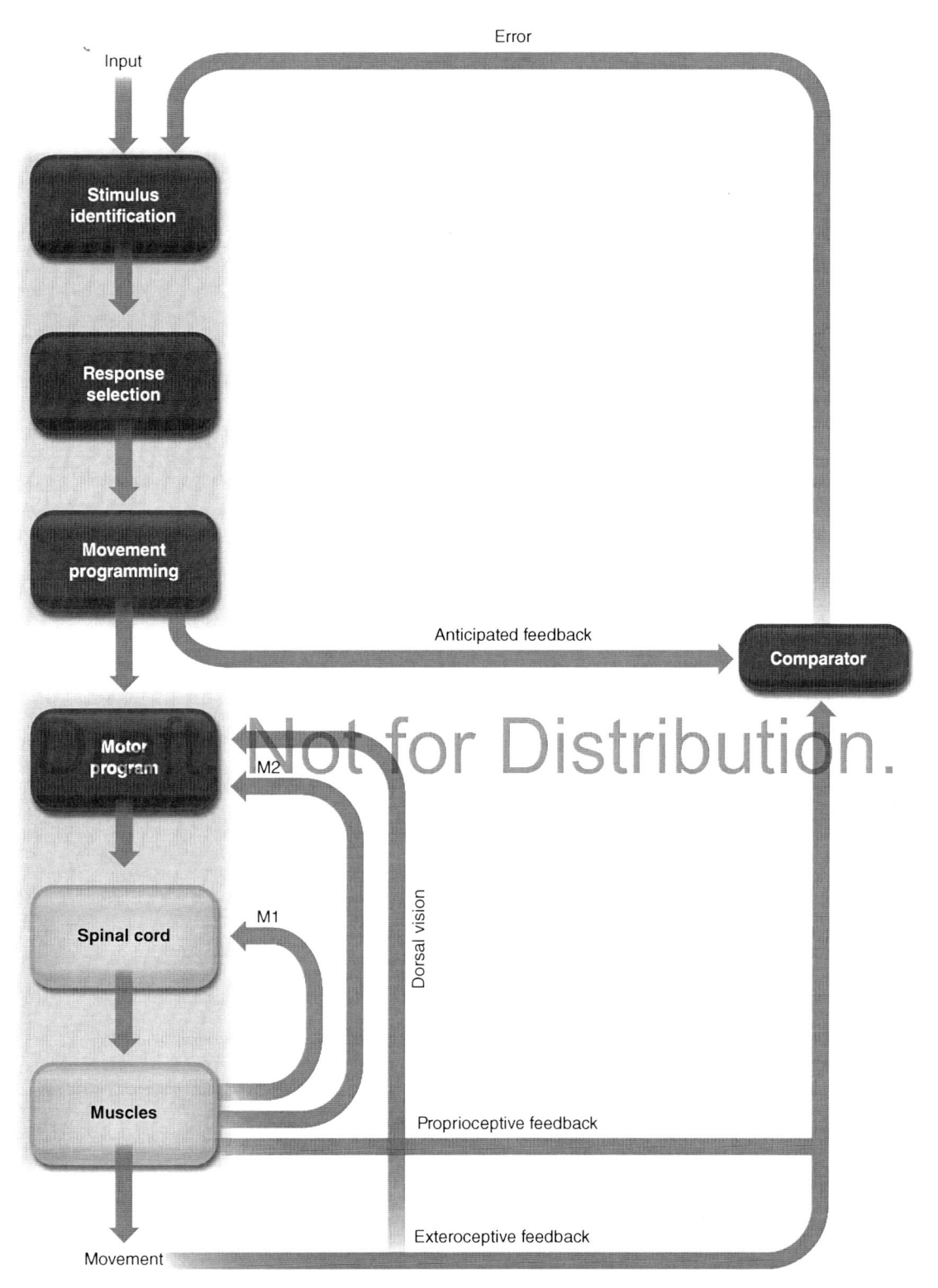

FIGURE 8.1 Conceptual model with the processes that improve with practice highlighted (in light green).

selected (during response selection) and parameterized (in movement programming); (c) building more effective generalized motor programs and effector processes; and (d) establishing more accurate references of correctness to aid in, for example, balance. In fact, learning can occur at all levels of the central nervous system, but the levels highlighted in figure 8.1 account for the biggest changes. Of course, all of these processes have been discussed before; now is simply added the notion that they can be improved in various ways through practice, leading to more effective performance.

Even though the underlying processes are not directly observable, we can usually observe and measure the products of the learning process by measuring changes in skill. Changes in underlying processes lead to more effective capability for skill, which then allows more skillful performances. Therefore, evidence about the development of these processes can be gained by examining carefully chosen performance tests. The performance gains on these tests are usually assumed to result from gains in skill.

Learning Requires Relatively Permanent Changes

One important qualification must be added to the previous section. In order for a change in skilled performance level to be regarded as due to learning, the change must be *relatively permanent*. Many different factors affect the momentary level of skilled performance, some of which are temporary and transient. For example, skills can be affected by drugs, sleep loss, mood, stress, motivation, and many other factors. Most of these variables alter performance only for the moment, and their effects soon disappear. Consider caffeine, for example; the performance gains from the caffeinated state to the de-caffeinated state are not due to learning because the changes are transient and reversible. There are many variations of practice that can be shown to affect performance greatly, but often these effects gradually wear off, allowing performance to return to its previous level. These changes were clearly not relatively permanent.

In studying learning, it is important to understand those practice variables that affect performance in a relatively permanent way. This changed capability is then a permanent part of the person's makeup and is available at some future time when the given skill is required.

An analogy might be useful. When water is heated to a boil, there are changes in its behavior (analogous to performance). Of course, these are not permanent because the water returns to the original state as soon as the effects of the variable (heating) dissipate. These changes therefore would not be analogous to learning changes because they are not relatively permanent. However, when an egg is boiled, its state is changed. This change is relatively permanent because cooling the egg does not reverse its state to the original. The relatively permanent changes in the egg are analogous to changes in the human due to learning. When people learn, relatively permanent changes occur that survive the shift to other conditions or the passage of time. After learning, you are not the same person you were before, just as the egg is not the same egg.

The realization that performance alterations due to learning must be relatively permanent has led to special methods for measuring learning and evaluating the effects of practice variations. Essentially, these methods allow scientists to separate relatively permanent changes (due to learning) from temporary changes (due to transient factors). We return to this idea in a subsequent section.

To emphasize the features of the definition of learning, the following statements are important to keep in mind:

- Learning results from practice or experience.
- Learning is not directly observable.
- Learning changes are inferred from certain performance changes.
- Learning involves a set of processes in the central nervous system.

- Learning produces an acquired capability for skilled performance.
- Learning changes are relatively permanent, not transitory.

How Is Motor Learning Measured?

For both the experimental effects of learning in the laboratory and the practical effects of learning in applications of daily living, measuring learning and evaluating progress are conducted in line with the same general principles. Some of these are presented in this section.

Performance Curves

By far the most common and traditional way to evaluate learning progress during practice is through **performance curves**. Assume that a large number of people are practicing some task, and performance measures for each of their attempts (called *trials*) have been collected. From these data, a graph of the average performance for each trial can be drawn, as in figure 8.2. These data were generated from a rotary pursuit tracking task, in which subjects attempted to keep a handheld stylus in contact with a constantly moving target. The measure of performance, time-on-target (the average number of seconds in contact during a 10 s trial), shows improvement as trials accumulate over five days of practice (Adams, 1952).

For practice with other tasks the curve slopes downward, such as those in which time or errors are the performance measures. Figure 8.3 involves a task in which the subjects attempted to match a complex goal pattern of arm movement. Error in making the proper pattern (termed root-mean-square error, or RMS error; see chapter 1) is the measure of performance, and it is reduced quickly at first, then more slowly as practice continues. Similar to what is seen in figure 8.2, there is a small regression in performance between practice days, due to forgetting and other processes (such as warm-up decrement; see chapter 9), but after a few trials the learners regained their earlier performance levels and continued to improve.

Comparing figures 8.2 and 8.3, one can readily see that performance curves slope upward or downward depending on whether the measured data increase (distance run, number of successful completions, and so on)

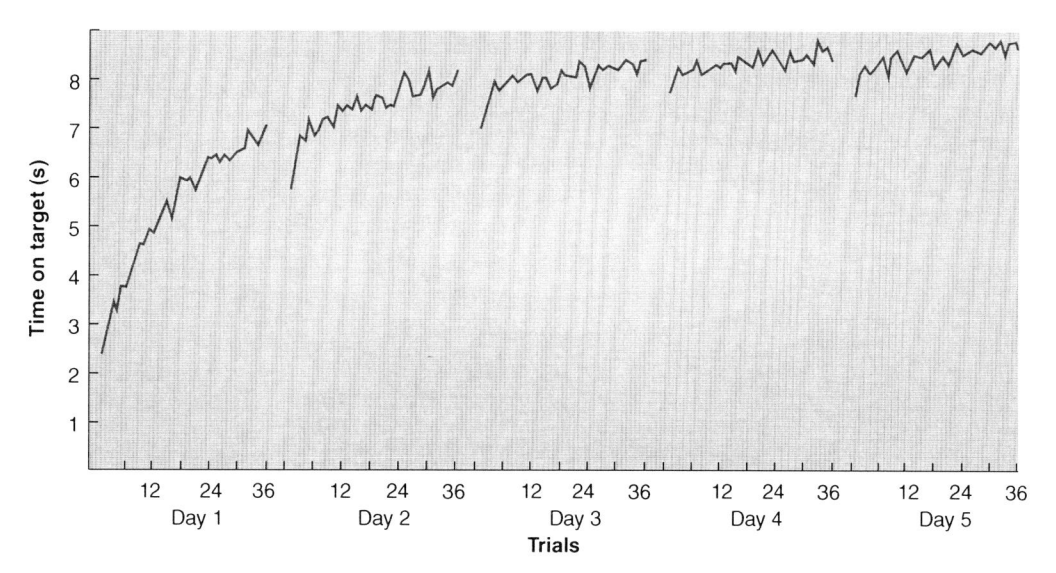

FIGURE 8.2 Performance curve for a group of subjects practicing a rotary pursuit tracking task. The score reflects the amount of time in contact with the object to be tracked during a 10 s trial.

From *American Journal of Psychology*. Copyright 1952 by the Board of Trustees of University of Illinois. Used with the permission of the University of Illinois Press.

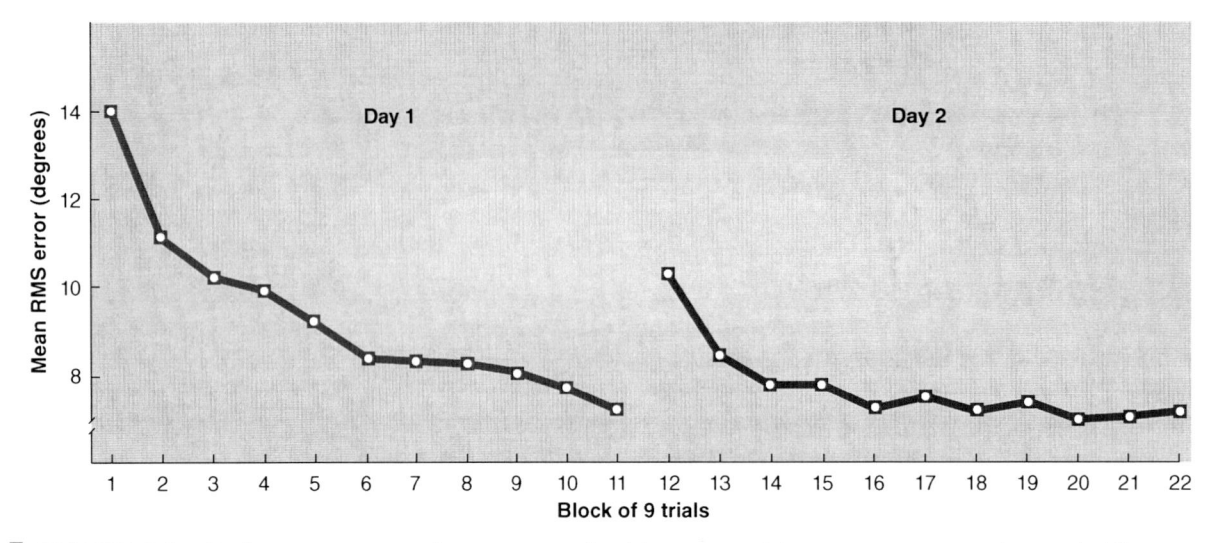

FIGURE 8.3 Performance curve for a group of subjects practicing an arm patterning task. The score reflects the amount of error (expressed as root-mean-square [RMS] error), which indicates how close the movements were to the goal pattern.

Reprinted by permission from Winstein and Schmidt 1990.

or decrease (errors, time) with practice and experience. Another feature of performance curves that is typified in both figures is that large changes occur early in practice and then more gradually later on. In some cases the improvements might be nearly completed after several dozen trials, whereas in other cases the improvements could continue for years, although such changes would be very small in later years.

This general form of performance curves—steep at first and more gradual later—is one of the most common features of learning any task and reflects a fundamental principle, called the "law of practice" (Snoddy, 1926). The mathematical form of these curves and how they change with various features of the task and the nature of the learners have been discussed in some detail by numerous writers in the skill area (e.g., Newell, Liu, & Mayer-Kress, 2001, 2009). Back in the 1960s, Franklin Henry (see chapter 1) was doing considerable logarithmic curve fitting, using data from both motor learning tasks and fatigue tasks, and he attempted to understand various changes in shapes of these performance curves (personal communication, University of California at Berkeley, 1962).

The major points so far about performance curves can be summarized as follows:

- Performance curves are plots of individual or average performance against practice trials.
- Such curves can either increase or decrease with practice, depending on the particular way the task is scored.
- The law of practice says that improvements are rapid at first and much slower later—a nearly universal principle of practice.

Limitations of Performance Curves

There are many useful ways to use performance curves, such as to display a given learner's performance gains or to chart the progress of a group of individuals. At the same time, several potential difficulties require caution in drawing interpretations from these curves.

Performance Curves Are Not Learning Curves.

As useful as performance curves are for illustrating learners' progress, several characteristics limit their usefulness. First, these are not "**learning curves**," as if they somehow charted the progress of learning. These

Focus on RESEARCH 8.1

Learning Curves: Facts or Artifacts?

In an important early article, Bahrick and colleagues (1957) identified a number of artifacts of so-called learning curves. Subjects practiced a tracking task in which hand movements of a lever were used to follow a variable cursor presented on a screen. The researchers recorded the performances for analysis and later scored them in three different ways. First they defined a narrow band of correctness around the track (5% of the screen's width) and counted the number of seconds out of each 90 s trial the subject was on that target. Such scores, called time-on-target (TOT) scores, measure the subject's accuracy. Next Bahrick and coauthors estimated TOT using a band of correctness that was somewhat larger (15% of the screen's width), and then they did it again for a very large target band of correctness (30% of the screen's width). Then they plotted these various TOT scores for each trial, giving the three curves shown in figure 8.4.

Remember that these curves came from the *same* performances from the same subjects, who were not aware of the scoring that Bahrick and colleagues did afterward. If you were

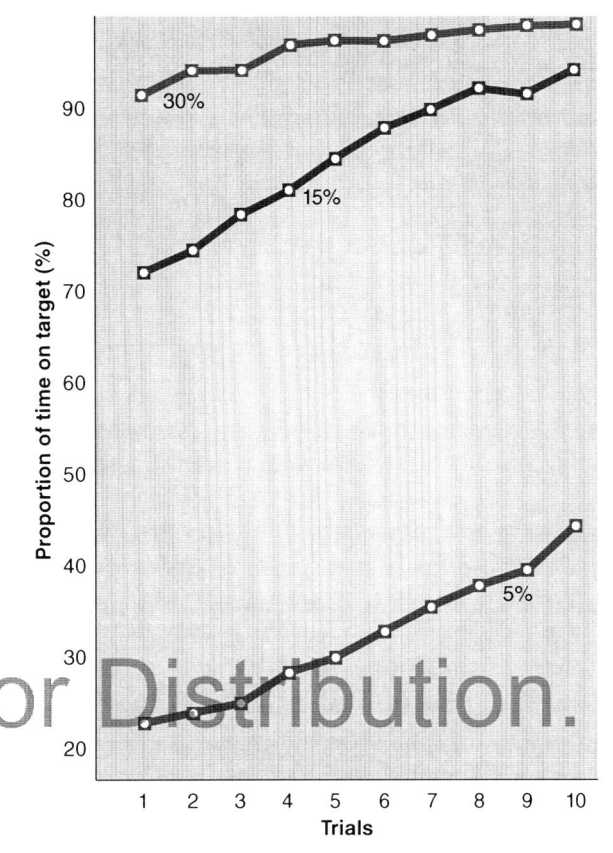

FIGURE 8.4 Proportion of time-on-target for a group of subjects practicing a tracking task, scored with three different criteria. Performance was considered to be "on-target" whenever the subject's response was near the cursor within 5%, 15%, or 30% of the screen's width.

Adapted by permission from Bahrick, Fitts, and Briggs 1957.

to think of these as learning curves, you would be forced into three contradictory conclusions: (a) The learning gains were rapid at first and slower later (30% curve); (b) the learning gains were linear across practice (15% curve); and (c) the learning gains were slow at first and more rapid later (5% curve). In fact, only one rate of learning was experienced by each subject, but it was estimated in three different ways, which led to three different conclusions about the changes with practice. These differences are caused by so-called scoring "artifacts". These artifacts occur whenever the measured scores become less sensitive to the gains in the internal capability for responding as they move closer to the best possible score on a trial. When the performance maximum is reached this is called a *ceiling* effect because a *higher* performance score is not possible. In this study, 100% TOT represents the

> continued

> continued

ceiling. Performance minima can also represent a scoring artifact. If tracking error had been measured in this study (say, using root mean square error, or RMSE), then zero error would be the minimum score possible, and would be called a *floor effect*, because a *lower* performance score than this is not possible. This experiment warns of the difficulties in using performance curves and the potential errors that can be made in making conclusions from these curves.

Exploring Further

1. Think of another motor learning task; describe how changes in the criterion for success could be made and how these changes might affect the shape of the performance curve over practice trials.

2. Provide an example of a floor effect and a ceiling effect in the task described for question 1.

---

curves are simply plots of (usually average) performance over practice trials, which (as seen in the next sections) do not necessarily indicate much about progress in the relatively permanent capability for performance, as learning was defined earlier (see also Focus on Research 8.1).

Between-Subject Effects Are Masked

One of the main reasons for using performance curves is that they average or "smooth out" the discrepant performances of different learners. Through averaging of a large group of people together, performance changes in the (mythical) average subject can be seen and, it is hoped, inferences can be made about changes in general proficiency. This is particularly useful in research settings, where the difference between two groups of subjects is studied as a function of different practice methods, for example.

The drawback is that this averaging process hides any differences between people, termed individual differences in chapter 7. Because of this, the averaging method gives the impression that all subjects improve at the same rate, or in the same way, which we know is not correct in most cases.

Within-Subject Variability Is Masked

A third drawback to performance curves is that the performance fluctuations *within* a single person tend to be obscured by averaging procedures. When examining "smooth" performance curves, such as those in figures 8.2 and 8.3, it is tempting to assume that the individual learners' performances contributing to the curves progressed smoothly and gradually as well. However, take another look at these figures, especially figure 8.3. Notice that the label on the horizontal axis specifies that each data point represents a block of nine trials. What this means is that nine separate trials for any single subject are averaged to produce a single score, which is then averaged over the group of subjects in an experimental condition. Thus, the averaging process produces a curve that masks both within- and between-subject variability.

Distinguishing Learning From Performance

Critically important, not only for the experimental study of learning but also for evaluating learning in practical settings, is the distinction between learning and performance. According to this view, practice can have two different kinds of influences on performance—one that is relatively permanent and due to learning, and another that is only temporary and transient.

Temporary and Relatively Permanent Effects of Practice

One product of practice is learning—the establishment of a relatively permanent improvement in the capability to perform. This effect produces a relatively permanent change in the person (which really could be the result of changes in a collection of processes, as seen in figure 8.1) that allows the individual to perform a particular action in the future and that endures over many days, or even many years. Essentially, the concern of researchers who study motor learning is the discovery of practice conditions that maximize the development of these relatively permanent changes, so that these conditions can be used in various practical settings to enhance learning.

It is important to remember, however, that many practice conditions have temporary effects as well as relatively permanent ones. Some effects are positive and contribute to increased performance levels (e.g., motivation), whereas others are negative and degrade performance somewhat (e.g., fatigue). A key concern is identifying what these effects are and distinguishing their impact on performance versus learning.

For example, various kinds of instructions or encouragement during practice elevate performance due to a motivating or "energizing" effect. As seen in chapter 11, giving the learner information about how he is progressing during the practice of a task can have an elevating effect on performance. Providing guidance in the form of physical help or verbal directions during practice can also benefit performance. Various mood states can likewise elevate performance temporarily, as can certain drugs. Other temporary practice factors can be negative, degrading performance temporarily. For example, sometimes practice generates physical or mental fatigue, which can depress performance relative to rested conditions. Lethargic performances can result if practice is boring or if learners become discouraged at their lack of progress; this effect is more or less opposite to the "energizing" effects just mentioned. Numerous other factors associated with practice could exert similar effects.

Practice can have numerous important effects on the learner:

- Relatively permanent effects that persist across many days, even years
- Temporary effects that vanish with time or a change in conditions
- Simultaneous temporary and relatively permanent effects

Separating Temporary and Relatively Permanent Effects

Suppose that you are interested in trying out a new teaching aid for improving the alignment skills of a golfer when setting up to make a putt. (The device is not legal for actual competition and can be used only during practice sessions.) Certainly your evaluation of this new teaching aid's benefits for learning will be based on whether it enhances performance in a relatively permanent way—that is, after the device has been removed (perhaps as in a golf game). After all, if the positive effects of the teaching aid disappear as soon as it is removed, the aid cannot have had much advantage as a teaching method.

Whenever learners practice, and especially when instructors intervene to enhance learning (e.g., by giving instructions and feedback), it is important to have a way to separate the relatively permanent practice effects from the temporary effects. Frequently in research settings, and sometimes in practical settings as well, learners are divided into two separate classes or groups. For example, let's suppose that one group of golfers practices trying to make 6 ft (1.8 m) putts with the alignment aid, and another group practices without the aid. The two groups might practice under these two different conditions for a period of time, perhaps over 10 sessions, and record the percentage of putts made. You might average all of the golfers' scores for each group separately and plot performance curves, essentially as was done in figures 8.2 and 8.3. Such a plot might look like the one in figure 8.5, where the average percentage of putts made from 6 ft away is plotted for the 10 sessions.

Which condition is more effective for learning—practice with the alignment aid or without it? This might seem like a silly question. Looking at the graph in figure 8.5 reveals that the golfers using the alignment aid improved their performance in practice more rapidly than the golfers without the aid, and their final performance level (in the last session) was also higher. It seems obvious that practice performance with the alignment aid was more accurate than without it, and the difference might be due to learning, which would be most interesting. As argued in the previous section, however, the difference between these two groups might be only a temporary performance effect, which could disappear as soon as the alignment aid is removed.

The problem can be posed more systematically in the form of hypotheses about the two conditions:

Hypothesis 1: The group that practiced with the alignment aid learned more than the group that practiced without it (a stronger relatively permanent capability for performance had been developed).

Hypothesis 2: Although the group that practiced with the alignment aid performed more accurately during the practice sessions than the group that practiced without it, they were no better in the relatively permanent capability for performance.

Which of these two hypotheses is correct? The answer, based only on the data in figure 8.5, is unknown. The information presented gives no way to tell whether the advantage of the new-device group is due to some relatively permanent (learning) effect or to some temporary (performance) effect that is likely to disappear once the alignment aid is no longer available. This is a critical problem because there is no real basis for deciding which learning method is better. Fortunately, additional procedures are available that permit separation of learning and performance effects.

Transfer Designs

A so-called transfer design can analyze whether a change that improves performance in practice also improves learning by separating the relatively permanent and temporary effects of a variable. This method has two important features. First, the temporary effects of the variable must be allowed to dissipate. In our golf example, the temporary effects of the alignment aid (if any) might be informational or physical (a type of guidance), operating mainly during actual performance, so very little time for dissipation would be needed. As a result, any other temporary effects (such as increased motivation) would dissipate relatively quickly, and certainly would dissipate before the next session. (Other variables could have temporary effects with much longer times for dissipation, such as a week or a month.) Second, the learners in both groups are tested again under common conditions in a transfer (or retention) test, either both with or both without the alignment aid. This is done to equalize any temporary effects that the test conditions themselves might have on retention performance. Otherwise, the results would be difficult to interpret.

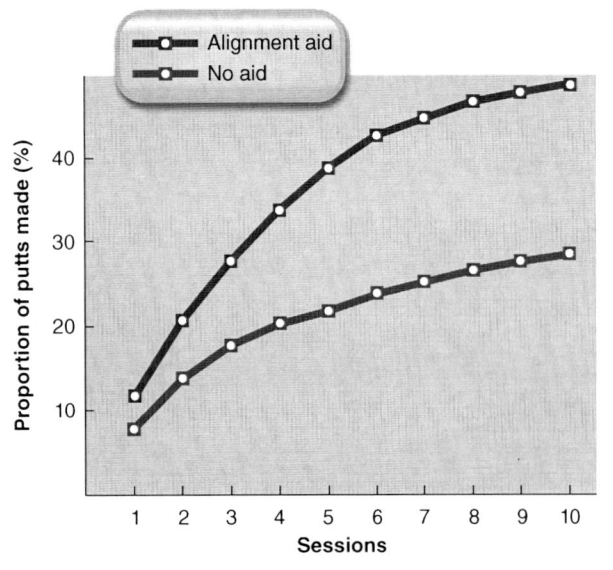

FIGURE 8.5 Hypothetical performance curves for two groups practicing the golf putt with or without an alignment aid.

> ### Focus on
> ### APPLICATION 8.1
>
> ### Self-Assessments of Learning
>
> In most activities of daily life, the learner is responsible for making the decisions about how to practice, such as session frequency and duration. Practice for a motor skills competition is no different than other types of studying—you determine how to practice and the practice duration, and stop practicing when you feel competent or confident in your *predicted* capability to perform when it counts (e.g., on an examination). The critical question is this: What is the basis for making this prediction?
>
> The problem is that most learners interpret temporary indicators of performance as permanent indicators of learning or remembering. Motor skills practice can also result in a similar feeling of overconfidence. One of the factors that is addressed in chapter 10 concerns blocked- versus random-practice scheduling. Drill-type or block-ordered practice generally produces better skilled performance than randomly-ordered practice trials. And, if asked to predict what their performance would be in a delayed **retention test**, subjects engaged in blocked practice predict that they will have achieved far more learning compared to subjects engaged in random practice. The reality is much different (actually reversed), however (see chapter 10 for details); and it illustrates that self-assessment judgments of learning can be quite unreliable, especially when they are based on *current* indicators of performance during practice. A good review of the research and applied nature of these memory and learning issues is provided by Bjork (2011).

In general, the term **transfer test** usually refers to a change of task conditions, whereas a *retention test* usually refers to a test given after an empty period without practice (in reality, though, the terms are often used interchangeably). The tests could be given a day or more after the last practice session or several minutes after the last session. Because the interest in the golf alignment aid example is mainly in the effect of the alignment aid on performance when the aid is no longer available (which is analogous to a competition), the decision is to test both groups without the aid. The logic that underlies a transfer or retention test is this: If the temporary effects have dissipated by the time of the test and any temporary effects are not allowed to reappear (or they do reappear but at the same rate in both groups), then any differences observed in the delayed test should be due to the relatively permanent effects acquired through training with the aid during the practice sessions. Thus, the learning effects of the alignment aid are not evaluated during practice, but rather in the transfer or retention test, when the temporary effects have disappeared, leaving the relatively permanent effects behind to be revealed on the test.

The essential features of a transfer design can be summarized as follows:

- Allow sufficient time (rest) for the supposed temporary effects of practice to dissipate. The amount of time will vary depending on the particular nature of the temporary effects.
- Evaluate learners again in a transfer or retention test, with all groups performing under identical conditions.
- Any differences observed in this transfer test are due to a difference in the relatively permanent capability for performance acquired during earlier practice, that is, in learning.

Consider the possible transfer test outcomes of the hypothetical experiment just described. A few of these possibilities are shown in figure 8.6, labeled A, B, C, and D in the right (transfer) portion of the figure. In transfer outcome A, the performances of the two groups are different by approximately the same amount as was present at the end of the practice sessions (compare performance on session 10 with transfer outcome A). In this case, the appropriate conclusion would be that all of the difference between groups achieved by the last session of practice was due to a relatively permanent effect because allowing the temporary effects (if any) to dissipate did not change the groups' relative status at all. *Conclusion:* The alignment aid was more effective for learning than was practice without the aid.

Now consider transfer outcome B in figure 8.6, where the transfer performance of the group practicing with the alignment aid is more accurate than that of the other group, but the difference is not as large as it was in the last practice session. From these test results one could argue that some of the difference between the practice session performances of these groups was due to temporary effects because dissipation reduced the difference somewhat. However, not all of the practice session difference was temporary because some of it remained in the transfer test, after the temporary effects dissipated. *Conclusion:* The alignment aid elevated performance temporarily, but it also produced some lasting effects on learning, compared to practice without the aid.

Next, examine transfer outcome C in figure 8.6, where the transfer performances of the two groups are essentially the same but at the level of the no-aid group at the end of practice. Here, when the temporary effects have dissipated, all of the differences that had accumulated between the groups during practice dissipated as well. This leads to the conclusion that all of the effect of the practice aid was due to some temporary elevating change, and none of it was due to learning. *Conclusion:* The alignment aid elevated performance compared to performance without the aid, but it had no lasting effect on learning.

Finally, examine outcome D, where the performance of the group that had practiced with the alignment aid resulted in transfer performance that was less accurate than that of the group that had practiced without the aid. This is a rather odd and counterintuitive result, for it reveals that not only did all performance advantages of the alignment aid disappear when the temporary effects dissipated, but that the alignment aid resulted in a learning effect that was smaller than practice without it. *Conclusion:* We will see some results that look like this in future chapters. The alignment aid elevated performance during practice, but had a degrading effect on learning compared to the group that practiced without the aid.

Measuring Learning in Practical Settings

The issues just discussed may seem, at first glance, to relate mainly to learning evaluation in research situations. However, transfer designs form the basis for learning evaluation in many teaching situations as well. For example, when a learner practices some skill, for example, producing the proper amount

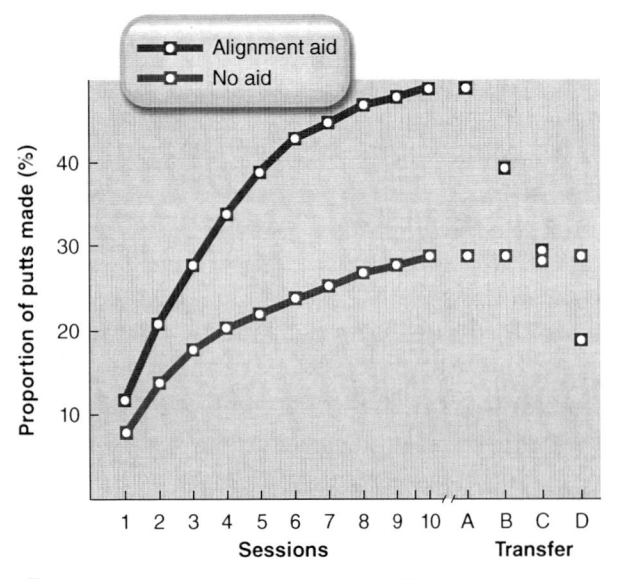

FIGURE 8.6 Hypothetical effects on transfer tests of two groups practicing the golf putt with or without an alignment aid. Four different possible outcomes on the transfer test are illustrated in transfer outcomes A, B, C, and D.

of pressure in cardiopulmonary resuscitation (CPR), the proficiency level reached at the end of a practice session may not reflect the actual performance capability achieved. Because practice and various factors involved in it may also affect performance temporarily, they may mask the underlying acquired capability for responding.

Practice conditions may also not reflect accurately the emotional conditions under which some skills are required. For example, CPR skills are usually needed in emergency situations, where the emotional stress may be elevated quite dramatically compared to the situations under which practice is typically done. Therefore, various types of retention and transfer tests may be required to assess the true level of skills learned during practice.

A related issue concerns evaluation for the purpose of grading. If a learner's grade in some activity is related to the *amount* learned, then basing the grade on performance toward the end of some practice session would be unwise. The learning level would tend to be masked by various temporary practice effects. A far better method would be to evaluate the learner's performance in a delayed retention or transfer test, administered sufficiently long after practice so that the temporary effects of practicing have dissipated.

In addition, people may be affected differently by these temporary factors—yet another form of individual differences (cf. chapter 7). For example, a learner who is more susceptible to fatigue than another will show larger temporary decrements in performance during practice, perhaps leading to the false conclusion that learning progress has been slow. Evaluating the learning level by a delayed test under relatively rested conditions provides a more complete representation of actual learning progress.

Transfer of Learning

An important variation of the ideas about learning addressed thus far requires further discussion—**transfer of learning**. As the name implies, this concept involves the learning achieved in one task or in one practice setting when it is applied to the performance of some other task, or in some other setting, or both. A good example involving transfer of learning is the handgun skills of a police officer. Transfer is a particularly important notion for instructors of police officers because the conditions under which practice is conducted are obviously quite different than the conditions in a real situation in which handgun involvement is required. However, for the safety of the public and the people involved, the skills acquired in practice must be maximally transferrable to the broadest range of "transfer" conditions imaginable. Therefore, teaching for transfer, or organizing practice and instruction to facilitate transfer of learning, is an important goal for most instructional programs.

Role of Transfer in Skill Learning Settings

Transfer is assumed whenever the skills learned in one task are applied successfully to the performance of some other task version. Consider police officers who undertake handgun shooting practice, for example. Shooting at targets at a practice range under rested, nonstressful conditions perhaps assumes that this experience will transfer to shooting in a life-or-death situation. In this situation, the transfer from practice to the transfer task skill situation must be substantial. If it is not, practicing the drills could be largely a waste of time.

Transfer is also involved when instructors modify skills to make them easier to practice. For example, relatively long-duration, serial skills, such as doing a gymnastics routine, can be broken down into their elements for practice. Practicing the stunts in isolation must benefit the performance of the whole routine (the *criterion task*), which is made up of the individual stunts. However, in more rapid skills, such as a tennis serve, it is usually not so clear that breaking down the skill into ball-toss and ball-strike portions for part practice will be effective for transfer to the whole task. The principles of transfer

Complex skills may be broken down into simpler elements for beginning learners, but to be valuable, this learning must eventually transfer to the criterion task.

applicable to such situations are dealt with in chapter 9.

How Is Transfer Measured?

Issues concerning the measurement of transfer are closely related to the learning measurement issues discussed earlier. Essentially, we want to estimate the performance level of the criterion task, with the relatively permanent effects of learning separated from any temporary performance effects. However, rather than asking how practice variations of a given task affect learning, transfer concerns how performance on the transfer task is influenced by practice on some other task.

Suppose you want to know whether practicing golf at the driving range transfers to the actual game of golf. Consider three hypothetical groups of subjects with different kinds of practice experiences. Group 1 practices for 4 h at the driving range; group 2 does not receive any practice; and group 3 practices for 4 h at miniature golf. After these various practice activities, all groups transfer to (are tested on) five rounds of golf on an actual golf course. The results of this hypothetical experiment are shown in figure 8.7, where the average scores for the five rounds of golf are plotted separately for the three groups. Assuming that the groups are equivalent at the start of the experiment, the only reason for the groups to be different on the first (and subsequent) rounds of golf is that the previous experiences have somehow contributed to, or detracted from, actual golf skill. Therefore, the focus for transfer would be on the relative differences among the groups on the criterion task.

Figure 8.7 shows that group 1, which had practiced at the driving range before five rounds of golf, performed more effectively

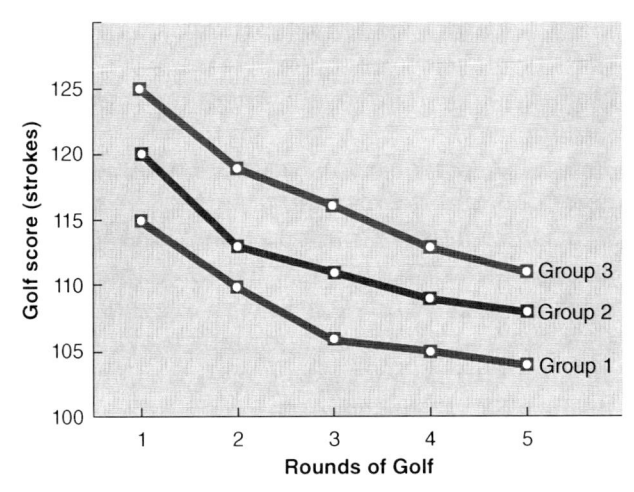

FIGURE 8.7 Hypothetical average scores for a round of golf as a function of prior practice experiences. Earlier, group 1 (red line) practiced at a driving range, group 3 (green line) practiced miniature golf, and group 2 (blue line) received no practice. The differences between groups 1 and 2 demonstrate positive transfer from practice at the driving range. The differences between groups 2 and 3 reveal negative transfer from practice at miniature golf.

than group 2, which received no previous practice. This difference is usually measured on the first trial, or at least on the first few trials, before the additional practice on the criterion task can alter the skill levels very much. In this case, we would have said that the driving range experience transferred *positively* to golf because it facilitated golf performance over and above no practice. If this were an actual experiment, you might conclude that the skills developed on the driving range were applicable in some way to those on the golf course.

Transfer can also be negative, as you can see by comparing groups 2 and 3 in figure 8.7. Notice that group 3, which had practice only on the miniature golf task, performed more poorly on the rounds of golf than group 2, which had no prior practice at all. In this case, miniature golf experience transferred *negatively* to golf performance. If this had happened in an actual experiment, you might conclude that the skills learned in miniature golf not only were different from those required on a golf course, but in fact led to disruption in the performance and learning of those skills needed in the golf game.

How much positive transfer occurred, and how can we put a measurement number on it? One way is through so-called percentage transfer. A means of doing this is to provide an estimate of the total amount of improvement of the group that had no prior practice on any task—in this case, group 2, and then compare that to the initial performance of the group that had the type of practice being evaluated. Simply taking the initial performance score of the no-practice group (120 strokes) and subtracting the final performance score (109 strokes) shows an improvement from 120 to 109 = 11 strokes. Then we see that group 1 (driving range practice) and group 2 (no prior practice) differ by about five strokes on the first session; that is, of the total 11 strokes of improvement that group 2 realized, five of them were gained in driving range practice. Researchers often describe these changes in terms of percentages—here, 5/11 = 45% transfer.

Alternatively, some researchers represent transfer in terms of a "savings score," where the amount of savings (here, in practice time) generated on the criterion task is the result of having practiced at the driving range. In this example, referring to figure 8.7 again, if we were to draw a horizontal line from group 1's initial performance (115 strokes) until it intersected the trend line for group 2, and then dropped a perpendicular line to the *x*-axis, we could compute a savings score—in this case about 1.7 rounds of golf for group 1. That is, as a result of having practiced on the driving range, group 1 "saved" about 1.7 rounds of golf practice.

These measures of amount of transfer are clearly confounded or flawed by concepts discussed already in this chapter. One of the fundamental ideas is that performance curves and their shapes are often arbitrarily defined by choices the experimenter makes before the study (e.g., the size of the target; see figure 8.4 and the related discussion). So, in terms of the percentage transfer measurement, basing the measurement of transfer on the changes that the no-prior-practice group produced is also arbitrary, producing an arbitrary percentage transfer score. A similar argument can be made for the savings score; as figure 8.7 shows, the initial shape of group 2's performance curve is also somewhat arbitrary. About the best we can say is that these measures provide useful ways of describing transfer results in relative terms, but they shouldn't be taken too seriously.

Specific Transfer

The previous sections on measuring learning have perhaps left the impression that the only way to measure the relative amount learned is by performance on some delayed retention test. This is probably the most important way to estimate learning, but other ways are possible, and some are even preferable in some situations.

The essential issue is what we want learners to be able to do after training. In some cases, learners are trained to be proficient at a specific task with a limited range of variations. For example, basketball players take foul shots using a set shot from a distance of 15 ft (4.6 m) to the basket (i.e., from the free-throw line). So, it seems perfectly reasonable to devote considerable set-shot practice from the free-throw line because the set shot is a specific type of basketball skill that is normally not performed at any other location

Because a basketball free throw is a closed skill that takes place at a set point on the court, specific transfer from practice is easy to achieve and measure.

on the court. Many closed tasks share these characteristics.

Generalized Transfer

One critical aspect of many training settings is the extent to which the practice transfers to different yet very similar settings in the real world. This is sometimes termed *near transfer*, the learning goal being a task relatively similar to the training task. A good example that contrasts nicely with the free throw is the jump shot in basketball. The jump shot can be taken from an infinite number of places on the court and under a variety of game situations. Being able to perform in such varied and unpredictable conditions is one mark of a highly skilled performer. Therefore, tests of transfer in which performance is measured on some variant of the task that is similar, yet different, from those in the practice conditions would be a reasonable test of generalized transfer.

Sometimes instructors want to train learners to develop more general capabilities for a wide variety of skills, only a few of which are actually experienced in practice. This is usually termed *far transfer* because the eventual goal is quite different from that in the original practice setting. For example, elementary school children are taught to throw, jump, and run; the main concern is the extent to which these activities transfer to future activities involving throwing, jumping, and running but occurring in very different settings.

In all these situations, the evaluation of training effectiveness is not based exclusively on how well the learners master the skills during actual practice. Rather, if transfer to relatively different activities is the goal, the most effective training program will be the one that produces the best performance on some transfer test performed in the future—one that may involve quite different skills from those actually practiced. Here, the effectiveness of a training program is measured by the amount of transfer to some different activity.

Summary

Motor learning is defined as a set of processes associated with practice. As such, the emphasis is on the determinants of this capability, which supports or underlies the performance. Hence, factors that affect performance only temporarily need to be distinguished from the factors affecting this underlying capability, which makes the use of "learning" curves somewhat risky for evaluating learning.

However, temporary and learning effects can be separated through the use of transfer or retention tests. In some experiments on learning, groups of learners practice under different conditions in acquisition; after a delay, they are tested on the same task but under conditions that are identical for all the groups. This procedure focuses attention on the relative performance in the retention tests as measures of learning.

Transfer, closely related to learning, is seen when practice on one task contributes to performance capability in some other task. Transfer can be positive or negative, depending on whether it enhances or degrades performance on the other task, usually as compared to a no-practice control condition. It can also be specific or generalized, depending on how different the transfer task is from the practice activities.

WEB STUDY GUIDE ACTIVITIES

Check Your Understanding

1. Define motor learning and indicate why each of the following terms is important to that definition.
   - Capability
   - Practice and experience
   - Performance

2. Distinguish between near transfer and far transfer and between positive transfer and negative transfer. Give one example of each.

3. List and describe two limitations of using performance curves to evaluate learning progress.

Apply Your Knowledge

1. List three essential features of a transfer design. How would these features be included in an experiment to examine if the use of a pole to aid in balance during a one-foot stance task is beneficial to learning?

2. Describe one practical setting where the proficiency level reached at the end of a practice session may not reflect the actual performance capability achieved under the conditions where the skill will eventually be required. How could you assess the true level of skills learned during practice?

Suggestions for Further Reading

Important cautions about the learning–performance distinction are provided by Kantak and Winstein (2012) and Cahill, McGaugh, and Weinberger (2001). An analysis of so called "learning curves" is given by Stratton and coauthors (2007). More information on the measurement of learning can be found in Schmidt and Lee (2011, chapter 11) and also on the retention and transfer of learning (chapter 14). See the reference list for these additional resources.

Skill Acquisition, Retention, and Transfer

How Expertise Is Gained

KEY TERMS

autonomous stage
cognitive stage of learning
criterion task
degree of freedom
degrees of freedom problem
error-detection capability
fixation (associative or motor) stage
forgetting
gearshift analogy
generalizability
lead-up activities
part practice
physical fidelity
progressive part practice
psychological fidelity
repetition
set
simulator
specificity of learning
warm-up decrement
whole practice

CHAPTER OUTLINE

Skill Acquisition
Skill Retention
Skill Transfer
Summary

CHAPTER OBJECTIVES

Chapter 9 describes the processes that influence skill acquisition, retention, and transfer. This chapter will help you to understand

- ▶ basic principles of the skill acquisition process,
- ▶ two conceptualizations of learning stages during skill acquisition,
- ▶ factors that influence the retention of skills after periods of no practice, and
- ▶ factors that influence the transfer of skills to new tasks or performance situations.

Playing the guitar provides a good example of how practice leads to the development of motor expertise. Consider the beginning chords of a song such as Link Wray's classic, "Rumble." The first three chords are D, D, and E. For a right-handed guitarist, the D chord is achieved by pressing down onto the third fret of the second string plus the second fret of the third string with the left hand while strumming the second, third, fourth, and fifth strings with the right hand. The D chord is played twice; then the fingers on the left hand shift to make an E chord, which requires fingers on the left hand to depress onto the first fret of the third string and the second fret of the fourth and fifth strings while the right hand now strums all six strings.

The beginner guitarist is faced with a number of problems to be solved simultaneously, such as knowing which fingers are placed on which frets, having to avoid strings that should not be touched, remembering what positions compose what chords and which strings the right hand should strum, then moving the hand and fingers to create a whole new chord. And this does not even consider the timing structure that must underlie these chords. It is very impressive, indeed, that anyone can learn to play the guitar given what we've just said; yet many do, and many do it very well.

Learning to drive a car provides another good example of the topics presented in this chapter. Typically, the beginning driver goes through changes in skill progression, called stages of motor learning. Certain principles of learning apply to almost all motor learning, and these principles result in the acquisition of a specific set of subskills that support driving performance. But that is not the whole story about motor learning. Time away from the task of driving has an impact on future performance because the *retention* of skills is expected to be different for different types of tasks; so, being able to classify driving as a member of one of several classes of skills is important. And lastly, motor learning would be very inefficient if we had to progress through the entire skill acquisition process for each and every vehicle that we drive and every situation in which we find ourselves. That is, we expect our driving skills to generalize (or *transfer*) to different vehicles, situations, and environments; therefore, information about the factors that are expected to affect transfer constitutes a critical component of any discussion of the learning process.

Skill Acquisition

Quite simply, the single most important factor leading to the acquisition of motor skill is *practice*. However, "practice" is also probably one of the most poorly understood and misused terms when applied to the concept of learning. In this section we describe some principles of practice, how they affect learning, and what occurs as the result of practice.

Basic Principles of Practice

It almost goes without saying that the most important variable for learning is practice itself. There's no easy way around it; and as a general rule, more practice produces more learning. But the amount of practice *time* is not the only concern here, and not all practice methods are equal in their impacts on learning. In this section we describe the basic principles of effective practice, and what might and (might not) lead to effective and efficient skill acquisition.

Practice Is More Than Just Repetition

A frequently misused substitute for the term practice is "repetition," and many well-intentioned instructors and coaches confuse the two concepts. To us, the term "**repetition**" invokes the idea of repeating a movement, and again, and again, and so on. The concept brings to mind the idea that repetitious movements somehow "groove" or "stamp in" a memory, with more repetitions leading to a deeper groove or more durable stamp in memory. The metaphor causes one to think (incorrectly, in our view) of learning as a concept similar to muscle hypertrophy, which results from repetitious exercise.

Consider the following quotes from two very influential theorists as counterpoints to the traditional view of "practice as repetition."

When I make the [tennis] stroke I do not . . . produce something absolutely new, and I never repeat something old. (Bartlett, 1932, p. 202)

The process of practice towards the achievement of new motor habits essentially consists in the gradual success of a search for optimal motor solutions to the appropriate problems. Because of this, practice, when properly undertaken, does not consist in [simply] repeating the . . . *solution* of a motor problem time after time, but [rather] in the *process of solving* this problem again and again by techniques which we changed and perfected from repetition to repetition. It is already apparent here that, in many cases, "practice is a particular type of repetition without repetition, and that motor training, if this position is ignored, is merely mechanical repetition by rote, a method which has been discredited in pedagogy for some time." (Bernstein, 1967, p. 134)

The conceptual model that we have developed throughout the book represents the most important components of the human information-processing system that are involved in movement control. These components fluctuate due to temporary factors, improve with development, and regress with advancing age. Importantly, though, the components of the processing system become more effective and efficient with learning. In our view, the most effective learning occurs when a repetition activates as many of the individual components of the system as possible. In this way, a repetition is successful to the degree that it engages the entire conceptual model presented in figure 8.1.

Specificity of Practice

Although transfer is a hallmark of learning (discussed in more detail later in this chapter, and in chapter 11), a consistent finding in the literature is that motor learning is quite specific. In general, **specificity of learning** suggests that what you learn depends largely on what you practice. Specificity effects are wide-ranging. This example might make the idea more clear: If you want your soccer team to perform well in the dark, in the rain, and in front of many noisy fans, then you must practice in the dark, in the rain, and in front of many noisy fans. Practicing in a particular environment or workspace often leads to better performance mainly in (sometimes only in) that workspace, compared to a different or altered workspace (this is perhaps one of the bases of the so-called home-field advantage; Carron, Loughhead, & Bray, 2005). Another important finding is that the sensory feedback (e.g., visual, auditory, tactile) resulting from performance during specific types or locations of practice becomes part of the learned representation for skill, such that later performance is more skillful when that *same* sensory information is available, compared to situations in which one or more of these feedback channels are altered (Proteau, 1992). Thus, while an important goal of practice is to facilitate transfer (i.e., performance enhancement for unpracticed situations or contexts), it is important to recognize that specificity of learning is the dominant characteristic.

Learning Versus Performance During Practice

Perhaps it is obvious that when learners acquire a new skill, they do so by doing something *different* than they had done earlier. The processes leading to learning require that the learner *change something* in the movement patterning, hopefully so the performance becomes more effective. Yet, when assisting learners during practice, many instructors encourage learners to "do your best" on each practice attempt. This generates two conflicting practice goals: performing as well as possible in practice versus learning as much as possible in practice by attempting to change movement patterning.

The learner who attempts to perform as well as possible in practice tends to be inhibited from modifying ("experimenting with") movements from attempt to attempt, which detracts from learning. The approach for maximizing performance, repeating the most effective pattern discovered so far, is not effective for learning in part because it discourages such experimentation. One way to separate these conflicting practice goals is to provide two fundamentally different activities during practice—practice sessions and test sessions.

First, provide practice sessions in which you instruct the learners simply to avoid repeating what they did earlier. Tell the learner to try different styles of movement control to discover some more effective pattern of action. You can guide the learning by suggesting specific ways to alter the movement, helping the learner eliminate inappropriate patterns. The learner should know that performance quality is not critical during this practice period, and that the only goal is to discover some new way to execute the skill that will be more effective in the long term.

Of course, the measure of the effectiveness of this learning progress is a *test* of some kind. After several minutes in the practice session, the instructor could announce a switch to a "test session," in which the next five attempts are treated as "a test." In the test session the learner is to perform as well as possible, using the best estimate gained so far of the movement pattern for the most proficient performance. After the test session, the learner has some idea of his progress and can return to the practice mode to continue searching for more effective movement patterning. Such tests could be formally evaluated and graded, but they can also be effective if given only for the student's own information. Evaluating progress by asking learners to compile their own test scores is an excellent method to help them assess their own progress; it is both motivating and educational.

Benefits of Practice

Obviously, a major goal of practice is effective performance, which can be thought of as developing the *capability* to perform some skill on future demand. However, there are several other benefits of practice that leave

Focus on
APPLICATION 9.1

Principles of Golf Practice

A frequent complaint of golfers who try to improve their skills through driving-range practice is that their performance on driving ranges is rarely matched on the golf course. In fact, the lament "But I was hitting the ball so well during practice" seems to summarize quite well the lack of progress that aggravates the "weekend warrior." The typical golfer rents a pail of balls at the local driving range, goes to a small booth that has an artificial hitting mat, and places a ball on the rubber tee. After a short warm-up, a golf club is withdrawn from the bag, an intended target out in the range is selected, the direction of the shot is determined, the stance is taken, and the shot is made. Then, with very little hesitation, a new ball is placed on the tee, and another shot is made. This process continues for 5, 10, or 20 more shots, until finally the golfer decides to try a different club. And on it goes. Let's take a look at this typical driving range practice behavior and compare it to the principles of practice discussed in this chapter.

1. *Repetitions.* The golfer's focus is on the swing, because that is the message of almost all of the instructional videos and infomercials that the golfer has seen on TV. If a successful shot is made, the golfer's immediate goal is now to repeat it. Repetition is key, and very little time and energy are spent either in preparation for the shot or in contemplating the result afterward.

2. *Practice design.* Our golfer really does not have the motivation to make a serious plan for the practice session. The only plan is to try to improve—usually with major emphasis on the swing.

3. *Specificity.* Although this is not a fault of the golfer, consider the very nature of the construction of most golf driving ranges. The hitting areas use rugs of artificial turf; the ball sits in a good, flat position; and there are no obstacles in front of the golfer to go around, over, or under. In other words, the typical driving range shot is taken under ideal conditions—conditions quite unlike those that the golfer will face on the course. So, the golfer learns to hit under nearly ideal conditions.

4. *Learning and performance goals.* Quite simply, the typical golfer equates good performance in practice with successful learning. And this illusion of progress, perhaps more than anything else, is what frustrates the golfer most.

To be fair, though, we shouldn't beat up our golfer too much. After all, these "violations" of the principles of practice are not uncommon in most types of sport skills, workplace training environments, and rehabilitation settings. And in reality, it would not take much effort to make golf range practice more effective for learning. Here are a few ideas:

▶ Make each shot "count." Try to create an image of each shot as it might look at your favorite course. Go through your typical preshot thinking routine before the ball is struck, and evaluate a number of different components of the shot afterward, perhaps in terms of a checklist (e.g., swing, ball contact, ball flight, final location in relation to target).

> *continued*

> *continued*

- Sketch out a plan for the practice session before going to the range. Establish clear goals and how you plan to achieve them.
- Try to create different types of shots to be made, even if they are just imaginary (e.g., a low shot into the wind or a high shot over a tree).
- Interject "tests" into practice, such as short games (chipping and putting from three locations around a green), either by yourself or in competition with a friend.

The bottom line here is that the skills needed to play the game of golf are the same skills that need to be practiced on the driving range. The frustrations that plague the typical golfer probably arise largely from the manner in which practice is undertaken.

---

the learner with capabilities not so directly related to actual task proficiency. Actually, the term "motor learning" is a bit of a misnomer, as what results from practice is much more than just "motor" learning. In this section we briefly describe some of the benefits to be expected from practice.

Perceptual Skills

The game of chess provided an unlikely beginning for this important research area. DeGroot (1946) and Chase and Simon (1973) showed chess experts and nonexperts either a partially played game of chess or a board that had a similar number of pieces placed randomly on the board (i.e., a grouping of chess pieces that was unlikely to occur in an actual game). After viewing the board for only about 5 s, the subjects were asked to recreate the scene they had just viewed by placing the pieces on another board. As expected, the experts were much better than the nonexperts at recreating the board that had a "game structure." But there was no difference between experts and novices when they recreated the randomly-arranged board. This study provided important evidence that the capability to remember briefly presented information is specific to the skills of the observer—here, for the chess experts, acquired over many years of practice.

The chess studies initiated a research paradigm that has since addressed the perceptual advantage that is gained with practice and experience. Different methods are used to assess this advantage. One example is showing video clips of specific activities (as in sporting events) in which a critical portion of the video (e.g., the pre–ball-release arm movements of a baseball pitcher) is clipped from viewing, and subjects (usually experts and nonexperts) are asked to predict something about the result of the occluded action (e.g., something about the ball's flight; see Williams, Ward, & Smeeton, 2004, for a review). Another research strategy is to monitor the eye and head movements made by performers of differing skill to assess whether the active search for information is changed by practice (e.g., Vickers, 2007). Results from this general research area tend to support the original findings with chess players—that this expertise is quite specific to the nature of the skill that has been practiced. The research also shows that experts tend to seek out more specific and narrowly focused information in a perceptual display, and to pick up that information much earlier in the action than nonexperts (see Abernethy et al., 2012, for an excellent review).

Attention

Attention represents a major focus of chapter 3. We presented several different concepts of attention, which can now be considered from a learning perspective—the effect of practice on these concepts of attention. We consider two of these in this section.

Reduced Capacity Demands One of the fundamental concepts from chapter 3 was

Expert chess players are able to better remember and recreate game-like arrangements of pieces on a board, demonstrating the perceptual advantages gained through practice.

that most tasks demand some attention for their performance, and performance suffers when the overall demand exceeds the available attentional capacity (e.g., see the discussion on distracted driving in Focus on Research 3.1). Thus, one benefit of practice is the reduced attention that is demanded by tasks that have been well learned. A wonderful study by Leavitt (1979) illustrates this concept well. In his study, Leavitt compared young hockey players of different ages, and different playing abilities within each age, in the performance of a skating task (which was the "main task"), done either without a stick and puck or when stick-handling a puck. The time required to skate over a fixed distance was measured. Ice skating without controlling a puck simultaneously would appear to be a much less attention-demanding task than when controlling a puck with a stick at the same time.

Leavitt's (1979) results are illustrated in figure 9.1. Some very interesting points are exemplified in this figure. First, note that skating times with the stick and puck are, in general, longer than during skating without the stick and puck. Second, the limitation in time due to skating with the puck becomes progressively smaller as children become older (i.e., as they advance from the Novice to Atom to Peewee to Bantam age groups). And, lastly, even within each age group, more highly skilled players suffered less decrement in speed when skating with the puck than did the Novice players. All of this evidence suggests that the decrement to skating performance that occurs when players must stick-handle a puck simultaneously with skating is reduced as skill improves.

Reduced Effector Competition Another important concept of attention is the interference that can arise when a task requires us to

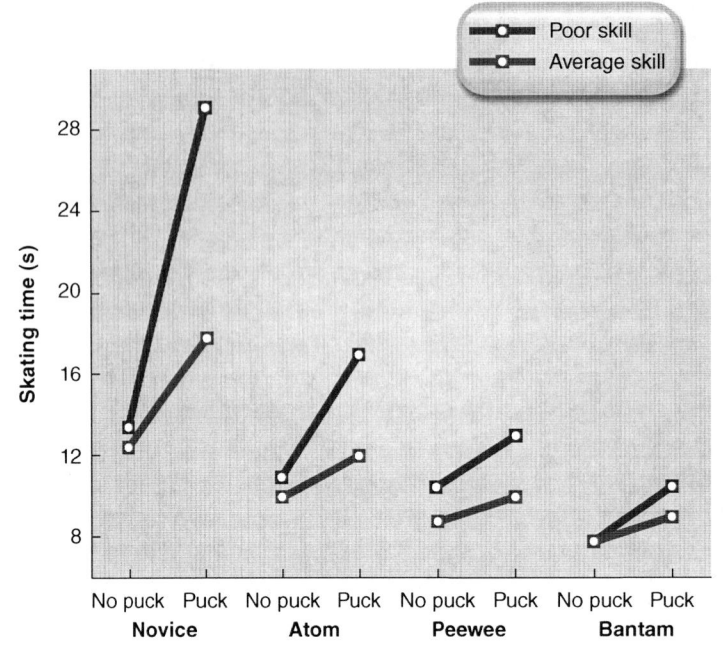

FIGURE 9.1 Skating times measured when subjects were skating alone (the "no-puck" condition) and when they were skating and stick-handling (the "puck" condition) simultaneously. (Atom = 10.1 years; Peewee = 11.3 years; Bantam = 14.1 years)

Data from Leavitt 1979.

do two or more different things at the same time. The classic example of patting your head and rubbing your stomach at the same time illustrates the problem here (see figure 9.2). The issue shares some similarities with the attention-demand concept, as discussed in the previous section and in chapter 3, but it is unique in the sense that one has no trouble rubbing (or patting) both the head and the stomach at the same time. So, it is not a matter of doing two things at once, but a matter of doing two *different things* at the same time.

Interference arises when one effector has a movement goal or pattern that is different from the goal (or movement pattern) of the other effector. The research of Bender (1987), discussed in chapter 6, illustrates nicely the problem and the benefits that result from practice. She found that producing the English letter "V" with one hand and the Greek letter "γ" with the other hand was nearly impossible when these actions were to be performed at the same time. Perhaps this is due to the competition between underlying motor programs (see figure 6.12). However, effector (or motor program) competition was reduced some with considerable practice,

FIGURE 9.2 A typical coordination problem that can be solved with practice.

perhaps due to the development of a single motor program that was responsible for controlling the two limbs as if they were a single limb (i.e., with a single motor program; see also Schmidt et al., 1998). The difficulty seems to be that the system is attempting to run two different programs at the same time (see chapter 6 for more discussion), and practice moves the learner closer to having a single motor program that governs both actions.

Motor Programs

A prominent theme in the motor learning literature suggests that many motor skills are learned through developing motor programs, as discussed in detail in chapter 5. How are these motor programs learned? The **gearshift analogy** provides a useful way to answer this question. When first learning to shift the gears of a standard-transmission car, the beginning driver goes through each of the seven steps illustrated in figure 9.3, the movement for each of these steps being controlled by separate motor programs. As some proficiency is gained, some of these steps are combined into larger motor programs that are capable of controlling the movements for two of more of the individual steps. At the highest level of skill (e.g., with a race-car driver) all seven steps are controlled by a single motor program.

Whether or not a sequence of actions is controlled by one, two, or perhaps more motor programs in sequence has been addressed by research designed to identify units of action. Imagine that a kinematic analysis of a movement allowed the measurement of the time of certain kinematic features (e.g., time of peak acceleration, time of maximum velocity). Since these kinematic features of movements are highly correlated in time over many individual trial executions (within subjects), then we assume that these actions were run off with a single motor program. A low correlation in time between any pair of such landmarks is evidence of separate programs (Schneider & Schmidt, 1995). This type of research can have many applications. For example, using this rationale, researchers analyzed childproof butane lighters and provided evidence that more than one motor program was required to complete all of the steps of igniting the lighter (Schmidt et al., 1996)—demonstrating that the safety feature was likely to be effective.

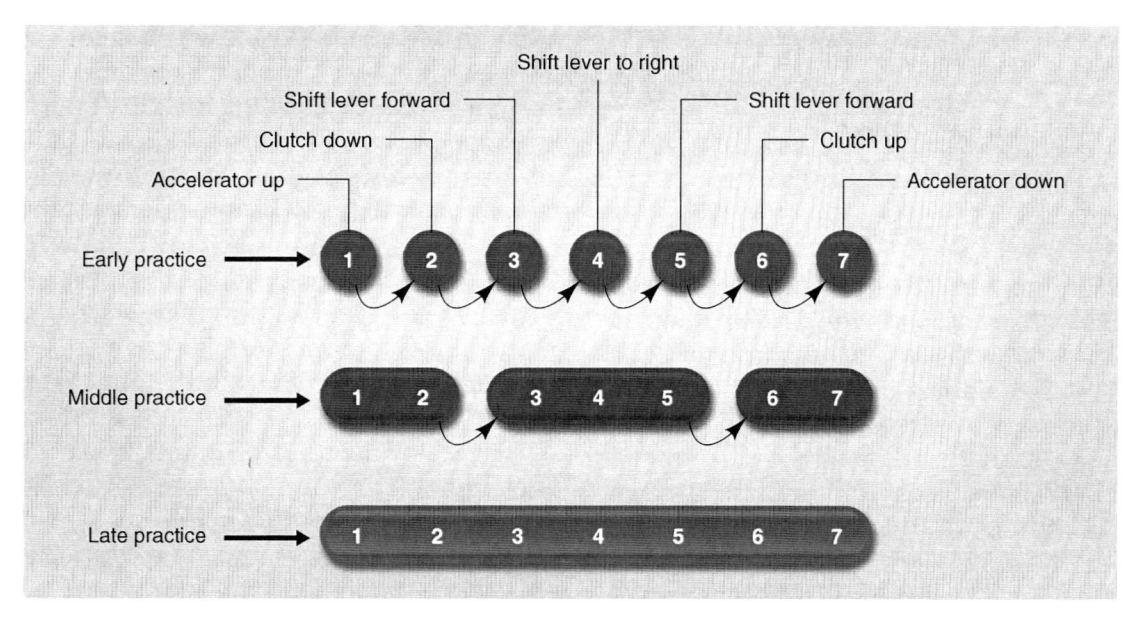

FIGURE 9.3 The gearshift analogy, using the example of shifting a standard-transmission car from second to third gear. Practice results in the reorganization of seven individual motor programs into one program (adapted from MacKay, personal communication, Los Angeles, 1976).

Reprinted by permission from Schmidt and Lee 2011; Adapted from MacKay 1976.

Error Detection

Error-detection capability represents another goal of practice. For example, when a student is learning cardiopulmonary resuscitation (CPR) skills, the instructor is usually present during practice. Therefore self-detection of errors is not critical because the instructor is there to point them out and suggest corrections. However, when the learner attempts to perform this skill in an actual emergency, the instructor will not be available to provide this corrective information. The learner who is able to detect and analyze her errors independently, and thus make corrections "in the moment," will be a far more skilled provider of CPR. This error-detection and correction capability tends to make the learner self-sufficient, which is one overall goal of practice. We will have much more to say in chapter 11 about how error-detection skills can be promoted (or discouraged) by the manner in which augmented feedback is presented.

Tasks differ with respect to the saliency of different types of sensory information, of course. The sound of the engine is particularly important to the race car driver, and the sound of the guitar is obviously important to the musician. Visual information is critical to the dentist, although when provided by a mirror, that information requires special translation skills. People who have lost their sight can become particularly adept at tactile discrimination using movement (e.g., using Braille).

Stages of Learning

It is useful to consider learning as a series of relatively distinct stages (or *phases*) that can be identified in the skill acquisition process. These stages should not be confused with the information-processing stages discussed in chapter 2. Rather, they are descriptors of the different levels of skill development. Two important stages-of-learning contributions have been made, one by Fitts and another by Bernstein, each from a very different perspective (see Anson, Elliott, & Davids, 2005, for further discussion).

Fitts' Stages

The stages suggested by Fitts (1964; Fitts & Posner, 1967) were specifically designed to consider *perceptual–motor* learning, with emphasis on both the perceptual and motor components involving skill acquisition. This perspective places heavy emphasis on how the cognitive processes invested in motor performance change as a function of practice.

Fitts' Stage 1: Cognitive Stage As the stage (**cognitive stage of learning**) name implies, the learner's first problem is cognitive, largely verbal (or verbalizable); the dominant questions concern goal identification, performance evaluation, what to do (and what not to do), when to do it, how to do it, and a host of other things. As a result, verbal and cognitive abilities (discussed in chapter 7) dominate at this stage. Figuring out what to look at in the environment (or listen to, or feel, and so on) and generating an appropriate movement attempt are critical.

Instructions, demonstrations, film clips, and other verbalizable information are also particularly useful in this stage. One goal of instruction is to have the learner transfer information from past learning to these initial skill levels. For example, many skills have similar stance requirements, so instructions that bring out already known stances should be useful for teaching a new one (e.g., "adopt a stance like you would in skill x"). Often, several previously learned movements can be sequenced together to approximate the desired skill (e.g., to shift gears, *push* in the clutch, *move* the gearshift down, and *let out* the clutch while gently *pressing* the accelerator), and can provide a start for later learning. Gains in proficiency in this stage are very rapid and large, indicating that more effective strategies for performance are being discovered. It is not of much concern that performance at this stage is halting, jerky, uncertain, and poorly timed to the external environment; this is merely the starting point for later proficiency gains.

Some learners engage in a great deal of self-talk, verbally guiding themselves through actions. However, this activity demands considerable attention and can interfere with the processing of other sensory events that may be going on at the same time. Verbal activity is effective for this initial stage, though, facilitating a rough approximation of the skill, and will likely drop out later.

Fitts' Stage 2: Fixation Stage The performer next enters the **fixation stage** (sometimes called the **associative stage** or **motor stage**). Most of the cognitive problems dealing with the environmental cues that need to be attended to and the actions that need to be made have been solved. So, now the learner's focus shifts to organizing more effective movement patterns to produce the action. In skills requiring quick movements, such as a tennis stroke, the learner begins to "build" a motor program to accomplish the movement requirements. In slower movements, such as balancing in gymnastics, the learner constructs ways to use movement-produced feedback.

Several factors change markedly during the fixation stage, associated with more effective movement patterns. Performance improves steadily. Some inconsistency from trial to trial is seen as the learner attempts new solutions to movement problems. Inconsistency gradually decreases, though; the movements involving closed skills begin to be more stereotypic, and those involving open skills become more adaptable to the changing environment (Gentile, 1972). Enhanced movement efficiency reduces energy costs, and self-talk becomes less important for performance. Performers discover environmental regularities to serve as effective cues for timing. Anticipation develops rapidly, making movements smoother and less rushed. In addition, learners begin to monitor their own feedback and detect their errors. This stage generally lasts much longer than the cognitive stage.

Fitts' Stage 3: Autonomous Stage After considerable practice, the learner gradually enters the **autonomous stage**. This is the stage usually associated with the attainment of expert performance—perceptual anticipation (chapter 2) is high, which speeds the processing of environmental information. The system generally programs longer movement sequences; this means that fewer programs need to be organized and initiated during a given interval of time, which decreases the load on attention-demanding movement initiation processes.

The decreased attention demanded by both perceptual and motor processes frees the individual to perform simultaneous higher-order cognitive activities, such as making higher-level decisions about strategies in sport, expressing emotion and affect in music and dance, and dealing with stress and chaos in emergency care activities. Self-talk about the actual muscular performance is almost absent, and performance often seems to suffer if self-analysis is attempted. However, self-talk could continue in terms of higher-order strategic aspects. Self-confidence increases and the capability to detect and correct one's own errors becomes more fine-tuned.

It is important to remember that performance improvements in the autonomous stage are slow, because the learner is already very capable when this stage begins. However, learning is far from over, as shown in many studies (see Focus on Research 9.1, for example).

Bernstein's Stages

In contrast to Fitts' emphasis on the information-processing aspects of perceptual and motor components of skill, Bernstein identified stages of learning from a combined motor control and biomechanical perspective.

Bernstein's Stage 1: Reduce Degrees of Freedom The initial problem facing the learner is what to do with all of the possible degrees of freedom of movement that are available for the body. A single **degree of freedom**, in Bernstein's view, refers to just one (out of all of the ways) in which the various muscles and joints are free to move. Bernstein considered that the solution to the so-called **degrees of freedom problem** (i.e., how can the system control all of the degrees of freedom) was to reduce the movement of nonessential or redundant body parts in the initial stage

Focus on RESEARCH 9.1

Learning Never Ends

The shape of the classic skill acquisition profile, sometimes erroneously termed a "learning curve," is illustrated by rapid gains early in practice, improvements slowing down as some proficiency is gained, then a gradual slowing to an eventual point where no further improvements in skill are detected. So, would it be correct to say that learning has ended as this point? Two classic studies in the motor learning literature suggest that the answer is no.

Bryan and Harter (1897, 1899) studied the perceptual–motor skill of telegraphy—involving the language of sending and receiving Morse code. They studied telegraphers of varying levels of experience and discovered many important findings. For example, the perceptual skill of receiving Morse code became faster and more efficient with practice. However, this was achieved not only through quantitative improvements (speed of letter detection), but also by means of qualitative change—as skill developed, telegraphers progressed by perceiving individual letters at first, then groupings of letters, then whole words, and then common phrases or groupings of words. The timing of dots and dashes is a critical component of sending Morse code, and Bryan and Harter found that the consistency in movement timing continued to improve over many years of experience (see Lee & Swinnen, 1993, for more analysis). In sum, there was no evidence that improvements stopped being made in either perceptual or motor skill. Rather, performance became more efficient and less variable with continued practice.

Crossman (1959) presented a very different type of analysis of a skill. He tracked the performance of cigar rollers who used a machine to combine leaves of tobacco into a finished product, a cigar. Crossman found that improvements in performance time leveled off only after seven years of experience (or 10 million cigars!) had been accumulated. However, the plateau in performance was not due to a limitation in human performance. Rather, performance leveled off because the limits of the cycle time of the machine had been reached. Presumably the cigar rollers would have continued to improve if they had not reached the cycle limit of the machine.

The illusion that learning has ended is almost always caused by the limits reached in the sensitivity of the measurement tool in revealing further changes. New measurement tools continue to be developed and to reveal the process of motor learning in more detail. For example, recent studies of motor learning have revealed markedly different effects of transcranial magnetic stimulation (TMS) on performance, depending on whether it was applied early (after 5 sessions) or late (after 16 sessions) in practice (Platz et al., 2012a, 2012b). We suspect that future studies using these and other measures of brain plasticity will provide clearer evidence that learning never stops.

Exploring Further

1. Consider a skill such as archery, which can be measured in terms of performance outcome (such as accuracy and consistency) and movement proficiency (e.g., steadiness). How might these different measures change at different rates as a function of practice?
2. Think of another motor task and describe how expertise might continue to evolve with continued practice. What measurement systems would be required to observe these continued changes?

Skill Acquisition, Retention, and Transfer

of learning—in essence, by *freezing* these degrees of freedom. In some ways, this solution achieved the same goal as Fitts' first stage of learning—since the number of degrees of freedom that need to be controlled is reduced, there are fewer motions of the body that require conscious control, which allows attention to be devoted to the few degrees of freedom that provide maximal control of the rudimentary aspects of the action.

Bernstein's Stage 2: Release Degrees of Freedom As control of a minimum number of degrees of freedom in stage 1 begins to result in some initial successes, the typical learner attempts to improve performance by *releasing* some of the degrees of freedom that had initially been "frozen." This release of degrees of freedom would seem to be particularly useful in tasks that require power or speed, as the degrees of freedom that have

As youth hockey players increase their skill level, the tasks of maintaining balance and handling the puck require less attention, allowing them to focus on other aspects of the game.

207

Focus on
APPLICATION 9.2

Fitts and Bernstein Learn to Play Ice Hockey

One way to conceptualize the different stages of learning perspectives proposed by Fitts and by Bernstein is with an example. Ice hockey involves two main tasks: skating (whole-body movements using two boots fitted with sharp blades that cut into the ice) and stick-handling (using a hockey stick to pass, shoot, and manipulate a flat rubber disk called the puck). What follows is an analysis regarding how the stages of learning might proceed according to Fitts and Bernstein.

Fitts' Stage 1

From Fitts' perspective, the process of maintaining balance is a primary concern, requiring massive amounts of attentional resources just to stay upright. Holding the stick is highly verbalizable, and doing so correctly is an important consideration. For right-handed players, the left hand holds the stick near the top of the shaft and the right hand holds it partway down the shaft. Shooting, passing, and manipulating the puck require considerable conscious resources since each of these activities perturb balance and pose a threat to the learner's posture.

Bernstein's Stage 1

For Bernstein, the same problem of staying upright and striking the puck is solved by reducing body motion. A steady base is critical; therefore movements that would destabilize that base, such as taking a long stride during the act of shooting or passing a puck, are largely avoided or reduced in magnitude. The motions of the body during skating are rather rigid, again to avoid destabilizing balance. The stick is used as a "crutch" during this stage to help maintain balance.

Fitts' Stage 2

Rudimentary skill has been achieved by the start of this stage—the learner has acquired the basic skills to skate, shoot, pass, and manipulate the puck, although these require considerable cognitive resources to coordinate at the same time. Attention to skating and stick handling has been reduced, however, allowing the learner to attend to other perceptual attributes of the situation, for example locating members of the opposing team and anticipating the movements of teammates.

Bernstein's Stage 2

For Bernstein, the learner's skating skills have improved dramatically due to the release of the body's degrees of freedom. Rather than appearing to "walk" on skates, the learner makes a sideward push with one skate and glides forward on the other skate. Considerably more trunk rotation is used to move, resulting in much faster skating speed. Control of the puck has also improved through more involvement of the wrist, forearm, and shoulder muscles. The result is greater force production and accuracy in shooting and passing the puck, as well as more effective stick-handling control.

Fitts' Stage 3

In Fitts' autonomous stage, very little attention is given to the processes involved in skating and puck control, or even the simultaneous control of these skills. Now the learner's cognitive involvement is invested in higher-order activities of the game—detecting patterns of game flow by members of both teams, planning strategic plays whereby the learner goes to locations on the ice that could provide an offensive or defensive advantage, or taking advantage of perceived weaknesses.

Bernstein's Stage 3

Bernstein's final stage exploits the energy that comes with the fast and dynamic play of the game. Players learn to stop, turn, accelerate, and decelerate with precision and use the passive dynamics of their own body but also the energy obtained from on-ice objects, both animate (other players) and inanimate (e.g., the rink's wall, or "boards"). Modern equipment (skates and sticks) are manufactured with composite materials, which are designed to be fully exploited by only the most highly skilled players.

Summary

This analysis represents just one example of how Fitts' and Bernstein's stages of learning might characterize the ways in which skill development proceeds. As you can readily tell from this comparison, the Fitts and Bernstein perspectives should not be seen as competing with each other. Rather, they represent two different theoretical approaches conceptualizing somewhat different sets of processes that change with practice.

been released could allow for faster and greater accumulation of forces.

Bernstein's Stage 3: Exploit Passive Dynamics In Bernstein's final stage, the performer learns to exploit the passive dynamics of the body—essentially, the energy and motion that come "for free" with the help of physics (such as gravity, spring-like characteristics of muscle, and momentum). Thus, in Bernstein's final stage, the movement becomes maximally skilled in terms of *effectiveness* (achieving the end result with maximum assuredness) and *efficiency* (minimum outlay of energy).

Limitations of Fitts' and Bernstein's Stages

One thing that is important to keep in mind about both the Fitts and the Bernstein perspectives is that neither was meant to describe learning as a series of discrete, nonlinear, and unidirectional stages. The progression from one stage to another is not categorical, such as leaving one room of a house and entering another. In many ways, these stages were meant to be considered as generic descriptions of performance capabilities and tendencies at any one time in the learning process, with the proviso that these capabilities change as learning progresses.

There are a number of other aspects of these two schemes that need to be considered. For example, Fitts considered performance change to be *regressive* as well as progressive, in the sense that performance, under conditions of high arousal or after a long layoff from practice, was expected to produce performance tendencies characteristic of a previous stage (Fitts et al., 1959).

Task differences also play an important role in the stage views of both Fitts and Bernstein. For instance, "automaticity" in Fitts' final stage might be achieved for some tasks but never achieved for other tasks. As one example, responding "automatically" to a specific stimulus with a specific response can be learned with many hours of devoted practice (e.g., Schneider & Shiffrin, 1977), although it might be impossible to ever develop automaticity for a novel, complex, serial, or continuous movement task.

Similarly, the nature of the task might limit the application of Bernstein's stages (Newell & Vaillancourt, 2001). We can think of two common examples of skills whose learning would seem to contradict Bernstein's stage 2 characterization. One of these involves doing a handstand on the still rings in men's gymnastics. The learner seems to begin learning this task using nearly all of the available degrees of freedom (e.g., maintaining balance with hip and trunk movements, using the arms). When the learner is clearly past the initial stage, rather than releasing degrees of freedom, the learner seems to *freeze* them. All of the wild hip and arm movements seem to drop out, leaving behind control of balance by the wrists only: this would seem to be just the opposite order from Bernstein's views, where the learner seems to gain proficiency by freezing, then freeing, degrees of freedom. Another example concerns the skill of learning to windsurf. At first, the learner uses wild hip, knee, and arm movements to maintain balance on the board, much as the gymnast does on the still rings at this stage. Then, when clearly past the first stage, the learner seems to freeze the hip, and knee movements so that the body is still and rigid, and control is due to very small movements of the sail with small elbow and wrist movements, again with freezing proceeding freeing. Konczak, vander Velden, and Jaeger (2009) found that, similar to these gymnast and windsurfer examples, expert violinists developed their skill by learning to reduce rather than release motions of their bowing arm.

In sum, we believe that the stage ideas of both Fitts and Bernstein retain considerable merit, and their longevity as descriptive analyses of the learning process attests to a continued prominence in the motor learning literature. However, one must not lose sight of the fact that these are rather generalized descriptions, not firm theories about the learning process.

Skill Retention

This section concerns the "fate" of motor skills after a period of time during which no further practice is undertaken, during which time **forgetting** may occur. This interval of time is often termed the "retention interval." As we will discuss, the absence of practice often is detrimental to skilled performance.

Forgetting

One of the truisms of life is that some skills seem never to be forgotten whereas others are lost rather quickly. The folklore example of the former is riding a bicycle, a skill that we seem to retain for very long periods of time during which we experience no intervening practice. In contrast, some memories are forgotten quite quickly, such as the number sequence of your first telephone number.

Consider the following two studies that are representative of this contrast. In the first study, conducted many years ago by Neumann and Ammons (1957), experimenters asked subjects to learn to match the locations of a series of eight paired switches and lights. This task seemed to have a relatively heavy verbal memory component to it, in that subjects had to learn and remember which switch went with which light. Practice continued until subjects performed two errorless trials, which, as illustrated in figure 9.4, required about 63 trials, on average. At that point the subjects were split into five subgroups, each defined by the length of time after which the retention test would be performed—retention intervals of 1 min, 20 min, two days, seven weeks, or a full year. The results illustrated in figure 9.4 are very clear. Retention performance was dramatically affected by the length of the retention interval, with one year of no practice both producing the least skilled performance on the first retention trial and returning this group essentially to the level at which they started on the first day. This decrement required the largest number of trials (as compared to the other groups) to regain the criterion of two errorless trials. It is of interest to note here that the rate of improvement after one year of no practice was somewhat larger than it was in original practice, suggesting that perhaps not all of the skill had been lost during this retention interval.

Now, contrast results from Neumann and Ammons study (figure 9.4) with the findings reported by Fleishman and Parker (1962), presented in figure 9.5. The task required production of complex tracking movements involving movement of the hands in the X (left-right) and Y (forward-backward) dimensions and movement of the feet in the X-dimension, using an aircraft-type stick and rudder controls. Retention tests were performed after nine months or one or two years. As illustrated in figure 9.5, the retention loss was remarkably small, even after two years of no practice. It is clear that the type of task influences retention performance.

What does the difference in the results of these two studies mean? We argue that long-term retention depends largely on the nature of the task—discrete tasks (especially those with a relatively large cognitive component such as the one used in Neumann and Ammons' study) are forgotten relatively quickly. On the other hand, continuous tasks, exemplified by the task in the Fleishman–Parker study, are retained very well over long periods of no practice. Of course, the amount of original practice will have much to say about the relative amount of retention for these tasks (e.g., Ammons et al., 1958). But, in general, continuous tasks, like riding a bicycle, are retained for much longer periods of time than are discrete tasks.

Warm-Up Decrement

The initial depression in motor activity at the very start of a performance represents what many researchers believe to be a different kind of retention deficit (Adams, 1961). Many

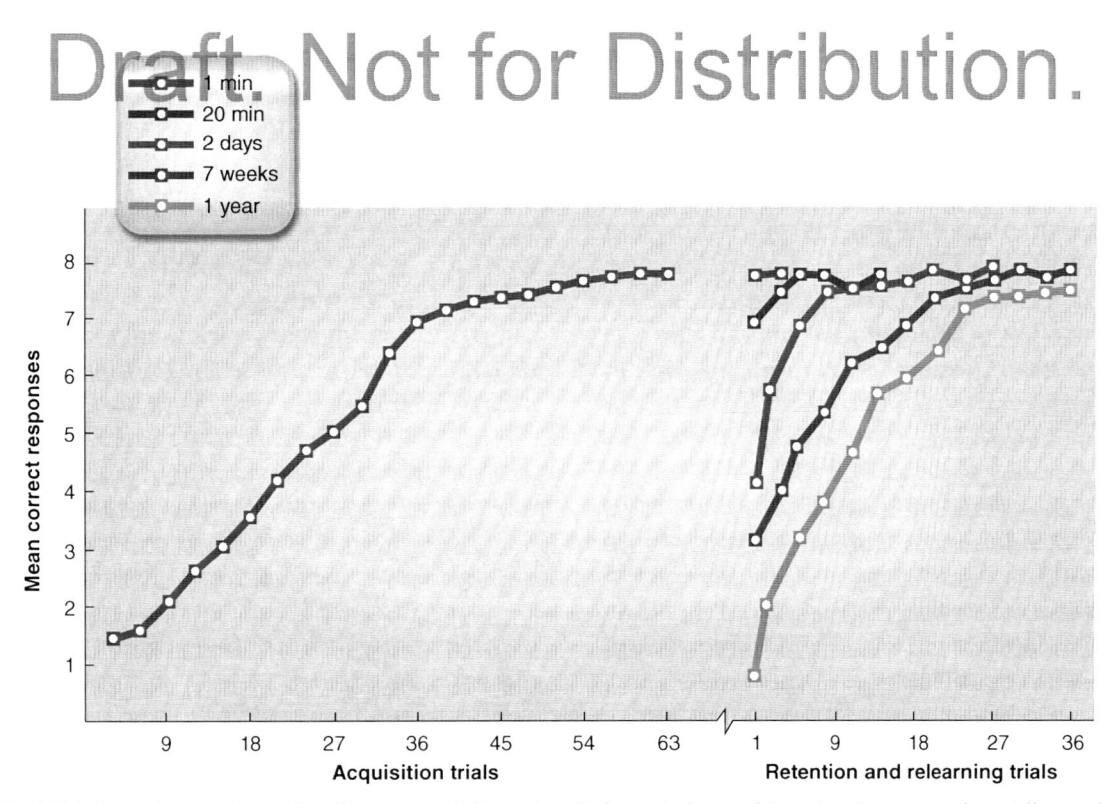

FIGURE 9.4 Forgetting of a discrete task (learning light switch combinations) occurred rapidly, and more additional practice trials were needed to reacquire the original criterion as the retention interval increased.
Reprinted by permission from Neumann and Ammons 1957.

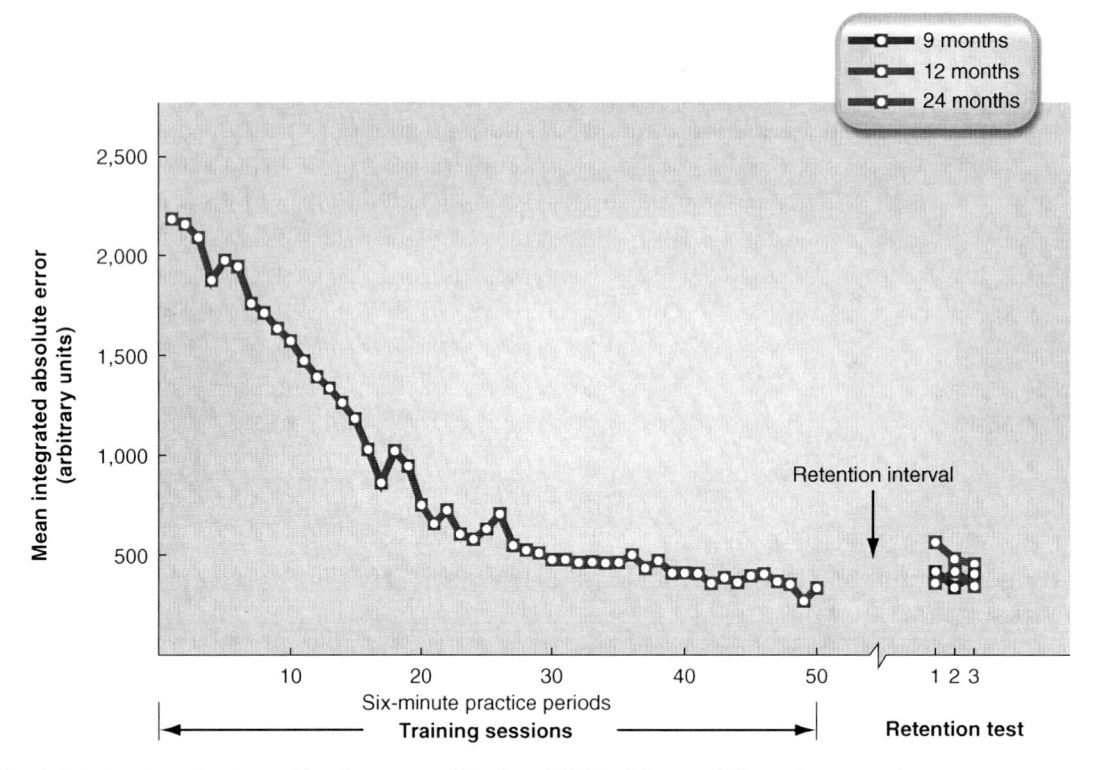

FIGURE 9.5 Results from Fleishman and Parker (1962). Motor skill tracking performance was retained well for periods of up to two years following original practice.

Reprinted by permission from Fleishman and Parker 1962.

examples exist. A musician may have trouble getting into the proper rhythm or mood to support optimal performance; a hockey goalie who is substituted late in the game may not be mentally prepared for the speed of play. In these cases the learner typically suffers a relatively large performance decrement and is temporarily prevented from performing at his maximum potential. This disturbance to performance is eliminated quickly once a few trials of practice are experienced—essentially as with the 20 min retention-interval condition in Neumann and Ammons' study (figure 9.4). Still, the facts that these decrements to performance are relatively large, and that they appear reliably in so many different tasks and under so many different circumstances, have earned this research area its very own term: *warm-up decrement*.

Note that the term "warm-up" is not used here in the same sense as "warming up" physiologically to run a race, for example. Rather, **warm-up decrement** is considered a psychological factor that is brought on by the passage of time away from a task and is eliminated when the performer begins again to perform a few trials. Many consider warm-up decrement the result of a loss of the "set" (a kind of tuning, or adjustment process not related to memory for the task itself) that facilitates performance before the retention break, and that, having been lost over the retention interval, now prevents a return to maximum performance potential for a short period of time. These decrements, being relatively large, have a large role in tasks for which the performer must respond as well as possible on the very first attempt after a layoff of a few minutes (e.g., free-throw shots in basketball).

The term "set," when referring to warm-up decrement, has very specific meaning (Adams, 1961). According to researchers, **set** is a collection of psychological activities, states, or adjustment and processes (for example, the target of attentional focus, one's

Some skills are retained, even with no practice, over long periods of time.

perceptual focus, and postural adjustments). These processes are appropriate for, and support performance while an activity is ongoing but are "lost" when a different set is adopted to support the activities undertaken during rest (e.g., a set of adjustments appropriate for resting).

One explanation for the occurrence of warm-up decrement is that it simply represents a type of motor forgetting. That explanation has not received much support from researchers, however, because so-called set-reinstating activities that do not influence memory for the task, undertaken near the end of the retention interval, have been shown to reduce or eliminate warm-up decrement. In contrast, activities (such as maximum-grip-force tests) that are deliberately designed to interfere with set for a task (such as delicate positioning of a lever on a trackway) produce increases in warm-up decrement (Nacson & Schmidt, 1971). These findings seem to argue against the idea that warm-up decrement is simply a form of memory loss (forgetting) in the main task.

Reinstatement of set before undertaking performance can eliminate much of the warm-up decrement that accrues over a retention interval, even a brief one. This finding likely helps to explain some of the benefit that occurs due to the preshot routine seen in many types of sporting events (e.g., golf shots, basketball free throws) when an athlete performs a highly individualized set of behaviors just before the "real" action. These may involve bouncing the basketball a certain way or following a set of procedures before hitting a golf ball. But most high-level athletes do these activities in a similar way each time. Successful performance has much to do with these preshot routines, and research suggests that overcoming the negative effects of warm-up decrement is part of the reason for this success (Boutcher & Crews, 1987).

Skill Transfer

Transfer, which is sometimes called *generalization*, is an important goal of practice. It refers to the idea that learning acquired during practice of a given task can be applied to, or transferred to, other task situations. An instructor cannot be satisfied if the students can perform only those task variations they have specifically practiced. The instructor wants them to be able to generalize specific learning to the many novel variations they will face in the future (see Focus on Application 9.3). The concern is how to organize practice to maximize generalization.

What Skills Will Transfer?

Recall from chapter 8 that transfer is defined as the gain or loss in the capability to perform one task as a result of practice or experience on another task. Transfer is task positive if it enhances performance in the other skill, negative if it degrades it, and zero if it has no effect at all. The issues surrounding transfer, and particularly maximizing transfer by adjusting teaching methods and styles, are far-ranging and need to be discussed briefly here.

Transfer and Similarity

An old idea in psychology and motor learning is that transfer of learning between two tasks increases as the "similarity" between them increases. One idea was that of identical elements (Thorndike & Woodworth, 1901), according to which learning certain elements in one situation transferred to another skill because the second skill used the same elements. As simple as this idea might sound, there have always been problems with it. One is that the concepts of "similarity" and "identical elements" are never explicitly defined. For example, is throwing a baseball more similar to passing a football than shooting a basketball? What exactly are the elements that are involved? This particular view of "similarity" has not been taken very seriously as a result. However, other views of similarity and transfer have been supported by research.

Fundamental Movement Patterning Many have suggested that the so-called overarm pattern underlies throwing a baseball, serving in tennis, spiking a volleyball, and many other actions requiring forceful overarm movements to strike or throw an object. All these involve rotation of the hips and shoulders and ballistic actions of the shoulder–arm–wrist, ending finally with wrist–hand action to accomplish the particular goal. An analogous idea common among gymnasts is that certain fundamental actions (e.g., the sharp hip extension in a kip) can be applied to many apparatus events. In both these examples, if practice is given at one variant of the class of movements sharing the same general pattern, then the learner should be able to transfer the learning to any other variant using this same pattern. Of course, practicing a kipping action would not transfer to an overarm action or vice versa, because these skills use very different patterns, belonging as they must to separate movement classes.

Perceptual Elements "Similarity" is also evident in the numerous perceptual elements underlying many tasks. For example, learning to intercept flying balls of various kinds (baseballs, footballs, tennis balls, and so on) depends on learning the common features of ball flight, which are based on the principles of physics. In a similar way, police trainees must be attuned to the perceptual cues that alert them to a dangerous situation. Learning to react appropriately to such cues in one situation facilitates transfer to other situations in which the perceptual elements are similar.

Strategic and Conceptual Similarities Similar strategies, rules, guidelines, or concepts are present in many different activities. For example, driving behaviors, signs, traffic lights, and general "rules of the road" are common within a restricted population or community, which facilitates driving performance when you travel to parts of the country that are new to you. However, one would expect much less transfer, or perhaps even some negative transfer, when the rules of the road differ dramatically, as when tour-

Focus on
APPLICATION 9.3

Teaching for Transfer of Learning

The general idea of "teaching for transfer" involves not only maximizing transfer from earlier learning but also selecting those methods and ways of organizing practice that maximize transfer and generalizability. This focus section considers several ways in which instructors can enhance generalization through practice organization and feedback.

Point Out Similarities (or Differences) Among Skills

Recall from earlier in the chapter that Fitts' first stage of learning is highly cognitive and verbal. The instructor can use this knowledge to advantage by pointing out to the learner that a particular skill being practiced for the first time is similar to another one learned earlier. For example, a surgical student learning to stitch an open wound can be reminded that these actions are similar to sewing together two pieces of cloth or two peach skins.

Pointing out fundamental differences can be useful too. An example is explaining the difference between a flop shot and a chip shot in golf—the former is like trying to score an underhanded shot through a basketball hoop (high arc, little roll) while the latter is like bowling a ball toward a target (low arc, considerable roll). Borrowing details of an action pattern from earlier learning gives the student an advantage in understanding how to perform a new skill, particularly in early learning.

Use Verbal Cues to Emphasize Transfer

Similarities can also be emphasized by various teaching cues. In gymnastics it is helpful to use consistent labels for skills. For example, it is a good idea to emphasize the fact that kips on the horizontal bar, on the rings, and on the parallel bars are really the "same" skill and to refer to them all as "kips." Also, many skills have similar mechanical principles, such as shifting momentum when beginning to walk or run or needing a wider base of support for maximum balance when walking on ice. Such cues are used commonly by physical therapists in rehabilitation, for example.

Emphasize Transfer to Future Skills

It is tempting to think of practice as contributing only to the skill that the learner is attempting at the moment. It works the other way, too. In the practice of a given skill, ask the learner how to apply a particular strategy or concept to this new setting. Some methods, such as variable practice (discussed in chapter 10), have this characteristic as a goal—today's specific techniques being at least partly directed to future **generalizability**. A physical therapist may ask the patient to get up out of a chair using as many different types and styles of chairs or actions as possible. The goal here is for the learner to acquire fundamental strategies that will transfer to new, not previously encountered chairs in the future.

ists drive on the opposite side of the road in a foreign country (e.g., Americans driving in Australia).

Overall, the concept of "similarity" among skills involves several classes of common features:

- Common movement patterning
- Common perceptual elements
- Common strategic or conceptual elements

Motor Transfer as Learning Progresses

The transfer principles just discussed apply best when the learner is just beginning to learn a skill. Recall from the discussion of Henry's specificity principle in previous chapters that the amount of transfer from earlier learning should drop markedly when the learner becomes more highly skilled in the to-be-transferred-to skill. This decrease in transfer occurs because, with continued practice and increased capability, a skill becomes more specific (see chapter 7 for a review) and shares less with other skills of the same movement type (Henry, 1968). In early practice an overarm throw and a tennis serve do seem similar, and relating them might help the novice get the idea critical to initial attempts. However, a tennis serve and an overarm throw are not the same thing, and at higher levels of proficiency the two skills become more distinct. What, then, are the principles of transfer for later stages of learning?

Motor Transfer Is Small Between two reasonably well-learned tasks that merely *appear* somewhat similar, there is usually very little transfer. The transfer that does appear is usually positive, the skills generally facilitating each other to some small extent. But the amount of transfer is generally so low that transfer ceases to be a major goal of practice; this is in contrast to the situation in the earliest practice stages, where transfer was a major goal. Therefore, teaching a particular skill A (which is not of major interest), simply because you would like it to transfer to skill B (which *is* of major interest), is not very effective, especially when one considers the time spent on skill A that could have been spent on skill B instead. Transfer is fine when received "for free" in early practice, but it usually requires too much time in later practice.

The principle just mentioned also applies to using various "**lead-up activities.**" These actions are usually not of interest in themselves but are considered only as means to another goal—the transfer to another skill. For example, learning to suture wounds by starting with grapes is a cost-effective lead-up activity to working with more realistic simulators or patients. In general, however, learning such preliminary activities tends to transfer to the degree that they are effectively "similar" to the goal conditions, which we will discuss in more detail shortly.

No Transfer of Basic Abilities A common misconception is that fundamental abilities (see chapter 7) can be trained through various drills or other activities. The thinking is that, with some stronger ability, the learner will see gains in performance for tasks having this underlying ability. For example, athletes are often given various "quickening" exercises, with the hope that these exercises will train some fundamental ability to be quick, allowing quicker responses in their particular sports. Coaches and physical therapists often use various balancing drills with the goal of increasing general balancing ability; eye movement exercises are used with the goal of improving general visual abilities; and there are many other examples. Such attempts to train fundamental abilities may sound fine, but usually they simply do not work (e.g., Abernethy & Wood, 2001; Lindeburg, 1949). Resources (time, money) would be better spent practicing the eventual goal skills.

There are two correct ways to think of these principles. First, there is no general ability to be quick, to balance, or to use vision, as discussed in chapter 7 on individual differences. Rather, quickness, balance, and vision are each based on many diverse abilities, so there is no single quickness ability, for example, even if it could be trained. Second, even if there were such general abilities, these are, by definition, essentially genetically-determined and are not subject to modification through practice. Therefore, attempts to modify an ability with a nonspecific drill are usually ineffective. A learner may acquire additional skill at the drill (which is, after all, a skill in itself), but this learning does not transfer to the main skill of interest.

Transfer of Part Practice to Whole Performance

Some skills are enormously complex, such as playing a musical instrument and performing a gymnast's routine. Clearly, in such situations the instructor cannot present all aspects of the skill at once for practice because the student would be overwhelmed and would likely grasp almost none of it. A frequent approach is to divide the task into meaningful units that can be isolated for separate part practice. The goal is to integrate these practiced units into the whole skill for later performance. This is not as simple as it may sound because there are several factors that make integrating the learned units back into the whole skill somewhat difficult.

The question is how to create subunits of skills and how they can be practiced for maximum transfer to the whole skill. It is a simple matter to divide skills into parts. You could separate a gymnastics routine into the component stunts; you could divide the left and right hands of piano practice into separate components for practice. And each subpart could be divided even further. But the real question is whether these parts, practiced in isolation, will be effective for learning the whole skill, which is the overall goal. Thus, **part practice** is based on the transfer-of-learning principles defined earlier: Will the subunit transfer to the whole task that contains it? How much (if any) time should be spent on part practice, and would this time be more effectively spent practicing the whole task?

At first glance the answers to these questions seem obvious. Because the part of the task practiced in isolation seems the same as that part in the whole task, the transfer from the part to the whole task would seem to be almost perfect. This may be so in certain cases, but there are many other situations in which transfer is far from perfect. These differences in part-practice effectiveness depend on the nature of the skill.

Serial Skills of Long Duration

In many serial skills, the learner's problem is to organize a set of activities into the proper order, as with the gymnast who assembles a routine of stunts. Practicing the specific subtasks is usually effective in transferring to whole sequences. Part transfer works best in serial tasks of very long duration and in cases in which the actions (or errors) of one part do

A gymnast putting together a routine (here, Richard Schmidt, the first author) must become skilled at performing the routine as a whole, since each movement must be modified in response to the previous movement.

not influence markedly the actions of the next part. That is, part practice is most effective for skills in which the parts are performed relatively independently. The learner can devote more practice time to the troublesome parts without practicing the easier elements, making practice time more efficient.

However, in many serial skills in sport, performance on one part frequently determines the movement that must be made on the next part. If the ski racer comes out of a turn too low and fast, this affects the approach for the next turn. Small positioning errors on the beam in one move determine how the gymnast must perform the next one. If a part-to-part interaction is large, as it might be if the sequence is run off quickly, modifying a given action as a function of performance on a previous action is an important component of the skill. However, these interactions between parts of the whole skill cannot be practiced and learned in isolated part practice; **whole practice** is necessary. The gymnast might be able to do all of the individual stunts in her routine, but she still might not be able to perform an effective routine in a meet because she never learned to modify each component movement based on the previous one.

Discrete Skills of Short Duration

Any skill is, in some sense, serial because certain pieces of it come before other pieces, such as hitting a baseball, which contains step, hip turn, and swing elements. At some point, though, these individual parts, when viewed separately, cease to be parts of the whole skill. Dividing a golf swing into smaller and smaller arbitrary parts destroys a critical aspect that allows the parts to be characterized as a component of a swing; that is, the division seems to disrupt the essential features of the action. Practice at these subparts could be ineffective, even detrimental, to learning the whole task.

Several experiments suggest that practicing parts of a discrete task in isolation transfers little if at all to the whole task (e.g., Lersten, 1968; Schmidt & Young, 1987), especially if the task is rapid and ballistic. This is probably related to the fact that the components in rapid tasks usually interact strongly, which means less effective transfer. In fact, transfer from the part to the whole can even be negative in certain cases, so practicing the part in isolation could be worse for the whole task than not practicing at all!

This evidence suggests that when very rapid skills are broken down into arbitrary parts, these parts become changed from the "same" parts in the whole task so that the part practice contributes very little to the whole. In tasks like hitting a golf ball, for example, practicing the backswing separately from the downswing changes the dynamics of the action at the top of the backswing, which is dominated by actively lengthening muscles whose spring-like properties allow the downswing to be smooth and powerful. Therefore, practicing the backswing in isolation, which eliminates the role of these spring-like muscle properties, is quite different from performing the same backswing in the context of the whole skill.

Motor Programs and the Specificity Principle

According to the motor program concept introduced earlier, quick actions are controlled essentially open loop, with the decisions about the action's structure programmed in advance. Performing only a part of this action in part practice, particularly if the part has different dynamics (e.g., in the golf swing) when performed in isolation, requires using a different program, or one that is responsible for only the part in isolation. Practicing such a part program contributes to performance of the part in isolation, but it will probably not contribute to production of the whole movement, which could be based on a different motor program. Thus, in part practice the learner develops two separate movement programs—one for the part and one for the whole task. This is consistent with Henry's (1968) specificity view of movement learning, in which isolating a part and changing it slightly to practice it separately shifts the underlying abilities to the point that it is no longer related to the original part in context of the whole skill.

Progressive Part Practice

Even with very rapid actions, though, some part practice might be helpful, particularly if the action's elements are many in number and provide initial difficulty for the learner to sequence them properly. Very early part practice might be beneficial in this case. However, to minimize the problems of learning actions that do not transfer to the whole, many instructors use **progressive part practice**. In this method the parts of a complex skill are presented separately, but the parts are integrated into larger and larger parts, and finally into the whole, as soon as they are acquired.

The principles of part practice can be easily summarized:

- For very slow, serial tasks with no component interaction, part practice on the difficult elements is very efficient.
- For very brief, programmed actions, practice on the parts in isolation is seldom useful and can even be detrimental to learning.
- The more the components of a task interact with each other, the less the effectiveness of part practice.

Simulation and Transfer

Transfer principles are commonly used in the area of simulation. A **simulator** is a practice device designed to mimic features of a real-world task. Simulators are often very elaborate, sophisticated, and expensive, such as devices to train pilots to fly aircraft (figure 9.6). But simulators need not be elaborate at all, such as wireless video game consoles (see Focus on Research 9.2). Simulators can be an important part of an instructional program, especially when the skill is expensive or dangerous (e.g., learning to fly a jetliner), where facilities are limited (e.g., cycling on a treadmill instead of in a velodrome), or where real practice is not feasible (e.g., using

FIGURE 9.6 An aircraft cockpit simulator.

Focus on RESEARCH 9.2

Game Systems for Virtual Training

One of the more recent advances in transfer-of-training research employs a common commercial product—gaming consoles, such as the popular Nintendo Wii system (figure 9.7). The advantages in using these systems are many, such as the relatively low price (specially created hardware and software research tools typically cost many tens of thousands of dollars, while game systems are available for a few hundred or less), the sophistication of the computing technology, and the intrinsic motivation to practice and learn that these gaming systems elicit (Levac, Rivard, & Missiuna, 2012).

In many ways, these gaming systems are nothing more or less than low-cost commercial simulators, although they were created for entertainment value rather than with a specific, transfer goal in mind. However, researchers have begun to use these highly motivating gaming systems to enhance specific end goals, such as physical rehabilitation for neurologically-challenged children (Levac et al., 2010) and adults who have had a stroke (Hijmans et al., 2011), as well as cognitive intervention for individuals with Alzheimer's disease (Fenney & Lee, 2010).

There is no doubt about the entertainment value of these gaming systems. However, their functional value, measured in terms of transfer of training, still remains to be assessed. To do so, we would use the same methods of evaluation as those applied to noncommercial simulators and training devices.

Exploring Further

1. Describe how a specific popular interactive game might be used in a poststroke rehabilitation setting.
2. Using the rationale presented in figure 9.8 (and described in the text), explain how you would assess the value of the gaming intervention described for question 1.

FIGURE 9.7 Video gaming systems engage people of all ages in performing activities and learning new motor skills.

Skill Acquisition, Retention, and Transfer

artificial patients rather than real humans for surgery practice).

Evaluating Simulator Effectiveness

Of course, a simulator must provide positive results in order to justify its use. Therefore, the amount of transfer resulting from the time spent in a simulator is an important consideration in determining its effectiveness and efficiency. Consider figure 9.8, showing the hypothetical performance curves on a novel motor learning task for two groups of subjects. The simulator group begins practice on the **criterion task** after having 3 h of practice on a simulator task, designed to provide positive transfer to the criterion task. The no-simulator group receives no prior practice on the simulator.

Figure 9.8 illustrates performance of both groups on the criterion task. Note that the point on the axis corresponding to 0 h of practice refers to the first trial on the criterion task for both groups (this point occurs after 3 h of practice on the simulator task for the simulator group). From figure 9.8 we can see that there is considerable positive transfer from the simulator to the criterion task, seen as the gain in probability of success from .30 to .50 (the difference labeled "A" in figure 9.8). Now look at the difference labeled "B" in figure 9.8. This difference suggests that the simulator group started at a level (.50) that took the no-simulator group 1.5 h of practice on the criterion task to achieve. So, in some respects, the simulator experience "saved" about 1.5 h of practice on the criterion task.

However, there is another way to look at this result. Remember that the simulator group had already spent 3 h of practice on the simulator. Since the simulator group spent 3 h of practice on the simulator but the no-simulator group "caught up" in 1.5 h, the simulation actually *cost* 1.5 h of real (sometimes very expensive) simulator time. Viewed in this way, simulator was not effective at all in reducing the time of training.

Time is not the only relevant factor here, though. The effectiveness of a simulator sometimes must also be judged in relation to the relative financial costs of simulator practice and criterion task practice, the availability of resources and facilities, safety, and so on. Relative to practice cost in a flight simulator, practice cost in an actual jetliner would be staggering, and there are obvious concerns for the safety of people, equipment, and so on. Thus, the evaluation of simulators in an instructional setting can be complicated, and it must take into account a number of important factors in making decisions about their use and effectiveness.

Physical Versus Psychological Fidelity

Remember that the overall goal of simulation is for the learning in the simulator to transfer to the criterion task. Scientists who conduct research in this area refer to the "quality" of the simulation in terms of *fidelity*—the degree to which the simulator mimics, or is "faithful to" the criterion task. But two different types of fidelity constructs have emerged in the literature. **Physical fidelity** refers to the degree to which the physical or surface features of the simulation and criterion tasks themselves are identical. In contrast, **psychological fidelity** refers the degree to which the behaviors and processes produced in the simulator

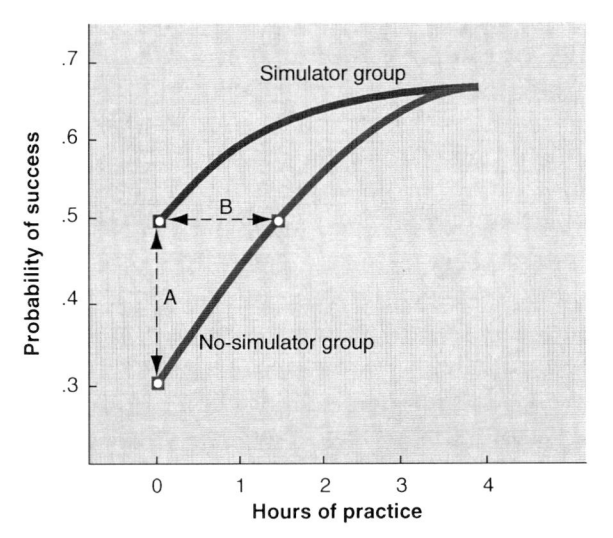

FIGURE 9.8 Hypothetical performance curves of two groups of learners on a novel motor learning task. The simulator group practiced a simulation task for 3 h before initial practice on the criterion task, whereas the no-simulator group did not.

replicate those required by the criterion task. Although these seem like similar constructs, in fact they are quite different and have the potential to result in quite different effects on transfer (e.g., Kozlowzki & DeShon, 2004).

Because transfer is expected to increase with task similarity, this idea has naturally led to the notion that physical fidelity should be as high as possible. Aircraft-cockpit simulators (figure 9.6, for example) replicate the cockpit of a real aircraft very closely (although doing so is often very expensive). Another example is cardiorespiratory resuscitation (CPR) mannequins, which are designed to be as anatomically correct as possible, for the purpose of training lifesaving skills. Physical fidelity refers to the degree to which the simulator replicates the physical features of the criterion task—possessing as much of the look, sound, and feel of the criterion task as possible.

Psychological fidelity is less concerned with the physical similarity between the simulator and criterion tasks and more concerned with the target skills and behaviors required to perform the criterion task. In the case of CPR mannequins, for example, simulator training might emphasize the perceptual and decision-making processes that are presented in an emergency situation, under high levels of stress, and perhaps under environmental challenges (e.g., extreme heat or cold). Psychological fidelity is concerned with training the skills that will be required of the end user in the criterion task.

Physical and psychological fidelity should be seen as complementary, not competing goals, according to Kozlowzki and DeShon (2004). Still, situations can arise in which too much faith is placed in the physical fidelity, without enough attention devoted to the psychological processes. Returning to our CPR example, some mannequins provide very exacting physical fidelity—the sights, sounds, and proprioceptive feedback that would appear to promote excellent perceptual and motor skill transfer. Yet just using the mannequin without considering how to structure the practice conditions and how to provide augmented feedback would be a major mistake, as the behaviors practiced during training would ultimately be expected to affect transfer to real emergency situations.

These issues of training motor skill behaviors are the major focus of the next two chapters. As we will see, how practice is structured and how feedback is augmented during practice determine the quality of motor learning that results from practice.

Summary

Motor learning is a fundamental necessity that we often take for granted, yet it is required for just about every facet of our daily existence. As people practice, they generally pass through stages of learning that describe the current state of their skill proficiency. Although some debate exists concerning how to best characterize these stages, practice results in some basic principles regarding how new motor skills are acquired and a specific set of benefits that result.

But periods of no practice are also a fact of life, and the retention of learned skills after a lengthy time away from them represents a critical area of research. Retention of skills is affected greatly by their classification; continuous skills are generally retained much more completely, and for longer periods of time, than discrete skills. Warm-up decrement refers to a specific type of retention deficit due to the loss of an activity set. Being able to perform a learned activity in a new situation concerns the issue of skill transfer. Simulators of various kinds can efficiently mimic important elements of a skill when practicing the actual skill would be too costly, dangerous, or impractical.

WEB STUDY GUIDE ACTIVITIES

Check Your Understanding

1. Contrast Fitts' and Bernstein's stages of learning. Name each stage and provide a brief description. Name one limitation of each of these perspectives.
2. Define warm-up decrement and explain how its effects can be reduced.
3. Distinguish between performance and learning during practice. How can they have conflicting goals, and how might this be overcome?

Apply Your Knowledge

1. List four benefits of practice discussed in this chapter and provide an example of how each might be illustrated by a karate student and a truck driver.
2. Your neighbor tells you that he will be learning to lead climb at a local rock-climbing gym. He tells about how lead climbing can be difficult because there are many parts to placing the safety gear properly while climbing and the decisions made can influence the next movement. From what he tells you about the lessons, it seems like the instructor will be using progressive-part practice. Why might the instructor have chosen this method? What alternatives would the instructor likely have considered, and why were these not chosen?

Suggestions for Further Reading

Specificity of learning, which remains an enduring topic in motor skills, was reviewed from different perspectives by Marteniuk (1974) and later by Proteau (1992). The development of expertise was the topic of a series of chapters in a volume edited by Starkes and Allard (1993). Differing views on stages of learning were explored by Anson, Elliott, and Davids (2005). And a range of topics on transfer of learning was reviewed by various authors in the book edited by Cormier and Hagman (1987). See the reference list for these additional resources.

Draft. Not for Distribution.

10

Organizing and Scheduling Practice

How the Structure of Practice Influences Learning

KEY TERMS

blocked practice
constant practice
demonstration
distributed practice
elaboration hypothesis
forgetting hypothesis
goal setting
massed practice
mental practice
modeling
observational learning
random (interleaved) prac
schema theory
self-regulation
variable practice

CHAPTER OUTLINE

Context and Considerations for Practice
Organizing Practice and Rest
Variable Versus Constant Practice
Blocked Versus Random Practice
Summary

CHAPTER OBJECTIVES

Chapter 10 describes the influence of the ways in which practice is structured and various conditions under which practice is conducted. This chapter will help you to understand

- key factors that occur while undertaking physical practice,
- basic concepts regarding the nature of practice,
- practice schedule organizations and their impact on performance and learning, and
- the role of practice variability in motor learning.

It comes as little surprise that increasing practice time, or increasing the efficiency of a given amount of practice time, is a major goal of instructors interested in practice effectiveness. Practice time is not the only factor, however; the *quality* of practice must also be considered. Thus, it is important to structure or organize a given amount of practice to maximize its effectiveness.

Imagine you are in charge of designing a plan for teaching a group of learners a particular set of skills. They may be prospective chiropractors learning different manipulation techniques, or a high school woodworking class, or perhaps a physical education class learning a set of tumbling exercises. Or perhaps there is no teacher involved at all, and you, the learner, are wondering how best to structure your music practice. How would you organize your time? How would you schedule physical practice and rest? In what order will you practice various skills, how much variation in skills would you introduce into your practice, and how much practice will you allow on one task variation before moving to the next? Questions like these affect how you would plan instruction, and this chapter presents the principles that help you solve these problems concerning how and when to practice.

Practice, or various kinds of experience, at particular skills is a broad concept, difficult to specify precisely. Practice can occur at many different times and places, under varying conditions, and it can be either almost unintentional or highly guided and structured. In experiments, many features of practice settings can be varied systematically, and these factors have been found to make practice more or less effective; many of these are under the direct control of the instructor. Of course, being armed as you are with principles of movement performance and learning will facilitate such decisions, equipping you to make wise choices about structuring practice to produce the most effective outcomes—usually the maximization of learning.

Off-Task Practice Considerations

Several important aspects of the practice setting occur very early in the process. In fact, many of these can occur in the absence of any physical practice at all (although they are generally more effective if they are interspersed with physical practice, as we discuss later). These considerations include concerns regarding motivation for learning, instructions, demonstrations, and mental practice (and imagery).

Motivation

Instructors often have the impression that the learner's motivation is not a problem—that a student would obviously want to learn a particular skill. However, students do not always share their instructors' enthusiasm for learning. An unmotivated learner is not likely to practice, and the result can be little or no learning. The motivated student devotes greater effort to the task, with more serious practice and longer practice periods, leading to more effective learning. How can instructors influence this motivation to learn?

Intrinsic motivation for learning concerns the learner's internalized drive—here, a drive to learn a skill. Considerable research has been conducted to understand how intrinsic motivation affects the learner in a wide variety of situations and skills, and has resulted in important advances in theory (e.g., Deci & Ryan, 2000) and application (e.g., Weinberg & Gould, 2011). For our purposes, however, we consider specifically the tools and techniques that may influence a learner's intrinsic motivation.

Deci and Ryan (2000) suggest that an individual's intrinsic motivation is largely determined by three basic needs: autonomy (control of one's own destiny), competence (skill mastery), and relatedness (being accepted within a social context). Of course, the relative weighting of each of these basic needs differs in every individual. Therefore, as an instructor, becoming familiar with the individual, and understanding how the acquisition of a motor skill fits into his needs, goes a long way in determining how best to respond in a learning context. The following sections discuss how motor learning may be affected by specific factors that influence motivation.

Goal Setting

An important motivational method is **goal setting**, whereby learners are encouraged to adopt specific performance goals. This method has had numerous applications, particularly in industry, and it has strong implications for learning in sport and physical education (Locke & Latham, 1985). In one experiment, Boyce (1992), either set specific goals or instructed participants to do so, or simply told participants to "do your best." Practice performance over a three-week period in which these goal-setting methods were applied is presented in figure 10.1, along with the results of a pretest (done before the goal setting was applied) and in a retention test. The findings clearly showed that adopting a specific goal improved performance compared to the "do-your-best" group. Moreover, this effect was maintained in a retention test. This is one of the few studies to demonstrate effects of goal-setting instructions on both performance (i.e., during practice) and learning (i.e., on a test of retention—see chapter 8 for a discussion of the use of retention tests to distinguish between performance and learning).

These results suggest that instructors encourage their learners to set realistic goals, ones that can be reasonably achieved with practice and effort. The learner can become discouraged by not even approaching goal levels that are too high. Yet goals that are too easily met can result in boredom and reduced motivation. Being encouraged to commit oneself to a specific, "challenging" (but not impossible) goal is strongly motivating and has positive benefits on performance and learning.

Augmented Feedback

Although augmented feedback—information that is provided to the learner from an external source—is the focus of the entire next chapter, we recognize here how it serves an important goal as a motivator. Lewthwaite and Wulf (2012) have recently reviewed a rapidly growing body of evidence suggesting that positive augmented feedback can provide

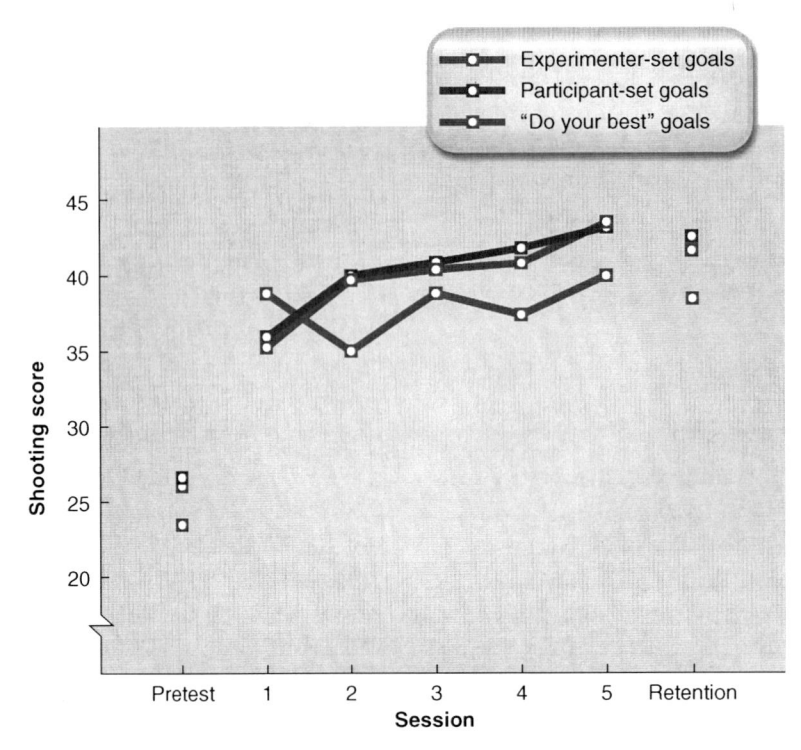

FIGURE 10.1 Results of the Boyce (1992) study in which learners practiced a shooting task after different goal-setting assignments.

Adapted by permission from Boyce 1992.

a boost to motor learning, even if the feedback is not entirely true.

For example, in one study by Lewthwaite and Wulf (2010, see figure 10.2), using a balance task, subjects in one group (red symbols in figure 10.2) were told that their performance was 20% more accurate than the average performance of others who had participated in the experiment (termed "false-positive-normative feedback"). The performance of this group was compared to that of another group (blue symbols) given similar false-negative normative feedback—they were told that their performance was 20% *less* accurate than average. A third (control) group (green symbols) was provided only their results, with no mention of the subjects' normative standing. The results of these feedback conditions are shown in figure 10.2, which illustrates clear benefits for the false-positive-normative feedback group throughout practice and in retention. Interestingly, there were no (significant) differences between the false-negative group and the control group, suggesting that the normative feedback provided a boost to learning when positive, but did not degrade learning reliably when it was negative. These and other studies of the effects of feedback on motivation are discussed in detail by Lewthwaite and Wulf (2012) and are revisited in the next chapter.

Self-Regulation of Practice

Providing some control over the learning environment is another factor thought to influence motivation and enhance learning. Researchers call this "**self-regulation**"; it refers to giving learners "ownership" over some of the components of practice. In studies of this type, learners are typically told that they can control how much practice to undertake, when augmented feedback will be provided, or how to organize the practice schedule (reviewed by Sanli et al., 2012). An important component of these studies is the inclusion of (yoked) control groups that provided the same schedule of feedback delivery as the self-selected group. However, these yoked conditions are determined entirely in advance and are not under the control of the

Organizing and Scheduling Practice

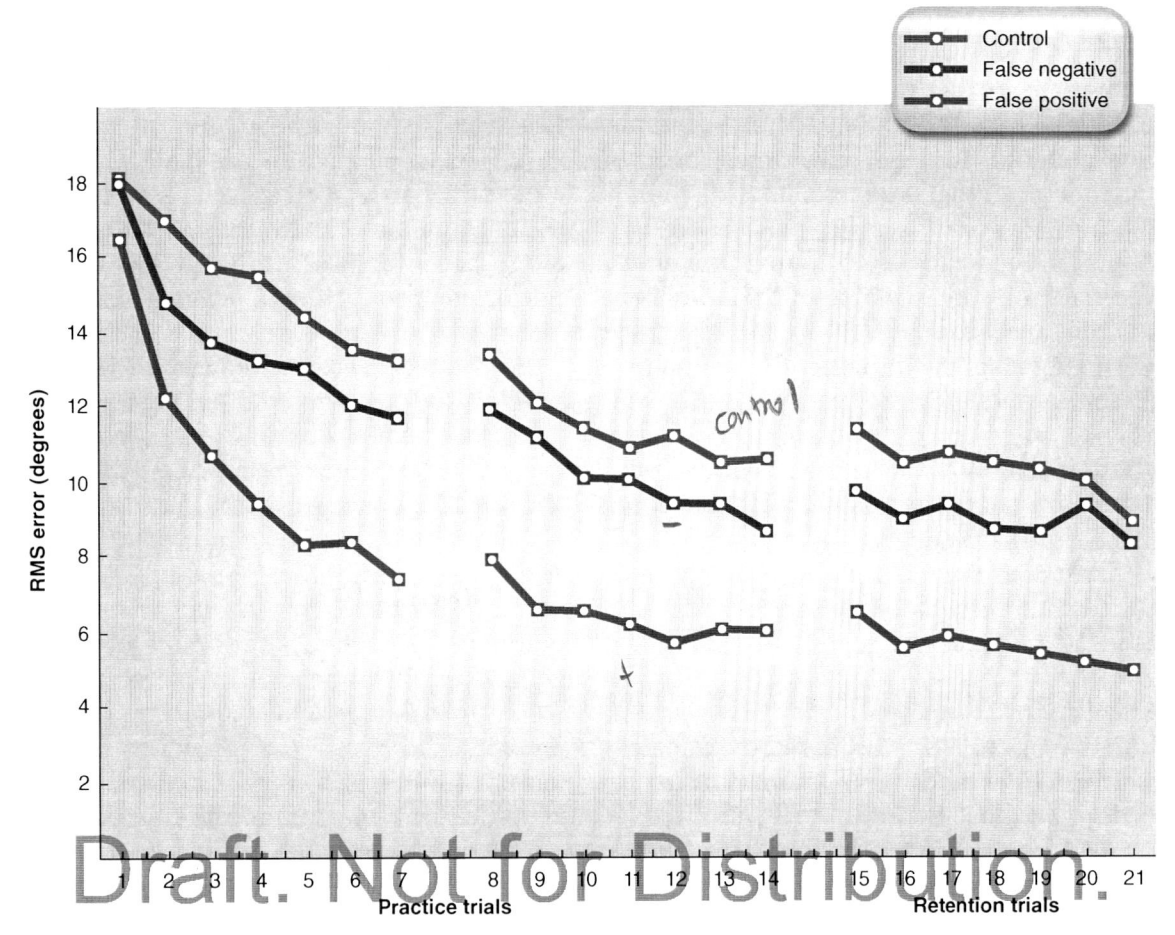

FIGURE 10.2 Results of the Lewthwaite and Wulf (2010) study, using a balance task. One group received false-positive feedback about their performance (red), another received false-negative feedback (blue), and one received only true feedback (green). RMSE = root-mean-square error (see chapter 1).

Reprinted by permission from Lewthwaite and Wulf 2010

learner. These studies have revealed more learning under self-regulated feedback conditions, leading some to speculate that giving learners control over their learning environment provides an extra incentive to learn. This seems to satisfy the need for autonomy, as suggested in Deci and Ryan's (2000) self-determination theory (see Lewthwaite & Wulf, 2012).

Instructions

Giving instructions is a feature of nearly every teaching setting. Instructions are usually spoken (although they can be written or demonstrated), and they provide information about the very first aspects of the skill. Tips on where and how to stand, how to hold the apparatus or other implement, what to look at, and what to do are frequently parts of typical instructions. Information about what is likely to happen also helps, such as a statement like "If you make this (chiropractic) manipulation correctly, you should feel this happen." Considering the difficulty students have with no instructions at all, these procedures are critical for raising skill level in very early practice. Simple, direct statements that start people off on the right track can be effective in reducing early confusion in the learning process. Effective instructors often even begin a **demonstration** by simply saying "Do this."

Instructions can be overdone, though. One problem is that words are a relatively crude, imprecise way of describing the subtle aspects of movements, so verbal descriptions are probably best suited only for the most elementary features. Try describing how to tie a shoelace in words, and the problem will be obvious. Along similar lines, many advocate explaining skills in terms of their biomechanical, or physical, bases, using concepts such as transfer of momentum and action–reaction forces. Some of this may be useful, but it assumes that learners understand the physical principles well enough to apply them to the new skills.

Two examples from motor learning research in which instructions have been determined to play a particularly strong role are discussed next. One of these concerns a largely verbal form of instruction (directing attentional focus); the other is mostly nonverbal (demonstrations and modeling).

Directing Attentional Focus

Earlier, in chapter 3, we discussed the effects on performance of directing a performer's attentional focus through verbal instructions. For most performers (perhaps with the exception of beginners), instructing them to pay attention to the intended *result* of an action (an "external focus") produces more skilled performance than an instruction to pay attention to aspects of the movement itself (an "internal focus"). This basic result has been replicated for many different sport activities, such as golf, baseball, basketball, and volleyball as well as other activities such as jumping and balancing (see Lohse, Wulf, & Lewthwaite, 2012, for a review), and this performance effect has also been extended to learners acquiring a new skill.

For example, groups of learners in a study by Wulf and colleagues (2003) practiced a balancing task while standing on a "teeter-totter" type of balance board (called a "stabilometer"). The balancing task was performed while also holding a cylindrical tube in their hands. A control group (green trace in figure 10.3) of subjects was given no instructions about where to direct their attentional focus while balancing. The other groups were instructed to try to balance while keeping a specific focus—either to keep their hands held horizontal (blue trace, an internal focus) or to keep the tube horizontal (red trace, an external focus). The results of these instructions, in figure 10.3, show the reduction in balance error over two days of practice and in tests of retention (where no attentional-focus instruc-

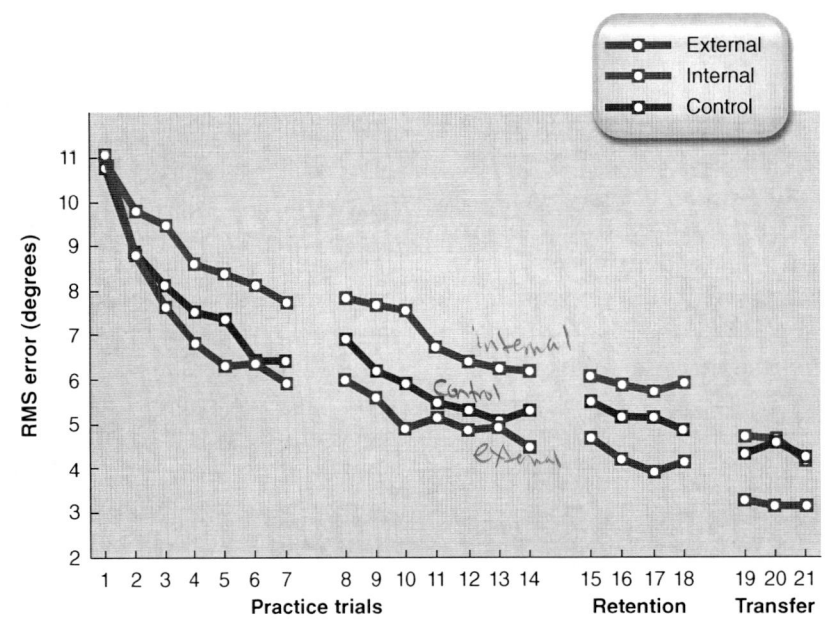

FIGURE 10.3 Effects of attentional focus in practice over two days (trials 1-14) and in retention and transfer tests. RMSE = root-mean-square error (see chapter 1).

Reprinted by permission from Wulf et al. 2003.

tions were given) and transfer (where none of the subjects held the tube). This finding is particularly remarkable in that holding the hands horizontal is almost exactly the same instruction as holding the tube horizontal (because the hands hold the tube).

The findings illustrated in figure 10.3 could be interpreted from two perspectives: (1) that external attentional focus instructions *facilitated* performance (during the practice trials) and learning (as measured in the retention and transfer tests), or (2) that internal attentional focus instructions *degraded* performance and learning (at least in retention). Or, perhaps the findings indicate some combination of these facilitation and degradation effects.

Demonstrations and Modeling

Good companions to prepractice instructions are various visual aids, such as still pictures, video clips, and live demonstrations by an instructor or by the learners themselves (sometimes called **modeling**). A clear advantage of transmitting information this way is seen, probably because modeling is not limited by words. This procedure comes under the general heading of **observational learning**, in which the learner gains information by watching another's performance.

The modeling process has been studied by researchers quite intensely over the past two decades. The result is a complex set of moderating variables that influence the observational learning process. The decision about how to maximize the effectiveness of a model seems to depend on a number of factors, which are summarized by Ste-Marie et al., 2012. How observational learning works without active movement on the part of the learner is a question that has raised plenty of debate. But there is little doubt that a considerable amount of learning, particularly early in practice, comes from studying and imitating others' actions. Capitalizing on this in instructional settings is a good procedure.

Mental Practice

One useful addition to the collection of activities in a practice session is to ask the learner to rehearse skills to be learned mentally, without performing actual, overt physical practice. In such **mental practice** the learner thinks about the skills being learned, rehearses each of the steps sequentially, and imagines doing the actions that would result in achieving the goal.

Can this method actually contribute to learning? For many years, scientists and educators in the motor learning field had very much doubted that *motor* learning could be accomplished through mental practice. The understanding of practice and learning at the time held that overt physical action was essential for learning. Most researchers thought that mental practice was producing gains in the cognitive–conceptual aspects of the task, and it was difficult to understand how any learning could occur without movement, active practice, and feedback from the movement to signal errors.

However, evidence from various experiments has demonstrated convincingly that mental practice procedures actually generate motor learning. Although mental practice does not result in as much learning as the same amount of physical practice, it does result in far more improvement than in no-practice control groups (see Feltz & Landers, 1983, for a review). Figure 10.4, from Hird and coauthors (1991), provides results from two separate tasks, the pegboard and pursuit rotor tasks. The fact that mental practice generates learning in the pursuit rotor (for example), which does not seem to have much cognitive learning involved beyond the first few trials, suggests strongly that the learning of motor control must be involved with mental practice.

How Does Mental Practice Work?

There are several views regarding how mental practice generates new task learning. One idea is that mental practice facilitates the learning of "what to do" (Heuer, 1985). For example, a tennis player could decide what shot to take; a baseball player could think how to grip the bat; and a skier could rehearse the sequence of turns in the ski run. These cognitive elements are thought to be pres-

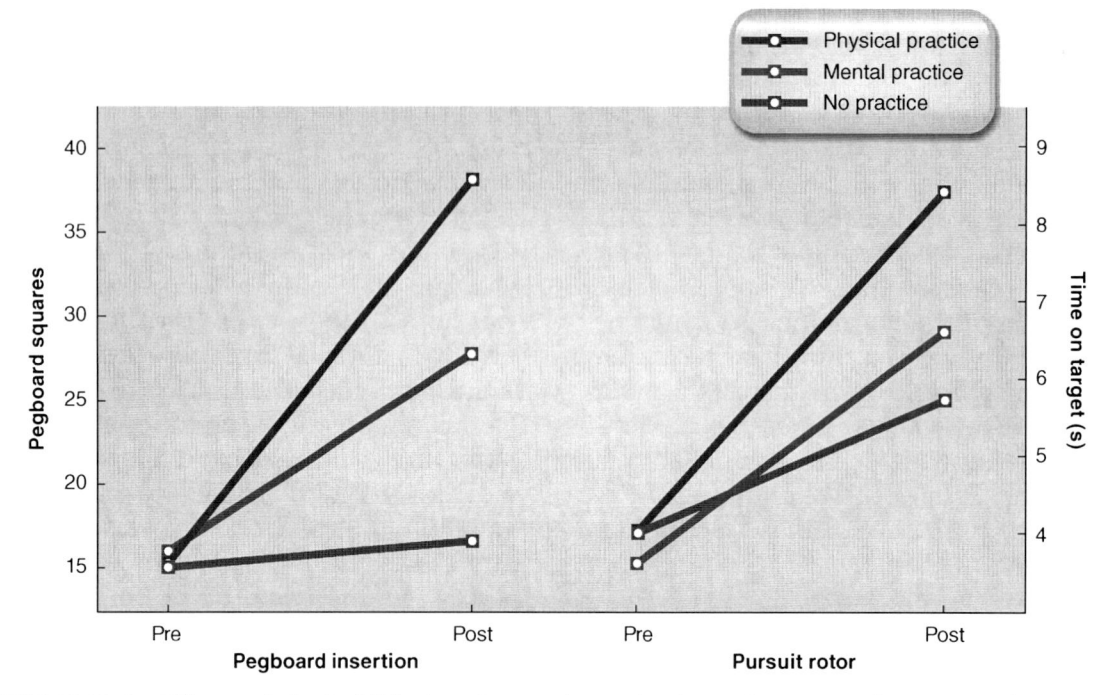

FIGURE 10.4 Effects of physical (blue) and mental practice (green) compared to a control, no-practice condition (red) on groups learning a pegboard-insertion task (left) and a pursuit-rotor task (right).

Data from Hird et al. 1991.

ent only in the very early stages of learning (the cognitive stage discussed earlier); thus, mental practice effects were predicted to apply only to early learning as well. Although learning cognitive elements is undoubtedly a major factor in mental practice, evidence such as that illustrated in figure 10.4 (and in Focus on Application 10.1) suggests that there is more to mental practice than just this. Beyond these early stages of practice, both the pegboard-insertion task and the pursuit-rotor task involve considerable motor control learning, as these tasks seem largely devoid of cognitive or conceptual components. Rawlings and coauthors (1972) also studied mental practice with the rotary-pursuit task, and their results were very similar to those of Hird and colleagues. Clearly, mental practice is not just cognitive or symbolic learning.

Another, older notion is that during mental practice, the motor system produces minute contractions of the participating musculature, with these contractions being far smaller in amplitude than those necessary to produce action. On this view, the "movement" is carried out in the central nervous system, providing "practice" even without overt body movement. Although EMGs (electromyograph recordings of the muscles' electrical signals) do show some evidence of weak activities during mental practice, the patterning of these EMGs does not resemble that of the actual movements very closely, making it difficult to understand how these electrical activities alone could be the basis for enhanced learning. This idea that mental practice produces minute muscular contractions has not generated much research support.

When and How to Use Mental Practice

The learner needs to be instructed carefully in the methods of mental practice. It is not enough simply to suggest that the learner go somewhere and "practice mentally"; systematic procedures are necessary. Weinberg and Gould (2011) provide additional tips for maximizing the use of imagery and mental practice, such as performing imagery and mental-practice activities in as many different

Mental practice does contribute to learning, though the exact way it does this is still unclear. One way may be allowing the learner to practice decision-making, such as a tennis player's choosing what shot to take.

settings as possible. Because mental practice and imagery require no apparatus; large groups of learners can practice at the same time. The clever instructor will find ways to interleave the two practice modes to provide maximal gains, for example by urging mental practice during the rest phase between trials of a fatiguing task or to break up a long string of repetitious physical practice trials.

Organizing Practice and Rest

Certainly, scheduling practice is a major concern in designing a program of instruction. This includes how many days per week skills should be practiced, whether to provide layoff days, how much practice to give on each day, and how much rest to provide during the practice period so fatigue does not

> **Focus on**
> **APPLICATION 10.1**
>
> ### Mental Practice in Stroke Rehabilitation
>
> The application of mental practice as a method to improve motor skills has been a part of sport for years. Sport facilities are limited in particular season, therefore mental practice would be a perfect fit for practicing sport in the off-season when facilities are not available. When research on mental practice, such as that shown earlier in this chapter, began to reveal positive effects on motor learning, instructors and therapists began to use these methods in their teaching and therapies, respectively—notably, in stroke rehabilitation they were justified in using these methods.
>
> Stroke is a medical condition that results in damage to the brain. Often the damage is to one side (hemisphere) of the brain, resulting in motor control impairments to the opposite side of the body. The goal of rehabilitation is to regain function by repairing the brain through goal-directed movements. Continued activations, from active physical practice, lead to restoration and compensation.
>
> But, there are limitations to the amount and frequency of rehabilitation treatments involving a therapist. Active movement outside therapy times may be encouraged, but unless specified and monitored, may not always be safe (e.g., for safety reasons). Fortunately, recent research has shown that mental practice (and imagery) generates neural activations of the brain that are similar to actual movement (Garrison, Winstein, & Aziz-Zadeh, 2010). Since mental practice cannot replace physical rehabilitation as an effective therapeutic technique, the combination of physical and mental practice is more effective than either form alone (Cha et al., 2012; Dickstein & Deutsch, 2007; Nilsen, Gillen, & Gordon, 2010). There appears to be little doubt that mental practice serves as an effective addition to the occupational and physical therapists' arsenal of rehabilitation tools.

become a problem. Some of these questions have been studied in the laboratory and in applied settings, revealing interesting and useful implications for skills learning.

There are countless ways to organize practice, of course, but how these variations affect learning and trade off with each other is complicated. Several common features of practice sessions have been well-studied, such as, the two research streams in this section: (1) research studying the effect of rest among periods of practice; and (2) research on mental practice and observation given during the intervals between periods of practice.

How Often to Practice

One of the first decisions concerns how often the learners will practice. On the one hand, a major goal of an instructor is usually to facilitate maximal learning before the first opportunity to perform the skills in a "real" situation. Most training schedules involve a limited period of time in which certain skills are practiced (e.g., a fixed number of weeks); one idea would be to provide as much practice as possible per week, concentrating it to maximize the practice time.

However, as shown by Baddeley and Longman (1978) with keyboard skills, there is likely some upper limit to the amount of practice per day that is effective for learning. In this study, postal workers were retrained for a total of 80 h of practice time (60 h only for one group). The practice was varied in terms of the amount of practice time per session (1 or 2 h) and the number of sessions per day (one or two), so among the three groups that received 80 total hours of training, two groups completed the training in 40 days (in either two, 1-h sessions or one, 2-h session per day) and one group completed it in 20 days (with two, 2-h sessions per day). The group that received 60 total hours of training completed the training in 60 days (one, 1-h session per day). The data in figure 10.5 present the results for the last part of the training period for all four groups, plus the results for three retention tests conducted months later. (Note that one peculiarity of this study was that the group having the least concentrated practice [1 h, once per day] received less total practice time than the other three groups.)

A consistent finding in figure 10.5 throughout practice and in retention was the relatively poor performance of the most concentrated practice group—the individuals who practiced for 4 h a day (2-h sessions, twice per day, red trace). Somewhat similar results, with concentrating practice into one session leading to less skill in a retention test than distributing practice across sessions, were obtained in a study of learning a golf skill (Dail & Christina, 2004).

Another interesting finding in the Baddeley–Longman study was that the practice schedule that produced the least learning (4 h per day, red trace), as measured in the retention tests, was the most popular among the trainees. This illustrates an important consideration: Learners do not always know which procedures work most effectively in terms of the overall goal of learning. (We will see more evidence of this less-than-optimal understanding of the learning process later in this chapter.)

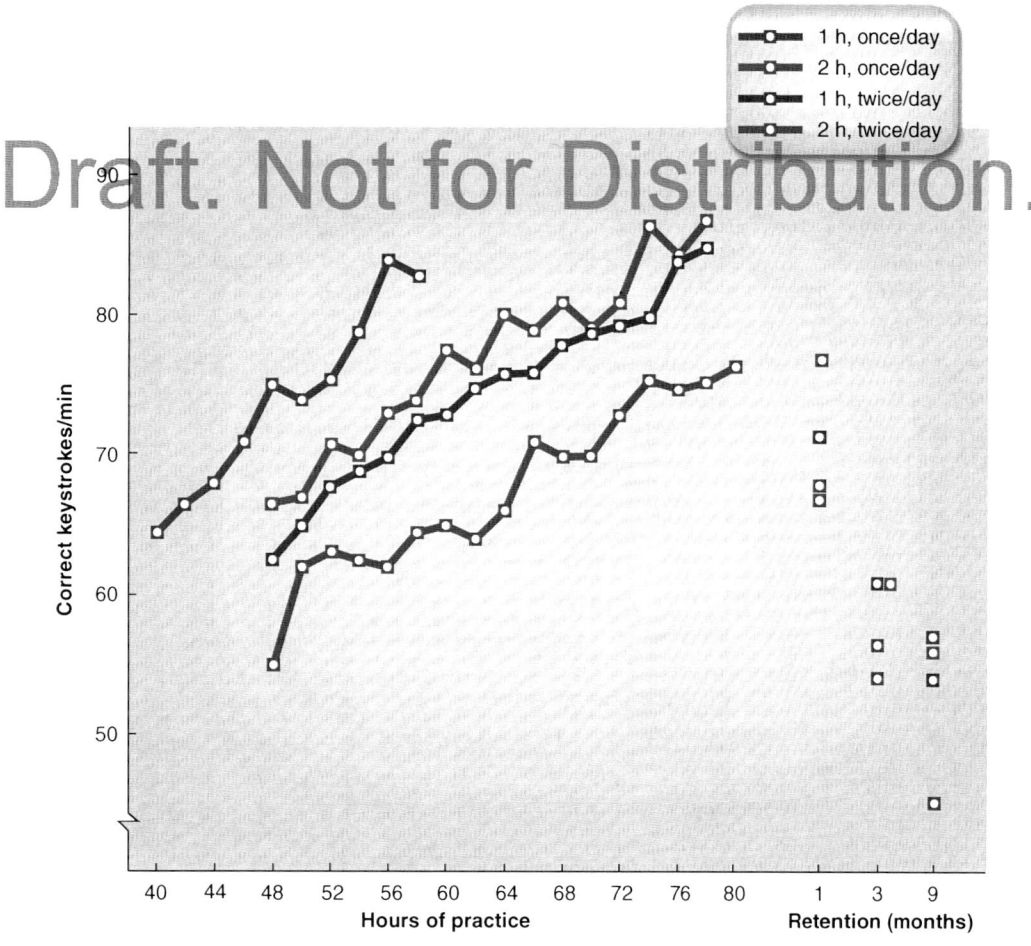

FIGURE 10.5 Results of the Baddeley and Longman (1978) study of retraining postal workers on keyboard tasks under different distributed-practice conditions.

Reprinted by permission from Schmidt and Lee 2011; Data from Baddeley and Longman 1978

The trainees' dissatisfaction with the short amounts of training in the 1 h a day condition highlights an important concern regarding the issue of practice *efficiency* versus practice *effectiveness*. The Baddeley and Longman study clearly demonstrated both: Although practicing 4 h a day was the least effective schedule in terms of learning, it was the most efficient in terms of total practice time (i.e., the least amount of time spent in the practice environment, working and resting). The decision to trade off effectiveness versus efficiency when determining how to distribute work and rest periods across days is not a simple one, and must take into account other factors, such as the likely motivational deficits that might occur with extended periods of practice and the fatigue-producing effects of the task.

Work and Rest Periods During a Practice Session

Unlike the questions concerning practice scheduling over a week, issues concerning organizing practice and rest during a single practice session have been studied a great deal in the laboratory. For the purposes here, we can define two classes of practice distribution, based on the relative amounts of practice and rest provided, called *massed* and *distributed* practice in the literature.

Massed practice provides relatively little rest between trials. For example, if a task has practice trials 30 s long, a massed-practice schedule might call for rest periods of only 5 s or perhaps no rest at all (so-called continuous practice). On the other hand, **distributed practice** calls for much more rest, perhaps with a rest period between trials that is as long as a trial itself (30 s in this example). There is no fixed dividing line between massed and distributed practice, but massed practice generally has reduced rest, as compared to distributed practice.

Researchers interested in massed and distributed practice (see Lee & Genovese, 1988, for a review) have generally been concerned with the effects of physical and mental fatigue-like states on learning effectiveness. For a given number of practice trials, decreasing the amount of rest between trials reduces the time available for dissipation of fatigue, degrading performance on the next practice trial and perhaps interfering with learning. Many experimenters have used a fixed number of practice trials in an acquisition session, varied the amount of rest between these trials, and then measured learning on a retention test. These work and rest schedules have different effects on performance and learning for discrete and continuous tasks.

Discrete Tasks

A few of the distribution-of-practice experiments have used relatively rapid discrete tasks. Generally, when the task involves performance trials that are only a few tenths of a second, as in a throw or a kick, it is very difficult to make the rest periods short enough to affect performance. In the laboratory, even when the rest periods were made as short as 300 ms, seemingly far shorter than for any real-world practice session, the result has been either no decrement in performance or learning or perhaps even slight advantages for massed conditions (see Carron, 1967; Lee & Genovese, 1989). It may be best to conclude that, for discrete tasks, there is no evidence that reducing the rest time through massed practice degrades learning.

Continuous Tasks

By far, most massed- and distributed-practice research has involved continuous skills analogous to real-world tasks such as swimming or typing. In these tasks, fatigue-like states have much more opportunity to build up within a trial, so decreasing the rest between trials has larger effects. This can be seen in a study by Bourne and Archer (1956), in which groups of subjects performed 30 s trials on a pursuit-rotor task that were separated by differing periods of rest between trials—either 0, 15, 30, 45, or 60 s. The results of the performance in the practice trials and in a retention test are illustrated in figure 10.6. Three general conclusions can be drawn from this figure; these typify the results seen generally with distribution-of-practice

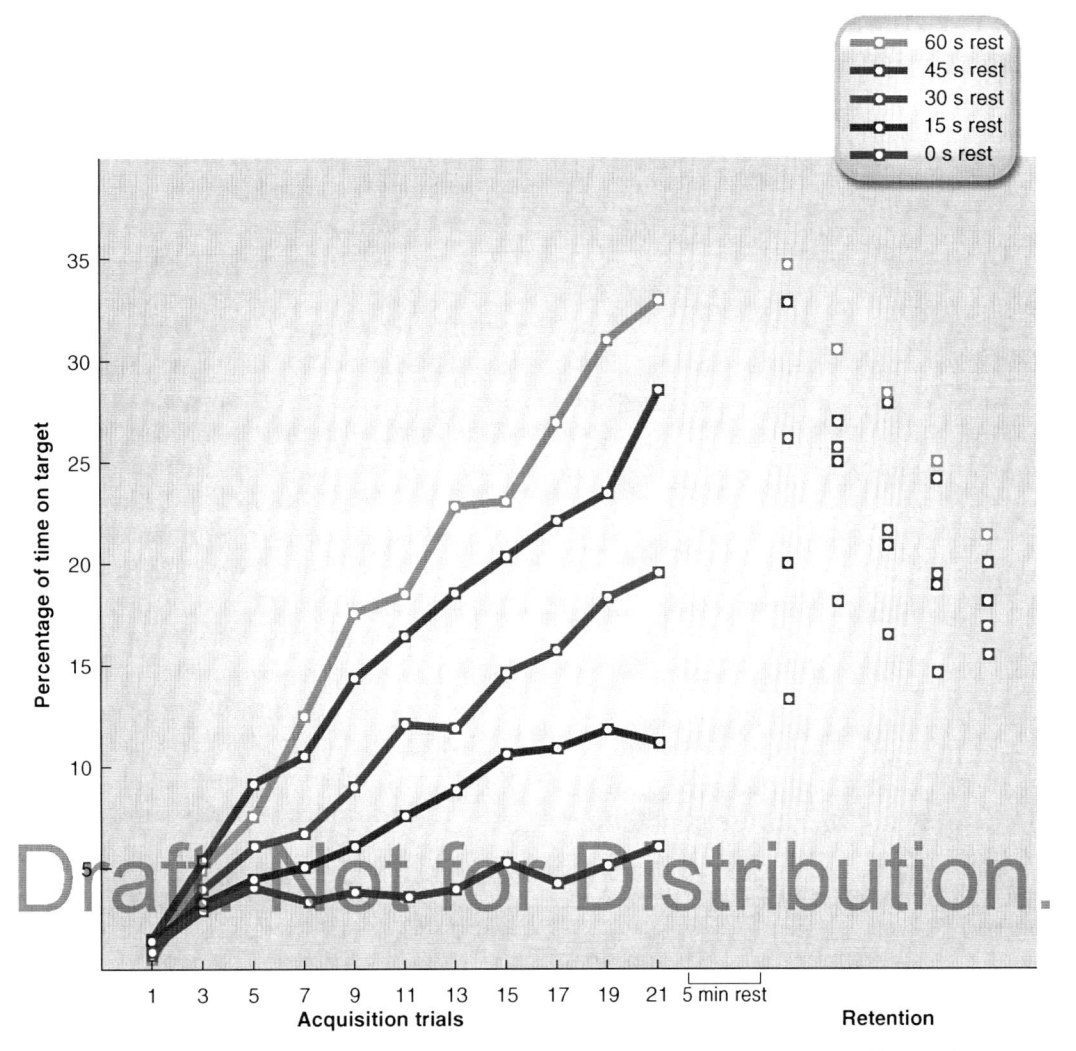

FIGURE 10.6 Results of the Bourne and Archer (1956) study examining the effects of rest intervals of differing length, inserted between 30 s periods of practice on a pursuit rotor task.

Reprinted by permission from Bourne and Archer 1956.

experiments using continuous tasks (Lee & Genovese, 1988):

1. Longer rest periods generally lead to more skilled performance during practice (i.e., distribution of practice has a performance effect).
2. When measuring learning, the size of the differences between groups is generally reduced as measured after a retention interval.
3. The positive effect of longer rest intervals on performance remains large on a retention test (i.e., distribution of practice has a learning effect).

Implications of Practice Distribution Effects

The effects of rest between trials have considerable importance when viewed from the standpoint of practice effectiveness versus practice efficiency. Clearly, longer rest periods have positive effects on both performance and learning. However, these effects come with a "cost," because essentially the rest periods are "lost time." In economic terms, the cost of introducing rest periods into a training application (e.g., in an airplane cockpit simulator) might outweigh the benefits to learning. Fortunately, there are alternatives to "resting" that can make the time between physical practice trials both effective *and* efficient from a learning standpoint. Two of these—mental practice and observation—were discussed earlier in this chapter. We consider these alternatives again in the next sections as a means to improve practice effectiveness and efficiency (Ong & Hodges, 2012).

Inserting Mental Practice and Observation

From the perspective of practice distribution, inserting periods of mental practice or observation during the "rest" between practice trials makes sense from a practice efficiency viewpoint. Rather than seeing rest as "lost time," one can use these intervals productively to enhance the motor learning at the same time the learners are recovering from fatigue. In effect, this strategy would make distributed practice both effective and efficient compared to massed practice. In this sense, both intervals of rest *and* mental practice or demonstrations would contribute positive effects on learning.

A second perspective concerns how rest during periods of physical practice should encourage the self-evaluation of performance outcomes, which should contribute to learning. One of the principles that we discuss in the next chapter concerns how using augmented feedback allows learners to become self-sufficient in their capability to assess their own performance and to learn to help themselves through error corrections. Interspersing periods of mental practice, demonstrations or observations, or both between periods of physical practice encourages learners to try to assess and better understand what makes their own performance effective at times and ineffective at other times.

Finally, mixing physical practice with periods of demonstration or observation and mental practice would likely have positive effects on motivation as well. These periods provide time for reflective thinking about the positive things that occurred during physical practice and about how the negative aspects might be improved upon in the next opportunity to perform.

Variable Versus Constant Practice

Ultimately, the goal of practice is to prepare a learner to perform to the highest possible level of skill when it counts—such as applying cardiopulmonary resuscitation (CPR) skills in an emergency. The task in these situations should be highly familiar to the learner because the action, as it was practiced, closely resembles the criterion task. However, these situations are few; by far, the more common situation occurs when the task changes somewhat between practice and the performance of the task in the criterion situation. Practice, in these cases, must prepare the learner to be highly adaptable to task requirements such that learners can perform in a way they have never performed before. How does one prepare for these different criterion tasks, and, more importantly, what are the features of practice that enable one to perform in such novel situations with skill and dexterity?

Review: Motor Programs and Parameters

Recall from chapter 5 that the skill of throwing, for example, represents a collection, or *class*, of movements. For example, in American football, skill in passing includes the skill to produce many different throwing distances, with arched or flat trajectories, and to stationary or moving targets, and also involves many other potential variations. Even with these variations, there is something fundamental, consistent, and characteristic about a football pass, such as the particular grip on the ball, the step and the follow-through, the arm action, and the wrist movement that produces a spiral. These features are called invariances (chapter 5). One can determine that an action is a member of a particular class of actions because it has the same invariant features as the other members of the class. Also, these features differ between classes, as there is no way to change a putting stroke into a football pass, for example. Members of a class have these characteristics:

- Common movement sequencing exists among the elements.
- Common temporal, or rhythmical, organization exists.
- The same action can usually be carried out with different effectors (e.g., limbs).
- The same action can differ in surface features (e.g., speed) on two different occasions, which is specified by different movement parameters.

Return now to the conceptual model of human performance developed earlier, for the example in figure 8.1. Action patterns are governed by generalized motor programs (GMPs), each with an almost invariant temporal organization. Once learned, a GMP for football passing can be applied to many specific throwing situations by specifying movement parameters in the movement programming stage, which define how the movement is carried. The learner evaluates the environment, decides what kind of pass is required in this particular case, and then specifying the proper parameters to the program (those that are likely to achieve the movement goals as assessed). The parts of the conceptual model involved in this process are

Passing a football accurately requires the player to throw with different speeds and trajectories under variable conditions. How can a learner practice to maximize the ability to perform this skill?

shown in figure 8.1. The questions are, How are the proper parameters selected, and how does the performer learn to *generalize* to all of the throwing distances in the class?

Schema Theory

One conceptualization to answer these questions is **schema theory** (Schmidt, 1975), in which the learner acquires a set of rules, called the schemas, that relate the surface features of throwing (e.g., distances, speeds) to the parameter values necessary to produce those actions. Figure 10.7 illustrates how this could work for the distance dimension in the football pass as an example. On the horizontal axis are all the possible distances the football has been thrown in the past, with a maximum of 40 m for this learner. Whenever a ball is thrown, the learner records briefly the distance the ball went as well as the parameter that was used for the GMP for that throw. Over time, with many such throws recorded, the learner then abstracts (or generalizes) the relationship between the past throwing distances and the task parameters that were used for the GMP (Schmidt, 1975). Figure 10.7 shows the abstraction. To avoid the storage problem the learner stores these values just long enough to update the schema after each throw, and then these are discarded or forgotten. According to schema theory, this process is responsible for motor learning associated with learning to parameterize the GMPs—a common problem for the player using the same GMP over and over again.

An important question for researchers is how the schema is learned. The learning process, according the schema theory, is also illustrated in figure 10.7. Suppose the learner begins the learning process by generating parameter A, which leads to a throwing distance of 29 m. On subsequent attempts, the learner chooses parameter B, which leads to a throw of approximately 18 m. Then, he issues parameter C, which leads to a throw of about 34 m, and so on. With each throw, the learner associates (abstracts or generalizes) the GMP parameter value used with the resulting distance thrown (seen as the collection of individual data points in figure 10.7). In the future when the person wants to make a throw of X_1 m, he chooses the distance of X_1 on the X-axis, where he uses the vertical red line to access the schema (blue line), and this results in using parameter value of Y. In

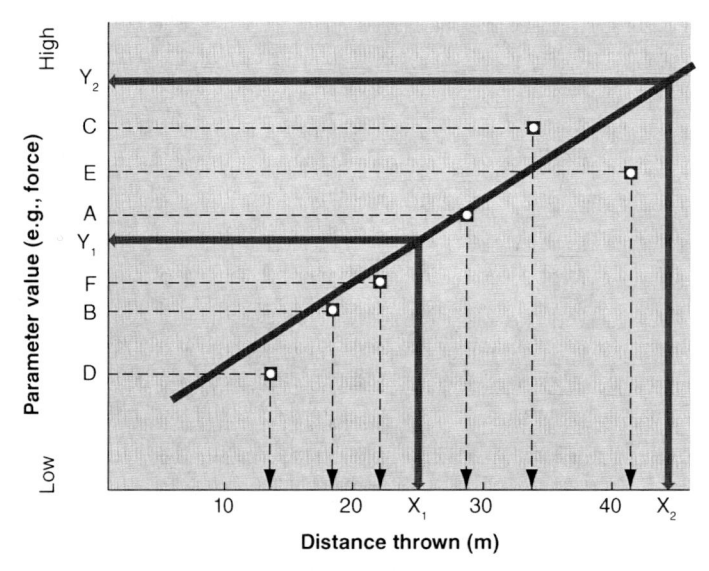

FIGURE 10.7 The schema relates parameter values to outcome distances. To produce a throw of 25 m (X_1) or 45 m (X_2), the learner relies on the schema to generate parameter values equal to Y_1 and Y_2, respectively.

the same way, desiring a throwing distance of X_2 m, he chooses a parameter value of Y_2.

This process generates a movement with parameter values based on the learner's past experience in using this program. Most important, this process allows the learner to make a movement that he has never made previously. Suppose that this learner has never produced a 45 m pass before (X_2 in figure 10.7). No problem: The learner simply provides the best estimate of the required parameter values from the schema, and then runs off the GMP with this parameter value (Y_2 in figure 10.7), thereby producing a novel action that has not been performed before.

Variable Practice Enhances Schema Learning

Considerable evidence suggests that variable practice should be particularly effective in cases like this. A basic research paradigm contrasts two groups of learners: One is a **constant-practice** group, practicing only a single member of a class of tasks; the second is a **variable-practice** group, practicing several members of the class of tasks (for the football passing example, this would mean practicing varying football passing distances). The two groups have the same amount of practice, but they differ in the amount of practice variability they receive.

The constant group typically outperforms the variable group during the acquisition phase. Typically a learner can produce instances of a single version of a movement more effectively than multiple versions, particularly if these versions are intermixed. However, when subjects in both groups are switched to a novel version of the task on a transfer test, the group that received variable practice performs at least as well as the constant group, and frequently they do so much more skillfully (e.g., McCracken & Stelmach, 1977). This evidence has been interpreted to mean that learners acquire schemas when they practice and that variable practice enhances their development, allowing more effective novel-task performance in the future. In other words, variable practice enhances *generalizability*, allowing the performer to apply past learning to actions not specifically experienced before in practice.

This generalization can be seen in figure 10.8 (from Catalano & Kleiner, 1984); groups practiced a coincident-timing task (predicting the arrival of a moving light simulating a moving ball by making a hand response) with target velocities of only one speed (5, 7, 9, *or* 11 mph [8, 11, 14.5, *or* 18 kph]) under constant-practice conditions; or another group practiced all speeds (5, 7, 9, *and* 11 mph) under variable-practice conditions, with the different target velocities presented in a random order over trials. Transfer tests were then given on task versions that were not experienced previously by either group (at 1, 3, 13, and 15 mph [1.6, 4.8, 21, and 24 kph]). In figure 10.8 three of the four transfer velocity tests, variable practice led to much smaller errors than did constant practice; hence variable practice produced generalization. Of course, many skills require us to produce variations that have never been produced before and practice is one means of maximizing the capability to move effectively in this way.

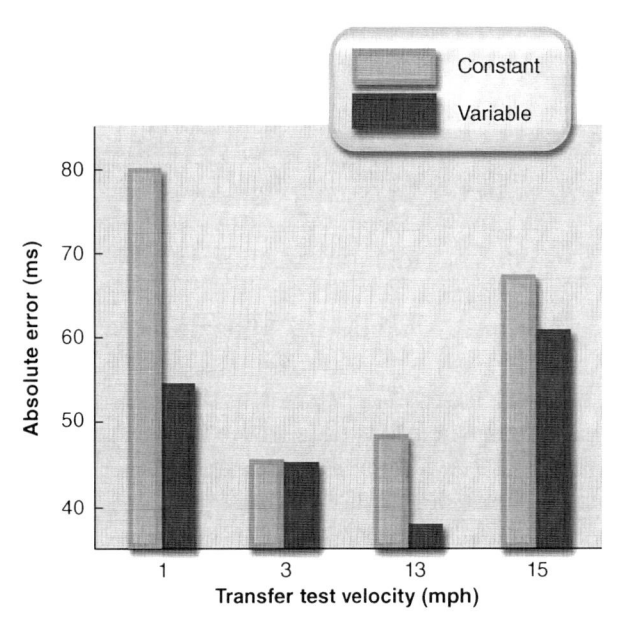

FIGURE 10.8 Mean absolute timing errors in four coincident-timing transfer target-speeds following practice in either a constant (gray)- or variable (blue)-practice condition.

Data from Catalano and Kleiner 1984.

Focus on RESEARCH 10.1

Especial Skills: An Exception to Variable Practice?

Schema theory, and indeed just common sense, suggests that if someone is faced with learning to produce a class of actions, that practice ought to be structured to be variable, taking into account the unlimited variations to be experienced in the criterion version of the skill. But how would practice be structured if only one variation of the criterion task would ever be experienced? In other words, are skills that are to be performed in only one way represented differently in memory than a class of skills that can be performed in infinite ways?

The latter question was addressed in a series of experiments involving basketball shooting skills (Keetch, Lee, & Schmidt, 2008; Keetch et al., 2005). Two types of shots are commonly used in basketball—jump shots (which, as the name implies, involve the player leaping into the air before releasing the ball), and set shots (in which the player remains in contact with the ground during the shot). Jump shots are usually taken anywhere on the court, but set shots are typically taken only at the foul (or free-throw) line.

Keetch and colleagues predicted that if variable (jump shot) practice results in the development of a schema for a class of actions, then performance at one location should be highly related to performance at all other locations, including shots at the free-throw line. In contrast, should constant practice (of the set-shot, practiced only at the free-throw line) result in a specific advantage for performance at that one particular location? And this prediction should be particularly strong for highly-experienced players, who have taken thousands of set-shot practice shots in the development of their expertise.

Data from college basketball players shooting set shots and jump shots from five locations (including one from 15 ft [4.57 m]—the foul line) are presented in figure 10.9. Jump shot accuracy decreased almost linearly as the player moved farther from the basket. In contrast, even though the set-shot decreased in accuracy as the distance increased generally, performance at the 15 ft mark was markedly more accurate than expected based on the performances at the other shot locations.

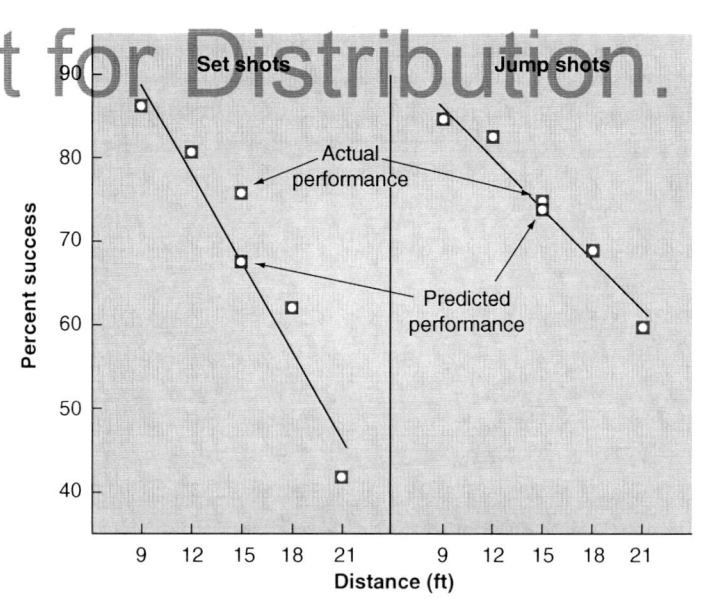

FIGURE 10.9 Performance of set and jump shots from five different locations. Set-shot performance shows an advantage at the foul line, whereas no specific advantage is seen for jump shots.

Reprinted by permission from Keetch, Schmidt, Lee, and Young 2005.

These findings have some interesting implications for learning, as they seem to suggest that practice be structured according to the criterion demands of the task—how the skills will be performed in the "test" situation. If flexibility in producing a variation of a class of skills is required, then it makes sense to continue with variable practice. However, if only one version of the task will ever be performed, then concentrating practice from the one location appears to have practical merit (Breslin et al., 2012).

Exploring Further

1. Name another skill, usually performed from only one specific location, that might show an effect similar to the set shot in basketball.
2. For the task named in question 1, describe an experimental methodology that would assess whether or not performance would show a specific advantage from that location.

Caveats to Variable Practice

Schema theory predicts that variable practice is best suited for performance that applies novel movement parameters to just a single version of the GMP, as in free-throw shooting a basketball. However, would variable practice also be optimal for learning in situations in which a criterion where only a single version of the GMP is needed? Recent evidence presented in Focus on Research 10.1 raises some doubts.

A second caveat regarding variable practice was alluded to earlier. A very important factor concerns how variable practice is scheduled; this issue was raised in a highly influential study by Shea and Morgan (1979). Studies in which variable practice was scheduled in a trial-by-trial random order showed rather large advantages compared to constant practice (e.g., Catalano & Kleiner, 1984; also Pigott & Shapiro, 1984). This broader concept of scheduling practice in general, not just variations of a single task, is the topic to which we now turn our attention.

Blocked Versus Random Practice

In many, if not most, real-world settings, the learner's goal is to acquire more than a single skill or task in a limited practice period, sometimes even in a single practice period. Physicians practice different skills related to surgery (such as suturing and knot-tying skills), musicians practice multiple songs at a time, tennis players practice serving and volleying as well as the more usual ground strokes during a single session, and so on. An important question confronting the learner or instructor is how to sequence the practice at these various tasks during the practice session so as to maximize learning. Two variations have powerful effects on learning: blocked and random practice.

Suppose that your student has three tasks (tasks A, B, and C) to learn in a practice session and that these tasks are fundamentally different, such as tennis serves, volleys, and ground strokes. That is, tasks are chosen such that one cannot argue that any of them are in the same class or use the same GMP. A commonsense method of scheduling such tasks would be to practice all trials of one task before shifting to the second, then to finish practice on the second before switching to the third. This is called **blocked practice**, in which all the trials of a given task (for that day) are completed before moving on to the next task. Blocked practice is typical of some drills in which a skill is repeated over and over, with minimal interruption by other activities. This kind of practice seems to make sense in that it allows the learners to concentrate on one particular task at a time and refine and correct it.

Another practice scheduling variation is called **random (interleaved) practice**; where the order of task presentation is mixed, or interleaved, across the practice period. Learners rotate among the three sample tasks so that, in the more extreme cases, they never (or rarely) practice the same task on two consecutive attempts. And from a common-sense perspective, the random method, with its high level of trial-to-trial variability, its high level of contextual interference would not seem optimal for learning.

The Shea and Morgan Experiment

John Shea and Robyn Morgan (1979) conducted a groundbreaking experiment that revolutionized the way scientists think of the processes involved in practice. Following some of the original ideas of William Battig (1966), Shea and Morgan had subjects practice three different tasks (A, B and C) that involved responding to a stimulus light with a correct series of rapid movements of the hand and arm, with each task having a different predetermined sequence. One group of subjects practiced the tasks in a blocked order, completing all task A practice before moving to task B, which they completed before moving to task C. A second group practiced in a random order; no more than two consecutive trials could occur for any one task. The two groups had the same amount of practice on tasks A, B, and C and had the same amount of total practice—they differed only in the order in which the tasks were presented.

The results are presented in figure 10.10. The goal was to respond to the stimulus and complete the movements as quickly as possible, so lower total times indicate more-skilled performance. Notice that, during acquisition, the blocked condition was far more effective for performance (with shorter times) than the random condition. But recall that differences during acquisition cannot be interpreted as differences in learning; rather, delayed retention (or transfer) tests are needed to evaluate learning (these concepts were presented in chapter 8).

Shea and Morgan tested for learning by conducting retention tests after 10 min and 10 days; these tests were conducted under either randomized or blocked conditions, which produced four subgroups. The following abbreviations indicate the condition in acquisition and the condition in retention, respectively: R-B, R-R, B-R, and B-B. The first character in the pair indicates the condition during acquisition (random or R and

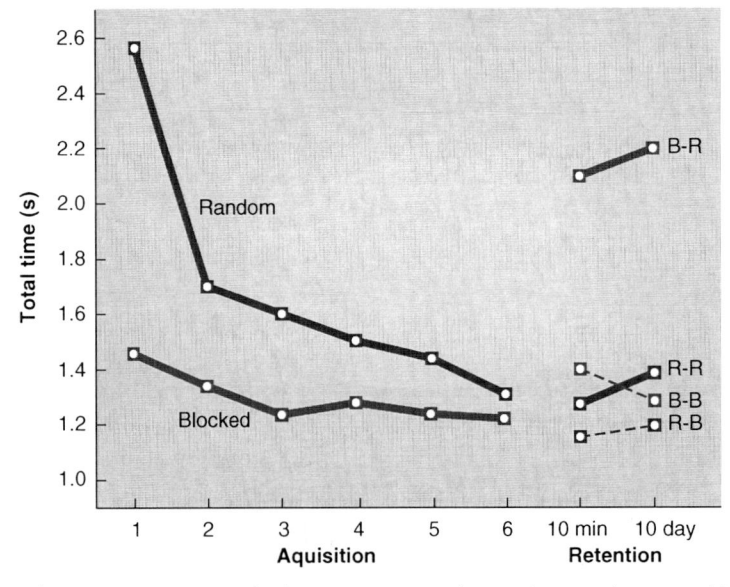

FIGURE 10.10 Performance on speeded movement tasks under random- and blocked-practice conditions during acquisition, and in random-ordered and blocked-ordered retention tests.

Adapted by permission from Shea and Morgan 1979.

blocked or B), and the second member of the pair indicates the performance conditions in retention.

When the retention tests were under random conditions, the group that had random practice in acquisition (R-R, solid blue) greatly outperformed the group with blocked conditions in acquisition (B-R, solid red). When the retention tests were under blocked conditions, again the random condition in acquisition (R-B) outperformed those who had blocked conditions in acquisition (B-B), but these differences were much smaller than for the random retention tests. Clearly, the random conditions in acquisition were always more effective for retention, but this benefit was clearly dependent on the nature of the retention test.

Why Random Practice Is So Effective

The Shea and Morgan findings surprised many scientists in the field by showing that, even though random conditions result in much less skilled performance than blocked conditions in acquisition, random-practice conditions produce more learning. The findings were a large surprise because most conventional viewpoints would suggest that learning should be maximized by those conditions that make learners most proficient *during* practice—there was no motor learning theorizing that could explain this opposite result. As a result, some interesting new hypotheses were offered to explain the findings.

Shea and Zimny (1983) argued that changing the task on every random-practice trial made the tasks more distinct from each other and more meaningful, resulting in more *elaborate* memory representations. As revealed in subject interviews after the experiment, random-practice subjects tended to relate the task structure to already learned materials (creating "meaningfulness"), such as discovering that task B had essentially the shape of an upside-down "Z." Also, they would make distinctions between tasks, such as "Task A is essentially like task C, except that the first part is reversed" (creating "distinctiveness"). The blocked-practice subjects, on the other hand, tended not to make such statements. Instead they talked of running off the performances more or less automatically, without thinking much about it, and blocked practice did not induce the kind of comparative and contrastive efforts in practice that were experienced during random practice. According to this **elaboration hypothesis**, increased meaningfulness and distinctiveness produce more durable memories for the tasks, and thus increased performance capabilities in tests of retention and transfer.

An alternative hypothesis explains the beneficial effects of random practice somewhat differently. Lee and Magill (1983) suggested that when the learner shifts from task A to task B, the "solution" that was generated (in short-term memory; see chapter 2) for performing task B causes the solution previously generated for task A to be forgotten. When task A is encountered again a few trials later, the learner must generate the solution anew; therefore, performance in practice is relatively poor. Yet this solution-generation process is assumed to be beneficial for learning (see also Cuddy & Jacoby, 1982). In blocked practice, on the other hand, the performer remembers the solution generated on a given trial and simply applies it to the next trial, which minimizes the number of times the learner must generate new solutions. Therefore, performance during practice in a blocked schedule is very effective because the solution, once generated, is remembered for a series of trials. Yet learning is poor because the learner is not required to generate a "new" solution to the task on every trial. In this way, the key focus of the forgetting hypothesis is the fact that new solutions are required frequently in random practice, but not in blocked practice; thus, the development of the solution for the task is the key feature that facilitates learning. Interestingly, the **forgetting hypothesis** suggests the somewhat ironic and counterintuitive idea that "forgetting facilitates learning."

A number of investigations have evaluated and supported both of the hypotheses.

For example, in a study by Wright (1991), members of a blocked-practice group were encouraged to make explicit comparisons of the task just practiced with one of the other tasks to be learned—essentially inducing this group to "mentally" practice the tasks with meaningful and distinctive processing. This special blocked-practice group outperformed the other practice groups that had a similar intervention but without the benefits of the explicit comparative and contrastive processing. The results supported the elaboration hypothesis predictions because of the insertion of these specific mental processing activities.

A key prediction of the forgetting hypothesis was that random practice forces more extensive planning operations on each trial compared to blocked practice. A study by Lee and colleagues (1997) attempted to reduce the need for these planning operations by presenting a powerful "model" just before each practice trial. This model was designed so that it would inform subjects how to perform the next trial, and because the model provided extremely strong memory guidance for the upcoming trial, the model was hypothesized to prevent the construction process (because the model provided the solution for the next trial). In the experiment, the presence of the model was combined with random practice. The model, eliminating as it did the subject's requirement to reconstruct the "solution" for the next trial, would interfere with performance in acquisition more or less as blocked practice does. As figure 10.10 shows, the model obliterated the usual benefits of random practice.

In the experiment, the random and blocked conditions are contrasted with this special "random + model" condition. Clearly, the model was beneficial for performance during acquisition (when the model was present), as seen on the left side of figure 10.11 where the "random + model" group was far more skilled than the group that had only random practice. However, in the retention tests, where the model was withdrawn, the random + model group regressed considerably, to the point that this condition led to the most error in the

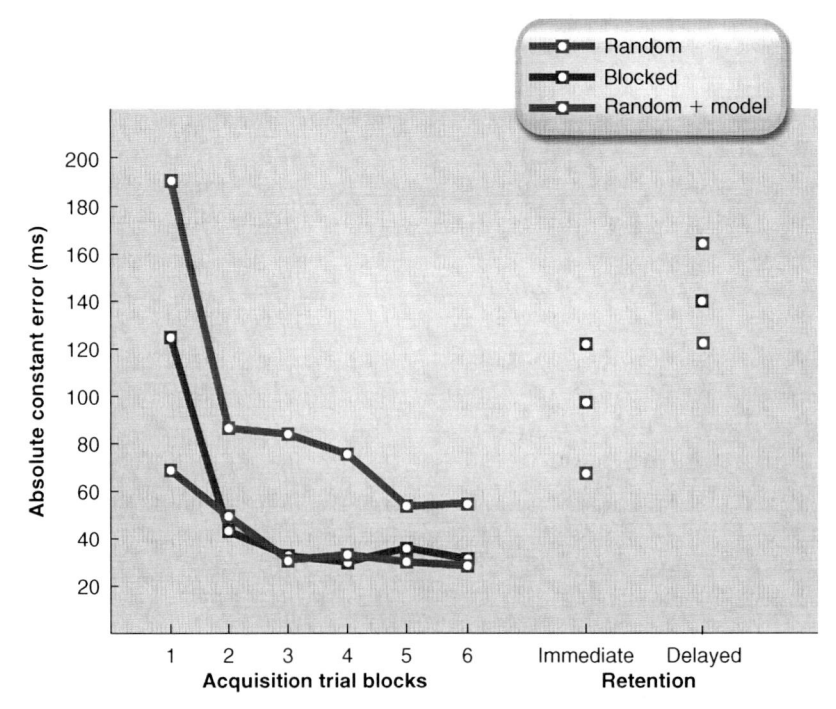

FIGURE 10.11 Providing a powerful guiding model reduced planning operations in a random + model practice group obliterated the usual random-practice benefit for learning (from Lee et al., 1997).

Reprinted by permission from Lee et al. 1997.

delayed retention test. Providing the powerful model before each practice trial, while it was beneficial for performance when it was present, was disastrous for learning – the model obliterated the beneficial advantages of random practice. These findings support strongly the forgetting hypothesis for the random- versus blocked-practice effect, and they show that random practice is not necessarily the "magic bullet" for effective motor learning.

A number of studies have provided evidence supporting the elaboration hypothesis, and a number have supported the forgetting hypothesis; but no clear "winner" has yet emerged. As a result, it is probably a better idea to consider these hypotheses as complementary, rather than competing, explanations of the random- versus blocked-practice effects. The beneficial effects of random practice over blocked practice appear to be due to several factors:

- Random practice forces the learner to become more actively engaged in the learning process by preventing simple repetitions of actions.
- Random practice gives the learner more meaningful and distinguishable memories of the various tasks, increasing memory strength and decreasing confusion among tasks.
- Random practice causes the learner to forget the short-term solutions (from working memory) to the movement problem after each task change.
- Forgetting the short-term solution forces the learner to generate the solution again on the task's next trial, which is beneficial to learning.

Further Research

Shea and Morgan's findings have been very influential. Hundreds of studies have been

This walking garden allows rehabilitation patients to practice walking with crutches over many surfaces, allowing for variable and random practice.

conducted on the random and blocked practice since their research was published, and many discussion articles have been written about how to conduct practice in everyday activities (e.g., Schmidt & Lee, 2012). The next sections summarize some of the research that has emerged in the years since the publication of this landmark study.

Contextual-Interference Effects in Nonlaboratory Tasks

As might be expected, the Shea and Morgan (1979) study motivated a large number of researchers to examine random- and blocked-practice schedules in non-laboratory tasks. Goode and Magill (1986) found similar random-blocked effects in participants who were learning three different types of badminton serves. Hall, Domingues, and Cavazos (1994) produced an analogous effect using a group of college baseball players who engaged in extra batting practice, hitting different types of pitches thrown in random or blocked order. And Ste-Marie and colleagues (2004) found similar beneficial effects for random practice in schoolchildren who were learning handwriting skills. The Shea and Morgan laboratory findings appear to extend to the acquisition of real-world tasks too.

Random-Practice Limitations

The beneficial effects of random practice are not universal, however, and some studies have resulted in no learning differences. Lee (unpublished data, Louisiana State University, 1981), using the pursuit-rotor task, failed to produce the expected random-practice benefits. The pursuit rotor, however, as a form of tracking task, does not require very much advance preparation between trials. Perhaps this can be taken as evidence that the random-practice benefits might only occur in tasks for which considerable pretrial preparation is needed.

Guadagnoli and Lee (2004) reviewed the varieties of evidence and suggested that random practice is likely to be least effective when the task demands are so high to begin with that performers have a very difficult time producing even a single trial of the behavior. This could occur when individuals are practicing a very "difficult" task, or when the learners themselves are in some way not "appropriate" for the task to be learned. A good example might be attempting to teach very young learners an "adult" task that demands too much. In such cases, random practice would make the practice environment too challenging and perhaps counterproductive to effective learning.

Alternatives to Blocked and Random Practice

Blocked and random practice represent "extreme" ends of the practice-schedule continuum—random practice involves very little (or no) repetition of the same task from one practice trial to the next, and blocked practice involves almost no interleaving of practice on other tasks. These scheduling extremes might be responsible for the rather dramatic shifts seen in performance and retention, with blocked practice facilitating performance in practice, but having a detrimental effect on retention (and vice versa for random practice). Thus, one need for seeking an alternative to a random- versus blocked-practice schedule concerns that fact that neither "optimizes" both performance *and* learning; that is, neither is a practice structure that facilitates learning without the degrading effects seen during the practice period.

There is another reason for seeking alternatives to blocked and random practice. Simon and Bjork (2001) asked their subjects to make predictions about their performance just before a retention test. The results, presented in figure 10.12, revealed an *illusion* about learning. Subjects with practice under random- or blocked-acquisition conditions were asked to predict how they would do on a retention test. The blocked practice "fooled" the learners into thinking that they had learned much more than they really had, whereas random practice led the learners to believe that they had learned less than they had. Thus, giving learners a more accurate sense of how learning is proceeding might be another reason to seek alternatives to blocked and random practice.

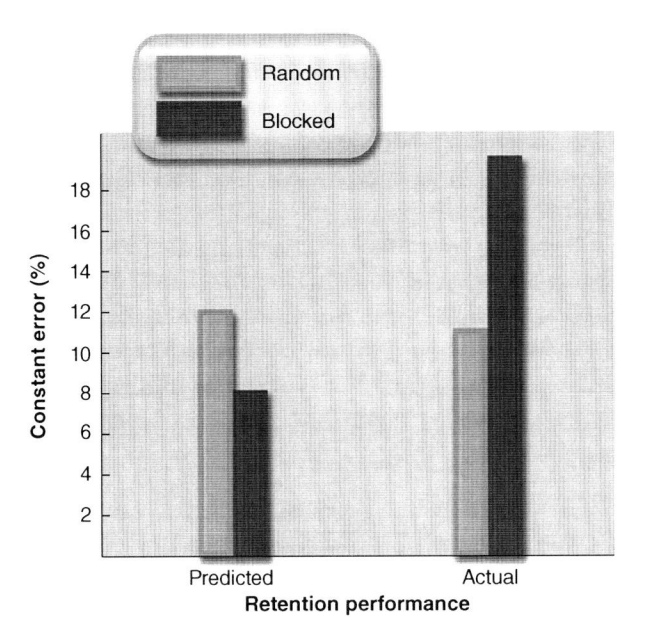

FIGURE 10.12 Before performance in a retention test (shown), individuals who had practiced in a blocked order (blue) predicted that they would be more skilled (the "predicted" bars) than those who practiced in a random order (gray), (the "predicted" bars). In reality, the retention performance of the blocked group was less skillful than that of the random group ("actual" bars).
Data from Simon and Bjork 2001.

Hybrid Schedules Some researchers have found that "moderate" levels of random practice, with the practice schedule including interleaved short strings of blocked practice for example, are beneficial for performance and learning. For example, Landin and Hebert (1997) had novices practice a basketball shooting task from different locations on the court according to either a blocked order, a serial order (a quasi-random condition, but more structured than purely random practice), or a "moderate" order in which practice rotated from task to task after "mini-blocks" of three attempts from the same distance were performed. As can be seen in figure 10.13, this "moderate" practice format was successful in reducing the performance deficit normally seen during purely random practice and facilitated learning as measured in both a blocked- and a random-retention test (see also Pigott & Shapiro, 1984).

Practice Contingencies Although the hybrid approach to practice would appear to represent the best of both worlds—it remains insensitive to individual differences. For example, although three blocked trials might

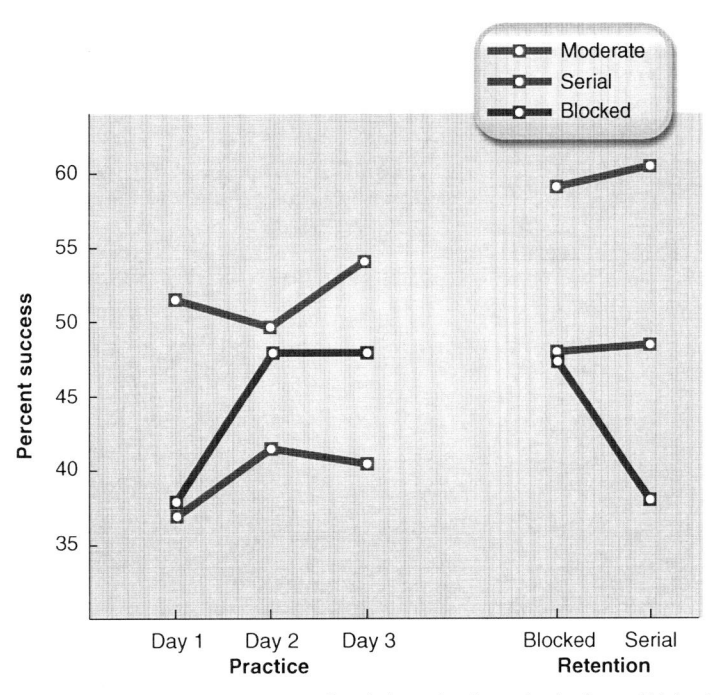

FIGURE 10.13 A hybrid (moderate) practice schedule, which included small blocks of blocked practice, facilitated basketball performance and learning compared to purely blocked and serial practice schedules.
Adapted by permission from Landin and Hebert 1997.

be optimal for one person, five blocked trials or no task repetitions might be optimal for two other people.

A type of schedule that is more sensitive to these individual differences is a "contingency" schedule, whereby the "difficulty" of the task (Choi et al., 2008) and the decision to repeat the same task or switch to an easier or more difficult task (e.g., Simon, Lee, & Cullen, 2008) depend on the performance success of the individual. These contingencies are just beginning to be examined by researchers and represent an exciting new approach to the topic.

Summary

Physical practice is just one way to "rehearse" a task. Several methods not involving physical rehearsals have also been shown to enhance learning. Observation (of a human model) provides objective information that learners can use to organize their thinking about the task. Mental practice and imagery reflect important methods to undertake this organization of thoughts.

Rest periods during physical practice (relative to no-rest conditions) produce gains in learning, especially so for continuous tasks. However, long rest periods have the disadvantage of making practice less time efficient. Research suggests that these rest periods can be used more efficiently if combined with periods of observation, mental practice, or both.

Variable practice involves intentional variations of a given task. Compared to constant practice, in which only a single variant is practiced, varied practice facilitates retention and generalizability to a novel situation whose specific variant has not received prior practice. Variable practice is thought to operate by generating stronger schemas, which define the relationship between parameters for a GMP and the movement's outcome.

Large learning gains can be made through effective practice organization and scheduling. An important concept is random practice, in which trials of several tasks are interleaved during acquisition. Relative to blocked practice, in which trials of a single given task are presented repeatedly, random practice produces far more skilled performance at retention (i.e., more learning). Random practice operates by preventing the learner from repeating the same movement output on successive trials and by interleaving experience gained from performing different activities on adjacent trials.

WEB STUDY GUIDE ACTIVITIES

Check Your Understanding

1. Explain how rest and cognitive activities between periods of practice influence motor learning.

2. Explain why including variable and random practice when teaching a person to play volleyball can be beneficial to learning. Are there any volleyball skills for which this type of practice would not be beneficial? Why or why not?

3. Discuss the differences between internal focus and external focus instructions. Give an example of each for someone learning to play the piano. Which of your examples would be more beneficial to learning for an intermediate student?

Apply Your Knowledge

1. Discuss three motivational tools or techniques that a physical therapist could use to help ensure a client is motivated during a recovery program. What factors would you consider in order to integrate observational learning or mental practice into the client's schedule?

2. You have volunteered to coach your nephew's soccer team for the summer. Two of the skills that you would like to work on with your team this season are penalty kicks and dribbling the ball down the field. How might you organize work–rest periods during practice for each of these skills? How might you include an amount of task variability appropriate to each skill? Are there any characteristics of your players that you would need to take into consideration when organizing practice? Why?

Suggestions for Further Reading

The review by Ste-Marie and colleagues (2012) provides a solid framework for considering various factors related to observational learning. A meta-analysis (statistical review) of the mental practice literature is provided by Feltz and Landers (1983). A distribution-of-practice meta-analysis and review was published by Lee and Genovese (1988). For more on variable practice and schema development, see Schmidt (1975) and Schmidt and Lee (2011; chapter 13). The variability-of-practice literature is reviewed in Shapiro and Schmidt (1982). And numerous reviews of the contextual-interference literature exist, including those by Magill and Hall (1990), Merbah and Meulemans (2011), and Lee (2012). See the reference list for these additional resources.

Draft. Not for Distribution.

Augmented Feedback
How Giving Feedback Influences Learning

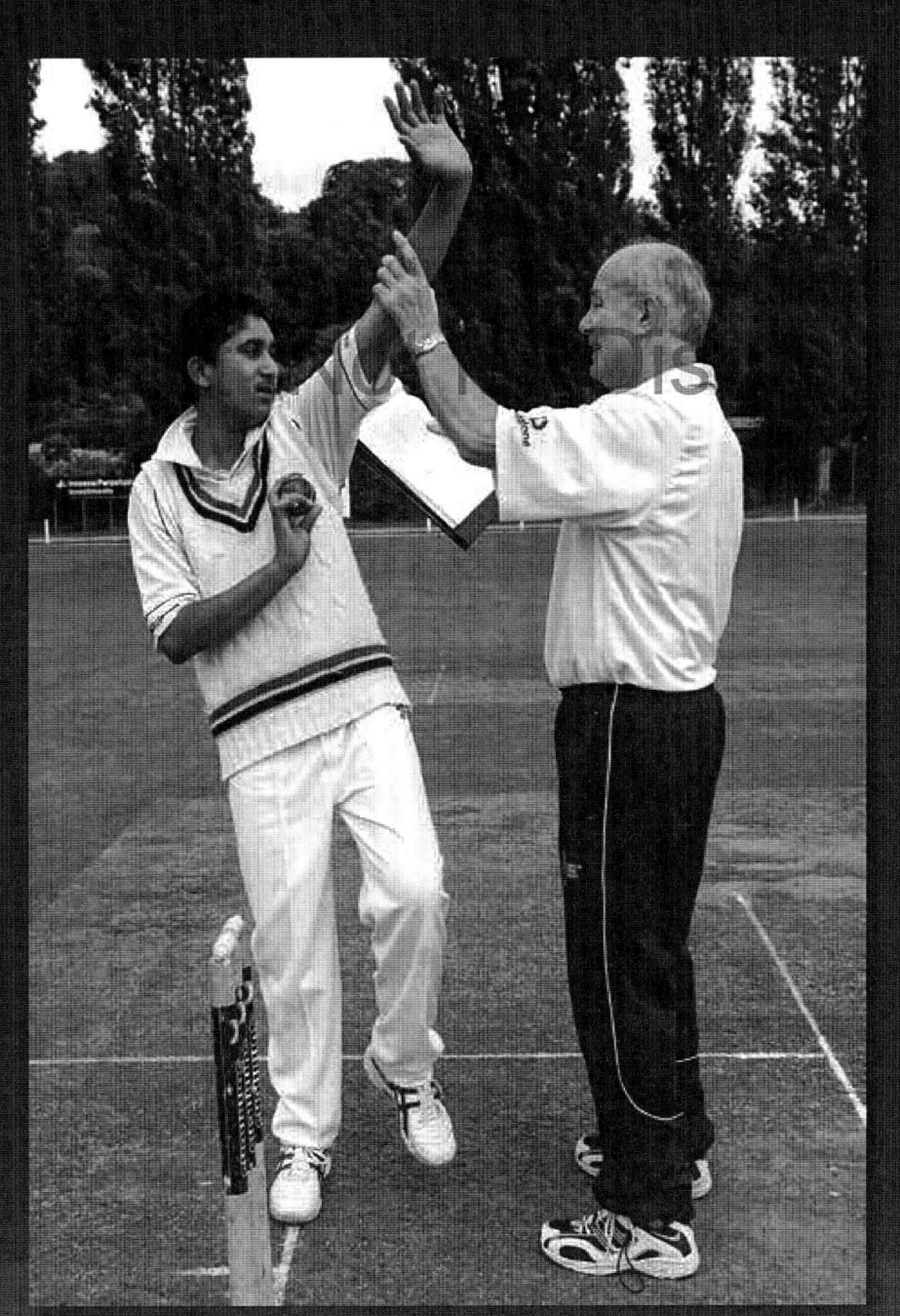

KEY TERMS

absolute frequency of feedback
augmented feedback
average feedback
bandwidth feedback
concurrent feedback
faded feedback
feedback
feedback delay interval
guidance
guidance hypothesis
inherent feedback
instantaneous feedback
intrinsic feedback
knowledge of performance (KP)
knowledge of results (KR)
post-feedback delay
precision of feedback
relative frequency of feedback
summary feedback
trials delay of feedback

CHAPTER OUTLINE

Feedback Classifications
Functions of Augmented Feedback
How Much Feedback to Give
When to Give Feedback
Summary

CHAPTER OBJECTIVES

Chapter 11 describes the influence of augmented feedback on motor performance and learning. This chapter will help you to understand

- ▶ the types of augmented feedback and their role in the conceptual model,
- ▶ how augmented feedback functions to influence performance and learning,
- ▶ the various properties of augmented feedback, and
- ▶ the influence of the various ways in which augmented feedback can be delivered.

This chapter can be considered an extension of chapters 9 and 10 because it also concerns the organization of practice. Here, though, the focus is on how an instructor organizes and delivers **feedback**—information about performance or errors that the learner can use for making future corrections. Here we discuss some principles of how feedback influences learning, examining questions about feedback frequency, feedback timing, and the most effective kinds of feedback for learning.

Without a doubt, one of the most important learning processes concerns the use of feedback about actions attempted in practice. As discussed in chapter 4, feedback may be a natural consequence of the movement, such as seeing a hammered nail become flush with a block of wood or hearing the sound of a key that has been depressed on a keyboard. Feedback can also be given in various "artificial" forms that are not so obvious to the learner, such as the performer's score in a driver's license examination or a comment about a swimmer's "whip kick" in performing the breaststroke. Of course, verbal feedback is under the instructor's direct control; thus, it makes up a large part of practice organization.

Feedback Classifications

The term "feedback" originally emerged from the analysis of closed-loop control systems (see chapter 4), referring to information about the difference between a performance and some desired goal-state. In closed-loop system terminology, feedback is considered to be information about error. In human performance systems, however, the term feedback takes on a more general meaning: information about the movement and movement outcomes, not just errors.

It is helpful to form a clear feedback classification system because many of the different kinds of feedback follow somewhat different principles. One system appears in figure 11.1, where the global category of all information available to the learner is divided into several subclasses. First, of course, there is a great deal of sensory information "out there," most of which is not related to the movement the person is learning. But of the information that is related to the movement, it is useful to categorize it as either available before the movement, during the movement, or after the movement. Information before action is critical for movement planning (discussed in chapters 4 and 5) and largely comes from the last practice attempt. This information influences the processes involved in anticipation, decision making, parameter selection, and so on. However, it is the information provided during the movement or after the movement that is commonly considered feedback. Feedback may be further divided into two main categories: *inherent* (or *intrinsic*) and *augmented feedback* (see figure 11.1).

Inherent Feedback

Sometimes also called "**intrinsic feedback**," **inherent feedback** is information provided as a natural consequence of making an action. When you take a swing at a tennis ball, you feel your hips, shoulders, and arms moving; you see the racket travel; you see, hear, and feel the ball's contact; and you see and hear where the ball travels. All these types of information are inherent to performing the task, and you can perceive them more or less directly, without special methods or devices. Other kinds of inherent information might be the sounds or smells made by a race car engine, or seeing the progress of a saw blade as it cuts through a piece of wood. This general class of feedback has been discussed throughout the text during the development of the conceptual model of human performance.

Augmented Feedback

Now it is time to finalize the conceptual model of human performance by adding augmented feedback, shown as the blue line in figure 11.2. Sometimes called "extrinsic

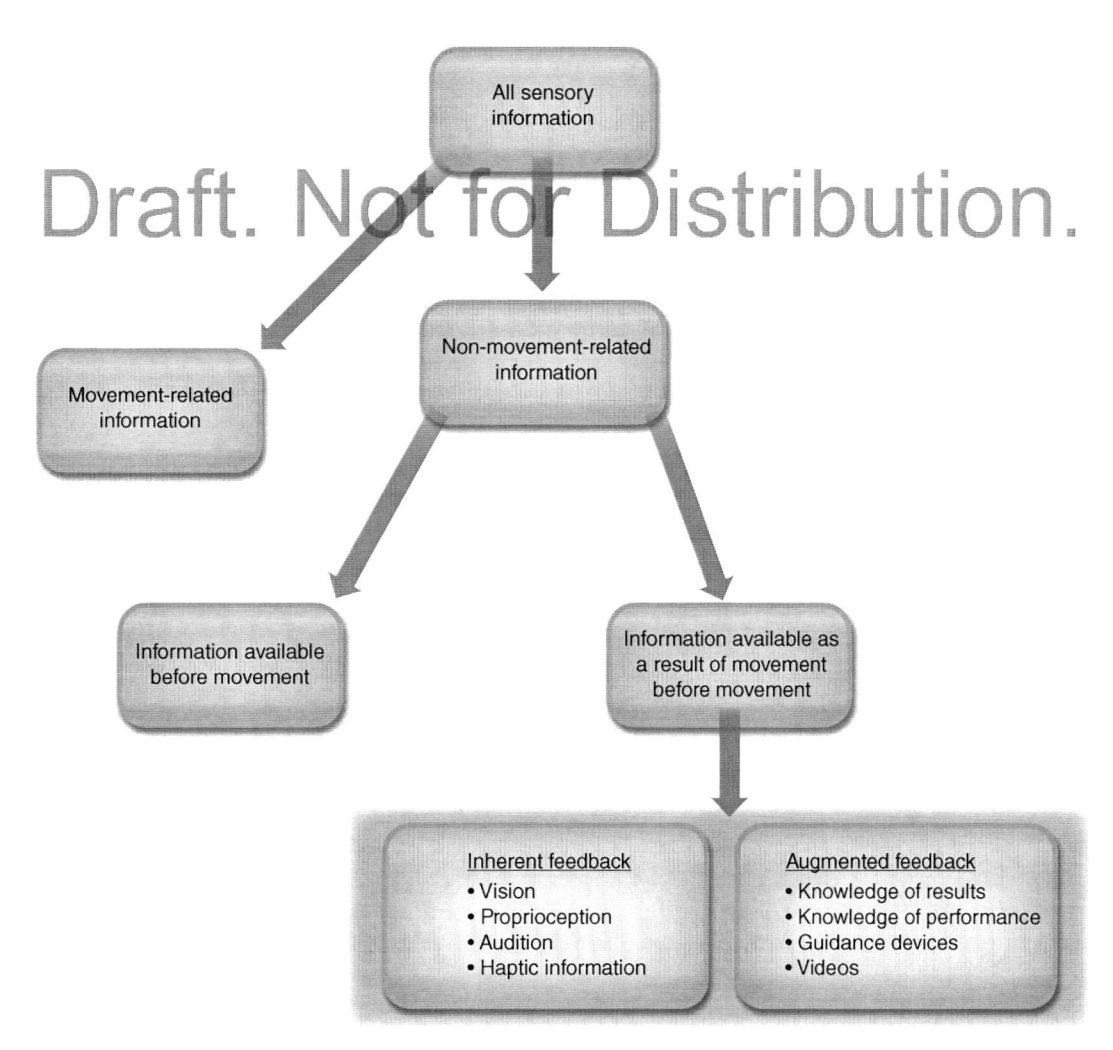

FIGURE 11.1 A feedback classification scheme.

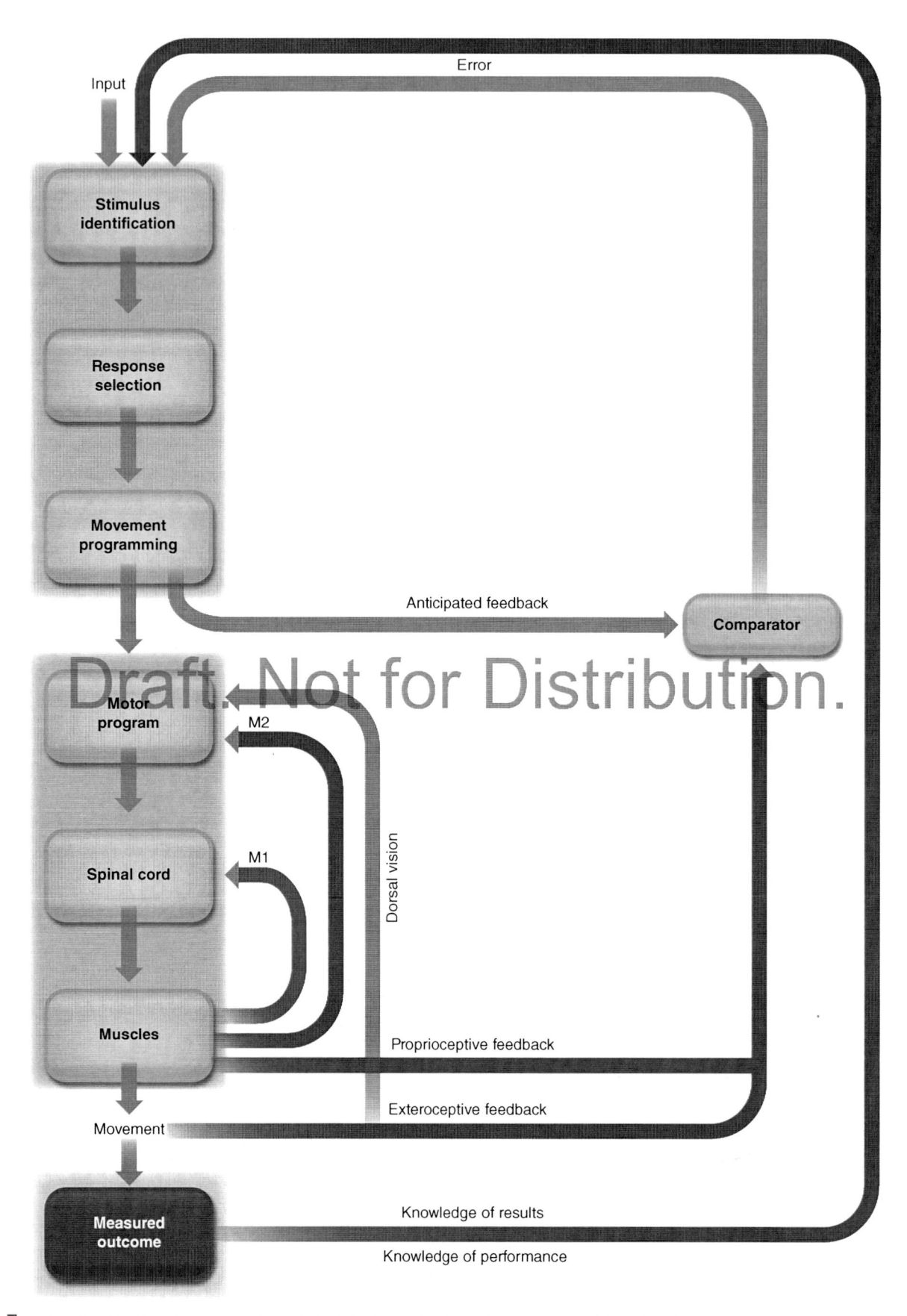

FIGURE 11.2 Conceptual model with the addition of augmented feedback.

feedback," **augmented feedback** consists of information from the measured performance outcome that is fed back to the learner by some artificial means, such as an instructor's voice or a video played on a computer or cell phone. Thus, augmented feedback is information supplied to the learner that is over and above that contained in inherent feedback. As the name suggests, augmented feedback serves to supplement the naturally available (inherent) information. Most importantly, this feedback is information over which the instructor has control; thus, it can be given or not given, given at different times, and given in different forms to influence learning. Scientists in motor learning tend to use the term "feedback" as shorthand for augmented feedback, and we use the term this way as well.

Knowledge of Results

Knowledge of results (KR) is a particularly important category of augmented feedback shown in figure 11.2 with the new blue line. KR is augmented, usually verbal (or at least verbalizable) information about the success of an action with respect to the environmental goal. In many daily activities, KR is redundant with the inherent information. Telling someone he missed the nail with the hammer and telling a basketball player she missed the free throw are examples of KR (the verbal information) that duplicates the information the performer received anyway.

However, KR is not always redundant with inherent feedback. Surgical residents, springboard divers, and dancers must wait for the assessment scores to know the success of their performance. In riflery and archery it is not always possible to see where the projectile hit the target area, so augmented KR information must be received from a coach or a scoring device. Musicians have to wait for the critic's reviews of their performances before they know how well it was accepted. In these cases, KR is critically important for performance and learning because, in tasks in which the inherent feedback is absent or incomplete, learners cannot know about the outcomes of their actions without some form of KR.

KR is frequently used in research, where specific aspects regarding how information is given to learners can be controlled. Researchers use this general method to examine how feedback processes influence learning. Earlier research was often conducted with very simple tasks, such as blindfolded limb-positioning tasks, in situations in which the learners could not use inherent feedback. These experiments generally showed that, without any KR, there was no learning at all (e.g., Thorndike, 1927; Trowbridge & Cason, 1932). On the other hand, providing KR about errors allowed rapid improvement across practice, such that performance improvements remained in retention tests even when KR was withdrawn. These results suggest that when learners cannot detect their own performance errors through inherent feedback, no learning occurs at all unless *some* form of feedback is provided. This is one of the reasons that feedback is considered the single most important variable for learning except for practice itself (Bilodeau, 1966).

This is not to say learning cannot occur without KR, however. You have probably learned many real-world tasks with no KR (as defined here) provided by an instructor, as in practicing free throws by yourself. You received goal achievement information (i.e., whether or not the ball went in the basket) through inherent feedback, and this feedback was the basis for your learning. Thus, the principle is as follows: Some information relative to goal achievement must be received, either through inherent sources or augmented sources, for any learning to occur.

Knowledge of Performance

Knowledge of performance (KP), sometimes referred to as "kinematic feedback," is augmented information about the movement pattern the learner has just made. It is frequently used by instructors in real-world settings. For example, you often hear coaches say things like "That pass was too slow" in ice hockey, "Your tuck was not tight enough" in a springboard dive, or "Your backswing was too short" in golf. Each of these forms of KP tells the learner something about kinematics (the movement or movement patterns). Note that KP information, unlike KR, does not necessarily tell about movement success in terms of meeting the environmental goal. Rather, kinematic feedback tells about the nature of the movement pattern that the learner actually produced. Some of the main similarities and differences between KR and KP are summarized in table 11.1.

Functions of Augmented Feedback

After a movement attempt, a music instructor says to the learner, "The rhythm was pretty good, but try to slow everything down a little next time." Think of all the meanings that such a simple statement could have to the learner. First of all, the feedback could have a motivating, energizing, or discouraging function: It could make the learner slightly more enthusiastic about the activity and encourage her to try harder. Second, there is of course the information about the rhythm and absolute timing of the movements, which can be combined with other information (e.g., how the movement felt) to generate new knowledge. Third, feedback helps to direct the learner's attention either toward the production of the movement (an internal focus of attention) or toward the end product or effect of the movement in the environment (an external focus). Finally, feedback can also produce a kind of dependency, such that performance is enhanced when feedback is present because of its influence on the following trial but causes performance to deteriorate when it is later withdrawn.

Generally in real-world settings, augmented feedback operates in four interdependent ways simultaneously; these functions are often very difficult to separate. To summarize, augmented feedback does these things:

- ▶ Produces motivation, or energizes the learner to increase effort
- ▶ Provides information about errors as a basis for corrections
- ▶ Directs the learner's attention toward the movement or the movement goal
- ▶ Creates a dependency, leading to problems at feedback withdrawal

Motivational Properties

The music instructor tells the struggling piano student, "Keep it up, you're doing fine." This casual comment motivates the student to keep going a little longer in practice. Certainly, one important function of feedback is to motivate the learner, for example, in helping a tired learner to bring more effort to bear on the task. In addition, early research revealed that, if performance was deteriorating (in so-called vigilance tasks), performers showed an immediate increase in proficiency, as if the feedback was acting as a kind of "stimulant" to energize them again (Arps,

TABLE 11.1 Similarities and Differences Between KR and KP

Knowledge of results (KR)	Knowledge of performance (KP)
Similarities	
Verbal (or verbalizable)	Verbal (or verbalizable)
Augmented	Augmented
Provided after movement (usually)	Provided after movement (usually)
Differences	
Information about goal outcome	Information about movement pattern
Often redundant with inherent feedback	Usually distinct from inherent feedback
Usually provided as a score	Usually kinematic information
Often used in laboratory research	Often provided in everyday activities

For a diver, augmented feedback could include a score provided by a judge or a coach's assessment of the diver's movement pattern.

1920; Crawley, 1926). In addition, learners who are given feedback say they like the task more, they try harder at it, and they are willing to practice longer. In short, unless it is overdone, learners seem to like feedback. Even when an instructor has another primary reason for giving feedback (e.g., to correct an error), this extra motivational benefit is achieved "for free."

You can capitalize on this feedback feature in practice. Think of ways to give learners feedback relatively frequently. This is not as simple as it sounds, though, because in large classes, one does not have much time to devote to a single learner. In any case, try to avoid long periods in which you give no feedback, because motivation can sag and practice can either be very inefficient or cease altogether. Keeping learners informed of their progress usually translates into their bringing more effort to the task, which can only benefit them in terms of increased learning.

The effects of feedback as a motivating tool just discussed are primarily *indirect* in their influence. For example, KR encourages the learner to keep practicing, and the results of this additional practice are what influences learning. However, recent research suggests that motivational feedback can also have a *direct* effect on learning. Consider the study by Chiviacowsky and Wulf (2007), for example. Learners in this study practiced a beanbag-tossing task in which vision of the end-result accuracy was obstructed, making feedback from the experimenter (KR) critical for improving performance. Subjects in the "KR good" group were provided with feedback about performance on the most skillful three performances out of the previous six trials, over repeated blocks of practice. In contrast, subjects in the "KR poor" group received information about their three least skillful performances over these same practice periods. Learning, as illustrated by the

Focus on RESEARCH 11.1
Revising Ideas About How Feedback Works

Research traditions that were established in the animal-learning literature early in the 20th century strongly influenced the thinking about how feedback must work in motor learning. In one example, a food reward was given if a hungry animal pressed a lever within 5 s of hearing a signal. Over trials, the animal learned to press the lever quite reliably when the sound occurred. Your new puppy quickly learns to sit on command if you give a biscuit or a friendly pat when the puppy performs the action. In this case, the food reward is serving as feedback for correctly responding to the stimulus (to sit on command).

Scientists realized that the nature and timing of the feedback had a marked influence on learning the desired response. These findings were captured and summarized by Thorndike's (1927) *Law of Effect*, in which reinforcement (or feedback) played a prominent role—associations (or "bonds") between the stimulus and the "correct" response were presumably strengthened when they were reinforced by (or were accompanied by) feedback. Factors that increased the immediacy or frequency of such feedback presentations presumably strengthened these bonds, further increasing learning. To view this another way, if feedback were withheld after a particular trial and the learner could not know the outcome from inherent feedback, then there could be no increment of bond strengthening for that trial, rendering that practice trial essentially useless for enhancing learning. These basic notions gave rise to the general idea that effective feedback is presented as immediately and as frequently as possible, which quickly became a standard belief in the movement skills literature.

Over the next few decades, scientists saw little in the literature that would contradict this basic viewpoint about feedback for skill learning. Gradually, based on Thorndike's ideas, a set of feedback generalizations emerged, suggesting that:

> *any variation of feedback during practice that makes the information more immediate, more precise, more frequent, more informationally rich, or generally more useful would be beneficial for learning.*

Such a view made good common sense—it just seems logical that giving more information to the learner should benefit learning—and this view became widely adopted as a result. The principle has strong implications for the structure of practice, encouraging just about anything that would provide more information to the learner.

As you will see throughout this chapter, however, the above generalization is probably wrong in several ways. One of the major difficulties with this principle emerged from research on the relative frequency of feedback—a key variable that defines how frequently feedback is scheduled in a learning session. Other variables, such as feedback delay, feedback summaries, and bandwidth feedback, failed to operate in ways predicted by Thorndike's views.

In the end, these early theoretical beginnings were important because they led to more research, new ideas, and a better understanding of feedback processes in motor learning. These more modern interpretations of the research constitute most of the theorizing presented in this chapter. An important review of the feedback literature by Salmoni, Schmidt, and Walter (1984) provides much more on the historical context of this work.

Exploring Further

1. Why does the typical experiment in animal conditioning provide an "extinction" period?
2. In what ways does augmented feedback in motor learning work similarly to the provision of feedback in animal conditioning studies? In what ways do the principles differ?

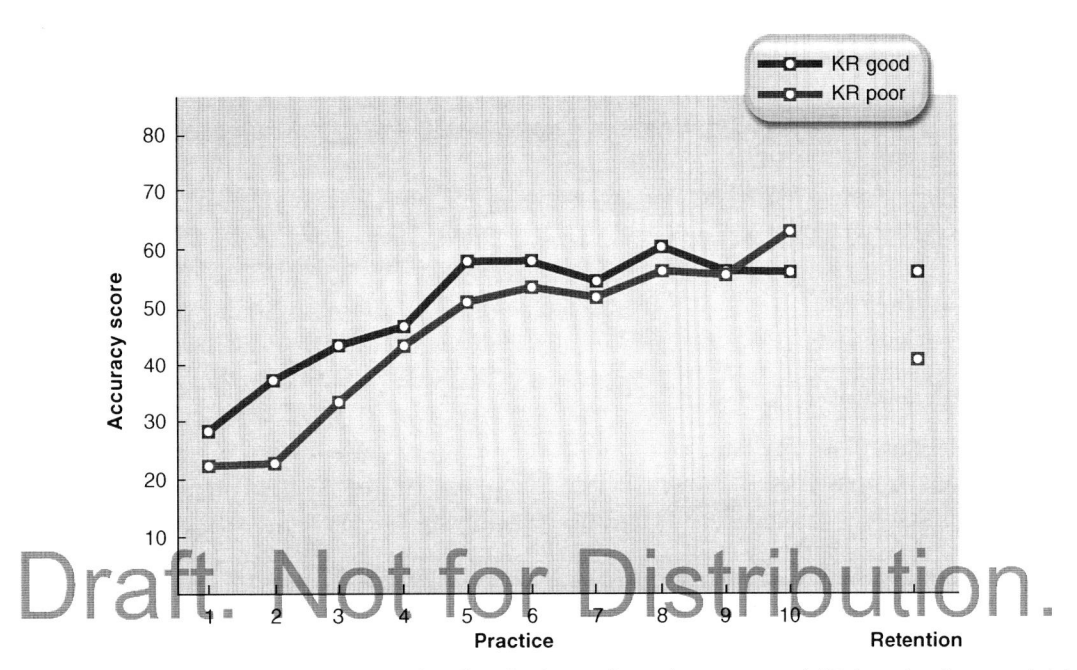

FIGURE 11.3 Providing learners with feedback about their three most skillful trials after each block of six trials (the "KR good" group, blue) resulted in stronger retention performance than providing learners with feedback about their three least skillful trials during practice (the "KR poor" group, red).

Reprinted by permission from Chiviacowsky and Wulf 2007.

retention performance in figure 11.3, was facilitated by the "good" feedback.

The findings of Chiviacowsky and Wulf (2007) underscore the beneficial effects of motivation on learning as discussed in chapter 10, and suggest that motivating feedback can also have a direct effect on learning. These and other recent findings on this new development in the feedback literature are discussed by Lewthwaite and Wulf (2012).

Informational Properties

Probably the most important component of feedback for motor learning is the information it provides about patterns of action. This feedback about errors, giving direction for modifying future performance, is the focus that makes the instructor so important for motor learning. Whereas a machine can give out jelly beans for effective performance, a skilled instructor can know the proper patterns of action for which feedback should be provided. Because of the importance of this component of feedback, most of the remainder of the chapter deals with the principles of its operation for learning.

Consider now the example mentioned earlier, in which the music instructor tells the student that the rhythm was fine but the tempo could be slower overall. This information defines clearly the basis for making corrections on the next attempt, bringing the performance closer to the values that characterize the "most-skilled" performance. There is no doubt that giving information guides the learner toward the movement goal. Continued use of this feedback keeps errors to a minimum and ensures that errors are corrected quickly, thus holding the movement pattern very near to the goal.

Recognizing that augmented feedback is mainly informational raises many important questions for the instructor. For example, what kind of information can the learner use most effectively (e.g., information about limb position, limb timing, coordination), in what form can it be presented (e.g., verbally, in video replays, graphically), when can it be presented (immediately after an action, delayed somewhat), and how often can it be presented (on every trial, only some trials)? These questions are addressed in detail later in this chapter.

Attentional-Focusing Properties

An important discussion in two previous chapters addressed the role of attentional focus on performance (chapter 3) and learning (chapter 10). In many situations, it is likely to be the case that performance and learning are enhanced when the learner's attention is directed to the product of movement (or the movement's goal achievement)—typically referred to as an external focus of attention. In contrast, an attentional focus that is directed toward the movement itself (an internal focus) often leads to poor performance and learning.

Now consider the roles of KR and KP in this discussion. By its very nature, KR provides information about success of performance relative to the movement goal. Put differently, KR directs the learner to think about externally-directed information. The informational content of KP, on the other hand, is about the nature of the *movement* that was produced, such as the spatial or temporal form of the action. Thus, the information content of KP directs the learner's attention to process movement-related information—an internally-focused process.

The attentional-focusing properties of KR and KP set up the learner for a potential conflict in practice goals. Since KP is acknowl- edged to be the preferred form of feedback for making changes in the kinematics and kinetics of the action itself (e.g., Newell & Walter, 1981), how can it be used without the detrimental impact of an internally-focused attention? Fortunately, researchers have studied ways of scheduling the provision of feedback so that the most useful information content can be delivered without the potentially detrimental effects that might occur when (an internal) attentional focus is created by that feedback. We discuss some of that literature in the sections that follow.

Dependency-Producing Properties

When feedback that contains information for error correction is given frequently, it tends to guide behavior toward the goal movement. In a sense, this process operates in very much the same way guidance procedures do, as we discuss later in this chapter. Physical **guidance** acts very powerfully to reduce errors, sometimes preventing them completely. This is fine as long as the guidance is present, but the learner can also become dependent on the guidance, allowing performance to deteriorate markedly when the guidance is removed and the learner attempts to perform without it (Salmoni, Schmidt, & Walter, 1984).

Just as with physical guidance, augmented feedback tends to hold the movement at the goal, allowing the learner to correct errors quickly and thereby maintain the movement's correct form or outcome. The problem led to the **guidance hypothesis** (Salmoni, Schmidt, & Walter, 1984), which holds that the learner can become dependent on such feedback, so that he uses this augmented source of information instead of internally generated processes to keep the movement on target. If the instructor's feedback is then removed on a retention test, the performance could suffer markedly if the learner has not developed the capability to produce the movement independently. Various ways have been developed to structure feedback to minimize dependency-producing effects, as discussed in the sections that follow.

How Much Feedback to Give

An instructor could give feedback about countless features of the action after every performance attempt. Thus, overloading the learner with too much information is a potential problem. Information-processing and memory capabilities of the learner—particularly a child—are limited, so it is doubtful that the youthful learner can take in and retain very much information during multiple feedback presentations. It is also doubtful that the learner can be very effective in correcting the next action in more than one way, particularly with feedback about motor patterning. Feedback (perhaps leading to many other comments and thoughts) such as the kind processed by the learner in figure 11.4 would be very difficult to translate into an effective correction.

In general, too much information is generally not useful. For example, video replay is only moderately effective as a feedback tool, despite its widespread appeal (see Focus on Research 11.2) probably because there's too much information for video replay. A good rule of thumb is to decide what error is most fundamental and focus the feedback on that.

Precision of Feedback

Feedback about movement errors can be expressed in terms of either the direction of the error, the magnitude of the error, or both, and with varying levels of precision. The following are some of the principles involved.

Qualitative information about the direction of the learner's error (early vs. late, high vs. low, left vs. right, and so on) is critical to bring the movement into line with the goal. In

FIGURE 11.4 Providing more feedback than can be processed effectively for movement correction is probably detrimental to performance and learning.

©Bob Scavetta. Reproduction is forbidden without the written permission of the copyright holder.

Focus on RESEARCH 11.2

Augmented Feedback From Video Replays

Knowledge of performance (KP) has a long history in motor skills research. Early pioneers in feedback methods recorded force–time tracings in sprint starts on stripchart paper (Howell, 1956). The recordings were then displayed to the learner as KP feedback with the correct tracing superimposed over the learner's tracing (see Tiffin & Rogers, 1943, for a very early study using similar methods with industrial tasks).

Films were also popular, particularly involving professional and collegiate sport teams; these were used as feedback so that a player could analyze mistakes and determine more effective actions to use next time. As learning tools, though, films were limited because the time required for developing film was usually quite long, troublesome, and costly. Also, many events intervened between a given action and the feedback from it, making it difficult for the learners to remember what they did to produce particular errors and how to avoid making those errors the next time.

Videotape solved many of the problems with film: Feedback about whole performances could be viewed after only a few seconds of tape rewind, and these replays would capture the details of the movement very well. And, of course, digital imagery has taken this kind of feedback to a whole new level. Crisp, clear, high-definition recordings of performances can be captured with nothing more than a cell phone and can then be distributed to others around the world in seconds. Providing "live" feedback to the user has never been easier, cheaper, or more informative.

But, an important question remains: Is presenting video replays an effective method of providing augmented feedback? Early on, Rothstein and Arnold (1976) reviewed the evidence on videotape replays and, surprisingly, found that this feedback was not always useful for learning. An explanation might be that videotape replays provide too much information, so the learner becomes confused about what to extract as feedback. This leads to the suggestion that *cuing*, in which the instructor directs the learner to examine some particular feature of the movement as feedback, could be an effective technique.

Kernodle and Carlton (1992) provided evidence to support Rothstein and Arnold's suggestions. Subjects in each of four groups practiced a throwing task (using a very lightweight foam ball) with their nondominant limb and were given retention tests for learning immediately before five separate practice sessions. One group received only KR about the distance of the throw. The other three groups all received videotape replays of their performances—one group with no additional feedback, another group with cues to direct attention to certain parts of the video, and a third group with supplemental cues indicating what changes to make on the next attempt. The results, illustrated in figure 11.5 were quite clear. Providing video feedback KP without additional information was no panacea—learning was no more effective than when only KR was provided. However, providing video feedback with the addition of attention-directing cues, or even better, with cues about what errors to correct, was indeed effective for learning.

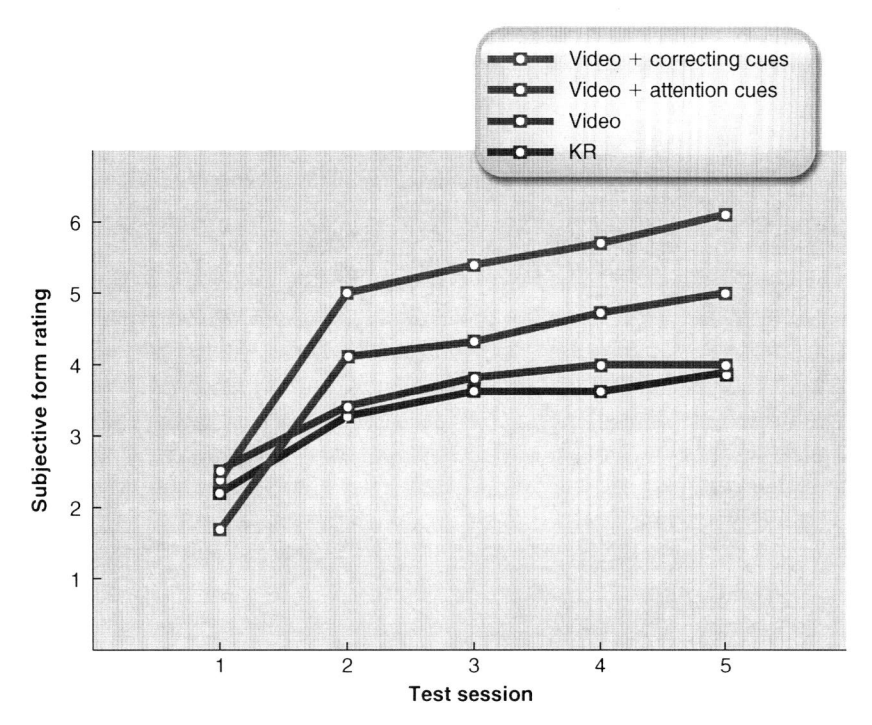

FIGURE 11.5 Providing real-time augmented feedback facilitates learning only if supplemented with additional cuing, as indicated by five retention tests conducted before practice over several days.

Reprinted by permission from Schmidt and Lee 2011; Data from Kernodle and Carlton 1992.

Exploring Further

1. Describe how you might conduct an experiment, similar to Kernodle and Carlton's (1992), using a task from physical rehabilitation, such as correcting an asymmetric walking gait.
2. Most of the video replay research has been conducted using older technology (videotape feedback). Would you expect newer video technology to produce similar or different results than those from Kernodle and Carlton's (1992) study?

---

addition, it is generally helpful to report some quantitative magnitude of the errors as part of the feedback, such as "Your movement was 2 cm to the left of the target." **Precision of feedback** is based on the level of accuracy with which the feedback describes the movement or outcome. You can imagine feedback that only roughly approximates the movement feature, as in learning to do partial weight bearing on crutches. Feedback such as "You put a little too much weight through your left leg that time" would be considered less precise (and produce less effective learning) than "you put 4.3 pounds too much weight through your left leg that time" (Trowbridge & Cason, 1932).

The level of feedback precision to provide seems to depend on the learner's skill. Early in practice, the learner's errors are so large that precise information about the exact size of the errors does not matter, simply because the learner does not have the movement-control precision to match the precision of correction specified by the feedback. By the same argument, movement control will be much more precise at higher levels of skill, and more precise feedback can be used effectively as a consequence. Of course, the effective

Technology has made providing video feedback to athletes easier than ever, but it is more effective when accompanied by cues to help the athlete focus on the relevant details.

instructor will be well-schooled in the proper form of the action and in how to detect errors in order for the feedback to describe the important movement aspects well.

Absolute and Relative Frequency of Feedback

The feedback literature has defined two general descriptors for feedback scheduling. **Absolute frequency of feedback** refers to the total number of feedback presentations given to a learner across a set of trials in practice. If there are 400 trials and the instructor gives feedback on 100 of them, then the absolute frequency is 100—simply the total number of feedback presentations. **Relative frequency of feedback**, on the other hand, refers to the percentage of trials receiving feedback. In this example, the relative frequency of feedback is 25% (100 feedback trials out of a total of 400 trials).

Consider this situation: A learner practices a task such as rifle shooting to a distant target, where errors cannot be detected without augmented feedback. Because the instructor is busy giving feedback to other students, information about the performances can be given only occasionally. We have discussed the learning benefits of the trials that actually receive feedback, but what about the no-feedback trials in between? Are they useful for learning? Do these so-called blank (no-feedback) trials have any function for learning at all, or are they simply a waste of time? Earlier, instructors suspected that no-feedback trials were generally ineffective, which led to the development of a number of artificial (and expensive) methods to give feedback about performance when the instructor was occupied. What are the issues here?

Such questions about so-called "blank trials" can be answered by examining the effect of relative frequency of feedback for learning. Research has shown that blank trials can be actually beneficial for learning, even though subjects receive no feedback on them and cannot detect their errors for themselves (Winstein & Schmidt, 1990). This can be seen in figure 11.6. Using a limb patterning task, the 100% group received feedback after every trial (100% relative frequency), and the 50% group received feedback after only half of the trials (50% relative frequency), with the same total number of trials. The groups improved at about the same rate in acquisition. However, in the tests of learning performed without any feedback, there was a strong effect for the 50% group to have learned more than the 100% group, even though half of the 50% group's trials involved no feedback. This finding challenges Thorndike's perspective that trials without feedback should produce no learning (see Focus on Research 11.1).

Faded Feedback

A key feature in the Winstein and Schmidt (1990) study was that reduced feedback frequency was achieved using faded feedback. In this method, the learner is given feedback at high relative frequencies (essentially 100%) in early practice, which has the effect of guiding the learner strongly toward the movement goal. The instructor then gradually reduces the relative frequency of feedback as skill develops in order to prevent the learner from developing a dependency on this feedback. With advanced skill, the performance does not deteriorate very much when feedback is totally withdrawn for a few trials. If performance does begin to drop off, the instructor can give feedback again for a trial or two to bring behavior back to the target, then withdraw the feedback again. The instructor can adjust feedback scheduling to the proficiency level and improvement rate of each learner separately, thus tailoring feedback to individual differences in capabilities. The ultimate goal is to generate the capability for the learner to produce the action on her own, without a dependency on feedback. Even though feedback is critical for developing the movement into a skilled pattern, it appears that it must be eventually removed to accomplish permanent skill learning.

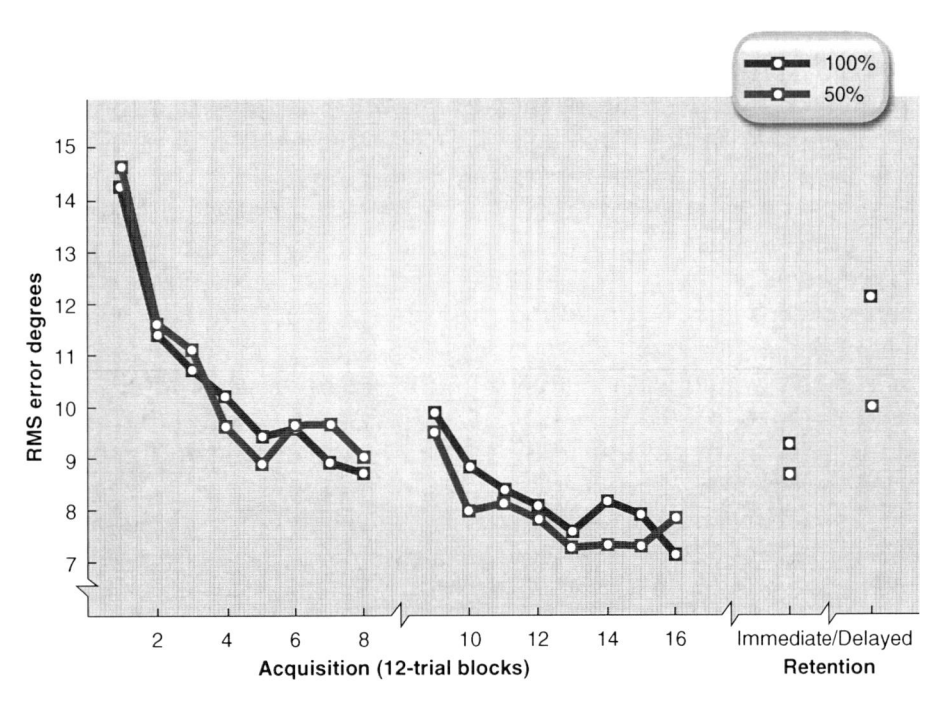

FIGURE 11.6 Reducing relative frequency of feedback from 100% to 50% during acquisition has beneficial effects on learning. RMSE = root-mean-squared error (see chapter 1).
Reprinted by permission from Winstein and Schmidt 1990.

Bandwidth Feedback

A method that combines both qualitative and quantitative types of information, discussed earlier, as well as the faded method of reducing the relative proportion of feedback, is known as **bandwidth feedback** (Sherwood, 1988). In this method, the decision to provide a learner with feedback is based on a preset degree of acceptability of performance. For example, if a resident is suturing a wound after a surgery, the instructing physician might say "good job" if the stitches were performed satisfactorily or the time to perform the surgery was acceptable. If either the accuracy or time was not acceptable, however, the physician might provide precise feedback about the nature of the errors made and what aspects of the performance need to be improved.

There are two general rules in using the bandwidth method (Sherwood, 1988). First, no feedback is given if some measure of performance falls within an acceptable level (or "band") of correctness. However, for the bandwidth method to work properly, the learner must be told ahead of time to interpret the absence of feedback to mean that performance was essentially "correct" (Lee & Carnahan, 1990). Second, precise feedback indicating the amount and direction of the error is given if and when performance falls outside the range of acceptability. In this way, the bandwidth method combines both qualitative and quantitative forms of feedback.

You may have guessed by now that a key issue in using the bandwidth method is deciding what level of error tolerance is appropriate for a learner. A simple illustration of this concept is presented in figure 11.7. The darker orange band in the figure illustrates a narrow bandwidth (−1 to +1 mm). In this case, the learner would receive no feedback on trials 5, 8, 9, and 10 (but would have been instructed that receiving no feedback would mean that those movements were essentially correct) and given precise feedback on the other trials. The orange band (−2 to +2 mm) illustrates a larger bandwidth that could be used instead. Here, the learner would not be

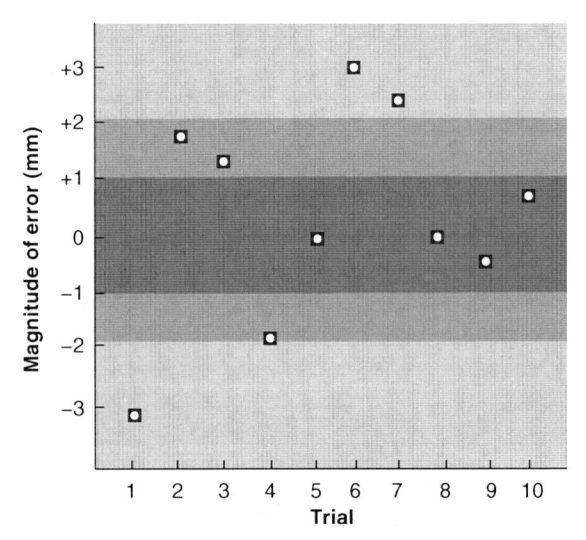

FIGURE 11.7 The bandwidth-feedback method. Establishing a preset level of tolerance (the two orange bands) determines what type of feedback is given to the learner. Two potential bands of correctness are shown here – a narrow band (the lighter orange) and a wider band (which includes both the lighter and darker orange). If performance falls outside of the tolerance band chosen, then and only then is error feedback given. Performance that falls within the band chosen results in no feedback, which the learner has been told beforehand means that performance was "correct."

given feedback on trials 2, 3, 4, 5, 8, 9, and 10 and given precise error feedback only on trials 1, 6, and 7.

Obviously, the size of the bandwidth will have a determining influence on how frequently the learner is given precise error feedback versus feedback that performance was "correct." And indeed, the bandwidth size itself has an important effect on learning. For example, Sherwood (1988) found that a larger bandwidth (10% of the target goal) produced more learning than smaller bandwidths (5% or 1%).

The bandwidth method is consistent with a number of well-established principles for learning. First, the method produces reduced faded-feedback frequency as a by-product (which Winstein & Schmidt [1990] found to be an important feedback variable in itself). When the learner is just beginning, the movements often tend to be outside the tolerance level, leading to frequent feedback from the instructor. As skill improves, more performances fall within the band, leading to less frequent error feedback on the error trials that are outside the band (which, as we will discuss later, has an important positive influence on learning in itself). Second, with improvements in performance (resulting in more performances inside the bandwidth), the increased absence of error feedback can also be viewed as a form of rewarding feedback. And as we have discussed twice previously, rewarding learners with motivating feedback has a strong learning function. Finally, withholding information on a set of trials that fall within the bandwidth fosters more stable, consistent actions. Eliminating these small trial-to-trial corrections has a stabilizing influence on performance, because the learner is not encouraged to change the action on every trial.

Summary Feedback

Another way to avoid the detrimental effects of every-trial feedback is to give feedback *summaries*. In this method, feedback is withheld for a series of trials—say, following a series of 5 to 20 performance attempts—after which feedback for the entire series is summarized for the learner, perhaps by providing a graph of all of the previous performance attempts in that block of trials. On the surface, summary feedback would seem to be particularly ineffective for learning. The informational content of the feedback would be seriously degraded because the learner wouldn't be able to associate the feedback with any particular practice attempt, and thus would have no basis for making trial-to-trial corrections to improve performance.

Even so, research has shown that **summary feedback** can be particularly effective for learning (e.g., Lavery, 1962; Schmidt et al., 1989). Generally, even though summary feedback is less effective than every-trial feedback for performance during practice, when feedback was withdrawn in retention tests, subjects who had received summary feedback performed more skillfully than subjects who had received every-trial feedback. Therefore, summary feedback is more effective for learning than every-trial feedback. How can summary feedback be so effective? For us, the better question is why is every-trial feedback so ineffective for learning?

How Many Trials to Summarize?

How many trials should you include in summary feedback? Can there be too many summarized trials? Evidence suggests that there is an optimal number of trials to include in summary-feedback reports, with either too few or too many trials decreasing learning. Why? With every-trial feedback (a one-trial summary), the learner is guided strongly to the goal; but this also maximizes the dependency-producing effects. On the other hand, if the feedback summarizes a very large number of trials (say 100), the dependency-producing effects are greatly reduced, but the learner also benefits less from the informational properties of the feedback that guide him to the goal. This rationale suggests the existence of an optimal number of summary-feedback trials in which the benefits from being guided to the goal are balanced just right with costs of the dependency-producing properties.

This prediction was confirmed in experiments by Schmidt, Lange, and Young (1990), who studied different numbers of summary feedback trials on a laboratory task resembling batting in baseball. As seen in figure 11.8, there was an optimal relationship between summary length and learning, with the 5-trial summary feedback length begin optimal. Again, even though the 1-trial condition (every-trial feedback) was best for performance during earlier practice, when feedback was being presented, the 5-trial condition was optimal for learning.

How Does Summary Feedback Work?

What are the processes behind the benefits of summary feedback? The following are three ways summary feedback (relative to every-trial could function to aid learning:

1. Summary feedback might prevent the dependency-producing effects of fre-

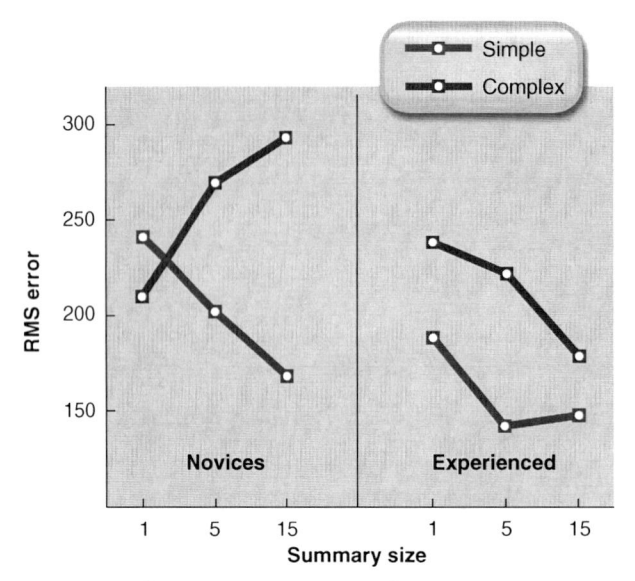

FIGURE 11.8 Performance score for various numbers of trials included in a summary-feedback presentation for acquisition (left) and immediate and delayed retention (right).

Reprinted from *Human Movement Science*, Vol 9, R.A. Schmidt, C. Lange, and D.E. Young, "Optimizing summary knowledge of results for skill learning," p. 334, copyright 1990, with permission of Elsevier.

quent feedback because it causes the learner to perform independently for several trials before finally receiving feedback. Then the learner can make corrections to the general movement pattern produced in the earlier trials.

2. Summary feedback might produce more stable movements because feedback is withdrawn for several trials, giving the learner no basis for a change in the movement from trial to trial. Frequent feedback, on the other hand, more or less encourages the learner to change the movement on every trial, which prevents the movement from achieving the stability needed for subsequent performance.

3. Summary feedback appears to encourage learners to analyze their inherent movement-produced feedback (kinesthetic, visual, and so on) to learn to detect their own errors (this concept was discussed in chapter 9). Frequent feedback tells learners about errors, eliminating the need to process inherent feedback, so the learners do not need to process information about their errors, as KR provides this for them.

Average Feedback

In a variant of summary feedback called **average feedback**, the learners wait for a series of trials before receiving feedback information about their scores (as with summary feedback), but now receive only the *average* score on those trials instead of a trial-by-trial (e.g., graphical) summary. For example, the golf instructor might watch the learner make 10 swings before commenting, "Your backswing was about 6 inches too short on those last 10 shots." Results from studies by Young and Schmidt (1992) and Yao, Fischman, and Wang (1994; illustrated in figure 11.9) showed that average feedback (green and purple) was far more effective for learning (i.e., retention) than every-trial feedback (red). And average feedback appeared to be slightly more effective for learning than summary feedback.

Average feedback and summary feedback might operate in the same general way—by blocking the detrimental, dependency-producing effects of every-trial feedback. Average feedback also allows the instructor to formulate a more complete idea of what the learner's error tendency happens to be. On any one attempt, just about anything can occur by chance alone (because performances

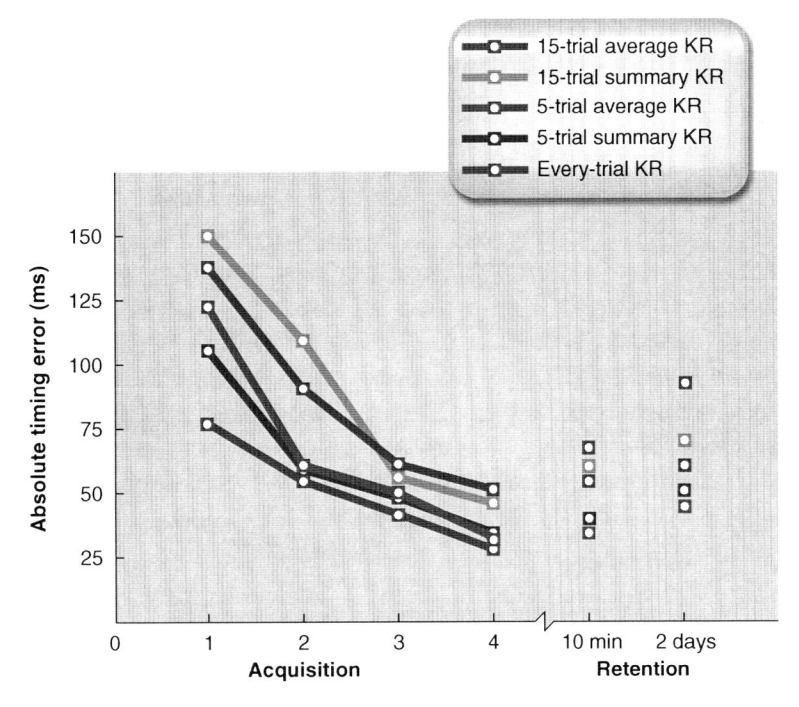

FIGURE 11.9 Average feedback produced benefits similar to summary feedback.
Reprinted by permission from Yao, Fischman, and Wang 1994.

vary greatly from trial to trial). However, by watching the performer do several trials, the instructor can "filter out" this within-subject variability (i.e., by averaging) to detect the error that a learner *typically* (i.e., on average) tends to make. Thus, average feedback gives the learner more reliable information about what to change, and how much to change it, on the next few practice attempts.

Learner-Determined Feedback Schedules

A different approach to the study of scheduling feedback gives the learner control over when to receive feedback, instead of having this determined by the instructor. In many ways this makes good common sense—the learner is often in the best situation to know when feedback would be most beneficial. In a study conducted by Janelle and coworkers (1997), subjects practiced throwing with their nondominant limb, with two groups receiving KP about the quality of the throwing motion. In one group, each subject received feedback whenever the learner requested it.

For each subject in the other group, the feedback schedule was matched to (i.e., yoked to) that of a member of the self-determined group, thereby ensuring that the amount of feedback and its scheduling were identical for the two groups—only the *determination* of feedback delivery was different (i.e., learner- vs. experimenter-determined). A third, control group received no KP feedback.

Consider the results of Janelle and colleagues' (1997) study, shown in figure 11.10, and focus first on the bottom part of the figure. The symbols here represent the frequency with which learners in the self-determined group requested feedback in each of the 20 blocks of practice trials over the two days in the experiment. Note that the learners tended to request feedback relatively infrequently (on 11% of the trials, overall, orange, lower), and also that they tended to fade (or "wean" themselves off) feedback as practice continued (ranging from 21% on the first block of practice to 7% on the last block).

Now consider these feedback manipulations on performance and learning, represented in the top half of figure 11.10.

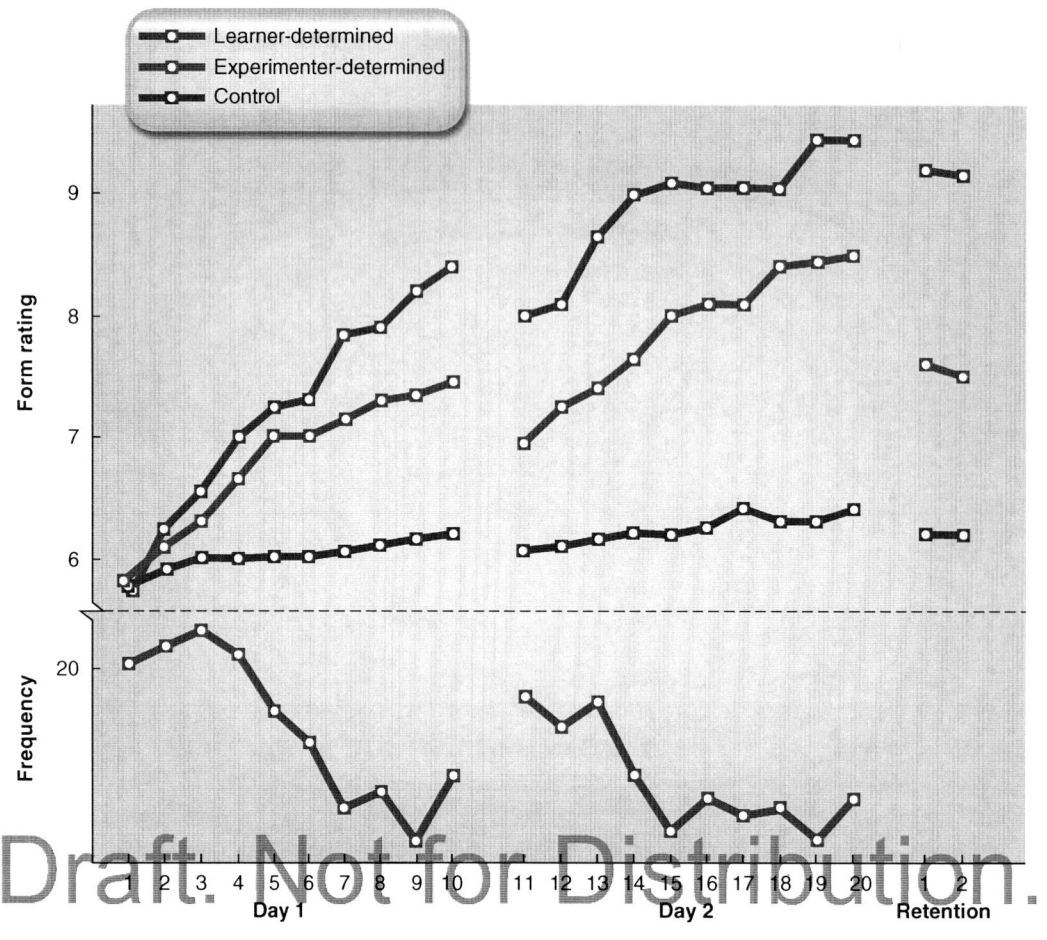

FIGURE 11.10 Self-determined feedback (purple) compared to a yoked control condition (green) and a no-feedback control condition (blue) for optimizing learning.

Adapted from Janelle et al. 1997.

First, compare the experimenter-determined (yoked) group (green) and the control group (blue). Clearly, giving KP feedback, which was also faded over trials for this yoked group, was beneficial to performance and learning. Now compare the experimenter (green)- and learner (purple)-determined groups. Giving the decision to the learner to determine when feedback would be delivered provided a boost to performance and learning that was above and beyond that generated by fading feedback. Why might this be so?

One implication from this study is that learners likely need (or at least request) feedback far less frequently than instructors tend to provide it. But there is another aspect of learner-determined feedback that should be mentioned. Research conducted by Chiviacowsky and Wulf (2002) revealed that learners tend to request feedback more frequently following trials that they perceived they performed well, as compared to trials that they thought they performed poorly. Thus, as discussed previously in this chapter (see also figure 11.3), there may be an important motivational component driving the request for feedback, which in turn has a beneficial effect on learning when that feedback is delivered.

When to Give Feedback

Assuming that it is desirable to provide feedback about a particular performance, an important question that remains is this: To maximize learning, when would it be given? We often hear that "immediate feedback" is desirable (see the subsequent section on this), leading to the idea that an instructor would strive to give feedback as quickly as possible after a performance to maximize learning (again, review Focus on Research 11.1). What is the role, if any, of the timing of the information that we give?

Feedback timing can be described in terms of three intervals, shown in figure 11.11. When delivered during the ongoing movement, it is typically called **concurrent feedback**. (Note that *physical guidance* falls within this definition too, since it consists of augmented information, though not verbal information, that helps to signal errors and is provided during an ongoing movement.) The interval of time after the completion of movement until feedback is presented is called the **feedback delay interval**. And the interval after the provision of feedback until the next movement starts is the **postfeedback delay** interval.

Feedback During the Movement

One of the most powerful ways to deliver feedback is to provide it while the movement is ongoing. The information can be used to regulate ongoing (particularly long-duration) actions by giving a basis for correcting errors and "pushing" the movement closer to the action goals. Two methods are typically used to provide ongoing information: (1) concurrent feedback, in which augmented information about the movement error (or the correct movement) is provided by verbal, visual, or auditory means; and (2) physical guidance, in which haptic or kinesthetic information is signaled to the learner by means of a physically restricted guidance device or a person (e.g., therapist) who physically restricts the movement. Despite their apparent differences, the two methods influence similar processes that govern motor learning.

Concurrent Feedback

A classic experiment, providing considerable insight into some of the processes involved in concurrent feedback, was conducted by Annett (1959). He asked subjects to learn to produce a given amount of pressure against a hand-operated lever. During the movement, one group of subjects received concurrent visual feedback on a display showing the amount of pressure they exerted in relation to the goal pressure whereas another group did not. As expected, the concurrent feedback facilitated performance greatly during practice. However, on a retention test with the feedback removed, this group performed very poorly, with some subjects pressing so hard that they damaged the apparatus! Subjects who had learned the task with this concurrent feedback were unable to perform without it. Similar results, showing enhanced performance but poor retention, were shown in Schmidt and Wulf (1997).

Physical Guidance Techniques

Concurrent feedback, such as that provided in the studies just cited, provides information that helps the learner to avoid making errors, to correct errors quickly, or both. Guidance techniques often work in a more direct way—to *prevent* the learner from making errors by physical means (e.g., see Focus on Application 11.1).

Physical guidance techniques represent a large class of methods in which the learner is "forced to" produce the correct movement patterning. Guidance devices have several goals; the main one is to reduce or eliminate

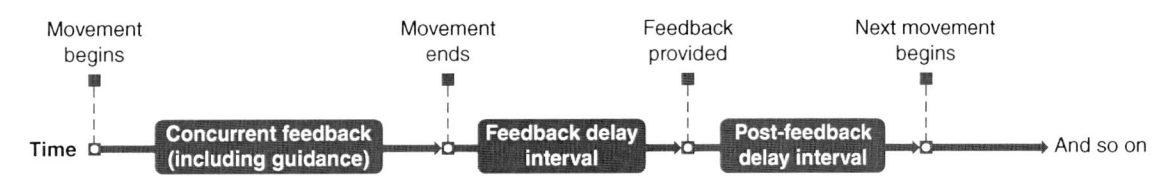

FIGURE 11.11 Labels for the various times at which feedback can be delivered.

errors and ensure that the proper pattern is carried out. This is particularly important when the movement is dangerous, as in gymnastics, where harmful falls can be prevented by various spotting methods, or in swimming, where fearful beginners can use flotation devices. Guidance is also useful for training with expensive equipment, where mistakes can be costly as well as dangerous, as with learning to drive a car or fly an airplane.

Guidance methods vary widely across settings. Some forms of guidance are very loose, giving the learner only slight aids to performance. An example is the instructor who provides very slight hand pressure to guide the learner or talks the learner through the action. Other forms of guidance are far more powerful and invasive. An instructor can constrain the learner's movements physically, as when the physical therapist "forces" the patient's movements into the proper path, preventing a serious fall. Physical-guidance devices are particularly popular in sports such as golf, where the aids constrain the movement pattern physically in several ways, with the hope that subjects will learn it.

Each method provides the learner with some kind of temporary aid during practice. The desire, of course, is that learning, as measured by performance in the future without the aid, will be enhanced. But the research suggests that while learning might be facilitated by small amounts of guidance, the negative impact on learning accrues quickly (Hodges & Campagnaro, 2012).

A study by Armstrong (1970) provides an important statement about the effects of guidance and an empirical comparison of concurrent feedback and terminal feedback as well. Over three days of practice, subjects learned to move a lever with elbow extension and flexion movements in order to produce a specific, timed kinematic sequence, or movement pattern (see also Focus on Research 5.3). As illustrated in figure 11.12, most of the movement error was prevented

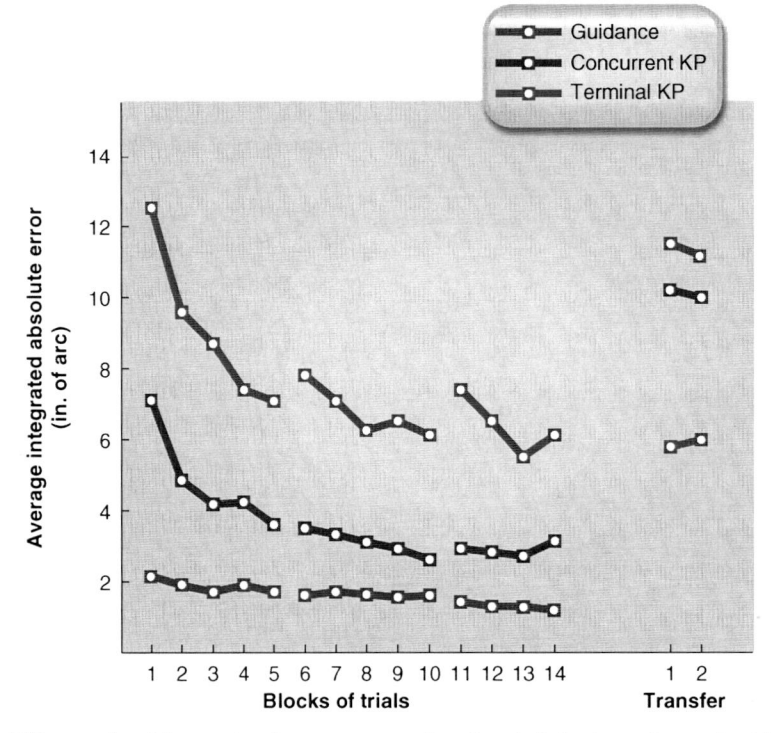

FIGURE 11.12 Effects of guidance (red), concurrent feedback (blue), and terminal feedback (green) on performance and on a no-feedback retention/transfer test of learning.
Reprinted by permission from Schmidt and Lee 2011; Adapted from Armstrong 1970.

in a guidance group that received a physically restricted patterning produced by light haptic (i.e., touch) restrictions to errorful actions. Movement error was not prevented entirely but was eliminated quickly in a concurrent-feedback group, whose subjects were able to see the ongoing movement's kinematic trace on a computer screen, overlaid on the

Focus on
APPLICATION 11.1

Physical Guidance in Stroke Rehabilitation

The effects of acute stroke are often devastating, and many individuals who experience a stroke never fully regain the motor capability that was lost due to the brain damage. But many individuals do indeed recover. Some of this recovery is spontaneous, as the brain heals itself following the trauma. And some of the recovery can also be attributed to intense therapeutic interventions involving movement.

Physical guidance is a frequently used technique in rehabilitation and is typically based on two basic fundamental assumptions: (1) that learning is a process of repetition and (2) that repeating an optimal or "correct" movement pattern results in more learning than repeating a movement that is suboptimal, incorrect, or errorful. Physical guidance techniques are designed with both of these assumptions in mind. Both of these assumptions have questionable validity, though, that we'll cover in a later section.

Patients who have had a stroke often tire easily because of extreme weakness. One advantage of upper limb guidance techniques, for example, is that they can be used to move the limb for the patient ("passive" movement) or to support the weight of the limb at least partially so that active movement can be done with minimized effort. An advantage, therefore, is that much less fatigue occurs during a therapy session with a guidance device, and more repetitions can be performed as a result, satisfying the first principle. By this view, then, more practice should lead to more complete rehabilitation outcomes. But see Barnett, et.al (1973).

The second principle is more contentious. The view of optimizing learning as a process of repeating a "correct" or desirable movement pattern is basically an extension of Thorndike's Law of Effect (see Focus on Research 11.1). This view characterizes learning as a process of strengthening the association between a goal (e.g., to move in a certain way, "correctly") and a response (e.g., actually moving correctly). For Thorndike, augmented feedback, in the form of "reward," was the agent that served to increase the repetition of this association. So, in theory, physically restricting the response so that *only* the correct movement can be performed should optimize the Law of Effect.

As we discuss in this chapter, however, the evidence from studies with healthy adults suggests that physical guidance is an ineffective method of practice, for several important reasons. Moreover, the use of physical guidance as a therapy intervention in stroke rehabilitation has come under increasing criticism (Mehrholz et al., 2008; Timmermans et al., 2009). The result is that new techniques are now being devised, with the aim of maximizing the positive benefits conferred by guidance devices that provide assistance only when needed—allowing the patient to make and experience some errors in movement, but not ones that would lead to further injury (Banala et al., 2009).

target template. And error was eliminated gradually over practice in a group that received KR feedback after the completion of a trial. Figure 11.12 shows that, even after three days of practice, subjects in the terminal-feedback group did not achieve the level of performance of the other groups. Clearly, this guidance procedure did its job, insisting that the learners remain on target.

But now consider the respective performances of these groups in a retention test, in which all groups were transferred to a test condition without the benefit of any augmented guidance or augmented feedback (far right side of figure 11.12). Several things are of interest to note here. First, the terminal-feedback group, which had been the most errorful of the three groups during practice, clearly showed the most learning as measured in these retention trials. Second, in the absence of augmented feedback, the terminal feedback group maintained the level of performance that had been achieved at the end of the practice trials. And finally, the performance of the physical-guidance group was most errorful of all in retention, showing that guidance during practice was particularly horrible for learning. Note also that both the guidance group and the concurrent-feedback group deteriorated remarkably over the retention interval. In fact, the performance of both of these groups deteriorated almost to the level of performance displayed by the terminal-feedback group on their very first block of practice, suggesting that guidance and concurrent feedback were almost completely ineffective for learning.

As mentioned previously, however, not all physical guidance is detrimental to learning. Guidance certainly plays an important role in dangerous or frightening situations; here it would be undesirable to continue practice in the absence of guidance. And guidance may also serve a useful function in the beginning stages of learning a skill; here, the communication of information to a learner is particularly difficult unless the learner is also led through the motions. Recent research also suggests that reducing or withdrawing guidance as the learner develops skill at the task is a fruitful learning procedure (see also Focus on Application 11.2).

Common Processes in Concurrent Feedback and Physical Guidance

The evidence discussed in the previous sections points to an important principle. Guidance and concurrent feedback, almost by definition, are effective for performance when present during practice. After all, these supplements are designed to help the performer make the correct action, to prevent errors, to aid in confidence, and so on, so there is little surprise that performance benefits from guidance. But the real test of guidance effectiveness is how well subjects do when the intervention is removed, and here is where these procedures often fail. When the ongoing information source is removed for retention tests, performance usually falls to the level of, or sometimes below, that of learners who had no guidance at all. That is, guidance is not a very effective variable for learning if it is not used wisely.

How can these principles of guidance be understood? Probably the best interpretation is that, during practice where guidance is present, the learner relies too strongly on its powerful performance-enhancing properties, which actually changes the task in several ways. Physical guidance can modify the "feel" of the task. Decision-making processes change when the instructor or the guidance tells the learner what to do. Also, the learner does not have the opportunity to experience errors, or to correct errors, during the guided movement or on the next movement. The learner will have failed to acquire the capability necessary to perform in a retention test or in a competition when the guidance is not present.

Notice that this interpretation is really a statement of the specificity view discussed in previous chapters. If guided practice changes the task requirements markedly (as it does), the task is not really the same task it was under the unguided conditions. If these modifications are large (as in very strong

Focus on
APPLICATION 11.2

Physical Guidance in Learning to Swim

In the text, we perhaps leave the impression that all physical guidance is detrimental for learning. Actually, there are a few situations in which physical guidance turns out to be very useful. Here's just one of them.

When one of us (RAS) was a graduate student at the University of Illinois, he was assigned to teach a course in beginning swimming. This course should have been called something like "Teaching the Persistent Nonswimmer to Swim," as many of these students could not swim a stroke, and many were truly terrified of the water.

After a week or so of learning to become familiar with water (e.g., in the shallow end of the pool, blowing bubbles, learning to open one's eyes underwater, counting fingers of a partner underwater), the next task was for the students to learn the elementary backstroke as a lifesaving stroke in case they were to fall into the water somewhere. This process involves the usual techniques (in the shallow end of the pool): learning to float on the back, gliding on the back after a push-off from the side of the pool, then adding a "frog kick" and eventually adding an arm stroke.

Then came the terrifying part: swimming with the elementary backstroke from the shallow end to the deep end of the pool. Naturally, most of the students were quite apprehensive about this task, so we developed various methods to alleviate their fear. One of these involved the use of long (15 ft or 4.57 m) wooden poles, about an inch (2.5 cm) in diameter. On the first attempt the instructor would walk along the poolside adjacent to the swimmer in the water just touching the pole against the swimmer's far-side hip. This did two things: First, it provided a measure of assurance for the swimmer, since all he had to do in an emergency was to grasp the pole, and the instructor could pull him to the pool edge. Second, though, this method did not interfere with the swimmer's own strokes allowing him to gain confidence and to learn the stroke.

This method was enormously successful. In fact, as a "final exam," the students had to swim a mile without touching the sides or ends of the pool. By this time most of them had been "weaned" from the assistance of the wooden pole, and they were quite capable of swimming relatively long distances (albeit very slowly). Over the course of about 10 years in which this course was taught, the average percentage of students who completed the 1 mi (about 2.5 km) swim was over 70%! The faculty proudly presented to each successful swimmer a fancy certificate with a gold star on it (suitable for framing), saying essentially, "I swam a mile at the University of Illinois." The look of pride on these students' faces was impossible to describe.

These were the two major keys to the success of this procedure:

- Alleviating nearly completely the learner's fear so that the student could learn the stroke
- Doing so in a very noninvasive way so that the guidance did not interfere with the actions the student was trying to produce

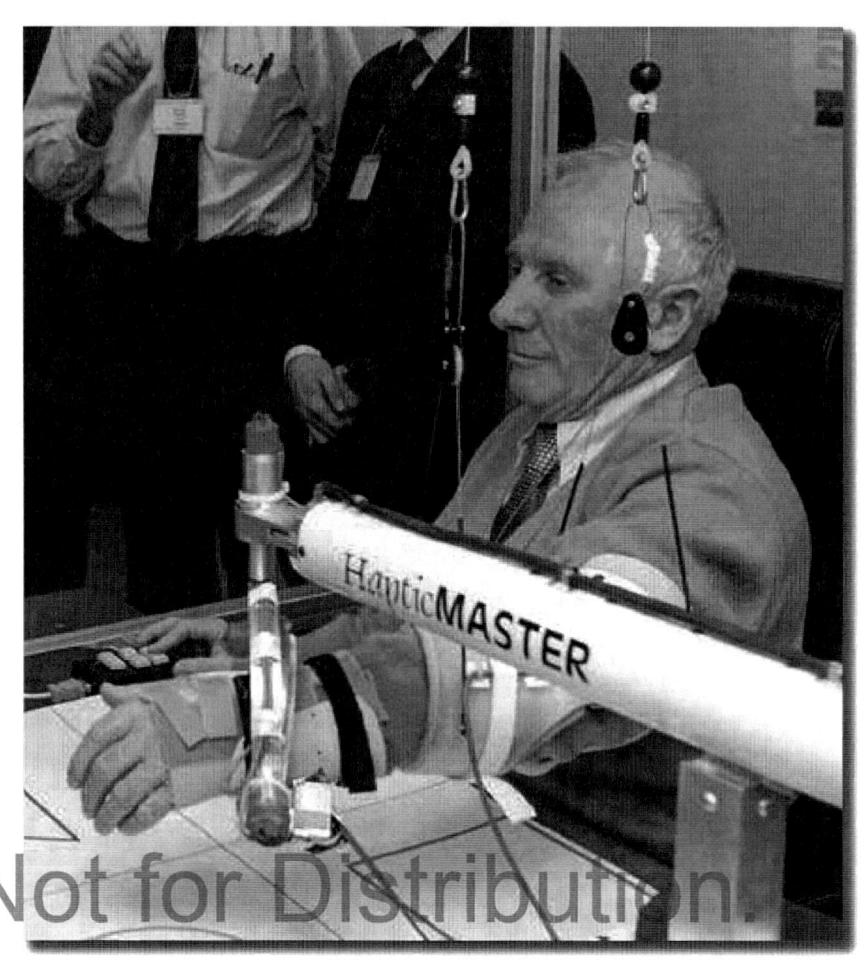

Special devices are being developed to assist stroke patients in their attempts to recover motor function, where factors such as amount of practice and practice variability come into effect.

physical guidance procedures), then practice on the guided version can be thought of as involving practice on a different task rather than practice on the unguided version. Under the specificity view, practice on the guided version will be effective for a retention test only under guided conditions; it will not be effective for a retention test performed under unguided conditions. This fits with the principle that transfer tends to be maximized when the two tasks are similar. Guided and unguided versions of the same task are thought of as dissimilar, leading to poor transfer between them.

Feedback After the Movement

The information-processing perspective about feedback holds that the learner uses feedback to correct errors. If the feedback presentation is separated in time (feedback delay) from the action and the learner forgets various aspects of the movement by the time feedback arrives, wouldn't the feedback be less useful in making corrections? In animal conditioning experiments, laboratory rats learning to press a bar after a presented tone suffer much from feedback delays; and, if the delay is long enough, there is no learning at all. Some researchers believed that the same would apply to humans and motor learning. But what does the evidence say?

Empty Feedback Delays

First, consider simply lengthening the time interval between a movement and its feedback, with the interval free of other attention-demanding activities (conversations, other trials, and so on). The information-processing view would expect longer intervals to interfere with learning. Yet when empty feedback delays have been examined in human research, scientists have almost never found systematic effects on learning (Salmoni, Schmidt, & Walter, 1984) with delays ranging from several seconds to several minutes. The lack of any degraded learning when the feedback delays are lengthened has been surprising. In any case, the evidence seems to suggest that, without other activities in the interval between a movement and its feedback, the instructor doesn't need to worry about the delay in giving feedback.

Instantaneous Feedback

There is one exception to this generalization about feedback delay, however—situations in which feedback is presented *very* soon after a movement. Under the belief that feedback given quickly will be beneficial for learning, many instructors have tried to minimize feedback delays, essentially giving feedback that is *almost simultaneous* with the completion of movement. Instantaneous feedback is common in many simulators, for example, such as medical mannequins, in which feedback about pressure is displayed immediately after a chest compression is performed.

Note that **instantaneous feedback** is not, technically, the same as concurrent feedback, because feedback is being delivered after the movement has finished. But the effects on performance and learning are remarkably similar to those for concurrent feedback. Research shows that giving feedback instantaneously, as opposed to delaying it by a few seconds, is actually detrimental to learning (Swinnen et al., 1990). This can be seen in figure 11.13: Subjects in the instantaneous-feedback condition (blue) performed a simulated batting task more poorly than the delayed group (red) on the second day of practice and on several retention tests given up to four months later. One interpretation is that feedback given instantaneously blocks the subject from processing inherent feedback (i.e., how the movement felt, sounded, looked). Attending to the augmented feedback from the instructor likely restricted the learning of error-detection capabilities, as discussed in chapter 9.

An interesting extension of these findings is that blocking instantaneous *inherent* (or *intrinsic*) feedback for a few seconds after a trial should also be effective for learning.

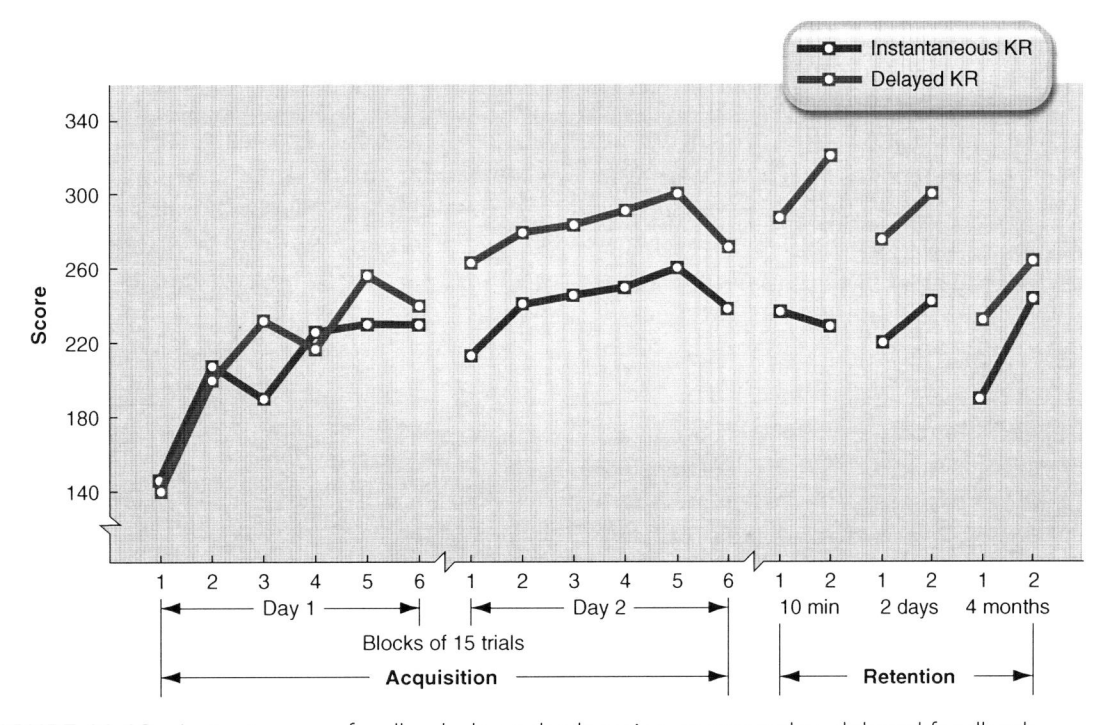

FIGURE 11.13 Instantaneous feedback degrades learning compared to delayed feedback.
Reprinted by permission from Swinnen et al. 1990.

This could be done by blocking the golfer's view of the ball's flight at a driving range, or using a blindfold for basketball dribbling practice. Curiously, one quite old study by Griffith (1931) used exactly this method to teach golf. After several weeks, learners who had practiced without the aid of vision of the club's contacting the ball were outperforming another group who had practiced with vision. To our knowledge, these methods have not been studied very thoroughly, so this extension of the findings should be regarded cautiously.

Filled Feedback-Delay Intervals

When the delays are long in many real-world settings, other attention-demanding activities can occur between a given movement and its feedback. These intervening activities may include conversing with a friend, practicing some other task, or even attempting other trials of the given movement as with the summary- and average-feedback methods discussed earlier in this chapter. The research findings fall into two classes, depending on the nature of the intervening task.

Intervening Activities of a Different Task Imagine that the activity occurring between a given movement and its feedback is a different task that interferes in some way. This activity could be a trial of a different motor task or even a task involving mental operations, such as recording one's scores or giving feedback to a friend. These events during the interval from the movement until feedback generally degrade learning as measured on retention tests (Marteniuk, 1986; Swinnen, 1990).

Trials-Delay Technique But what if the intervening activity is just another trial of the same motor task? For example, the instructor might give the learner several minutes to practice a skill, then give feedback about the first movement after the learner has completed several more attempts in the interim. For instance, feedback from a therapist to a patient when practicing to stand from a seated position might include statements such as "On your first attempt you started to stand before your feet were properly positioned under your knees," but this is provided after several more attempts at the sit-to-stand have already been completed. This has been called **trials delay of feedback**, with other trials of a given action intervening between the movement and its feedback.

Although the trials-delay procedure would seem to prevent the learner from associating the movement and the corresponding feedback, the evidence says that it is not detrimental at all; and it may be more effective for learning than presenting feedback after each trial (Lavery & Suddon, 1962). In fact, researchers have suggested that the performance of intervening trials before the delivery of feedback has the effect of raising awareness of the inherent feedback available after performing the task, perhaps making it more important or valuable when it is then presented to the learner (Anderson et al., 2005).

Intervening Subjective Estimations The conclusions of Anderson and colleagues (2005) just discussed support a view that learning is enhanced when processing of the inherent feedback occurs before augmented feedback is provided. This idea has been examined more directly in studies that promoted subjective estimation of task performance during the KR-delay period. For example, learners who practiced a throwing task with their nondominant limb performed more skillfully in retention tests if they made subjective estimates of their throwing technique during practice (Liu & Wrisberg, 1997). And a study by Guadagnoli and Kohl (2001) revealed that the negative effects of 100% KR frequency were reversed if learners made subjective estimates of error before the delivery of the feedback on each trial (see figure 11.14). Note, however, that a group (blue) that benefitted from having feedback presented on only 20% of their trials (the remaining trials received no feedback) received no further benefit (compared to the purple group) from error estimation, perhaps because this 20%

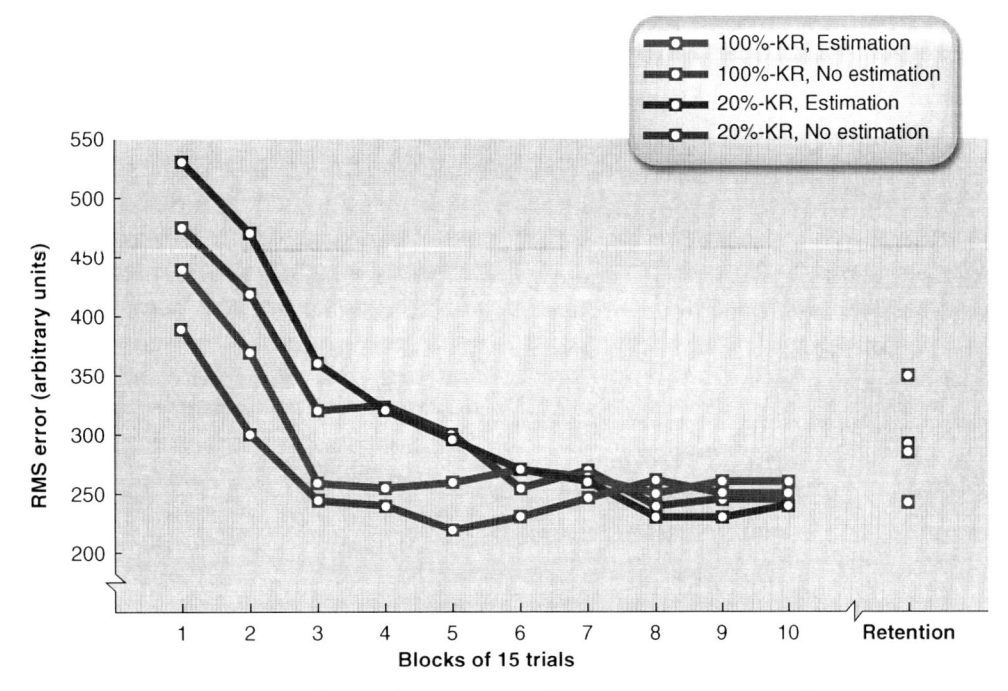

FIGURE 11.14 The negative effects of presenting feedback on every trial (100% KR) were reversed when subjects performed an error-estimation procedure. RMSE = root-mean-square error (see chapter 1).
Reprinted by permission from Guadagnoli and Kohl 2001.

group was estimating spontaneously on the no-feedback trials.

Together with the results of the trials-delay studies, these findings support a strong role for processing inherent (intrinsic) feedback information. It is important to remember that retention tests in all of these studies were performed without augmented feedback. Thus, the only information that a learner could use to check on performance accuracy in numerous trials of retention was the inherent sources of feedback that are always available, with inherent feedback being the basis for trial-to-trial corrections. Conditions of practice that encourage a more thorough appreciation and use of the information provided by inherent feedback promote learning that is more suited to performance in both (a) these no-augmented-feedback tests and (b) most real-world applications of these ideas.

Postfeedback Delay Intervals

After receiving feedback for one movement, in the postfeedback delay (see figure 11.11) the learner attempts to create another movement that is at least somewhat different from the previous one—a movement that will eliminate the errors signaled by feedback. How much time is required for processing this information, and how soon can the next movement begin? The research on these questions shows that if this interval is too short (less than 5 s), performance on the next trial will suffer, probably because of insufficient time to plan it. However, if the interval is somewhat longer (say, greater than 5 s), there is no advantage to giving the learner even more time to plan and generate the next movement (Weinberg, Guy, & Tupper, 1964). The interval would probably be a little longer in a task that is relatively complex or where many different decisions have to be made about alternative movement strategies and methods. Overall, though, the postfeedback interval is not particularly powerful in determining learning, and you can focus on more important aspects of the learning environment.

Summary

A learner can receive various kinds of sensory information, but augmented feedback about errors from the instructor is one of the most critical aspects of the learning environment. This kind of information can have several simultaneous roles: It can serve as an "energizer" to increase motivation; it can provide information, in which case it signals the nature and direction of errors and how to correct them; and it can produce a learner dependency, in which case performance suffers when the information is withdrawn. Feedback can take on many forms, such as videotape replays, films, and, of course, verbal descriptions. Verbal feedback is best when it is simple and refers to only one movement feature at a time, a movement feature that the learner can control.

The largest errors can be corrected in early learning with frequent feedback. After a few trials, however, learning is stronger if feedback frequency is gradually reduced (i.e., faded) across practice. Summary feedback, whereby a set of trial-results is described by a graph shown to the learner only after the set is completed, is particularly effective for learning; but the optimum number of trials included in the summary will decrease as task complexity increases. An early principle—that anything making feedback more frequent, accurate, and useful enhances learning—is being replaced by newer viewpoints that focus on the subtle aspects of feedback's nature and scheduling.

WEB STUDY GUIDE ACTIVITIES

Check Your Understanding

1. Define inherent and augmented feedback, highlighting the differences between them. Define knowledge of results and knowledge of performance, highlighting the differences between them. Provide an example of each of these types of feedback that a beginner watercolor artist might experience.

2. Briefly explain how each of the following can affect learning:
   - Frequency of feedback
   - Precision of feedback
   - Feedback schedules
   - Timing of feedback presentation

3. List and briefly discuss four properties of augmented feedback.

Apply Your Knowledge

1. A university wrestling coach is teaching his team some new ways to finish a takedown. One wrestler has been competing for 10 years and is the current national champion, while another is in her first year of university and has much less experience. Discuss some factors that the coach might consider when providing feedback to each of the wrestlers. Explain how the coach might provide feedback in order to benefit learning of the new skills and transfer to a wrestling match.

2. A physical education teacher is beginning a new unit, teaching the game of goalball to her high school class. In the game of goalball each player is blindfolded, and the ball used for play emits an auditory signal. Discuss three types of augmented feedback the teacher can use to provide feedback to the students during the class. Would the amount, precision, and frequency of feedback change from her earlier unit teaching handball? If so, how would it change?

Suggestions for Further Reading

A thorough review of the published research on feedback and motor learning by Salmoni, Schmidt, and Walter (1984) offers fuller details of the principles discussed here. An excellent review of the guidance research was written by Hodges and Campagnaro (2012). An important early review on videotape replays for motor learning was presented by Rothstein and Arnold (1976). And chapter 12 of Schmidt and Lee (2011) provides more detail on each of the sections presented in this chapter. See the reference list for these additional resources.

Draft. Not for Distribution.

Glossary

ability—A stable, enduring, mainly genetically-defined trait that underlies skilled performance, is largely inherited, and is not modifiable by practice.

absolute constant error (|CE|)—The absolute value of CE for a subject; a measure of amount of bias without respect to its direction.

absolute error (AE)—The average absolute deviation of each of a set of scores from a target value; a measure of overall error.

absolute frequency of feedback—The actual number of feedback presentations given in a series of practice trials.

Adams (closed-loop) theory—A theory of motor learning proposed by Adams (1971), focusing heavily on the learning of slow positioning movements.

ambient vision—See *dorsal stream*.

amplitude—The distance between the two target centers in aiming tasks ("A" in Fitts' Law).

anti-phase—A coordination timing pattern in which two movement components oscillate in opposition (180° relative phase).

arousal—An internal state of alertness or excitement.

attention—A limited capacity or set of capacities to process information.

augmented feedback—Information from the measured performance outcome that is fed back to the learner by some artificial means; sometimes called extrinsic feedback.

automatic processing—A mode of information processing that is fast, is done in parallel, is not attention demanding, and is often involuntary.

autonomous stage—The third of three stages of learning proposed by Fitts, in which the attention demands of performing a task have been greatly reduced.

average feedback—A type of augmented feedback that presents a statistical average of two or more trials, rather than results on any one of them.

bandwidth feedback—A procedure for delivering feedback in which errors are signaled only if they fall outside some range of correctness.

blindsight—A visual medical condition in which the patient can respond to certain visual stimuli while being judged legally blind by other criteria.

blocked practice—A schedule in which many trials on a single task are practiced consecutively; low contextual interference.

capability—The internal representation of skill, acquired during practice, that allows performance on some task.

central pattern generator (CPG)—A centrally-located control mechanism that produces mainly genetically defined actions such as walking.

choice reaction time—A variation in RT procedure in which the performer, when a particular stimulus is given, must choose one response (the "correct" response) from a number of possible predetermined responses; the temporal interval between the presentation of a given stimulus and the start of its associated response.

choking—Scenario in which a performer changes a normal routine or fails to adapt to a changing situation, resulting in a failed performance.

closed-loop control—A type of system control involving feedback, error detection, and error correction that is applicable to maintaining a system goal.

closed skill—A skill for which the environment is stable and predictable, allowing advance organization of movement.

cocktail-party effect—A phenomenon of attention in which humans can attend to a single conversation at a noisy gathering, neglecting most (but not all) other inputs.

cognitive stage of learning—The first of three stages of learning proposed by Fitts, in which the learners' performances are heavily based on cognitive or verbal processes.

comparator—A component of closed-loop control that compares anticipated feedback with actual feedback, finally outputting an error signal.

concurrent feedback—Augmented (usually continuous) feedback that is presented simultaneously with an ongoing action.

constant error (CE)—The signed difference of a score on a given trial from a target value; a measure of bias for that trial.

constant practice—A practice sequence in which only a single variation of a given class of tasks is experienced.

contextual interference—The interference in performance and learning that arises from performing one task in the context of other tasks; blocked practice has low contextual interference, and random practice has high contextual interference.

contextual-interference effect—The finding that groups of subjects who practice under high contextual interference do not perform well relative to blocked-practice subjects during acquisition, but outperform blocked-practice subjects when evaluated in transfer or retention tests; see *contextual interference*.

continuous skill—A task in which the action is performed without any recognizable beginning or end.

controlled processing—A mode of information processing that is relatively slow, serial, attention demanding, and voluntary.

correlation coefficient *(r)*—A statistical method that evaluates the strength of a relationship between two variables; it does not imply causality.

criterion task—The ultimate version, condition, or situation in which the skill learned in practice is to be applied; the ultimate goal of practice.

cutaneous receptor—A receptor located in the skin that provides inherent information about touch (haptic sensations).

deafferentation—A surgical procedure that involves cutting one or more of an animal's dorsal roots, preventing nerve impulses from the periphery from traveling to the spinal cord.

degrees of freedom—The collection of separate movements of a system that need to be controlled; see *degrees-of-freedom problem*.

degrees of freedom problem—The problem of explaining how a movement with many degrees of freedom is controlled or coordinated; see *degrees of freedom*.

demonstration—Performance of a skill by an instructor (or a model) to facilitate observational learning.

differential method—A method of understanding behavior by focusing on individual differences and abilities.

discrete skill—A task that has a recognizable beginning and end; usually brief in duration.

distributed practice—A practice schedule in which the duration of rest between practice trials is "relatively long"; the time in practice is often less than the time at rest.

dorsal stream—Visual information, used specifically for the control of movement within the visual environment, that is sent from the eye to the posterior parietal cortex; sometimes called ambient vision.

double stimulation paradigm—A method for studying information processing in which a given stimulus (leading to one response) is followed closely by a second stimulus (leading to another response).

effective target width (W_e)—The amount of spread, or variability, of movement end points about a target in an aiming task; represents the performer's "effective" target size; the within-subject standard deviation of the movement distances for a set of trials.

elaboration hypothesis—The idea that frequent switching among tasks (e.g., in random practice) renders the tasks more distinct from each other and more meaningful, resulting in stronger memory representations; one explanation of the contextual-interference effect.

error-detection capability—The learned capability to detect one's own errors through analyzing inherent feedback.

especial skills—A specific representation for one skill (e.g., free throw in basketball) within a broader class of skills (e.g., set shots in basketball).

experimental method—A method of understanding behavior emphasizing common principles among people and through the use of experiments.

external focus of attention—Attention directed outside the body to an object or environmental goal.

exteroception—Sensory information arising primarily from outside the body.

extrinsic feedback—See *augmented feedback.*

faded feedback—The practice in delivering feedback whereby the frequency of feedback is decreased systematically across trials.

faded frequency—A feedback schedule in which the relative frequency is high in early practice and reduced in later practice.

false-negative normative feedback—An experimental procedure in which learners are (mis)informed that their performance is less skilled than that of others.

false-positive normative feedback—An experimental procedure in which learners are (mis)informed that their performance on some task is more skilled than that of others.

far transfer—Transfer of learning from one task to another, very different task or setting.

feedback—Information provided to the learner about the action just made; often synonymous with augmented feedback.

feedback delay interval—The interval of time from the end of the movement until the feedback is presented.

feedforward—Anticipated sensory consequences of movement that should occur if the movement is correct.

Fitts' Law—The principle that movement time in aiming tasks is linearly related to the $Log_2(2A/W)$, where A = amplitude and W = target width.

fixation (associative or motor) stage—The second of three stages of learning proposed by Fitts, in which learners establish motor patterns.

focal vision—See *ventral stream.*

foreperiod—In a reaction time task, the interval of time between a warning signal and a stimulus to respond.

forgetting—The loss of an acquired capability for responding; loss of memory.

forgetting hypothesis—The hypothesis that frequent task switching in random practice causes forgetting of the planning done on the previous trial, therefore leading to more next-trial planning and resulting in stronger memory representations; a hypothesis to explain the contextual-interference effect.

gearshift analogy—A model regarding the learning of motor programs using the analogy of learning to shift gears in a standard-transmission automobile.

generalizability—The process of applying what is learned in the practice of one task to one or more other unpracticed tasks.

generalized motor program (GMP)—A motor program whose output can vary along certain dimensions to produce novelty and generalizability in movement.

general motor ability—An older, incorrect view in which a single, general ability was thought to underlie individual differences in motor behavior; sometimes called motor educability.

goal setting—A motivational procedure in which the learner is encouraged to set personal performance goals during practice.

Golgi tendon organs—Small stretch receptors located in the tendons that provide precise information about muscle tension.

guidance—A procedure used in practice in which the learner is physically or verbally directed through the performance in order to improve performance.

guidance hypothesis—A view emphasizing the guidance properties of augmented feedback, which promotes effective performance when it is present but has dependency-producing (guidance-like) effects on retention tests of learning.

Hick's Law—The mathematical descriptor showing a linear relationship between choice reaction time and the logarithm (to the base 2) of the number of stimulus–response alternatives.

hypervigilance—A heightened state of arousal that leads to ineffective decision making and poor performance; panic.

inattention blindness—A failure to perceive objects in the visual environment when attention is directed to other objects or events.

index of difficulty (ID)—The theoretical "difficulty" of a movement in the Fitts tapping task, or ID = $\text{Log}_2(2A/W)$, where A is target amplitude and W is target width.

individual differences—Stable, enduring differences among people in terms of some measurable characteristic (e.g., age) or performance of some task (e.g., reaction time).

information-processing approach—Approaches to the study of behavior that treat the human as a processor of information, focusing on storage, coding, retrieval, and transformation of information.

inherent feedback—Information provided as a natural consequence of making an action; sometimes called intrinsic feedback.

in-phase—A coordination timing pattern in which two movement components oscillate in synchrony (0° relative phase).

instantaneous feedback—Augmented feedback delivered immediately after completion of movement (with no delay).

internal focus of attention—Attention directed to locations inside the body, or to motor or sensory information.

interstimulus interval (ISI)—See *stimulus-onset asynchrony.*

intrinsic feedback—See *inherent feedback.*

invariant feature—A feature of a class of movements that remains constant, or invariant, while surface features change (e.g., relative timing).

inverted-U principle—The principle that increased arousal improves performance only to a point, with degraded performance as arousal is increased further.

joint receptors—Sensory receptors located in the joint capsule that provide information about joint position.

knowledge of performance (KP)—Augmented information about the movement pattern the learner has just made; sometimes referred to as kinematic feedback.

knowledge of results (KR)—Augmented verbal (or at least verbalizable) information fed back to the learner about the success of an action with respect to the environmental goal.

lead-up activities—Special tasks designed to be learned before the practice of a more complicated or dangerous criterion task.

learner-determined feedback—A schedule in which the provision of feedback is determined by the learner.

learning curves—A label sometimes applied to a performance curve (a plot of average performance against trials), in the mistaken belief that the changes in performance mirror changes in learning.

long-term memory (LTM)—A virtually limitless memory store for information, facts, concepts, and relationships; presumably storage for movement programs.

looked-but-failed-to-see accidents—Traffic accidents in which the driver looked at, but failed to notice (to see) the presence of a cyclist or pedestrian; believed to be related to inattention blindness.

M1 response—The monosynaptic stretch reflex, with a latency of 30 to 50 ms.

M2 response—The polysynaptic, or functional, stretch reflex, with a latency of 50 to 80 ms.

M3 response—The voluntary reaction-time response to a stimulus, with a latency of 120 to 180 ms.

massed practice—A practice schedule in which the amount of rest between practice trials is relatively short; in massed practice, the amount of rest between trials is often less than the time for a trial.

mental practice—A practice procedure in which the learner imagines successful action without overt physical practice.

modeling—A practice procedure in which another person demonstrates the skills to be learned.

motor learning—A set of internal processes associated with practice or experience leading to relatively permanent gains in the capability for skilled performance.

motor program—A prestructured set of movement commands that defines the essential details of skilled action, with minimal (or no) involvement of sensory feedback.

movement programming—The third stage of information processing in which the motor system is readied for the planned action.

movement time (MT)—The interval from the initiation of a movement until its termination.

muscle spindle—Structure located in parallel with muscle fibers that provides information about muscle length.

near transfer—Transfer of learning from one task or setting to another that is very similar.

novelty problem—The concern that simple theories cannot account for the production of novel, unpracticed movements.

observational learning—The process by which the learner acquires the capability for action by observing model demonstrations.

open-loop control—A type of system control in which instructions for the effector system are determined in advance and run off without feedback.

open skill—A skill for which the environment is unpredictable or unstable, preventing advance organization of movement.

optical array—The collection of rays of light that are reflected from objects in the visual environment.

optical flow—The change in patterns of light rays from the environment as they "flow" over the retina during continuous movement of the eye through the environment, allowing perception of motion, position, and timing.

parameterized—The process whereby parameters are supplied to the general motor program to define its surface features.

parameters—Values applied to a generalized motor program that determine a movement's surface features, such as speed, amplitude, or limb used.

part practice—A procedure in which a complex skill is broken down into parts that are practiced separately.

perceptual narrowing—The tendency for the perceptual field to "shrink"; sometimes called tunnel vision, or "weapon focus" in police work.

performance curve—Plots of average performance for an individual or a group plotted against practice trials; sometimes incorrectly called a learning curve.

physical fidelity—The degree to which the surface features of a simulation and the criterion task are identical.

population stereotypes—Habitual stimulus–response relationships that dominate behavior due to specific cultural learning.

postfeedback delay—The interval of time between the presentation of augmented feedback and the start of the next movement.

precision of feedback—The level of precision with which augmented feedback describes the movement or outcome produced.

prediction—The process of using people's abilities to estimate their probable success in various occupations or sports.

probe-task technique—A method that uses an RT task as a secondary task during the performance of a primary, criterion task to assess the attention demands of the criterion task.

progressive part practice—A procedure in which parts of a skill are gradually integrated into larger units.

proprioception—Sensory information arising from within the body, resulting in the sense of position and movement; sometimes called kinesthesis.

psychological fidelity—The degree to which the behaviors produced in a simulator are identical to the behaviors required by the criterion task.

psychological refractory period (PRP)—The delay in responding to the second of two closely spaced stimuli.

quiet-eye effect—The period of time when a performer fixates the eyes on a target just before movement onset.

random (or interleaved) practice—A schedule in which practice trials on several different tasks are mixed, or interleaved, across the practice period; high contextual interference.

reaction time (RT)—The interval from presentation of an unanticipated stimulus until the beginning of the response.

reference tests—Well-studied tests thought to measure abilities of various kinds (e.g., reaction time, movement time, spatial relations).

reflex-reversal phenomenon—The phenomenon by which a given stimulus can produce two different reflexive responses depending on the function of the limb in a movement.

relative-age effect—Phenomenon in which members of an age-normative team who are born early in a given year are "relatively older" than teammates born late in the year.

relative frequency of feedback—The proportion of trials during practice on which feedback is given; absolute frequency divided by the number of trials.

relative timing—The temporal structure or rhythm of action; the durations of various segments of an action divided by the total movement time.

repetition—A type of ineffective practice in which a movement is repeated again and again.

response selection—The second stage of information processing in which the system selects a response from a number of alternatives.

response time—The sum of reaction time plus movement time; sometimes called total time.

retention test—A performance test on a given task provided after a retention interval without practice; sometimes called a transfer test.

root-mean-square error (RMSE)—The square root of the average squared deviations of a set of values from a target value; typically used as a measure of overall tracking proficiency.

schema—A learned rule relating the outcomes of members of a class of actions to the parameters that were used to produce those outcomes.

schema theory—A theory of motor control and learning based on generalized motor programs and schemata.

self-organization—A view that describes motor control as emerging from the interaction of the components of the movement system and the environment.

self-regulation—Technique used in motor learning studies in which the learners determine how to schedule practice or feedback or some other aspect of scheduling.

sensory neuropathy—A medical condition in patients who are unable to process and respond to most of their own sensory feedback.

serial skill—A task composed of several discrete actions strung together, often with the order of actions being critical for success.

set—A collection of psychological activities or adjustments that underlie performance but that can be "lost" after a rest.

short-term memory (STM)—A memory store with a capacity of about seven elements, capable of holding information briefly (perhaps up to 30 s); sometimes called "working memory."

short-term sensory store (STSS)—A functionally limitless memory store for holding literal, sensory information from the various senses very briefly (for only about 1 s).

simple RT—A reaction-time situation in which there is only one possible stimulus and one response.

simulator—A training device that mimics various features of some real-world task.

skill—The capability to bring about an end result with maximum certainty, minimum energy, or minimum time; task proficiency that can be modified by practice.

spatial anticipation—The anticipation of which of several possible stimuli will occur; sometimes called event anticipation.

specificity of individual differences—A view of motor abilities holding that tasks are composed of many unrelated abilities.

specificity of learning—A view that what you practice is what you learn. See *specificity of hypothesis*.

speed–accuracy trade-off—The tendency for accuracy to decrease as the movement speed or velocity of a movement increases and vice versa.

startle RT—A rapid (<100 ms latency) reaction to an unexpected, often very loud, stimulus; used to study the involuntary release of motor programs.

stimulus-onset asynchrony (SOA)—The interval between the onsets of the two stimuli in a double-stimulation paradigm; sometimes called the interstimulus interval (ISI).

stimulus identification—The first stage of information processing in which a stimulus is recognized and identified.

stimulus–response (S-R) compatibility—The degree of "naturalness" (or directness) between the stimulus and the response assigned to it.

storage problem—The concern that simple program theories would require an almost limitless storage capacity for nearly countless different movements.

summary feedback—Information about the effectiveness of performance on a series of trials that is presented only after the series has been completed.

superability—A weak general ability thought to contribute to all tasks.

surface feature—An easily changeable aspect of a movement, such as movement time or amplitude, that does not affect the "deep structure" (the invariant features).

sustained attention—Maintenance of attention over long periods of work, such as monitoring a radar-based aircraft detection device; sometimes called vigilance.

Tau τ—A variable providing optical information about time-to-contact; the size of the retinal image divided by the rate of change of the image.

temporal anticipation—The anticipation of when a given stimulus will arrive or when a movement is to be made.

tracking—A class of tasks in which a moving track must be followed, typically by movements of a manual control.

transfer of learning—The gain or the loss in proficiency on one task as a result of practice or experience on another task.

transfer test—A performance test in which the task or task conditions have changed; often provided after a retention interval without practice.

trials delay of feedback—A procedure in which the presentation of feedback for a movement is delayed; during the delay the learner practices one or more other trials of the same task.

triggered reactions—Coordinated, learned reactions to perturbations that are manifest in large segments of the body; the triggered reaction has a latency shorter than RT yet longer than the long-loop reflex (50 to 80 ms).

unintended acceleration—Sudden, uncommanded, violent acceleration of a vehicle accompanied by the perception of a loss of braking effectiveness.

variable error (VE)—The standard deviation of a set of scores about the subject's own average (CE) score; a measure of movement (in)consistency.

variable practice—A schedule of practice in which many variations of a class of actions are practiced.

ventral stream—Information useful for the identification of an object that is sent to the inferotemporal cortex; sometimes called focal vision.

vestibular apparatus—Receptors in the inner ear that are sensitive to the orientation of the head with respect to gravity, to rotation of the head, and to balance.

warm-up decrement—Temporary worsening of performance that is brought on by the passage of time away from a task and that is eliminated quickly when the performer begins again.

whole practice—A procedure in which a skill is practiced in its entirety, without separation into its parts.

width—The size of a target in aiming tasks ("W" in Fitts' Law).

yoking—A type of control procedure in which a practice schedule is determined by a learner in a different experimental group or condition.

References

Abbs, J.H., Gracco, V.L., & Cole, K.J. (1984). Control of multimovement coordination: Sensorimotor mechanisms in speech motor programming. *Journal of Motor Behavior, 16,* 195-232.

Abernethy, B., Farrow, D., Gorman, A., & Mann, D. (2012). Anticipatory behavior and expert performance. In N.J. Hodges & A.M. Williams (Eds.), *Skill acquisition in sport: Research, theory, and practice* (2nd ed.) (pp. 287-305). London, UK: Routledge.

Abernethy, B., & Wood, J.M. (2001). Do generalized visual training programmes for sport really work? An experimental investigation. *Journal of Sports Sciences, 19,* 203-222.

Ackerman, P.L. (2007). New developments in understanding skilled performance. *Current Directions in Psychological Science, 16,* 235-239.

Adams, J.A. (1952). Warmup decrement in performance on the pursuit-rotor. *American Journal of Psychology, 65,* 404-414.

Adams, J.A. (1953). *The prediction of performance at advanced stages of training on a complex psychomotor task.* Res. Bull. 5349. Lackland Air Force Base, TX: Human Resources Research Center.

Adams, J.A. (1956). *An evaluation of test items measuring motor abilities.* Research Rep. AFPTRCTN5655. Lackland Air Force Base, TX: Human Resources Research Center.

Adams, J.A. (1961). The second facet of forgetting: A review of warmup decrement. *Psychological Bulletin, 58,* 257-273.

Adams, J.A. (1971). A closedloop theory of motor learning. *Journal of Motor Behavior, 3,* 111-150.

Adams, J.A. (1976). *Learning and memory: An introduction.* Homewood, IL: Dorsey.

Adams, J.A. (1987). Historical review and appraisal of research on the learning, retention, and transfer of human motor skills. *Psychological Bulletin, 101,* 41-74.

Adams, J.A., & Dijkstra, S. (1966). Short-term memory for motor responses. *Journal of Experimental Psychology, 71,* 314-318.

Alexander, R.M. (2003). *Principles of animal locomotion.* Princeton, NJ: Princeton University Press.

Allard, F., & Burnett, N. (1985). Skill in sport. *Canadian Journal of Psychology, 39,* 294-312.

Ammons, R.N., Farr, R.G., Block, E., Neumann, E., Dey, M., Marion, R., & Ammons, C.H. (1958). Long-term retention of perceptual motor skills. *Journal of Experimental Psychology, 55,* 318-328.

Anderson, D.I., Magill, R.A., Sekiya, H., & Ryan, G. (2005). Support for an explanation of the guidance effect in motor skill learning. *Journal of Motor Behavior, 37,* 231-238.

Annett, J. (1959). Learning a pressure under conditions of immediate and delayed knowledge of results. *Quarterly Journal of Experimental Psychology, 11,* 3-15.

Anson, J.G., Elliott, D., & Davids, K. (2005). Information processing and constraints-based views of skill acquisition: Divergent or complementary? *Motor Control, 9,* 217-241.

Armstrong, T.R. (1970). *Training for the production of memorized movement patterns.* Tech. Rep. No. 26. Ann Arbor, MI: University of Michigan, Department of Psychology.

Arps, G.F. (1920). Work with knowledge of results versus work without knowledge of results. *Psychological Monographs, 28,* 1-41.

Asundi, K., & Odell, D. (2011). Effects of keyboard keyswitch design: A review of the current literature. *Work, 39,* 151-159.

Ayres, T.J., Schmidt, R.A., Steele, B.D., & Bayan, F.P. (1995). Visibility and judgment in car-truck night accidents. In D.W. Pratt (Ed.), *Safety engineering and risk analysis—1995* (pp. 43-50). New York: American Society of Mechanical Engineers.

Baddeley, A.D., & Longman, D.J.A. (1978). The influence of length and frequency of training session on the rate of learning to type. *Ergonomics, 21,* 627-635.

Bahrick, H.P., Fitts, P.M., & Briggs, G.E. (1957). Learning curves—facts or artifacts? *Psychological Bulletin, 54,* 256-268.

Banala, S.K., Kim, S.H., Agrawal, S.K., & Scholz, J.P. (2009). Robot assisted gait training with active leg exoskeleton (ALEX). *IEEE Transactions on Neural Systems and Rehabilitation Engineering, 17,* 2-8.

Barnett, J.L., Ross, D., Schmidt, R.A., & Todd, B. (1973). Motor skills learning and the specificity of training principle. *Research Quarterly, 44,* 440-447.

Barnsley, R.H., Thompson, A.H., & Legault, P. (1992). Family planning: Football style, the relative age effect in football. *International Review for the Sociology of Sport, 27,* 77-78.

Bartlett, F.C. (1932). *Remembering: A study in experimental and social psychology.* Cambridge: Cambridge University Press.

Battig, W.F. (1966). Facilitation and interference. In E.A. Bilodeau (Ed.), *Acquisition of skill* (pp. 215-244). New York: Academic Press.

Beilock, S.L. (2010). *Choke: What the secrets of the brain reveal about success and failure at work and at play.* New York: Simon & Schuster.

Beilock, S.L., Carr, T.H., MacMahon, C., & Starkes, J.L. (2002). When paying attention becomes counterproductive: Impact of divided versus skill-focused attention on novice and experienced performance of sensorimotor skills. *Journal of Experimental Psychology: Applied, 8,* 6-16.

Belen'kii, V.Y., Gurfinkel, V.S., & Pal'tsev, Y.I. (1967). Elements of control of voluntary movements. *Biofizika, 12,* 135-141.

Bender, P.A. (1987). *Extended practice and patterns of bimanual interference.* Unpublished doctoral dissertation, University of Southern California.

Bernstein, N.A. (1967). *The co-ordination and regulation of movements.* Oxford: Pergamon Press.

Bilodeau, I.M. (1966). Information feedback. In E.A. Bilodeau (Ed.), *Acquisition of skill* (pp. 255-296). New York: Academic Press.

Bjork, R.A. (2011). On the symbiosis of learning, remembering, and forgetting. In A.S. Benjamin (Ed.), *Successful remembering and successful forgetting: A Festschrift in honor of Robert A. Bjork* (pp. 1-22). London, UK: Psychology Press.

Blouin, J., Gauthier, G.M., Vercher, J.L., & Cole, J. (1996). The relative contribution of retinal and extraretinal signals in determining the accuracy of reaching movements in normal subjects and a deafferented patient. *Experimental Brain Research, 109,* 148-153.

Bourne, L.E. Jr., & Archer, E.J. (1956). Time continuously on target as a function of distribution of practice. *Journal of Experimental Psychology, 51,* 25-33.

Boutcher, S.H., & Crews, D.J. (1987). The effect of a preshot attentional routine on a well-learned skill. *International Journal of Sport Psychology, 18,* 30-39.

Boyce, B.A. (1992). Effects of assigned versus participant-set goals on skill acquisition and retention of a selected shooting task. *Journal of Teaching in Physical Education, 11,* 220-234.

Brace, D.K. (1927). *Measuring motor ability.* New York: A.S. Barnes.

Breslin, G., Hodges, N.J., Steenson, A., & Williams, A.M. (2012). Constant or variable practice: Recreating the especial skill effect. *Acta Psychologica, 140,* 154-157.

Bridgeman, B., Kirch, M., & Sperling, A. (1981). Segregation of cognitive and motor aspects of visual information using induced motion. *Perception & Psychophysics, 29,* 336-342.

Brown, I.D. (2005). *Review of the "looked but failed to see" accident causation factor.* Road Safety Res. Rep. No. 60. Cambridge, England: Ivan Brown Associates.

Brown, I.D., Tickner, A.H., & Simmons, D.C.V. (1969). Interference between concurrent tasks of driver and telephoning. *Journal of Applied Psychology, 53,* 419-424.

Bryan, W.L., & Harter, N. (1897). Studies in the physiology and psychology of the telegraphic language. *Psychological Review, 4,* 27-53.

Bryan, W.L., & Harter, N. (1899). Studies on the telegraphic language: The acquisition of a hierarchy of habits. *Psychological Review, 6,* 345-375.

Cahill, L., McGaugh, J.L., & Weinberger, N.M. (2001). The neurobiology of learning and memory: Some reminders to remember. *Trends in Neurosciences, 24,* 578-581.

Card, S.K., English, W.K., & Burr, B.J. (1978). Evaluation of mouse, rate-controlled isometric joystick, step keys, and text keys for text selection on a CRT. *Ergonomics, 21,* 601-613.

Carlsen, A.N., Maslovat, D., Lam, M.Y., Chua, R., & Franks, I.M. (2011). Considerations for the use of a startling acoustic stimulus in studies of motor preparation in humans. *Neuroscience and Biobehavioral Reviews, 35,* 366-376.

Carron, A.V. (1967). *Performance and learning in a discrete motor task under massed versus distributed conditions.* Unpublished doctoral dissertation, University of California, Berkeley.

Carron, A.V., Loughhead, T.M., & Bray, S.R. (2005). The home advantage in sport competitions: Courneya and Carron's (1992) conceptual framework a decade later. *Journal of Sports Sciences, 23,* 395-407.

Catalano, J.F., & Kleiner, B.M. (1984). Distant transfer in coincident timing as a function of practice variability. *Perceptual and Motor Skills, 58,* 851-856.

Cha, Y.J., Yoo, E.Y., Jung, M.Y, Park, S.H., & Park, J.H. (2012). Effects of functional task training with mental practice in stroke: A meta analysis. *NeuroRehabilitation, 30,* 239-246.

Chabris, C.F., & Simons, D.J. (2010). *The invisible gorilla: And other ways our intuitions deceive us.* New York: Crown.

Chase, W.G., & Simon, H.A. (1973). Perception in chess. *Cognitive Psychology, 4,* 55-81.

Cherry, E.C. (1953). Some experiments on the recognition of speech, with one and two ears. *Journal of the Acoustical Society of America, 25,* 975-979.

Chiviacowsky, S., & Wulf, G. (2002). Self-controlled feedback: Does it enhance learning because performers get feedback when they need it? *Research Quarterly for Exercise and Sport, 73,* 408-415.

Chiviacowsky, S., & Wulf, G. (2007). Feedback after good trials enhances learning. *Research Quarterly for Exercise and Sport, 78,* 40-47.

Choi, Y., Qi, F., Gordon, J., & Schweighofer, N. (2008). Performance-based adaptive schedules enhance motor learning. *Journal of Motor Behavior, 40,* 273-280.

Christina, R.W. (1992). The 1991 C.H. McCloy research lecture: Unraveling the mystery of the response complexity effect in skilled movements. *Research Quarterly for Exercise and Sport, 63,* 218-230.

Chun, M.M., Golomb, J.D., & Turk-Browne, N.B. (2011). A taxonomy of external and internal attention. *Annual Review of Psychology, 62,* 73-101.

Cobley, S., Baker, J., Wattie, N., & McKenna, J. (2009). Annual age-grouping and athlete development: A meta-analytical review of relative age effects in sport. *Sports Medicine, 39,* 235-256.

Cormier, S.M., & Hagman, J.D. (Eds.) (1987). *Transfer of learning: Contemporary research applications.* New York: Academic Press.

Crawley, S.L. (1926). An experimental investigation of recovery from work. *Archives of Psychology, 13,* 85.

Crossman, E.R.F.W. (1959). A theory of the acquisition of speed skill. *Ergonomics, 2,* 153-166.

Cuddy, L.J., & Jacoby, L.L. (1982). When forgetting helps memory. An analysis of repetition effects. *Journal of Verbal Learning and Verbal Behavior, 21,* 451-467.

Dail, T.K., & Christina, R.W. (2004). Distribution of practice and metacognition in learning and retention of a discrete motor task. *Research Quarterly for Exercise and Sport, 75,* 148-155.

Davies, D.R., & Parasuraman, R. (1982). *The psychology of vigilance.* New York: Academic Press.

Davis, R. (1988). The role of "attention" in the psychological refractory period. *Quarterly Journal of Experimental Psychology, 11,* 127-134.

Deci, E.L., & Ryan, R.M. (2000). The "what" and "why" of goal pursuits: Human needs and the self-determination of behavior. *Psychological Inquiry, 11,* 227-268.

de Gelder, B., Tamietto, M., van Boxtel, G., Goebal, R., Sahraie, A., van den Stock, J., Stienen, B.M.C., Weiskranz, L., & Pegna, A. (2008). Intact navigation skills after bilateral loss of striate cortex. *Current Biology, 18,* R1128-R1129.

deGroot, A.D. (1946/1978). *Thought and choice in chess.* The Hague: Mouton. (Original work published in 1946).

Dickstein, R., & Deutsch, J.E. (2007). Motor imagery in physical therapist practice. *Physical Therapy, 87,* 942-953.

Diedrich, F.J., & Warren, W.H. Jr. (1995). Why change gaits? Dynamics of the walk-run transition. *Journal of Experimental Psychology: Human Perception and Performance, 21,* 183-202.

Donders, F.C. (1969). On the speed of mental processes. In W.G. Koster (Ed. & Trans.), *Attention and performance II.* Amsterdam: North-Holland. (Original work published in 1868).

Drowatzky, J.N., & Zuccato, F.C. (1967). Interrelationships between selected measures of static and dynamic balance. *Research Quarterly, 38,* 509-510.

Easterbrook, J.A. (1959). The effect of emotion on cue utilization and the organization of behavior. *Psychological Review, 66,* 183-201.

Elliott, D., Hansen, S., & Grierson, L.E.M. (2010). The legacy of R.S. Woodworth: The two-component model revisited. In D. Elliott & M. Khan (Eds.), *Vision and goal-directed movement: Neurobehavioral perspectives* (pp. 5-19). Champaign, IL: Human Kinetics.

Elliott, D., Helsen, W.F., & Chua, R. (2001). A century later: Woodworth's (1899) two-component model of goal-directed aiming. *Psychological Bulletin, 127,* 342-357.

Elliott, D., & Khan, M. (Eds.) (2010). *Vision and goal-directed movement: Neurobehavioral perspectives.* Champaign, IL: Human Kinetics.

Eysenck, M.W., Derakshan, N., Santos, R., & Calvo, M.G. (2007). Anxiety and cognitive performance: Attentional control theory. *Emotion, 7,* 336-353.

Farrell, J.E. (1975). The classification of physical education skills. *Quest, 24,* 63-68.

Feltz, D.L., & Landers, D.M. (1983). The effects of mental practice on motor skill learning and performance: A meta-analysis. *Journal of Sport Psychology, 5,* 25-57.

Fenney, A., & Lee, T.D. (2010). Exploring spared capacity in persons with dementia: What Wii can learn. *Activities, Adaptation & Aging, 34,* 303-313.

Fischman, M.G., Christina, R.W., & Anson, J.G. (2008). Memory drum theory's C movement: Revelations from Franklin Henry. *Research Quarterly for Exercise and Sport, 79,* 312-318.

Fitts, P.M. (1954). The information capacity of the human motor system in controlling the amplitude of movement. *Journal of Experimental Psychology, 47,* 381-391.

Fitts, P.M. (1964). Perceptual-motor skills learning. In A.W. Melton (Ed.), *Categories of human learning* (pp. 243-285). New York: Academic Press.

Fitts, P.M., Bahrick, H.P., Noble, M.E., & Briggs, G.E. (1959). *Skilled performance.* Contract No. AF 41 [657]-70. Columbus, OH: Ohio State University, Wright Air Development Center.

Fitts, P.M., & Peterson, J.R. (1964). Information capacity of discrete motor responses. *Journal of Experimental Psychology, 67,* 103-112.

Fitts, P.M., & Posner, M.I. (1967). *Human performance.* Belmont, CA: Brooks/Cole.

Fleishman, E.A. (1956). Psychomotor selection tests: Research and application in the United States Air Force. *Personnel Psychology, 9,* 449-467.

Fleishman, E.A. (1957). A comparative study of aptitude patterns in unskilled and skilled psychomotor performances. *Journal of Applied Psychology, 41,* 263-272.

Fleishman, E.A. (1964). *The structure and measurement of physical fitness.* Englewood Cliffs, NJ: Prentice Hall.

Fleishman, E.A., & Bartlett, C.J. (1969). Human abilities. *Annual Review of Psychology, 20,* 349-380.

Fleishman, E.A., & Hempel, W.E. (1955). The relation between abilities and improvement with practice in a visual discrimination task. *Journal of Experimental Psychology, 49,* 301-312.

Fleishman, E.A., & Parker, J.F. (1962). Factors in the retention and relearning of perceptual motor skill. *Journal of Experimental Psychology, 64,* 215-226.

Fleishman, E.A., & Stephenson, R.W. (1970). *Development of a taxonomy of human performance: A review of the third year's progress.* Tech. Rep. No. 726-TPR3. Silver Spring, MD: American Institutes for Research.

Forssberg, H., Grillner, S., & Rossignol, S. (1975). Phase dependent reflex reversal during walking in chronic spinal cats. *Brain Research, 85,* 103-107.

Fritsch, G., & Hitzig, E. (1870). Über die elektrischeErregbarkeit des Grosshirns. *Archiv Anatomie Physiologie, 37,* 300-332.

Fullerton, G.S., & Cattell, J. (1892). On the perception of small differences. *University of Pennsylvania Philosophical Series,* No. 2.

Furley, P., Memmert, D., & Heller, C. (2010). The dark side of visual awareness in sport: Inattentional blindness in a real-world basketball task. *Attention, Perception & Psychophysics, 72,* 1327-1337.

Garrison, K.A., Winstein, C.J., & Aziz-Zadeh, L. (2010). The mirror neuron system: A neural substrate for methods in stroke rehabilitation. *Neurorehabilitation and Neural Repair, 24,* 404-412.

Gentile, A.M. (1972). A working model of skill acquisition with application to teaching. *Quest, 17,* 3-23.

Gentile, A.M. (2000). Skill acquisition: Action, movement, and neuromotor processes. In J.H. Carr & R.H. Shepherd (Eds.), *Movement science: Foundation for physical therapy in rehabilitation* (2nd ed.) (pp. 111-180). Gaithersburg, MD: Aspen.

Gentner, D.R. (1987). Timing of skilled motor performance: Tests of the proportional duration model. *Psychological Review, 94,* 255-276.

Ghez, C., & Krakauer, J. (2000). The organization of movement. In E.R. Kandel, J.H. Schwartz, & T.M. Jessell (Eds.), *Principles of neural science* (pp. 653-673). New York: McGraw-Hill.

Gibson, J.J. (1966). *The senses considered as perceptual systems.* Boston: Houghton Mifflin.

Gladwell, M. (2000). *The tipping point: How little things can make a big difference.* New York: Little, Brown.

Gladwell, M. (2008). *Outliers: The story of success.* New York: Little, Brown.

Goode, S., & Magill, R.A. (1986). Contextual interference effects in learning three badminton serves. *Research Quarterly for Exercise and Sport, 57,* 308-314.

Gray, R. (2009). How do batters use visual, auditory, and tactile information about the success of a baseball swing? *Research Quarterly for Exercise and Sport, 80,* 491-501.

Griffith, C.R. (1931). An experiment on learning to drive a golf ball. *Athletic Journal, 11,* 11-13.

Grillner, S. (1975). Locomotion in vertebrates: Central mechanisms and reflex interaction. *Physiological Reviews, 55,* 247-304.

Guadagnoli, M.A., Dornier, L.A., & Tandy, R.D. (1996). Optimal length for summary knowledge of results: The influence of task-related experience and complexity. *Research Quarterly for Exercise and Sport, 67,* 239-248.

Guadagnoli, M.A., & Kohl, R.M. (2001). Knowledge of results for motor learning: Relationship between error estimation and knowledge of results frequency. *Journal of Motor Behavior, 33,* 217-224.

Guadagnoli, M.A., & Lee, T.D. (2004). Challenge point: A framework for conceptualizing the effects of various practice conditions in motor learning. *Journal of Motor Behavior, 36,* 212-224.

Guthrie, E.R. (1952). *The psychology of learning.* New York: Harper & Row.

Haken, H., Kelso, J.A.S., & Bunz, H. (1985). A theoretical model of phase transitions in human hand movements. *Biological Cybernetics, 51,* 347-356.

Hall, K.G., Domingues, D.A., & Cavazos, R. (1994). Contextual interference effects with skilled baseball players. *Perceptual and Motor Skills, 78,* 835-841.

Helmuth, L.L., & Ivry, R.B. (1996). When two hands are better than one: Reduced timing variability during bimanual movement. *Journal of Experimental Psychology: Human Perception and Performance, 22,* 278-293.

Henry, F.M. (1968). Specificity vs. generality in learning motor skill. In R.C. Brown & G.S. Kenyon (Eds.), *Classical studies on physical activity* (pp. 331-340). Englewood Cliffs, NJ: Prentice Hall. (Original work published in 1958).

Henry, F.M., & Rogers, D.E. (1960). Increased response latency for complicated movements and a "memory drum" theory of neuromotor reaction. *Research Quarterly, 31,* 448-458.

Heuer, H. (1985). Wiewirktmentale Übung? [How does mental practice operate?] *Psychologische Rundschau, 36,* 191-200.

Heuer, H. (1988). Testing the invariance of relative timing: Comment on Gentner (1987). *Psychological Review, 95,* 552-557.

Heuer, H., Schmidt, R.A., & Ghodsian, D. (1995). Generalized motor programs for rapid bimanual tasks: A two-level multiplicative-rate model. *Biological Cybernetics, 73,* 343-356.

Hick, W.E. (1952). On the rate of gain of information. *Quarterly Journal of Experimental Psychology, 4,* 11-26.

Hijmans, J.M., Hale, L.A., Satherley, J.A., McMillan, N.J., & King, M.J. (2011). Bilateral upper-limb rehabilitation after stroke using a movement-based game controller. *Journal of Rehabilitation Research and Development, 48,* 1005-1014.

Hird, J.S., Landers, D.M., Thomas, J.R., & Horan, J.J. (1991). Physical practice is superior to mental practice in enhancing cognitive and motor task performance. *Journal of Sport and Exercise Psychology, 13,* 281-293.

Hodges, N.J., & Campagnaro, P. (2012). Physical guidance research: Assisting principles and supporting evidence. In N.J. Hodges & A.M. Williams (Eds.), *Skill acquisition in sport: Research, theory and practice* (2nd ed.) (pp. 150-169). London, UK: Routledge.

Hollerbach, J.M. (1978). *A study of human motor control through analysis and synthesis of handwriting.* Unpublished doctoral dissertation, Massachusetts Institute of Technology, Cambridge.

Howell, M.L. (1953). Influence of emotional tension on speed of reaction and movement. *Research Quarterly, 24,* 22-32.

Howell, M.L. (1956). Use of force-time graphs for performance analysis in facilitating motor learning. *Research Quarterly, 27,* 12-22.

Hubbard, A.W., & Seng, C.N. (1954). Visual movements of batters. *Research Quarterly, 25,* 42-57.

Humphrey, N. (1974). Vision in a monkey without striate cortex: A case study. *Perception, 3,* 241-255.

Hyman, I.E. Jr., Boss, S.M., Wise, B.M., McKenzie, K.E., & Caggiano, J.M. (2010). Did you see the unicycling clown? Inattentional blindness while walking and talking on a cell phone. *Applied Cognitive Psychology, 24,* 597-607.

Hyman, R. (1953). Stimulus information as a determinant of reaction time. *Journal of Experimental Psychology, 45,* 188-196.

Irion, A.L. (1966). A brief history of research on the acquisition of skill. In E.A. Bilodeau (Ed.), *Acquisition of skill* (pp. 1-46). New York: Academic Press.

Ishigami, Y., & Klein, R.M. (2009). Is a hands-free phone safer than a handheld phone? *Journal of Safety Research, 40,* 157-164.

Jackson, G.M., Jackson, S.R., & Kritikos, A. (1999). Attention for action: Coordinating bimanual reach-to-grasp movements. *British Journal of Psychology, 90,* 247-270.

James, W. (1890). *The principles of psychology* (Vol. 1). New York: Holt.

James, W. (1891). *The principles of psychology* (Vol. 2). New York: Holt.

Janelle, C.M., Barba, D.A., Frehlich, S.G., Tennant, L.K., & Cauraugh, J.H. (1997). Maximizing performance feedback effectiveness through videotape replay and a self-controlled learning environment. *Research Quarterly for Exercise and Sport, 68,* 269-279.

Kahneman, D. (2011). *Thinking, fast and slow.* New York: Farrar, Straus, and Giroux.

Kantak, S.S., & Winstein, C.J. (2012). Learning–performance distinction and memory processes for motor skills: A focused review and perspective. *Behavioural Brain Research, 228,* 219-231.

Keele, S.W. (1968). Movement control in skilled motor performance. *Psychological Bulletin, 70,* 387-403.

Keele, S.W., & Posner, M.I. (1968). Processing of visual feedback in rapid movements. *Journal of Experimental Psychology, 77,* 155-158.

Keetch, K.M., Lee, T.D., & Schmidt, R.A. (2008). Especial skills: Specificity embedded within generality. *Journal of Sport and Exercise Psychology, 30,* 723-736.

Keetch, K.M., Schmidt, R.A., Lee, T.D., & Young, D.E. (2005). Especial skills: Their emergence with massive amounts of practice. *Journal of Experimental Psychology: Human Perception and Performance, 31,* 970-978.

Kelso, J.A.S. (1995). *Dynamic patterns: The self-organization of brain and behavior.* Cambridge, MA: MIT Press.

Kelso, J.A.S., & Engstrøm, D.A. (2005). *The complementary nature.* Cambridge, MA: MIT Press.

Kelso, J.A.S., Putnam, C.A., & Goodman, D. (1983). On the space-time structure of human interlimb co-ordination. *Quarterly Journal of Experimental Psychology, 35A,* 347-375.

Kelso, J.A.S., Scholz, J.P., & Schöner, G. (1986). Nonequilibrium phase transitions in coordinated biological motion: Critical fluctuations. *Physics Letters A, 118,* 279-284.

Kelso, J.A.S., Scholz, J.P., & Schöner, G. (1988). Dynamics governs switching among patterns of coordination in biological movement. *Physics Letters A, 134,* 8-12.

Kelso, J.A.S., Southard, D.L., & Goodman, D. (1979). On the coordination of two-handed movements. *Journal of Experimental Psychology: Human Perception and Performance, 5,* 229-238.

Kelso, J.A.S., Tuller, B., Vatikiotis-Bateson, E., & Fowler, C.A. (1984). Functionally specific articulatory cooperation following jaw perturbations during speech: Evidence for coordinative structures. *Journal of Experimental Psychology: Human Perception and Performance, 10,* 812-832.

Kernodle, M.W., & Carlton, L.G. (1992). Information feedback and the learning of multiple-degree-of-freedom activities. *Journal of Motor Behavior, 24,* 187-196.

Klapp, S.T. (1996). Reaction time analysis of central motor control. In H.N. Zelaznik (Ed.), *Advances in motor learning and control* (pp. 13-35). Champaign, IL: Human Kinetics.

Konczak, J., vander Velden, H., & Jaeger, L. (2009). Learning to play the violin: Motor control by freezing, not freeing degrees of freedom. *Journal of Motor Behavior, 41,* 243-252.

Kozlowski, S.W.J., & DeShon, R.P. (2004). A psychological fidelity approach to simulation-based training: Theory, research, and principles. In E. Salas, L.R. Elliott, S.G. Schflett, & M.D. Coovert (Eds.), *Scaled worlds: Development, validation, and applications* (pp. 75-99). Burlington, VT: Ashgate.

Lachman, R., Lachman, J.L., & Butterfield, E.C. (1979). *Cognitive psychology and information processing: An introduction.* Hillsdale, NJ: Erlbaum.

Landin, D., & Hebert, E.P. (1997). A comparison of three practice schedules along the contextual interference continuum. *Research Quarterly for Exercise and Sport, 68,* 357-361.

Langham, M., Hole, G., Edwards, J., & O'Neil, C. (2002). An analysis of "looked but failed to see" accidents involving parked police vehicles. *Ergonomics, 45,* 167-185.

Lashley, K.S. (1917). The accuracy of movement in the absence of excitation from the moving organ. *American Journal of Physiology, 43,* 169-194.

Lashley, K.S. (1942). The problem of cerebral organization in vision. In J. Cattell (Ed.), *Biological symposia. Vol. VII. Visual mechanisms* (pp. 301-322). Lancaster, PA: Jaques Cattell Press.

Lavery, J.J. (1962). Retention of simple motor skills as a function of type of knowledge of results. *Canadian Journal of Psychology, 16,* 300-311.

Lavery, J.J., & Suddon, F.H. (1962). Retention of simple motor skills as a function of the number of trials by which KR is delayed. *Perceptual and Motor Skills, 15,* 231-237.

Lawrence, M., & Barclay, D.M. (1998). Stuttering: A brief review. *American Family Physician, 57,* 2175-2178.

Leavitt, J.L. (1979). Cognitive demands of skating and stickhandling in ice hockey. *Canadian Journal of Applied Sports Science, 4,* 46-55.

Lee, D.N. (1980). Visuo-motor coordination in space-time. In G.E. Stelmach & J. Requin (Eds.), *Tutorials in motor behavior* (pp. 281-295). Amsterdam: North-Holland.

Lee, D.N., & Aronson, E. (1974). Visual proprioceptive control of standing in human infants. *Perception & Psychophysics, 15,* 529-532.

Lee, D.N., & Young, D.S. (1985). Visual timing of interceptive action. In D. Ingle, M. Jeannerod, &

References

D.N. Lee (Eds.), *Brain mechanisms and spatial vision* (pp. 1-30). Dordrecht: Martinus Nijhoff.

Lee, T.D. (2012). Contextual interference: Generalizability and limitations. In N.J. Hodges & A.M. Williams (Eds.), *Skill acquisition in sport: Research, theory, and practice* (2nd ed.) (pp. 79-93). London, UK: Routledge.

Lee, T.D., & Carnahan, H. (1990). Bandwidth knowledge of results and motor learning: More than just a relative frequency effect. *Quarterly Journal of Experimental Psychology, 42A*, 777-789.

Lee, T.D., & Genovese, E.D. (1988). Distribution of practice in motor skill acquisition: Learning and performance effects reconsidered. *Research Quarterly for Exercise and Sport, 59*, 277-287.

Lee, T.D., & Genovese, E.D. (1989). Distribution of practice in motor skill acquisition: Different effects for discrete and continuous tasks. *Research Quarterly for Exercise and Sport, 60*, 59-65.

Lee, T.D., Ishikura, T., Kegel, S., Gonzalez, D., & Passmore, S. (2008). Do expert golfers really keep their heads still while putting? *Annual Review of Golf Coaching, 2*, 135-143.

Lee, T.D., & Magill, R.A. (1983). The locus of contextual interference in motor-skill acquisition. *Journal of Experimental Psychology: Learning, Memory, and Cognition, 9*, 730-746.

Lee, T.D., Magill, R.A., & Weeks, D.J. (1985). Influence of practice schedule on testing schema theory predictions in adults. *Journal of Motor Behavior, 17*, 283-299.

Lee, T.D., & Swinnen, S.P. (1993). Three legacies of Bryan and Harter: Automaticity, variability and change in skilled performance. In J.L. Starkes & F. Allard (Eds.), *Cognitive issues in motor expertise* (pp. 295-315). Amsterdam: Elsevier.

Lee, T.D., Wishart, L.R., Cunningham, S., & Carnahan, H. (1997). Modeled timing information during random practice eliminates the contextual interference effect. *Research Quarterly for Exercise and Sport, 68*, 100-105.

Lee, W.A. (1980). Anticipatory control of postural and task muscles during rapid arm flexion. *Journal of Motor Behavior, 12*, 185-196.

Lersten, K.C. (1968). Transfer of movement components in a motor learning task. *Research Quarterly, 39*, 575-581.

Levac, D., Pierrynowski, M.R., Canestraro, M., Gurr, L., Leonard, L., & Neeley, C. (2010). Exploring children's movement characteristics during virtual reality video game play. *Human Movement Science, 29*, 1023-1038.

Levac, D., Rivard, L., & Missiuna, C. (2012). Defining the active ingredients of interactive computer play interventions for children with neuromotor impairments: A scoping review. *Research in Developmental Disabilities, 33*, 214-223.

Lewthwaite, R., & Wulf, G. (2010). Social-comparative feedback affects motor skill learning. *Quarterly Journal of Experimental Psychology, 63*, 738-749.

Lewthwaite, R., & Wulf, G. (2012). Motor learning through a motivational lens. In N.J. Hodges & A.M. Williams (Eds.), *Skill acquisition in sport: Research, theory and practice* (2nd ed.) (pp. 173-191). London, UK: Routledge.

Lindeburg, F.A. (1949). A study of the degree of transfer between quickening exercises and other coordinated movements. *Research Quarterly, 20*, 180-195.

Liu, J., & Wrisberg, C.A. (1997). The effects of knowledge of results delay and the subjective estimation of movement form on the acquisition and retention of a motor skill. *Research Quarterly for Exercise and Sport, 68*, 145-151.

Locke, E.A., & Latham, G.P. (1985). The application of goal setting to sports. *Sport Psychology Today, 7*, 205-222.

Lohse, K.R., Wulf, G., & Lewthwaite, R. (2012). Attentional focus affects movement efficiency. In N.J. Hodges & A.M. Williams (Eds.), *Skill acquisition in sport: Research, theory and practice* (2nd ed.) (pp. 40-58). London, UK: Routledge.

Lotter, W.S. (1960). Interrelationships among reaction times and speeds of movement in different limbs. *Research Quarterly, 31*, 147-155.

Mackworth, N.H. (1948). The breakdown of vigilance during prolonged visual search. *Quarterly Journal of Experimental Psychology, 1*, 6-21.

MacLeod, C.M. (1991). Half a century of research on the Stroop effect: An integrative review. *Psychological Bulletin, 109*, 163-203.

Magill, R.A., & Hall, K.G. (1990). A review of the contextual interference effect in motor skill acquisition. *Human Movement Science, 9*, 241-289.

Marteniuk, R.G. (1974). Individual differences in motor performance and learning. *Exercise and Sport Sciences Reviews, 2*, 103-130.

Marteniuk, R.G. (1976). *Information processing in motor skills*. New York: Holt, Reinhart & Winston.

Marteniuk, R.G. (1986). Information processes in movement learning: Capacity and structural interference effects. *Journal of Motor Behavior, 18*, 55-75.

McCloy, C.H. (1934). The measurement of general motor capacity and general motor ability. *Research Quarterly, 5* (Suppl. 5), 45-61.

McCracken, H.D., & Stelmach, G.E. (1977). A test of the schema theory of discrete motor learning. *Journal of Motor Behavior, 9,* 193-201.

McLeod, P. (1980). What can probe RT tell us about the attentional demands of movement? In G.E. Stelmach & J. Requin (Eds.), *Tutorials in motor behavior* (pp. 579-589). Amsterdam: Elsevier.

Mehrholz, J., Platz, T., Kugler, J., & Pohl, M. (2008). Electromechanical and robot-assisted arm training for improving arm function and activities of daily living after stroke. *Cochrane Database of Systematic Reviews, 4.* CD006876. doi:10.1002/14651858.CD006876.pub2.

Merbah, S., & Meulemans, T. (2011). Learning a motor skill: Effects of blocked versus random practice. A review. *Psychologica Belgica, 51,* 15-48.

Merkel, J. (1885). Die zeitlichen Verhaltnisse der Willensthaütigkeit. *Philosophische Studien, 2,* 73-127. (Cited in Woodworth, R.S. [1938]. *Experimental psychology.* New York: Holt.)

Merton, P.A. (1972). How we control the contraction of our muscles. *Scientific American, 226,* 30-37.

Meyer, D.E., Abrams, R.A., Kornblum, S., Wright, C.E., & Smith, J.E.K. (1988). Optimality in human motor performance: Ideal control of rapid aimed movements. *Psychological Review, 95,* 340-370.

Meyer, D.E., Smith, J.E.K., Kornblum, S., Abrams, R.A., & Wright, C.E. (1990). Speed-accuracy tradeoffs in aimed movements: Toward a theory of rapid voluntary action. In M. Jeannerod (Ed.), *Attention and performance XIII* (pp. 173-226). Hillsdale, NJ: Erlbaum.

Nacson, J., & Schmidt, R.A. (1971). The activity-set hypothesis for warm-up decrement. *Journal of Motor Behavior, 3,* 1-15.

Nashner, L., & Berthoz, A. (1978). Visual contribution to rapid motor responses during postural control. *Brain Research, 150,* 403-407.

Neisser, U., & Becklen, R. (1975). Selective looking, attending to visually specified events. *Cognitive Psychology, 7,* 480-494.

Neumann, E., & Ammons, R.B. (1957). Acquisition and long-term retention of a simple serial perceptual-motor skill. *Journal of Experimental Psychology, 53,* 159-161.

Newell, K.M., Liu, Y.-T., & Mayer-Kress, G. (2001). Time scales in motor learning and development. *Psychological Review, 108,* 57-82.

Newell, K.M., Liu, Y.-T., & Mayer-Kress, G. (2009). Time scales, difficulty/skill duality, and the dynamics of motor learning. In D. Sternad (Ed.), *Progress in motor control* (pp. 457-476). Berlin: Springer.

Newell, K.M., & Vaillancourt, D.E. (2001). Dimensional change in motor learning. *Human Movement Science, 20,* 695-715.

Newell, K.M., & Walter, C.B. (1981). Kinematic and kinetic parameters as information feedback in motor skill acquisition. *Journal of Human Movement Studies, 7,* 235-254.

Nilsen, D.M., Gillen, G., & Gordon, A.M. (2010). Use of mental practice to improve upper-limb recovery after stroke: A systematic review. *American Journal of Occupational Therapy, 64,* 695-708.

Norman, J. (2002). Two visual systems and two theories of perception: An attempt to reconcile the constructivist and ecological approaches. *Behavioral and Brain Sciences, 25,* 73-144.

Ong, N.T., & Hodges, N.J. (2012). Mixing it up a little: How to schedule observational practice. In N.J. Hodges & A.M. Williams (Eds.), *Skill acquisition in sport: Research, theory and practice* (2nd ed.) (pp. 22-39). London, UK: Routledge.

Pearson, K., & Gordon, J. (2000). Spinal reflexes. In E.R. Kandel, J.H. Schwartz, & T.M. Jessell (Eds.), *Principles of neural science* (pp. 713-736). New York: McGraw-Hill.

Perkins-Ceccato, N., Passmore, S.R., & Lee, T.D. (2003). Effects of focus of attention depend on golfers' skill. *Journal of Sports Sciences, 21,* 593-600.

Peterson, L.R., & Peterson, M.J. (1959). Short-term retention of individual verbal items. *Journal of Experimental Psychology, 58,* 193-198.

Pfordresher, P.Q., & Dalla Bella, S. (2011). Delayed auditory feedback and movement. *Journal of Experimental Psychology: Human Perception and Performance, 37,* 566-579.

Pigott, R.E., & Shapiro, D.C. (1984). Motor schema: The structure of the variability session. *Research Quarterly for Exercise and Sport, 55,* 41-45.

Plamondon, R., & Alimi, A.M. (1997). Speed/accuracy tradeoffs in target-directed movements. *Behavioral and Brain Sciences, 20,* 279-349.

Platz, T., Roschka, S., Christel, M.I., Duecker, F., Rothwell, J.C., & Sack, A.T. (2012a). Early stages of motor skill learning and the specific relevance of the cortical motor system—a combined behavioural training and theta burst TMS study. *Restorative Neurology and Neuroscience, 30,* 199-211.

Platz, T., Roschka, S., Doppl, K., Roth, C., Lotze, M., Sack, A.T., & Rothwell, J.C. (2012b). Prolonged motor skill learning – a combined behavioural training and theta burst TMS study. *Restorative Neurology and Neuroscience, 30,* 213-224.

Polanyi, M. (1958). *Personal knowledge: Towards a post-critical philosophy.* London: Routledge and Kegan Paul.

Posner, M.I., & Keele, S.W. (1969). Attentional demands of movement. *Proceedings of the 16th Congress of Applied Psychology.* Amsterdam: Swets and Zeitlinger.

Poulton, E.C. (1957). On prediction in skilled movements. *Psychological Bulletin, 54,* 467-478.

Poulton, E.C. (1974). *Tracking skill and manual control.* New York: Academic Press.

Proteau, L. (1992). On the specificity of learning and the role of visual information for movement control. In L. Proteau & D. Elliott (Eds.), *Vision and motor control* (pp. 67-103). Amsterdam: Elsevier.

Raibert, M.H. (1977). *Motor control and learning by the state space model.* Tech. Rep. No. AI-TR-439. Cambridge: Massachusetts Institute of Technology, Artificial Intelligence Laboratory.

Rasmussen, J. (1986). *Information processing and human-machine interaction: An approach to cognitive engineering.* New York: North-Holland.

Rawlings, E.I., Rawlings, I.L., Chen, S.S., & Yilk, M.D. (1972). The facilitating effects of mental rehearsal in the acquisition of rotary pursuit tracking. *Psychonomic Science, 26,* 71-73.

Redelmeier, D.A., & Tibshirani, R.J. (1997). Association between cellular-telephone calls and motor vehicle collisions. *New England Journal of Medicine, 336,* 453-458.

Robinson, G.H., & Kavinsky, R.C. (1976). On Fitts' law with two-handed movement. *IEEE Transactions on Systems, Man, and Cybernetics, 6,* 504-505.

Rothstein, A.L., & Arnold, R.K. (1976). Bridging the gap: Application of research on videotape feedback and bowling. *Motor Skills: Theory Into Practice, 1,* 35-62.

Salmoni, A.W., Schmidt, R.A., & Walter, C.B. (1984). Knowledge of results and motor learning: A review and critical reappraisal. *Psychological Bulletin, 95,* 355-386.

Sanli, E.A., Patterson, J.T., Bray, S.R., & Lee, T.D. (2013). Understanding self-controlled motor learning protocols through the self-determination theory. *Frontiers in Movement Science and Sport Psychology, 3,* 611. doi:10.3389/fpsyg.2012.00611.

Schmidt, R.A. (1969). Movement time as a determiner of timing accuracy. *Journal of Experimental Psychology, 79,* 43-47.

Schmidt, R.A. (1975). A schema theory of discrete motor skill learning. *Psychological Review, 82,* 225-260.

Schmidt, R.A. (1982). *Motor control and learning: A behavioral emphasis.* Champaign, IL: Human Kinetics.

Schmidt, R.A. (1985). The search for invariance in skilled movement behavior. *Research Quarterly for Exercise and Sport, 56,* 188-200.

Schmidt, R.A. (1989). Unintended acceleration: A review of human factors contributions. *Human Factors, 31,* 345-364.

Schmidt, R.A., Heuer, H., Ghodsian, D., & Young, D.E. (1998). Generalized motor programs and units of action in bimanual coordination. In M. Latash (Ed.), *Progress in motor control, Vol. 1: Bernstein's traditions in movement studies* (pp. 329-360). Champaign, IL: Human Kinetics.

Schmidt, R.A., Lange, C., & Young, D.E. (1990). Optimizing summary knowledge of results for skill learning. *Human Movement Science, 9,* 325-348.

Schmidt, R.A., & Lee, T.D. (2011). *Motor control and learning: A behavioral emphasis.* Champaign, IL: Human Kinetics.

Schmidt, R.A. & Lee, T.D.(2012). Principles of practice for the development of skilled actions: Implications for training and instruction in music. In A.Mornell (ed.), Art in motion II: Motor skills, motivation, and musical practice. (pp.17-41). Frankfurt am Main, Germany. Peter Lang.

Schmidt, R.A., & Sherwood, D.E. (1982). An inverted-U relation between spatial error and force requirements in rapid limb movements: Further evidence for the impulse-variability model. *Journal of Experimental Psychology: Human Perception and Performance, 8,* 158-170.

Schmidt, R.A., Wood, C.T., Young, D.E., & Kelkar, R. (1996). *Evaluation of the BIC J26 child guard lighter.* Tech. Rep. Los Angeles: Failure Analysis Associates, Inc.

Schmidt, R.A., & Wulf, G. (1997). Continuous concurrent feedback degrades skill learning: Implications for training and simulation. *Human Factors, 39,* 509-525.

Schmidt, R.A., & Young, D.E. (1987). Transfer of movement control in motor learning. In S.M. Cormier & J.D. Hagman (Eds.), *Transfer of learning* (pp. 47-79). Orlando, FL: Academic Press.

Schmidt, R.A., Young, D.E., Swinnen, S., & Shapiro, D.C. (1989). Summary knowledge of results for skill acquisition: Support for the guidance hypothesis. *Journal of Experimental Psychology: Learning, Memory, and Cognition, 15,* 352-359.

Schmidt, R.A., Zelaznik, H.N., Hawkins, B., Frank, J.S., & Quinn, J.T. Jr. (1979). Motor-output variability: A theory for the accuracy of rapid motor acts. *Psychological Review, 86,* 415-451.

Schneider, D.M., & Schmidt, R.A. (1995). Units of action in motor control: Role of response complexity and target speed. *Human Performance, 8,* 27-49.

Schneider, W., & Shiffrin, R.M. (1977). Controlled and automatic human information processing: I. Detection, search, and attention. *Psychological Review, 84,* 1-66.

Scripture, C.W. (1905). *The new psychology.* New York: Scott.

Selverston, A.I. (2010). Invertebrate central pattern generator circuits. *Philosophical Transactions of the Royal Society B, 365,* 2329-2345.

Shapiro, D.C., & Schmidt, R.A. (1982). The schema theory: Recent evidence and developmental implications. In J.A.S. Kelso & J.E. Clark (Eds.), *The development of movement control and co-ordination* (pp. 113-150). New York: Wiley.

Shapiro, D.C., Zernicke, R.F., Gregor, R.J., & Diestel, J.D. (1981). Evidence for generalized motor programs using gait pattern analysis. *Journal of Motor Behavior, 13,* 33-47.

Shea, J.B., & Morgan, R.L. (1979). Contextual interference effects on the acquisition, retention, and transfer of a motor skill. *Journal of Experimental Psychology: Human Learning and Memory, 5,* 179-187.

Shea, J.B., & Zimny, S.T. (1983). Context effects in memory and learning movement information. In R.A. Magill (Ed.), *Memory and control of action* (pp. 345-366). Amsterdam: Elsevier.

Sherrington, C.S. (1906). *The integrative action of the nervous system.* New Haven, CT: Yale University Press.

Sherwood, D.E. (1988). Effect of bandwidth knowledge of results on movement consistency. *Perceptual and Motor Skills, 66,* 535-542.

Sherwood, D.E., Schmidt, R.A., & Walter, C.B. (1988). The force/force-variability relationship under controlled temporal conditions. *Journal of Motor Behavior, 20,* 106-116.

Simon, D.A., & Bjork, R.A. (2001). Metacognition in motor learning. *Journal of Experimental Psychology: Learning, Memory, and Cognition, 27,* 907-912.

Simon, D.A., Lee, T.D., & Cullen, J.D. (2008). Win-shift, lose-stay: Contingent switching and contextual interference in motor learning. *Perceptual and Motor Skills, 107,* 407-418.

Simons, D.J., & Chabris, C.F. (1999). Gorillas in our midst: Sustained inattentional blindness for dynamic events. *Perception, 28,* 1059-1074.

Simons, D.J., & Levin, D.T. (1998). Failure to detect changes to people in a real-world interaction. *Psychonomic Bulletin & Review, 5,* 644-649.

Slater-Hammel, A.T. (1960). Reliability, accuracy and refractoriness of a transit reaction. *Research Quarterly, 31,* 217-228.

Snoddy, G.S. (1926). Learning and stability: A psychophysical analysis of a case of motor learning with clinical applications. *Journal of Applied Psychology, 10,* 1-36.

Snyder, C., & Abernethy, B. (Eds.) (1992). *The creative side of experimentation: Personal perspectives from leading researchers in motor control, motor development, and sport psychology.* Champaign, IL: Human Kinetics.

Sperling, G. (1960). The information available in brief visual presentations. *Psychological Monographs, 74* (11, Whole No. 498).

Starkes, J.L., & Allard, F. (Eds.) (1993). *Cognitive issues in motor expertise.* Amsterdam: Elsevier.

Ste-Marie, D.M., Clark, S.E., Findlay, L.C., & Latimer, A.E. (2004). High levels of contextual interference enhance handwriting skill acquisition. *Journal of Motor Behavior, 36,* 115-126.

Ste-Marie, D.M., Law, B., Rymal, A.M., O, J., Hall, C., & McCullagh, P. (2012). Observation interventions for motor skill learning and performance: An applied model for the use of observation. *International Review of Sport and Exercise Psychology, 5,* 145-176.

Stephen, L., Macknik, S.L., King, M., Randi, J., Robbins, A., Teller, J.T., & Martinez-Conde, S. (2008). Attention and awareness in stage magic: Turning tricks into research. *Nature Reviews: Neuroscience, 9,* 871-879.

Sternberg, R.J. (Ed.) (1989). *Advances in the psychology of human intelligence* (Vol. 5). Hillsdale, NJ: Erlbaum.

Stratton, S.M., Liu, Y.T., Hong, S.L., Mayer-Kress, G., & Newell, K.M. (2007). Snoddy (1926) revisited: Time scales of motor learning. *Journal of Motor Behavior, 39,* 503-515.

Strayer, D.L., & Johnston, W.A. (2001). Driven to distraction: Dual-task studies of simulated driving and conversing on a cellular telephone. *Psychological Science, 12,* 462-466.

Stroop, J.R. (1935). Studies of interference in serial verbal reactions. *Journal of Experimental Psychology, 18,* 643-662.

Swinnen, S.P. (1990). Interpolated activities during the knowledge-of-results delay and post-knowledge-of-results interval: Effects on performance and learning. *Journal of Experimental Psychology: Learning, Memory, and Cognition, 16,* 692-705.

Swinnen, S.P., Schmidt, R.A., Nicholson, D.E., & Shapiro, D.C. (1990). Information feedback for skill acquisition: Instantaneous knowledge of results degrades learning. *Journal of Experimental Psychology: Learning, Memory, and Cognition, 16,* 706-716.

Taub, E. (1976). Movement in nonhuman primates deprived of somatosensory feedback. *Exercise and Sport Sciences Reviews, 4,* 335-374.

Taub, E., & Berman, A.J. (1968). Movement and learning in the absence of sensory feedback. In S.J. Freedman (Ed.), *The neuropsychology of spatially oriented behavior* (pp. 173-192). Homewood, IL: Dorsey.

Temprado, J.J. (2004). A dynamical approach to the interplay of attention and bimanual coordination. In V.K. Jirsa & J.A.S. Kelso (Eds.), *Coordination dynamics: Issues and trends* (pp. 21-39). Berlin: Springer.

Thompson, L.L., Rivara, F.P., Ayyagari, R.C., & Ebel, B.E. (in press). Impact of social and technological distraction on pedestrian crossing behaviour: An observational study. *Injury Prevention.*

Thorndike, E.L. (1927). The law of effect. *American Journal of Psychology, 39,* 212-222.

Thorndike, E.L., & Woodworth, R.S. (1901). The influence of improvement in one mental function upon the efficiency of other functions. *Psychological Review, 8,* 247-261.

Tiffin, J., & Rogers, H.B. (1943). The selection and training of inspectors. *Personnel, 22,* 3-20.

Timmermans, A.A.A., Seelen, H.A.M., Willmann, R.D., & Kingma, H. (2009). Technology-assisted training of arm-hand skills in stroke: Concepts on reacquisition of motor control and therapist guidelines for rehabilitation technology design. *Journal of Neuroengineering and Rehabilitation, 6,* 1. doi:10.1186/1743-0003-6-1.

Trowbridge, M.H., & Cason, H. (1932). An experimental study of Thorndike's theory of learning. *Journal of General Psychology, 7,* 245-260.

Turvey, M.T. (1977). Preliminaries to a theory of action with reference to vision. In R. Shaw & J. Bransford (Eds.), *Perceiving, acting, and knowing* (pp. 211-265). Hillsdale, NJ: Erlbaum.

Umiltà, C., Priftis, K., & Zorzi, M. (2009). The spatial representation of numbers: Evidence from neglect and pseudoneglect. *Experimental Brain Research, 192,* 561-569.

Ungerleider, L.G., & Mishkin, M. (1982). Two cortical visual systems. In D.J. Ingle, M.A. Goodale, & R.J.W. Mansfield (Eds.), *Analysis of visual behavior* (pp. 549-586). Cambridge, MA: MIT Press.

Valls-Solé, J., Kumru, H., & Kofler, M. (2008). Interaction between startle and voluntary reactions in humans. *Experimental Brain Research, 187,* 497-507.

Verbruggen, F., & Logan, G.D. (2008). Response inhibition in the stop-signal paradigm. *Trends in Cognitive Sciences, 12,* 418-424.

Vickers, J. (2007). *Perception, cognition, and decision training.* Champaign, IL: Human Kinetics.

Vidmar, P. (1984). *Public-domain comments.* New York: American Broadcasting Company.

Wadman, W.J., Denier van der Gon, J.J., Geuze, R.H., & Mol, C.R. (1979). Control of fast goal-directed arm movements. *Journal of Human Movement Studies, 5,* 3-17.

Weinberg, D.R., Guy, D.E., & Tupper, R.W. (1964). Variation of postfeedback interval in simple motor learning. *Journal of Experimental Psychology, 67,* 98-99.

Weinberg, R.S., & Gould, D. (2011). *Foundations of sport and exercise psychology* (5th ed.). Champaign, IL: Human Kinetics.

Weinberg, R.S., & Ragan, J. (1978). Motor performance under three levels of trait anxiety and stress. *Journal of Motor Behavior, 10,* 169-176.

Weiskrantz, L. (2007). Blindsight. *Scholarpedia, 2* (4), 3047. www.scholarpedia.org/article/Blindsight.

Weiskrantz, L., Warrington, E.K., Sanders, M.D., and Marshall, J. (1974). Visual capacity in the hemianopic field following a restricted occipital ablation. *Brain, 97,* 709-728.

Welford, A.T. (1952). The "psychological refractory period" and the timing of high-speed performance—a review and a theory. *British Journal of Psychology, 43,* 2-19.

Welford, A.T. (1980). *Reaction times.* London: Academic Press.

Weltman, G., & Egstrom, G.H. (1966). Perceptual narrowing in novice divers. *Human Factors, 8,* 499-505.

Wickens, C.D., & McCarley, J.S. (2008). *Applied attention theory.* Boca Raton, FL: CRC Press.

Williams, A.M., Ward, P., & Smeeton, N.J. (2004). Perceptual and cognitive expertise in sport: Implications for skill acquisition and performance enhancement. In A.M. Williams & N.J. Hodges (Eds.), *Skill acquisition in sport: Research, theory and practice* (pp. 328-347). London: Routledge.

Wing, A.M. (2002). Voluntary timing and brain function: An information processing approach. *Brain and Cognition, 48,* 7-30.

Wing, A.M., & Kristofferson, A.B. (1973). The timing of interresponse intervals. *Perception & Psychophysics, 13,* 455-460.

Winstein, C.J., & Schmidt, R.A. (1990). Reduced frequency of knowledge of results enhances motor skill learning. *Journal of Experimental Psychology: Learning, Memory and Cognition, 16,* 677-691.

Wolfe, J.M., Horowitz, T.S., & Kenner, N.M. (2005). Rare items often missed in visual searches: Errors in spotting key targets soar alarmingly if they appear only infrequently during screening. *Nature, 435,* 439-440.

Woodworth, R.S. (1899). The accuracy of voluntary movement. *Psychological Review Monographs, 3* (Whole No. 13).

Woodworth, R.S. (1938). *Experimental psychology.* New York: Holt.

Wright, D.L. (1991). The role of intertask and intratask processing in acquisition and retention of motor skills. *Journal of Motor Behavior, 23,* 139-145.

Wulf, G. (2007). *Attention and motor skill learning.* Champaign, IL: Human Kinetics.

Wulf, G., Weigelt, M., Poulter, D.R., & McNevin, N.H. (2003). Attentional focus on supra-postural tasks affects balance learning. *Quarterly Journal of Experimental Psychology, 56A,* 1191-1211.

Yao, W., Fischman, M.G., & Wang, Y.T. (1994). Motor skill acquisition and retention as a function of average feedback, summary feedback, and performance variability. *Journal of Motor Behavior, 26,* 273-282.

Yerkes, R.M., & Dodson, J.D. (1908). The relation of strength of stimulus to rapidity of habit-formation. *Journal of Comparative Neurology and Psychology, 18,* 459-482.

Young, D.E., & Schmidt, R.A. (1990). Units of motor behavior: Modifications with practice and feedback. In M. Jeannerod (Ed.), *Attention and performance XIII* (pp. 763-795). Hillsdale, NJ: Erlbaum.

Young, D.E., & Schmidt, R.A. (1992). Augmented kinematic feedback for motor learning. *Journal of Motor Behavior, 24,* 261-273.

Zehr, E.P. (2005). Neural control of rhythmic human movement: The common core hypothesis. *Exercise and Sport Sciences Reviews, 33,* 54-60.

Index

\to come\

Draft. Not for Distribution.

Index

Draft. Not for Distribution.

Index

Draft. Not for Distribution.

Index

Draft. Not for Distribution.

About the Authors

Richard A. Schmidt, PhD, is professor emeritus in the department of psychology at UCLA. He currently runs his own consulting firm, Human Performance Research, working in the area of human factors and human performance. Known as one of the leaders in research on motor behavior, Dr. Schmidt has more than 35 years of experience in this area and has published widely.

The originator of schema theory, Schmidt founded the *Journal of Motor Behavior* in 1969 and was editor for 11 years. He authored the first edition of *Motor Control and Learning* in 1982 and the first edition of *Motor Learning and Performance* in 1991, and he has since followed up with new editions of both texts.

Schmidt received an honorary doctorate from Catholic University of Leuven, Belgium, in recognition of his work. He is a member of the North American Society for the Psychology of Sport and Physical Activity (NASPSPA), where he served as president in 1982 and received the organization's two highest honors: the Distinguished Scholar Award for lifetime contributions to research in motor control and learning (in 1992) and the President's Award for significant contributions to the development and growth of NASPSPA (in 2013). He is also a member of the Human Factors and Ergonomics Society and the Psychonomic Society and received the C.H. McCloy Research Lectureship from the American Alliance for Health, Physical Education, Recreation and Dance. His leisure-time activities include sailboat racing, amateur Porsche racing, and skiing.

\INSERT Photo E5868_photo to come\

Timothy D. Lee, PhD, is a professor in the department of kinesiology at McMaster University in Hamilton, Ontario, Canada. He has published extensively in motor behavior and psychology journals since 1979. More recently, he has contributed as an editor to both *Journal of Motor Behavior* and *Research Quarterly for Exercise and Sport* and as an editorial board member for Psychological Review. Since 1984 his research has been supported by grants from the Natural Sciences and Engineering Research Council of Canada. Lee is a member and past president of the Canadian Society for Psychomotor Learning and Sport Psychology (SCAPPS) and a member of the North American Society for the Psychology of Sport and Physical Activity (NASPSPA), the Psychonomic Society, and the Human Factors and Ergonomics Society. In 1980 Lee received the inaugural Young Scientist Award from SCAPPS, and in 2011 he was named a fellow of the society—its highest honor. In 1991-92 he received a senior research fellowship from the Dienst Onderzoekscoordinatie, Catholic University in Leuven, Belgium, and in 2005 he presented a prestigious senior scientist lecture at NASPSPA.

In his leisure time, Lee enjoys playing hockey and golf. He has maintained a lifelong fascination with blues music and is currently putting years of research into practice by learning to play blues guitar.

\INSERT Photo E5868_photo to come\

You'll find other outstanding motor behavior resources at

www.HumanKinetics.com

In the U.S. call

1-800-747-4457

Australia	08 8372 0999
Canada	1-800-465-7301
Europe	+44 (0) 113 255 5665
New Zealand	0800 222 062

HUMAN KINETICS
The Information Leader in Physical Activity & Health
P.O. Box 5076 • Champaign, IL 61825-5076 USA